Yasukuni Shrine

A Study of the Weatherhead East Asian Institute

YASUKUNI SHRINE

History, Memory, and Japan's Unending Postwar

Akiko Takenaka

UNIVERSITY OF HAWAI'I PRESS
HONOLULU

Paperback edition 2017

Printed in the United States of America

22 21 20 19 18 17 6 5 4 3 2 1

Library of Congress Cataloging-in-Publication Data

Takenaka, Akiko, author.
Yasukuni Shrine : history, memory, and Japan's unending postwar / Akiko Takenaka.
pages cm—(Studies of the Weatherhead East Asian Institute, Columbia University)
Includes bibliographical references and index.
ISBN 978-0-8248-4678-7 (hardcover : alk. paper)
1. Yasukuni Jinja (Tokyo, Japan) 2. War memorials—Japan. 3. Shinto and state.
I. Title. II. Series: Studies of the Weatherhead East Asian Institute, Columbia University.
BL2225.T62T35 2015
299.5'61350952135—dc23

2015001006

ISBN 978-0-8248-7380-6 (pbk.)

STUDIES OF THE WEATHERHEAD EAST ASIAN INSTITUTE, COLUMBIA UNIVERSITY

The Studies of the Weatherhead East Asian Institute of Columbia University were inaugurated in 1962 to bring to a wider public the results of significant new research on modern and contemporary East Asia.

University of Hawai‘i Press books are printed on acid-free paper and meet the guidelines for permanence and durability of the Council on Library Resources.

Designed by Milenda Nan Ok Lee

CONTENTS

ACKNOWLEDGMENTS

This project took one and a half decades to complete and benefited tremendously from the generosity of more people than I can name here. I first encountered Yasukuni Shrine as an object of scholarly inquiry in my first year of graduate work at Yale University, during a seminar offered by James Crowley. Mimi Yiengpruksawan subsequently encouraged me to pursue the topic for this book. I thank her for the guidance through these years. I spent some postdoctoral years overwhelmed by a topic as large as Yasukuni Shrine and contemplated other ways to present my research on war and memory. A chance encounter with Mark Selden, his interest in and series of questions about my work on Yasukuni Shrine, and a subsequent request that I write a short piece on the topic for the *Japan Focus* reinvigorated my attention toward Yasukuni Shrine.

Jordan Sand has offered a steady stream of precious advice and encouragement for over a decade, and right up to the present. Carol Gluck inspired me to keep writing and presented my prospectus to the Weatherhead East Asian Institute for its book series. Without the generosity of these two scholars, this project would not have taken the shape that it has and would have been the lesser for it. The theoretical foundation for this work was shaped with the help of two architectural historians: Mark Jarzombek and Sandy Isenstadt. The manuscript has benefited from valuable comments by a number of scholars at conferences, workshops, and other academic opportunities; I thank the participants for their feedback in faculty writing workshops at the University of Michigan and the University of Kentucky, the Midwest Japan Seminar, and a work-in-progress meeting of the Committee for Social Theory at the University of Kentucky. Special thanks go to E. Taylor Atkins, Takashi Fujitani, Alison Goebel, Helen Hardacre, Laura Hein, Andrew Herscher, Marro Inoue, Liang Luo, Brian Masshardt, Wallis Miller, Michael Molasky, John Nelson, Jonathan Reynolds, Jeffery Richey, Stephen Wrinn, and Takashi Yoshida. The comments of three anonymous readers for the Weatherhead East Asian Institute and the University of Hawai'i Press were tremendously useful for improving the manuscript. My appreciation also goes to my colleagues in the Department of History at the University of Kentucky and especially to the current department chair, Karen Petrone, for her unfailing support of this project in particular and my career as a scholar in general.

In Japan I benefited tremendously from activities by the late Nishiha Kiyoshi and members of the "No More War" mailing list, which he established in 2000. I learned a great deal from conversations with a number of *taikensha* at lectures, meetings, and other events. Hasegawa Jun'ichi, Tōkairin Tsuguo, and Miwa Yūji provided me with valuable resources and opportunities. Iki Hiroshi, curatorial staff at the Yūshūkan Museum, gave me helpful insights during a 2005 interview. In the shrine's publicity office, Hayashi Noritaka arranged my use of the beautiful prints in this book. At the distribution office of the documentary film *Annyeong, Sayonara,* Tsukamoto Mitsunori contributed a copy of the DVD to my research.

I am indebted to Dan Rivero at the Weatherhead Institute and to Stephanie Chun and Patricia Crosby at the University of Hawai'i Press for their guidance throughout the revision and publication process of this book. Lise McKean transformed the manuscript line by line. I also extend a special thanks to Jason Karlin for hosting me at Tokyo University during the final stages of the book production. The project has benefited from generous grants from multiple institutions: Dissertation Research Grant and Dissertation Writing Fellowship, Yale University; Postdoctoral Fellowship, Center for Art of East Asia, University of Chicago; Postdoctoral Fellowship, Michigan Society of Fellows; University of Michigan Center for Japanese Studies; Office of Vice President of Research, University of Kentucky; and the Japan Foundation.

This book is dedicated to the two most important people in my life: my father, Fumihiro Takenaka, who has nurtured and stimulated my intellectual curiosity throughout my life and followed with interest all the vicissitudes of this journey; and Doug Slaymaker for intellectual companionship, for reading and editing endless drafts of the manuscript, and most of all for love and laughter and for being there for me the entire time.

All dates up to December 31, 1872, are in accordance with the lunar calendar. Japanese names appear family name first, with the exception of those who have published primarily in English. All translations are mine unless otherwise noted.

INTRODUCTION

Yasukuni no
miya ni mitama wa
shizumaru mo
Oriori kaere
haha no yumeji ni

Your noble spirit rests
In the shrine of Yasukuni,
My son.
But why don't you come visit
Your mother every now and then
At least in her dreams.

EULOGY FOR A YOUNG SOLDIER KILLED IN CHINA

This short poem about a mother whose son fell in battle during the Asia-Pacific War (1931–1945)[1] was popularized throughout Japan in 1937 by the song "Yasukuni no" (Of Yasukuni). The song is just ninety-three seconds long.[2] Sung by a choir with piano accompaniment in G major, the melody would sound uplifting if it were not for the slow tempo and solemn vocals. The words, in the *tanka* poem structure, are minimalist. Yet, they eloquently convey both the mother's attempt to contain her overwhelming sadness and the reverence that she must now express for her late son. The music for "Yasukuni no" is credited to composer Nobutoki Kiyoshi, and the words are by Ōe Hifumi. Ōe, a career soldier in the Japanese Army, originally wrote the poem as a eulogy for a young comrade killed on a reconnaissance mission in August 1937, just three weeks into active duty. Found in the pocket of the young man's bloodstained uniform was a photograph of his mother with the word *okāsan* (mother) handwritten twenty-four times on the back.[3]

"Yasukuni no" quickly became a familiar requiem. It was featured in the NHK (Japan Broadcasting Corporation) *National Songs* (Kokumin Kayō) radio series.[4] In addition to frequent radio broadcasts, the song was popularized through live radio coverage of the enshrinement rituals at Yasukuni Shrine.[5] Soon after Japan's defeat in 1945, however, most of these national songs (including "Yasukuni no"), which were frequently sung and broadcast during the war years, faded from the nation's collective memory.

The song began its second life in 1984—amid the controversies generated by then Prime Minister Nakasone's repeated visits to Yasukuni Shrine—when its lyrics were reintroduced as a cultural artifact that symbolized the problem of Yasukuni Shrine. Ōe's son, the late historian Ōe Shinobu, invoked it in the afterword of his 1984 publication, *Yasukuni Jinja* (Yasukuni Shrine) as the inspiration for conducting his own research on the monument. The younger Ōe points out that the mother in the poem, unable to keep the spirit of her fallen son at her side, is hesitantly asking him to visit her from time to time in her dreams. To Ōe, the passage demonstrates how Yasukuni Shrine controlled the lives of Japanese men to the extent that they could not return home even after death and, further, how the shrine indoctrinated people to believe that dying in battle was an act worthy of aspiration and a source of pride.[6] The poem is an apt opening for my discussion of Yasukuni Shrine not only because of its significance during wartime and today but also because of the parallel trajectories of both the poem and the shrine during the war and subsequent decades.

Ōe's analysis of the poem brings up just one of several problems that Yasukuni Shrine has posed in recent decades. Another key issue concerns the Class-A war criminals enshrined there.[7] In commemorating men who were charged with the maximum level of guilt for conspiring to start and wage the war, Yasukuni Shrine has, for its critics, also come to symbolize Japan's militarism in general and the multitudinous war crimes committed during the Asia-Pacific War in particular. It has thus been (and continues to be) the focus of intense political controversy, which on occasion has led to major international-relations crises. Books, articles, and editorials are continually published in Japan on the "Yasukuni issue" (*Yasukuni mondai*). Almost all of them treat it as a political issue in need of resolution.[8] In this book I analyze Yasukuni Shrine as a war memorial. I examine its role in waging war, honoring the dead, promoting peace, and especially in building a modern national identity. Through my study of Yasukuni Shrine, I reflect on the making and unmaking of a modern militaristic Japan and consider the shrine within the context of memory studies—that is, in terms of the varying ways that contemporary Japanese remember the Asia-Pacific War.

My analysis of Yasukuni Shrine grapples with two larger issues relating to war and memorialization. The first is the problem of how a nation-state that was defeated in war acknowledges its military dead. It is a relatively uncomplicated matter for a victorious nation to commemorate its fallen soldiers as sacrifices to a worthy cause. But how does a nation legitimately acknowledge its military dead not only when the war was lost but also when an international tribunal deemed the war a criminal event? The prolonged and heated debate over the design and implementation of the United States' Vietnam Veterans Memorial offers some parallels and demonstrates the difficulties associated with forming a consensus on how to pay tribute to those who died in a controversial and unpopular war.[9]

War inevitably produces death. Military dead have been memorialized at both the personal and the national level throughout the modern era. The dead of victorious wars are commemorated as heroes: Eulogies are written, names are inscribed, monuments are constructed. Heroicizing the war dead is key to mythmaking, which is a vital component of modern nation building.[10] However, the treatment of those who died for the losing side is considerably more complicated. How does it officially remember its war dead? Moreover, how might survivors and succeeding generations remember those who fought and died in what was deemed a war of aggression? Are their deaths devalued when the cause for which they were fighting is discredited? Japan has had to face this issue following its failed imperialist conquests in Asia, which began in the late nineteenth century and culminated in the Asia-Pacific War.

Yasukuni Shrine is central to these questions as it epitomizes the dilemma of how to remember those who fell during this problematic war. At once a Shinto shrine and a war memorial, it is where all of the military-related war casualties of modern Japan (1868–1945) are collectively memorialized as the protective deity of Japan.[11] Until the end of the Asia-Pacific War, an elaborate ritual was conducted once or twice a year to summon the spirits of the war dead from all of the battlefields so that they might be enshrined there as heroes. Children growing up during the war were taught that enshrinement at Yasukuni Shrine was the highest honor a Japanese could receive. Regardless of the soldiers' actions on the battlefield, once they died, they were commemorated as god. However, everything changed after Japan's defeat. If it is unacceptable to commemorate the victims of a wrongful war, in what way should the Japanese state publicly recognize these sacrifices? Further, as seen with the Vietnam Veterans Memorial, reaching a consensus on how to memorialize these individuals is a difficult task, as there is no one single, national memory of the war. For many, Yasukuni Shrine represents all of the wrongdoings of the Japanese wartime state. Yet for others, it honors the memory of loyal Japanese who gave their lives for their country.

The second issue that this analysis addresses is the relationship between religion and war memorialization in a secular state. Religion typically plays a key role in memorial rituals. In modern Japan, Shinto and Buddhism co-existed in rituals for the dead. As a Shinto shrine, the physical form of Yasukuni Shrine is typical of such monuments. A large *torii* gate stands at the entrance, while a central approach (*sandō*) of approximately five hundred meters connects the main entrance and the worship hall. Along this path, a series of smaller *torii* gates creates hierarchical layers of sacred spaces. The main hall (*honden*), where the spirits of gods are believed to reside, is behind the worship hall. But as I demonstrate in the following chapters, Shinto as a religion was not always consistently visible, mainly because of the ways in which the shrine's spaces were used. Furthermore, the conflation of religion and war memorialization was not problematic until 1945 as Shinto was, until then, considered the official doctrine of the Japanese state.[12] However, the postwar Japanese Constitution prohibits state support of religious institutions and guarantees freedom of religion to all. These constitutional provisions make Yasukuni Shrine's status as a religious institution problematic. At the same time, for current visitors, the spatial configuration as a shrine continues to anchor memories that are colored by religion.

In most critics' discussions, Yasukuni Shrine typically is portrayed as the official propaganda machine of the wartime government. For example, Ōe Shinobu argues that Yasukuni Shrine is problematic because, during the Asia-Pacific War, it was a "political and ideological instrument of the state . . . [that] indoctrinated people into believing that war death was not tragic or distressing but in fact glorious and honorable."[13] Numerous other scholars have similarly portrayed Yasukuni Shrine. In discussions about the controversies surrounding the shrine, the term "Yasukuni" (often interchangeable with "Yasukuni Shrine") alone can refer to anything from the political controversy to beliefs associated with shrine rituals and decisions made by the Council of Worshipers' Representatives (Sūkeisha Sōdaikai).[14] For example, the presence of the names of seven executed Class-A war criminals on the shrine's register is said to glorify militarism. To many East Asian and Southeast Asian countries that suffered from Japan's military aggression during the Asia-Pacific War, interactions between the Japanese state and Yasukuni Shrine signals Japan's desire for rearmament and future military enterprise. Furthermore, the shrine representatives' refusal to grant requests from family members to remove those who are enshrined demonstrates the unconstitutionality of the shrine's activities. All of these discussions ambiguously use "Yasukuni" to describe the cause or source of the issue. In these narratives, "Yasukuni" is responsible for most, if not all, of Japan's unresolved issues from the Asia-Pacific War. What, then, does "Yasukuni" really stand for?

This conflation of the shrine—a group of buildings in central Tokyo—with the discourse on Japan's unsettled war responsibilities is at the heart of the Yasukuni issue. That is, the shrine's compound and the physical structures situated within it did not, on their own, create all of the problems currently associated with this matter. Rather, Yasukuni Shrine was a tool—and one of many—that the Japanese state and the military used to propagate ideological messages associated with warfare in general and dying in battle in particular. The shrine compound provided a space in which to perform rituals and other practices that popularized these ideas among both visitors and those who vicariously experienced the events through mass media.[15] Since 1955 the Liberal Democratic Party (LDP) has capitalized on the shrine to appeal to particular voting blocs, heightening the shrine's political significance as a result. Nevertheless, it is the physical presence of the shrine that was and continues to be the focus of intense criticism. One proposed solution highlights this fact: the suggested construction of a new national war memorial to replace (or at least divert attention from) Yasukuni Shrine[16]—as if destroying or turning attention away from the physical site would eliminate all of the problems associated with it.[17] Scholars of history, philosophy, international relations, and religious studies, as well as journalists and critics, have written extensively about Yasukuni Shrine. However, most of this writing frames Yasukuni Shrine as a "political problem that needs to be resolved": a framework that conflates the shrine with the political problems of postwar Japan. However, the debates have not yet posed this pertinent question: How would replacing Yasukuni Shrine with a new representative Japanese war memorial, making changes to the existing shrine, or completely severing ties between the Japanese state and the shrine solve the Yasukuni issue? That is, how can the removal of the symbol that represents a problem solve the problem itself? This book identifies and analyzes the strands of political, religious, and other issues that are intertwined with the shrine and its site, which have come to be known as "Yasukuni" or "Yasukuni Shrine."

As a starting point, I identify three components of "Yasukuni": Yasukuni the belief (Yasukuni shinkō), Yasukuni the site (Yasukuni Jinja), and Yasukuni the issue (Yasukuni mondai). The passage by Ōe cited earlier articulates Yasukuni the belief. The men who led the overthrow of the *bakufu*, or shogunate, developed the myth underlying this belief during the last years of the Tokugawa era. During Japan's international wars of imperialism, the myth was gradually formalized into a belief system and was propagated by the Japanese government and military. In the last years of the Asia-Pacific War, the idea that war death and the resulting enshrinement at Yasukuni Shrine was the highest honor a man could ever achieve reached its zenith. "Yasukuni the site" refers to the physical space that is both a Shinto shrine and a war memorial, as well as the spatial practices within it. Until 1945 it was a site where militarism was interwoven with technology and spectacle in ways that fascinated its visitors. It was also a site of mourning and remembrance for bereaved family members. In the postwar years, it became a site where the coexistence of political ideology and religious practice generated tension. Finally, "Yasukuni the issue" includes the postwar political problems currently associated with the shrine, such as the presence of the Class-A war criminals' names on the register as well as the other issues mentioned earlier. These three elements are not independent of each other. The shrine site and the associated spatial practices are intertwined with the beliefs and issues. The operators of "Yasukuni the site" are complicit in promoting "Yasukuni the belief" and therefore play a major role in intensifying "Yasukuni the issue."

In this book I examine these three elements on their own and in association with each other, and I scrutinize the complex and dynamic relationships among them over a century and a half. Most discussions of Yasukuni Shrine, and particularly those by its critics, reduce the complex history and memories of Japan's wartime past into one ambiguous "Yasukuni," giving the impression that an intervention into (or severing state ties with) the physical presence of the shrine could resolve all of the issues associated with the Asia-Pacific War. This focus on the shrine—and by extension the wartime military and political leaders who created and supported it—ironically reinforces the narrative of victimhood prevalent in Japan today. Namely, that during the Asia-Pacific War, ordinary Japanese were victims of the wartime state (embodied by Yasukuni Shrine and the Class-A war criminals enshrined there). This stark separation of victim and perpetrator roles in wartime Japan obstructs a necessary effort to reconcile with non-Japanese victims of the war. I explicate this point in the chapters covering the postwar period.

MEMORY AND SPATIAL PRACTICE

Two concepts—memory and spatial practice—are central to my analysis of Yasukuni Shrine. One of the shrine's key roles is that of a war memorial. Particularly in the modern era, memories and sentiments assigned to war memorials vary as much as the monuments themselves. In addition to the collective memories that these monuments are meant to evoke, individual visitors can have their own memories that they bring to these memory markers.[18] As a nationally sanctioned war memorial, Yasukuni Shrine preserved a particular kind of collective war memory for Japan until 1945. Officially, it commemorated the "honorable sacrifices" made to advance modern Japan's imperialist goals and was pivotal in promoting a certain kind of national identity. At the same time, individual visitors, whether or not they were personally associated with any of those memorialized, could have their own memories of and relationships with the shrine. For example, in its early years, some associated the spaces of the shrine with novelty and entertainment; for others, the shrine was a place where they could communicate with sons, brothers, or fathers who died in one of Japan's wars. Even during the postwar years, when the shrine fueled political controversy, it still served as a site for mourning and remembrance. Yet most critics today regard the shrine only in terms of its offensive role in Japan's wartime past. Assigning a single meaning to Yasukuni Shrine obstructs efforts to acknowledge and work through Japan's wartime past. Singling out Yasukuni Shrine in this way overemphasizes the role of one institution and distracts attention from important issues such as reconciliation with China, South Korea, and other Asian countries. Furthermore, it ignores the memorial function, which has been important for many. I suggest a different approach, one that is derived from a more complex and nuanced understanding of Yasukuni Shrine and involves both an appreciation of the dynamic relationship between memory and space and an acknowledgment of the multiplicity of memories and meanings that can be derived from a single space.[19]

In a posthumous essay originally published in 1950,[20] Maurice Halbwachs assumes a precise relationship between memory and space and argues that collective memory is a social construction, shaped by the concerns of the present.[21] But Halbwachs also notes the tension, or perhaps contradiction, that this presentist construction of collective memory engenders: If the presentism of memory were pushed to its limit, there would be no memory at all, no continuity in the representation of the past, and perhaps even no past as such. The so-called past would be no more than a blank screen on which to project the contingencies of an ever-changing present. Theorizing the limit to memory's presentism, Halbwachs invokes space as the fundamental medium of memory, approaching it as a "physical and sensory" presence upon which memories can be projected.[22] Through the medium of space the past takes on an objectified form in the immediacy of spatial cognition and experience. For Halbwachs, to change space is to change memory, and to change memory is to change space: "[T]he altars of the ancient gods must be overturned, and their temples destroyed, if remembrances of a more primitive worship are to be obliterated from the memory of men."[23] Succeeding scholars of memory have also sought to anchor memory in particular sites—Pierre Nora, for example, identified *lieux de mémoire* as sites "where memory crystallizes and secretes itself."[24]

If Halbwachs' assertion holds true, the destruction of Yasukuni Shrine anticipates the obliteration of inconvenient war memories in Japan. Recent theorizations of space, however, suggest a more complex and fraught relationship between memory and space.[25] Space is not the "reality that endures" and that preserves our past, as Halbwachs imagined.[26] Henri Lefebvre, for example, contends that space is a social formation that is produced not only materially but also through representations and social practices.[27] Furthermore, space is not inherently instrumental because it is a result of social practices that take place within.[28] Multiple events affect our understanding of the space of Yasukuni, including the revelation of Class-A criminals' enshrinement, visits by prime ministers, and debate over a new national memorial, to cite some key examples. Over the past four decades, "Yasukuni the issue" has become conflated with "Yasukuni the site," leading the site to become a politically charged issue and resulting in debates that focus on the site's removal or preservation. As collective memory is a social construct shaped by present concerns, the current understanding of Yasukuni is significantly influenced by contemporary political trends. The mediation of collective memory, whether through narration and visualization on the one hand or ritual and ceremony on the other, forms and transforms social space as much as the same space defines and stabilizes memory. Thus, memory can not only reproduce the meanings encoded in social space but also resist, subvert, repress, or displace those meanings. It can even produce novel meanings and spaces. Unlike for Halbwachs and others, a precise relationship between memory and space cannot be assumed but rather must be derived from analyses that incorporate the temporal dimension and consider spatial mediations.

Investigation of the three strands I introduced—belief, site, and issue—not only independently but also together, with particular attention to the shifting dynamics in their relationship, will help us understand how they have become inextricably one concern in recent decades.[29] The physicality of the site has created the impression that both the belief and the resulting issue have always been a singular, unchanging entity fully embedded within the site. Recent debates on this unspecified "Yasukuni" have further reinforced the idea of Yasukuni the site as a Halbwachsian medium that holds memories intact. But the wartime belief, of which the site was an intricate part, should be understood separately from the postwar issue, over which both the site and the belief hold sway.

Representations and social practices, which are instrumental in the production of space, also play a key role in shaping memory. As I outline in chapter 1, in the early conceptualization of Yasukuni Shrine, the belief and the site developed together and, at times, independently of each other. In chapters 2 and 3 I detail the period of Japan's earlier wars of imperialism, during which the site flourished mainly as a space for popular entertainment for Tokyoites, while the belief developed throughout the rest of Japan primarily through ritual, education, and mass media. At the height of Japan's militarism (chapter 4), the site on which rites of commemoration took place was projected throughout Japan via mass media alongside messages bolstering the belief. The spatial practices that took place within the site, therefore, were not always the same as the mediated representations that were consumed by those far from Tokyo. In the postwar decades (chapters 5 and 6), the issue emerged not only from the site itself but also alongside unresolved matters associated with crimes committed by the Japanese military. If the occupation forces had scrapped Yasukuni Shrine—a move that they seriously contemplated—I am certain that we would still have been left with the same problem concerning Japan's unresolved wartime past, only with a different name.

When pundits argue over a replacement for Yasukuni today, they are arguing not about the actual physical space that exists in Tokyo but about an imagined site on which the issue is projected. Of course the issue will not go away with the destruction of the physical space. Fused with the site that currently functions as a screen on which particular kinds of memories are projected, however, the belief and the issue, both of which have continuously changed with the social and political milieu throughout the shrine's existence, seem instead to have frozen in time. Although popular perception of

Yasukuni has never been unitary, Yasukuni the site, as it is represented in most postwar literature, continues to reproduce a very particular memory of the Asia-Pacific War—an official memory of wartime Japan, in which all Japanese were proud to sacrifice their lives for the emperor. Indeed, this strong narrative was associated with Yasukuni Shrine. And according to the shrine's opponents, this is the narrative that indoctrinated wartime Japanese.

But for many others, Yasukuni Shrine does not represent the deception these opponents speak of. For example, in his best-selling book on Yasukuni Shrine, philosopher Takahashi Tetsuya introduces gripping testimony by a widow who lost her husband during the Asia-Pacific War. As a part of the defense for Yasukuni Shrine during a 2002 lawsuit filed at Osaka District Court, war widow Iwai Masuko pleaded as follows: "If you must dishonor Yasukuni Shrine, kill me a million times instead. Hearing just one word that disparages Yasukuni Shrine, I feel my body shredded into pieces. And all the blood from my entire body gushes out and spreads as far as the eye can see—it is the ocean created by blood of the [Japanese] troops."[30] For Takahashi, this statement exemplifies what Yasukuni Shrine does best: It fundamentally alters one's feelings, a change that he called "emotional alchemy (*kanjō no renkinjutsu*)." Because of this, he argues, the emotions of the bereaved family are transformed "from sadness to happiness," training those left behind to be grateful to have had a family member who was able to die in the service of the emperor. He further speculates that this system instilled a sense of desire among Japanese during wartime: the desire to die at war, the desire to have a family member die at war.[31] The widow's comment demonstrates one of the most powerful sentiments on Yasukuni Shrine to be verbalized so many decades after 1945, and it can certainly be used convincingly to condemn the shrine as Takahashi has done. At the same time, it is possible that these powerful emotions of gratitude and pride sustained this widow for decades after the war. It is also possible that the act of holding on to similar emotions made it possible for many other women to survive through the immediate postwar years, impoverished without the family's breadwinner and often with very young children. In the postwar climate in which any association with the Japanese military was an uncomfortable concept in popular consciousness, it is possible that Yasukuni Shrine functioned as a strong consolation, as a sanctuary for those left behind. This does not necessarily mean that these women believed in this myth prior to the death of their husbands, but they perhaps embraced it to help them survive after their loss. I do not mean for this factor to legitimize the existence of the shrine or to defend the wartime ideologies attached to it. I want to emphasize instead the presence of important memories that do not conform to the critics' discourse in order to present the complexities involved in the significance of Yasukuni Shrine.

THE DISCOURSE OF VICTIMHOOD AND COUNTERMEMORY

Teasing apart the issues currently associated with Yasukuni Shrine provides an opportunity to reflect on important matters beyond wartime propaganda and the Class-A war criminals. One postwar by-product of Yasukuni the belief is what Carol Gluck has referred to as the "victims' history": the narrative in which the Japanese suffered from the prolonged war due to the actions of their reckless leaders.[32] It is important to note that this discourse is different from the revisionist narrative (e.g., Japan fought a war of self-defense) in many important ways. I emphasize this for clarification because the use of the term "victim," at least as it relates to Yasukuni issues, is easily misunderstood. That is, it tends to generate an instant response that the narrator of the victims' history is aligned with the kind of history that, for example, the Yūshūkan museum (on the shrine grounds) narrates.[33] In the discourse of victimhood, the Japanese state, as the aggressor, committed numerous war crimes during the fifteen-year war; the people, including generally everyone except the leaders of the wartime government and those found guilty of Class-A war crimes by the Tokyo War Crimes Tribunal, are victims of the Japanese state. Such a discourse contributes to the current predicament, where, although many acknowledge the aggressive and criminal nature of Japan's fifteen-year war, few seem ready to be held accountable for, or willing to act on, Japan's war responsibilities themselves. This reluctance has become even more problematic in recent years, as there are now few Japanese citizens who actively participated in the war. Although most hold their government responsible, lawmakers also seem unwilling to accept responsibility for events that happened before they were born.

In the postwar decades, Yasukuni Shrine has become the perfect scapegoat for the defunct wartime government. In this scenario the victims are not only civilians at home but also members of the military who killed their enemies. I summarize the connection later on. "Yasukuni the belief" also justified military violence by placing little value on human life and bestowing the status of a noble spirit (*eirei*) on all military dead regardless of what they did.[34] Wartime violence, in the Japanese case, yielded two results, both of which involved the loss of numerous lives: massive atrocities inflicted against the enemy and the deaths of many Japanese troops. The violence inflicted on the enemy—most prominently in the Nanjing Massacre, but also characteristic of the reckless strategies in the Pacific Islands warfare—was made possible by devaluing human life. Death on the battlefield made a soldier an *eirei* regardless of his previous actions. Reckless fighting and killing with little regard for one's own survival resulted in massive loss of life for both the Japanese and their enemies.[35]

This ideology, which justified wartime violence, fueled huge losses and enormous grief both domestically and internationally. Of course, this "justification" of violence was not presented or perceived as such during the war. According to official wartime discourse, a soldier's motivation was the honor (i.e., Yasukuni enshrinement) given to those who made the ultimate sacrifice. The concept of honorable sacrifice was vigorously disseminated through popular culture, with frequent references to Yasukuni Shrine. The postscript of this narrative in the postwar years led to a different conclusion: Because of Yasukuni, members of the Japanese military perpetrated such wartime violence, which ultimately resulted in the attacks on the homeland; because of Yasukuni, all Japanese (both on the battlefield and at home) suffered during the war. In this narrative, the Japanese are the wartime victims. Only the top government and military leaders are blamed for Japan's colonial ambitions in the Asia-Pacific War and the associated aggression against the enemy. Although few openly expressed dissent, the fact that not everyone fully subscribed to the cult of militarism is also absent from this formulation.

If the majority of Japanese believed themselves to be victims of the wartime government and military, now that the wartime leaders are deceased, there is little popular will in Japan today to address the issues of war responsibility and reconciliation. The conflation of belief, shrine, and issue is pertinent to this point. For Yasukuni's critics in Japan, the shrine represents the wrongdoings of the wartime government and military, which resulted in the suffering of the Japanese people. Internationally, Yasukuni Shrine represents Japan's failure to "adopt a correct view of history," namely, a view that recognizes Japan's war crimes, as well as the threat of future aggression by Japan associated with its rearmament. Although these issues can and should be treated separately, they are currently intertwined in the problematic concept of Yasukuni and give rise to intense criticism that focuses on the shrine and its existence rather than specific unresolved issues of Japan's wartime past.

The discourse of victimhood and the conflation of the shrine and the issue have led many to consider Yasukuni Shrine as the cause of Japan's wartime violence. As a result, war responsibility and blame have shifted from human actors to an inanimate physical structure. Many have condemned the shrine as an institution that forcefully indoctrinated members of the Japanese military to act with wanton disregard for the value of human life and converted unwilling people to members of a cult who uncritically believed in the honor of sacrificing their life for the emperor. In the discourse of victimhood, the prospect of enshrinement at Yasukuni seduced or coerced the Japanese people. To use a term popularized by postwar peace promoters, they were "brainwashed (*sennō sareta*)" or "deceived (*damasareta*)" into participating in the national war effort.[36] They were trained to subscribe to the myth of the honorable fallen, which the wartime government and military propagated. My analysis of Yasukuni Shrine complicates this victims' narrative by blurring the boundary between victim and perpetrator.

In his seminal work on overcoming the German past, Theodor Adorno expressed his apprehension for postwar German society, which, in his view, lacked the capacity to fully and critically reflect on what had happened during the reign of National Socialism. For Adorno, this inability to reflect was a kind of forgetting, a "destruction of memory."[37] I suggest that Japan is still experiencing a similar phenomenon and that the presence of Yasukuni Shrine functions as a convenient tool that aids in this forgetting. In lieu of critical reflection, complex past events are reduced to a simplified and convenient narrative that lays all blame on Yasukuni Shrine. Ironically, arguments by Yasukuni critics, who reduce the complexities of the wartime past, including the suffering inflicted both domestically and internationally, to one institution, result in a form of memory destruction that Adorno had apprehended. And for Japan, highlighting the deception—the brainwashing and the trickery—facilitated the construction of a narrative that conveniently placed the blame on Yasukuni Shrine and the wartime state. Here I am not arguing that deceit did not occur. For many Japanese born during the war, lessons on topics such as Japan's holy war and reverence for the emperor shaped their young minds. Many felt deceived when, in the immediate postwar years, the same teachers, without adequate explanation, began to preach democracy. At the same time, reducing Japan's wartime experience to that of deception does not yield a better understanding of the war period or a productive solution for the future.

Another issue that concerned Adorno was the idea of democracy in postwar Germany. Writing in the 1950s, Adorno believed that because democracy was introduced by the Allied victors, it lacked emotional connections with contemporary Germans. The history of democracy in Japan is similar: The Allied occupation forces introduced the idea, primarily through the new constitution.[38] In the immediate postwar period, the deception narrative helped many to accept this constitution, as well as the fact that nothing positive ensued from all of the suffering and loss they had endured. At the same time, it allowed the Japanese to avoid squarely confronting what they had lived through—an all-out war in which they, too, had participated. The new democratic political structure, which was to transform the wartime government—and the leaders who had deceived them—was a welcome replacement.[39] It not only promised to change society but also validated blaming the government; little compelling reason remained for critical reflection on the wartime past. In Japan as in postwar Germany, the new democracy allowed the people to "turn the page and . . . wip[e the wartime past] from memory."[40]

It is also important to note that multiple motives and concepts were mobilized to advance the war effort, many of which had little to do with Yasukuni Shrine or the emperor. Numerous narratives exist that do not fit neatly into the "people brainwashed by Yasukuni Shrine" framework. Many opportunistically took advantage of the presence of war and used its violence for corporate or personal gain. Wartime Japan's view of the emperor, too, was not uniform. Songs mocking the emperor were enjoyed behind closed doors. Children secretly changed the words to the Imperial Rescript on Education, which they were forced to memorize at school. In most letters from the front, soldiers asked about the well-being of their family members and promised to fight for their country and their family. Most did not mention the emperor.[41] In a poll taken in November and December 1945 on people's reaction to the declaration of surrender on August 15, just 4 percent admitted that they were worried about the emperor or felt ashamed for the defeat or apologetic toward him.[42] Views of Yasukuni Shrine and the emperor were never uniform, even when limited to the fifteen-year period of the Asia-Pacific War. I examine a longer history—from years before its inception to today—in order to demonstrate the diverse ways that the Japanese (and in some cases Korean and Taiwanese nationals as well) have considered Yasukuni Shrine.

Generally, critics have viewed visits to Yasukuni Shrine by the emperor as the primary incentive for soldiers to sacrifice their lives in battle. Yasukuni enshrinement may certainly have functioned as a consolation for those left behind. But, for most soldiers, enshrinement was not in fact the primary motive to die; it was simply a widely accepted outcome of a soldier's death—a view that was cultivated through elementary school education in the decades following the Russo-Japanese War. To feel the obligation to go to war and fight—once conscripted or drafted or in response to a national emergency—is a view that can almost be considered a universal one: an outcome of an intense desire to protect one's own family and others important in one's life. In fact, opposition to the state and the war it waged was somewhat public as many people used rituals and prayer in their attempts to prevent conscription and war death.[43] What, then, did the presence of Yasukuni Shrine mean to the Japanese at war and at peace? In this book I pay attention not only to memories that conform to the mainstream narrative but also to countermemories—memories that construct what Foucault referred to as "effective history": an examination that attempts not to create a linear narrative from origin (Japan's imperialist aspirations, which began in the late nineteenth century) to conclusion (the Asia-Pacific War and Japan's defeat) but instead to "isolate the different scenes where they engaged in different roles."[44] Such an analysis demonstrates the complexity of history and memory associated with the Asia-Pacific War, a level of complexity that cannot and should not be reduced to one specific shrine.

WAR RESPONSIBILITY, POSTWAR RESPONSIBILITY

As a starting point for discussion of Japan's war responsibility, political theorist Maruyama Masao's 1949 point on Japan's "system of irresponsibility (*musekinin no kōzō*)" remains valid in its succinct portrayal of a system through which all Japanese evaded blame for the war—both its beginning and its ending (Japan's defeat).[45] This system of irresponsibility became apparent during the Tokyo War Crimes Tribunal, when military personnel of every rank testified that they were unable to interfere with what they described as the "force of circumstances." The locus of responsibility therefore remained nebulous. In the same essay, Maruyama pointed to the shrine as often being a "mere robot who affects other people by 'doing nothing' "—a point that identifies how agency was overly assigned to Yasukuni Shrine in the postwar period.[46] For the general public, however, the tribunals conveniently defined responsibility and identified the names of those responsible—most prominently by identifying Class-A war criminals—while overlooking other major crimes, including many committed in Korea, China, and elsewhere in Asia.[47] The idea that the wartime state was ruled by war criminals convicted by an international tribunal further reinforced support and appreciation for the idea of democracy. Thus, the opportunity for critical reflection was compromised once again. With Japan's normalization of international relations between Korea and China in 1965 and 1972, respectively, the question of war responsibility seemed to be settled. But the situation changed at the end of the twentieth century.

As Carol Gluck notes, the 1990s saw a shift in responsibility from state-to-state claims for compensation, to individuals demanding recognition of harm inflicted on them.[48] But by the time these voices arose in China and Korea, demanding Japanese accountability for crimes committed against their people, the majority of elected officials in the Japanese government had not played any role in the war. They protested that they were being held responsible for actions that had taken place before they were born. How can we begin discussions about coming to terms with wartime crimes in a country full of people born long after the crimes took place? Partly in response to these comments by the postwar generation, in 1998 Takahashi Tetsuya suggested the idea of recognizing the concept of responsibility in terms of "response-ability," or the willingness and ability to respond to others. The postwar generation should therefore respond to the demands from Korea and China, he argued.[49]

Takahashi's suggestion is part of a more recent trend in the topic of Japan's responsibilities for the Asia-Pacific War: what many scholars and activists refer to as "postwar responsibility."[50] Most Japanese today, however, argue that they have no obligation to engage in the war responsibility discourse as they were born after the Asia-Pacific War ended.[51] The lack of concern about both war and postwar responsibility is apparent in a survey that the *Yomiuri* newspaper conducted in 2005, on the sixtieth anniversary of Japan's defeat in the Asia-Pacific War. Responding to the question "Who do you think bears a significant amount of responsibility for the Asia-Pacific War?" 67.3 percent of the respondents pointed to military leaders, followed by prime ministers at 33.3 percent and politicians at 27.2 percent. A mere 5 percent attributed significant responsibility to the general public.[52] In the same *Yomiuri* survey, 44.8 percent responded that the Japanese people no longer have to feel responsible for the damage their country inflicted on the rest of Asia during the Asia-Pacific War; as many as 63.0 percent responded that Japanese prime ministers have apologized sufficiently to China and Korea.[53] For them, Yasukuni Shrine justifies and reinforces the idea that a handful of powerful people were responsible for what happened during the war.

The tendency to place responsibility on wartime leaders developed in the immediate postwar years, while many Japanese experienced days and months that were often more arduous than those during the war. Those who managed to live through the war now needed to survive in impoverished postwar conditions, facing even more severe shortages of food, shelter, and medical care. Fear of death lingered, and many died from hunger and illness.[54] The end of the war—or rather, Japan's defeat—created an air of despair, as victory, the all-encompassing goal and belief, had become defunct. It was unclear to many Japanese why they needed to repent. Furthermore, the Tokyo War Crimes Tribunal identification of specific Japanese as "war criminals"—and Class-A war criminals in particular—who were responsible for the war, simultaneously fostered among the Japanese people a sense of both freedom from responsibility and victimhood.

In his speech at the first national memorial tribute on August 15, 1963, which subsequently became an annual event, Prime Minister Ikeda Hayato cautioned that "although our nation experienced a remarkable development in the areas of culture and the economy that was built upon a foundation of peace, we must never forget that this success was only possible because of the numerous people who died with the belief that they were dying for the glory of our motherland."[55] Ikeda's speech is useful in considering another concept prevalent in postwar Japan: redemption. As John Breen points out, Yasukuni Shrine highlights this redemptive factor by referents such as "cornerstone (*ishizue*)"—a cornerstone of peace and prosperity in Japan today.[56] If the idea of honorable enshrinement at Yasukuni Shrine helped some to come to terms with their loss as individuals, the idea of a peaceful society built upon past sacrifices helped to define the war's meaning on a national level. People across the political spectrum could embrace the idea of peace and prosperity. However, the concept of responsibility is noticeably absent from this redemptive discourse. As Ienaga Saburō, a historian who made a lifework of responsibly representing the wartime past in school textbooks, cautioned that, if postwar prosperity came at the expense of the war, those who are able to enjoy this (including the postwar generations) should be willing to take responsibility for the war.[57]

The enshrinement of the Class-A war criminals at Yasukuni in 1978 forged a connection between those wartime military leaders and the shrine, further reinforcing the victim consciousness vis-à-vis not only those leaders but also Yasukuni Shrine. As Yoshikuni Igarashi and others have pointed out, the United States' virtual monopoly on the occupation policies of the Allied nations abetted the Japanese in reinterpreting their war experience as a conflict with the United States, thereby erasing the Asian component from Japanese memories of the war.[58] The United States' attack with atomic bombs intensified the perception among the Japanese people that they were victims of the war.[59] The erasure of war memories in Asia precipitated the ease with which responsibility was dismissed for major atrocities and war crimes, including the Nanjing Massacre, comfort women, and the Unit 731 biological experiments.

In the following chapters I explore this shift in popular consciousness and explicate the complex and often contradictory memories that have resulted in the current popular view of Yasukuni. Toward this end, I disassemble the term into the three elements I introduced earlier: the belief, the site, and the issue. Attention to the construction and destruction of memory, particularly in relation to temporal and spatial practice, is crucial to my critical reassessment of the relationship between Yasukuni Shrine and contemporary Japan's inability to confront its wartime past.

In an editorial on June 21, 2011, in the *Mainichi* newspaper, a Wakayama branch reporter drew attention to the idea that the Japanese people are responsible for the nuclear crises that followed the Great East Japan earthquake of March 11, 2011. Highlighting a Wakayama town that opposed the construction of nuclear reactors in 1988 because residents did not believe the government's assurances about the safety of the facilities, the reporter drew a parallel from discussions about the war responsibility of the Japanese people that followed the Asia-Pacific War. In particular, he referenced the late filmmaker Itami Mansaku, who argued in 1946 that the Japanese people were also responsible for allowing themselves to be deceived by their government: "If we are people that can be fine thinking that 'we were deceived,' we will most likely be deceived again and again in the future. It's likely that we are already beginning to be deceived by another lie."[60] This idea of taking responsibility for having allowed oneself to be deceived is worth exploring. An investigation of ways that people were deceived in the past is an important step toward preventing recurrences. My examination of Yasukuni Shrine's history contributes to this process.

OVERVIEW OF CHAPTERS

In chapter 1 I trace the beginnings of the myth that developed around Yasukuni Shrine during the Asia-Pacific War: that dying for the emperor results in enshrinement at Yasukuni as a god—the most highly valued of all achievements for a Japanese. I investigate the process through which the idea of a national memorial was developed using memorial practices observed by members of the Chōshū domain (central actors of the Meiji Restoration) in the decade leading up to the restoration. Existing beliefs and rituals associated with death were incorporated into the foundation of the shrine. My close analysis of these early memorial practices demonstrates, however, that the idea of encouraging death by attaching a particular value to it, which ultimately became the Yasukuni myth during the Asia-Pacific War, was not present at the time the shrine was established.

In chapter 2 I cover the two early successful wars of Japanese imperialism (the Sino-Japanese War, 1894–1895, and the Russo-Japanese War, 1904–1905) in order to examine the gradual process through which the Japanese people came to understand and identify with the ideas behind the shrine. At the time the shrine was conceived, most Japanese had little to do with the men memorialized there; the military conflicts associated with the restoration involved no more than a handful of men from domains far from Tokyo. The intent of the creators, then, was not apparent to most Japanese. But with each victory in the wars against China and Russia, the shrine's grounds were transformed into a key locus for celebrations of war. During these early wars of imperialism Yasukuni Shrine firmly established its position as a site for celebration of the expanding empire by situating itself at the center of a visible network of victory parades and other events that transformed Tokyo into a space of celebration. War death, at the time, was not highlighted.

Around the same time, discourses associated with Yasukuni Shrine began to be disseminated in areas outside Tokyo. (Chapter 3 examines the popularization of beliefs associated with Yasukuni Shrine in areas far from Tokyo, with a focus on local victory celebrations and memorial practices.) Two concepts in particular played a key role in the nationalization of the Yasukuni myth. One was the establishment of a parallel structure between the family and the nation-state. Just as all family members were to respect and obey the father as its head following the Confucian ideal, so all Japanese were instructed to consider their nation as one family with the emperor at the head and to whom they were to demonstrate the utmost respect and obedience. We see here the beginnings of the later idea of sacrificing one's own life for the emperor. Another discourse, more closely associated with Yasukuni Shrine, was the mobilization of the concept of *eirei* (honorable spirit) to urge ultimate reverence for those memorialized at the shrine. But the dissemination of these ideas was a comprehensive undertaking that involved a variety of venues, including education, mass media, and local rituals, as well as the Imperial Rescript on Education and the Meiji Constitution.

The use of performances and celebrations, analyzed in chapters 2 and 3, worked only under certain conditions: successful wars that did not involve a majority of the population. Chapter 4 covers the Asia-Pacific War period, during which all of Japan—both military and civilian—was mobilized for the war effort. I trace one soldier's fate after battlefield death, including cremation, return of the ashes, local memorial services, and Yasukuni enshrinement, with a particular focus on the bereaved family members. To give a fuller picture of cultural practices associated with death during the Asia-Pacific War period, I contextualize this particular soldier's journey using other Yasukuni-related episodes compiled from media sources and material produced by the shrine. During this war, grief over a family member's war death was institutionalized as a national event. Furthermore, participants came to perform an "acceptable" kind of emotional response to war death (e.g., pride rather than grief, joy rather than sorrow). I argue that such performances did not result merely from widespread and strong belief in the Yasukuni myth. Instead, these performances were shaped by organizations, including elementary schools, neighborhood associations, and patriotic women's groups, that exerted pressure on the bereaved to conform to specific conventions of behavior.

An important idea that emerges from this structure is the question of victim and perpetrator, which I deal with in chapter 5. This chapter opens the postwar period of Yasukuni Shrine with a discussion of the "Yasukuni issue." Although the components of the Yasukuni issue are closely intertwined, I focus on attempts to have the names of the dead removed from the Yasukuni register. In particular, I examine a recent lawsuit filed by Okinawans at the Naha District Court (Okinawa) in October 2010, seeking the removal of civilian deaths from the register. The Okinawa case is distinctive because it is the only place in Japan that was invaded by the enemy and simultaneously was the target of the aggressive behavior of Japanese soldiers who refused to protect the civilians. The Okinawa example thus presents an opportunity to examine the complex roles of victims and perpetrators in an all-out war. I also touch upon similar legal suits filed by Korean and Taiwanese families whose members are memorialized at Yasukuni Shrine against their will. The cases focus on Article 20 of the Japanese Constitution, which guarantees freedom of religion: Does Yasukuni Shrine's memorialization of the war dead interfere with freedom of religion, which is guaranteed to the family members of those memorialized? Through a close examination of the deliberations, I also consider the concept of mourning (*tsuitō*) a public death. Do family members possess exclusive rights to mourn? If, for example, Japan had not lost the Asia-Pacific War, those enshrined at Yasukuni would have remained national deaths. Would family members have demanded an exclusive right to mourn had the war been successful?

Memories and narratives of the Asia-Pacific War occupy an important place in Japan today, where many are concerned with the waning of its immediacy. Museums, exhibition halls, and oral history projects attempt to compile such memories and present them in a way relevant to today's youth—the postmemory generations that were born after 1945.[61] Yasukuni Shrine also participates in this effort. Chapter 6 examines recent attempts by the shrine administration and supporters to reintroduce their ideas of memorialization in ways that are relevant to postmemory generations. I introduce the ways that management and supporters of Yasukuni Shrine have attempted to reinvent the institution for the twenty-first century with the younger generation in mind. This revisionist history is finding an increasingly receptive audience in contemporary Japan. I find in this trend the postmemory generations' need for a conservative (and redemptive) discourse for the purpose of not only overcoming their inherited past but also, at the same time, evading the issue of war responsibility, which was inadvertently taken on from previous generations. I suggest here a reciprocal reinforcement between the attempt for the shrine to look back to (draw from) the past to entice its audience and the postmemory generations' desire to reconstruct an idealized past so that they may overcome their inherited trauma.

I conclude the book with a brief epilogue. In recent years, volunteers who consider themselves unofficial guides of Yasukuni Shrine have led tours through the shrine grounds to introduce various monuments and museum displays. Their mission is to use the shrine grounds as a way to discuss various acts of violence and crimes committed by the Japanese military. Through their activities, they reappropriate the space of the shrine and transform the shrine into a countermonument, a site that can be used to question the official narrative propagated by the shrine itself.[62] Through their spatial practice, these guides introduce a new, dynamic way to engage with both the political issues associated with the shrine and Japan's troubled postwar legacies. More specifically, the practices of these activist guides diverge from proposals to either alter the shrine or replace it with a new national war memorial, both of which suggestions have the implicit goal of erasing inconvenient memories by removing the monument that represents them. These practices also diverge from conservative supporters, who strive to maintain the shrine as it is. At the same time, the new narratives focus the blame for the Asia-Pacific War on the shrine, thereby reinforcing the narrative of victimhood and hindering Japan's much-needed efforts to reconcile with the rest of Asia.

ONE

MOBILIZING DEATH

Developing the Myth of Yasukuni

> Today on the way to the villa I passed through the temple grounds of Ueno. The two-story gate and most of the buildings were burned in the battle last summer; so now the grandeur of the past is but a dream. I want to purify this ground and dedicate it as a memorial to the war dead.
>
> *KIDO TAKAYOSHI*, THE DIARY OF KIDO TAKAYOSHI

On January 15, 1869, statesman Kido Takayoshi noted in his diary that the Kan'eiji site in Ueno, which he happened to walk through earlier that day, should be purified and transformed into a memorial for the war dead.[1] He was, in fact, proposing that Ueno, once bustling with patrons of the Kan'eiji temple but now left devastated after the Battle of Ueno the previous year, should house a memorial for the imperial loyalist men who fell during the restoration. In short, Kido was recommending that an institution akin to what would become Yasukuni Shrine be built at Ueno. Kido's proposal did not materialize, however. Ōmura Masujirō, who soon would become the vice minister of the newly created Army Ministry, opposed Kido's choice, arguing that the spirits of the dead bakufu soldiers—enemy casualties of that battle—haunted the site. Furthermore, the land was unavailable, as the Meiji government announced shortly thereafter that it had designated the Ueno site for a new university hospital. Instead, Ōmura selected a stretch of land atop Kudan Hill that had been controlled by the bakufu infantry—the site that Yasukuni Shrine currently occupies. He recommended it as the most auspicious location for the Imperial Palace: The site was situated to the northwest (*inui*) of the palace, the direction in need of protection.[2]

Ōmura had grand plans. He predicted that the Kudan site, with its proximity to the Imperial Palace and a commanding view of Tokyo, would become a strategic spot in case of armed domestic conflict. Thus, it was—at least symbolically—to function as more than a memorial for the fallen. At the time, the road that traveled up the hill comprised nine sloped steps (hence the name Kudan, or nine steps), and from the summit one could see as far as Tokyo Bay. As the original pathway up Kudan was narrow and steep, Ōmura planned to widen it and decrease the incline for easier travel by the military. Although they did not yet exist in Japan, he imagined horse-drawn carriages traveling along the street.[3] In addition to the memorial itself, Ōmura also proposed an expansive plan for the site (shown on a map dated June 1869) that would include a communal cemetery for those memorialized.[4]

These visions of Ōmura Masujirō became the foundation for the Yasukuni Shrine that we know today. But the shrine grounds do not include a cemetery, and Yasukuni Shrine has dealt only with the spirits—not the physical bodies—of the fallen. The decision to eliminate the cemetery was partly logistical. Ōmura's original plan included an expansion of the site into a large area of surrounding buildings, a proposal that did not materialize due to vehement opposition by local shopkeepers.[5] Nonetheless, the construction project for the memorial itself commenced in mid-June 1869. Temporary structures, which included the inner shrine, a worship hall, and two offering halls, were hurriedly completed in ten days, all in time for a memorial scheduled at the end of the same month.[6] In the evening of June 28, the first *shōkon* ritual (literally translated as a ritual to invite the spirits of the dead) took place, which memorialized the spirits of 3,588 imperialist men who had fallen during the Boshin War. For five days following the ritual, from June 29 to July 3, the shrine hosted festivities that featured sumo matches and fireworks. An imperial messenger paid tribute on June 29. Units of the Imperial Army took turns firing celebratory gun salutes. Visitors were treated to sacred sake.[7] Until the permanent inner shrine was completed three years later, three festivals per year took place at the site.[8]

At the time, these structures were known as the Tokyo Shōkonsha, or the "Tokyo shrine to invite in spirits of the dead," and together they comprised the immediate predecessor to Yasukuni Shrine.[9] As I detail in the next chapter, it was not a well-known site at first. Even the five-day festival to commemorate the first enshrinement of the imperial fallen seems to have captured little attention. Although the Kudan area quickly became a popular location, the shrine was generally absent from cultural representations of Tokyo in general and of the Kudan area in particular. The turning point was the 1872 spring festival, conducted immediately after the permanent structure was completed, during which numerous people visited the shrine grounds. An article reporting the festival in the *Yūbin hōchi* newspaper suggests one reason for the lack of attention in previous years:

> On May 15th, the annual Shōkonsha festival took place at the new building at Kudan Hill completed on May 10th. For the past couple of years, *few people visited this shrine and many had no respect for the facility, as enshrined here were only those from the Western domains*. . . . With the completion of the new building however, numerous people, both officials and the masses, have flocked to the shrine raising clouds of dust. The scene is unlike any seen here before.[10]

It was the new, permanent shrine that attracted Tokyoites, not the memorial function of the site. By this time, other novelties were perched atop Kudan Hill, including a pair of monumental stone lanterns completed in 1871. Together with the spectacular view of the bay, the shrine grounds inspired artists and attracted nearby residents. Festivals and other events on the shrine grounds quickly became popular.

There was a simple reason that people living within easy traveling distance of the shrine initially had little knowledge of the men who were memorialized: Most Tokyoites had no association with them and were uninterested in their cause. The antibakufu faction, which took political power away from the Tokugawas, was led by men from Chōshū and Satsuma, the "Western domains," as noted in the article. Other major participants were the domains of Aki, Inshū, and Tosa, also located in the Western half of Japan. While leaders quickly took over Tokyo to organize the new government, residents were not invested in the fate of the imperialist dead. Not only did the men come from the faraway "Western domains," but ordinary Tokyoites at the time also had little to do with armed conflict. Armed participation in a military cause was for the most part limited to the samurai class during the Tokugawa era. For most others, battles were spectacles in which deaths occurred to unknown and unrelated people. During the Battle of Ueno, for example, nearby residents gathered to watch the confrontation, while opportunistic shopkeepers wove their way through the crowd selling rice balls and pickled vegetables.[11] The significance of the shrine as a memorial to deaths that occurred at Ueno and other related battles was not apparent to most Tokyoites in the early Meiji era.

Of course, Tokyo Shōkonsha (and Yasukuni Shrine soon thereafter) did not remain an obscure institution for long, as can be observed by the prominent place it occupied in the last years of the Asia-Pacific War. The process that transformed it into a central institution of war memory, however, is not straightforward. Wars and the resulting loss of life in Japan's imperialist quest certainly played a key role in this transformation: Death was presented in a positive light in order to sustain a level of enthusiasm to support these wars.

Imperial Japan was certainly not alone in this effort. In analyzing the modern European experience of warfare (roughly contemporaneous with my work here), George Mosse discusses what he refers to as "the Myth of the War Experience," with a particular focus on how the concept was mobilized in post–World War I Germany.[12] In representations of war memory in prose, poetry, picture books, and film, Mosse identifies a strong urge to portray a higher meaning of the war experience that was shaped by encounters with mass death and argues that this Myth of the War Experience developed more significantly in defeated nations.[13] Redefining the meaning of the lives that were lost was central to this myth: War death was presented as sacrifice and resurrection rather than loss of life. Young soldiers were remembered as having fought courageously and dying for the homeland singing joyously (in striking parallel to the anecdotal accounts of Japanese troops shouting "Long live the emperor!" in the face of death). Mosse contends that these narratives were influential not so much for the soldiers in the trenches but, significantly, more for those waiting at home.[14]

Many parallels to Mosse's claim can be found in Japan during the first half of the twentieth century. I am interested here in exploring the development of such myths and their transformation into a sort of national belief (Yasukuni the belief). Yasukuni Shrine certainly played an important role in this process. However, these initial chapters examine the multiplicity of tools mobilized in the process of transforming this myth into a belief, of which Yasukuni Shrine was one. Over time, and certainly by the 1940s, Yasukuni Shrine came to occupy center stage in the Japanese myth of war experience. But the shrine's role in this myth was not always so apparent in the early years. In this chapter I focus on the earliest phase in the creation of this belief. What was the origin of the idea that dying in war for the emperor's sake is the greatest honor one could ever achieve? And who realized that this idea could be used to mobilize men for a common cause even in the face of death? "Yasukuni the belief," of course, is an invented tradition, just like national holidays, anthems, flags, and other conventions of nationhood.[15] But typically inventions that become traditions are based loosely on preexisting conventions. I am interested in exploring the origins of the myth and the ways in which they were reinvented.

THE ORIGINS OF YASUKUNI PRACTICE

In order to address these questions, I start in the years leading up to the Restoration, when the practice of commemorating war death was normalized. The early history of Yasukuni Shrine provided in key works by scholars such as Ōe Shinobu is straightforward and is summarized here.[16] The practice of memorializing the fallen imperial loyalists began several years before the Boshin War as rituals conducted by members of the Chōshū domain. What started as a local ritual developed into a national one when restoration-related dead from multiple domains were collectively enshrined in Kyoto on December 24, 1862. With the relocation of the imperial capital in 1868, the new government ordered a transfer of the spirits to the newly built shrine in central Tokyo (Tokyo Shōkonsha). Constructing the shrine in the middle of the new capital symbolized the central role this institution occupied in the newly constructed nation. And with the frequent wars Japan subsequently engaged in, as well as through its association with the emperor, Yasukuni Shrine attained its notorious status during the Asia-Pacific War years and beyond.

There are no inaccuracies in this narrative. Yet it does not explain the process through which the Japanese came to embrace the idea of dying for the emperor or the idea of transforming the war dead into a protector god for Japan—a process that closely aligns with the development of the Myth of the War Experience in modern Japan. In this and the next two chapters I explore the beginnings of this myth and how it was shaped during Japan's earlier wars of imperialism. Newly invented cultural practices can enjoy wider acceptance when they draw on existing customs. Memorializing military death at Yasukuni Shrine was no exception. Although the *shōkon* ritual conducted at Yasukuni Shrine was introduced during the last years of the Tokugawa era, planners of this ritual drew on precedents and customs.

According to modern ethnographic accounts, *shōkon* rituals in general draw from traditional death-related practices in Japan, which developed out of the belief in the close relationship between the living and the dead.[17] It was believed, for example, that the spirits of the dead lingered in the world of the living after death. It was commonly thought that spirits were confused about or unaccepting of their death. Rituals were designed to call back the wandering spirits to the world of the living or to attempt to communicate with the spirits, typically to placate them.[18] This kind of spirit, *aramitama* (spirit of the new dead) in Buddhist terminology, was considered to possess a great deal of energy, which made it capable of harming the living. Especially feared were spirits of those who were believed to have had special powers (whether psychic or political) while alive, those who felt contempt for humanity, those whose death rituals were not performed properly, and those who died an untimely death (including the military dead). Rituals were conducted in order to tame these spirits, based on the belief that, when properly appeased, the power of vengeful spirits is transformed and brings positive influence to the living. The imperial court historically followed this tradition to commemorate and posthumously promote men that had died a tragic death as a way to placate their spirits. Examples of such "promotion" include Sugawara no Michizane (845–903) and Kusunoki Masashige (c. 1294–1336), both of whom had shrines dedicated to them. As I will explain, Kusunoki, in particular, played a key role in the foundation of the Yasukuni myth.

In medieval times the fear of vengeful spirits (*goryō shinkō*) grew into a battlefield memorial practice. Warriors adopted this practice in order to memorialize battlefield deaths during the tumultuous period from the twelfth to the sixteenth century. According to this practice, all deaths were memorialized, whether enemy or ally.[19] Once the outcome of the battle was determined, the victors conducted a ritual called *dai segaki e* (the great rite to appease hungry ghosts) for all of the war dead from both sides. Following the ritual, the victors typically erected a memorial on the site for both enemy and ally (*teki mikata kuyō-hi*). This medieval practice is distinct from Yasukuni ritual in that both enemy and ally were memorialized together.[20] In fact, during these battlefield rituals, the dead from the defeated side were memorialized with particular attentiveness.[21] Previous accounts of the origins of Yasukuni practice conclude that the creators of Yasukuni Shrine appropriated and politicized this traditional ritual by selectively memorializing and commemorating war death for the emperor.[22]

A close examination of the ways that death rituals were conducted in the years leading up to and during the restoration suggests, however, that there was not yet an established arrangement to discriminate enemy dead. Some domains performed memorial rituals for their men. In some of the restoration-related battles, all dead were memorialized regardless of which side they had fought for. In other cases, concerted efforts were made to prevent the enemy from tending to their dead. But when Tokyo Shōkonsha was originally created, the idea of selective memorialization was not yet institutionalized. Instead, a move to politicize the war dead for a larger cause emerged during the last years of the Tokugawa era. Later on I outline the development of death rituals in some of the antibakufu domains and then introduce instances where death—encompassing both the physical bodies and the spirits of the dead—was mobilized for the construction of a collective identity. The idea of mobilizing death for a political cause is not unique to modern Japan, and thus my analysis is informed by scholars who have studied the politics of memorial, burial, exhumation, and reburial elsewhere.[23]

SON'NŌ JŌI AND THE LEGEND OF KUSUNOKI MASASHIGE

Two domains in particular hold the key to the modern practice of *shōkon,* which developed into the ideas behind Yasukuni Shrine: Chōshū, a key player of the Meiji Restoration and situated at the Western end of mainland Japan, and Mito, the birthplace of the Mito School of nativist thought, located much closer to Edo. During the final years of the Tokugawa era, men of samurai status in Chōshū began to collectively and publicly memorialize the deaths of samurai. Around the same time, some six hundred miles away, Mito ideologues were promoting the idea of *son'nō jōi* (revere the emperor; expel the barbarian) as a way to strengthen the national consciousness of Japan as a whole by uniting under the emperor. Both were responding to the emerging sense of crisis precipitated by the decline of bakufu influence, social unrest more generally, and the appearance of foreign ships in Japanese waters.

In the beginning the Chōshū practice was exclusively domain based. In October 1851 Chōshū leader Mōri Takachika ordered research on and the collection of the names of all samurai who died for a cause that benefited the domain—or should have benefited it. Two years later, in 1853, Chōshū men created a register of such domainal deaths, deposited it at the local Tōshunji temple, and performed a Buddhist-style memorial service on June 14. This practice was to be an annual ritual conducted on the same date. While the religious style differs, this ritual—a memorial service regularly performed for an exclusive group of people—bears striking resemblance to the Yasukuni practice. But little information exists on the reasons for this annual rite since *Kōhon mori no shigeri,* the official chronicle of Chōshū history, contains only brief entries on events.[24] For example, the 1851 entry simply notes that the names, as well as date and location of death, were recorded for "all war dead and loyal dead from long past (*ōko yori*)." The 1853 entry mentions a memorial ritual that was to take place on June 14 every year.[25]

The circumstances contributing to the reasons for these rituals, however, are open to interpretation. For instance, these rites became an annual event when foreign ships appeared in the waters surrounding Japan: Commodore Matthew Perry, a catalyst for Japan's dramatic shift in foreign policy, arrived at Uraga on June 5, 1853. Domestic politics also contributed to the situation. Because of a two-and-a-half-century-old history, Chōshū leaders held the bakufu in deep contempt throughout the Tokugawa regime.[26] Legend has it that, as an annual new year's tradition, a retainer would ask the daimyo, "should it be this year [that we attack the Tokugawas]?" to which the daimyo would always respond, "not yet." Retainers are said to have slept with their feet facing Edo to demonstrate their resentment.[27] By this time, with the political power of the bakufu waning, Chōshū leaders began to anticipate armed conflict, whether domestic or international, in the near future, with an eye to opportunities to overthrow the bakufu. A practice of collective memorial was thus useful. At a time when more deaths could be foreseen, ritualized treatment of the dead could help promote a collective identity.

Although there are similarities between the annual Chōshū memorials and Yasukuni practice, the Chōshū rituals were conducted in the Buddhist style. How did the shift to the Shinto style of Yasukuni enshrinement take place? Further, how was the concept of fighting for the emperor incorporated into the rituals? Here I turn to Mito, a domain that produced the thinkers who played a central role in shaping the political ideas behind the restoration, including *son'nō jōi*. The *Shinron* (The New Theses, 1825), by Mito scholar Aizawa Seishisai, is a key text that promotes the concept of *son'nō jōi* and highlights the emperor's importance. Written as a response to the bakufu order of the same year to expel foreigners from Japanese waters, *Shinron* attempted to strengthen a collective, national consciousness of Japan through unity under the emperor. *Shinron,* however, did not criticize bakufu authority. Its goal was to secure Japanese independence by establishing a strong political structure that maintained the bakufu politically, while creating a renewed identity around the traditional authority of the emperor. In short, the recommendation was to emphasize national consciousness of Japan as a whole (with both the bakufu and the court intact) over allegiance to individual domains.[28] Of course, this stance changed once the bakufu signed treaties to open Japanese ports: *Son'nō jōi* quickly came to include the idea of overthrowing the bakufu.

To promote a new brand of *son'nō jōi* that included restoring exclusive power to the emperor, Mito scholars used a fourteenth-century figure, Kusunoki Masashige (c.1294–1336), whom they could associate with a previous "restoration" of imperial power over a bakufu that occurred during the final years of the Kamakura period (1185–1333). At that time, when bakufu power was faltering in the hands of the Hōjō family, Emperor Go-Daigo took military measures to terminate the bakufu and establish his own rule: the short-lived Kenmu Restoration (1333–1336). Kusunoki fought for the emperor and played a key role in the court's success. But he was not as successful when, in 1335, Ashikaga Takauji led his army and wrested political power from the court and later started the next bakufu. In May 1336, after losing the decisive battle against Takauji, Kusunoki killed himself in Minatogawa, present-day Kobe.[29] The Kusunoki tragedy was popularized through the epic *Taiheiki,* which is considered to have been written in the fourteenth century and was used as the subject of *kōdan* (professional storytelling) during the Muromachi and Tokugawa periods.[30] But his grave was untended until 1692, when Mito daimyo Mitsukuni restored the burial site and constructed a new gravestone.[31] The Kusunoki figure proved useful for the Mito scholars' attempts to foster a sense of nationalism focused on the emperor. His initial success was reinterpreted in the late Tokugawa years as a historical example of the emperor asserting his authority with the help of a brave warrior to reclaim rule from a military leader. His tragic death—voluntary and by his own hand—came to symbolize ultimate loyalty to the emperor. Kusunoki quickly came to be revered as a hero in a historical "overthrowing of the bakufu" and as the emperor's loyal follower who sacrificed his life for the imperial cause.

Kusunoki also appears in *Shinron,* in which Aizawa Seishisai advocated the deification of people who accomplished extraordinary deeds for Japan. The connection with Shinto is also introduced here. In *Shinron,* Aizawa mentions Shinto shrines that are dedicated to people whose deeds were significant (e.g., Kitano and Kasuga) and argues that reviving the tradition of deifying loyal warriors would encourage commoners to pay reverence to the gods. He even suggests a series of holidays, many of which are for Shinto rites, but also includes several dates on which people who accomplished great feats would be celebrated. One such figure was Kusunoki. In his 1834 text, *Sōen wagen*—a commentary on court-related events and rituals—Aizawa proposed gathering comrades on the anniversary of Kusunoki Masashige's death for training and morale building.[32] Here we see a communal identity beginning to develop via the death rituals.

Aizawa's follower Maki Izumi went one step further in his 1859 text, *Keii gusetsu,* in which he argues for the deification of loyal warriors in history and their posthumous promotion. In addition, he suggests dedicating shrines to these figures as a way of inspiring contemporary warriors.[33] On May 25,

1862, Maki conducted a ritual for Kusunoki, during which he also memorialized eight spirits of antibakufu Satsuma warriors who died during the Teradaya incident.[34] Around this time, Kusunoki rituals began taking place in other domains as well. In 1865, residents of the Yamaguchi domain, for example, began regularly conducting a Kusunoki ritual and soon incorporated the dead from their own domain into the ceremony.[35] Through these combined memorials, the Kusunoki legend shifted its emphasis from a narrative of successful imperial restoration to one of a brave hero who sacrificed his life for an imperial cause. His death was thus mobilized for a larger political objective: to rally around the emperor in order to unseat the Tokugawa regime from power. This new interpretation of the Kusunoki legend became popularized in late Tokugawa Japan and, consequently, in the modern years as well.

CHŌSHŪ MEMORIAL PRACTICES

The idea of Kusunoki worship traveled to the Chōshū domain early on. In the mid-1850s, Yoshida Shōin, scholar and son of a Chōshū samurai, preached passionately on the heroic self-sacrifice of Kusunoki to pupils in his private school while he was under house arrest.[36] A strong dissenter of the bakufu's passive foreign policies, Shōin encouraged his students to follow Kusunoki's lead and defy the bakufu in order to restore power to the court. Through his fervent instruction he cultivated many enthusiastic followers, including Takasugi Shinsaku and Kusaka Gensui, who would play central roles in the movement to overthrow the bakufu. In addition to these men's contempt for the bakufu, as a domain Chōshū also had reasons for supporting the imperial court: It was believed that the Mōri family (the daimyo of Chōshū) had blood ties with the imperial court.[37]

In the early 1860s, Chōshū leaders began developing a more encompassing memorial practice. By this time clashes between the antibakufu and probakufu factions led to bloodshed such as the Ansei purges (1858–1859) and the Sakurada Gate incident (1860).[38] Shōin was executed in October 1859 as a part of the Ansei purges. Also by this time, Kyoto was emerging as the key site for antibakufu supporters who were not limited by domain boundaries; many converged in the imperial capital to plan an overthrow of the Tokugawa regime. Because heroic sacrifices would inspire their men, Chōshū leaders conspired to hold a collective memorial rite in Kyoto to commemorate their dead. But the bakufu forbade a proper memorial for these dead. From the bakufu's viewpoint, the imperial loyalist dead were criminals who had been executed or killed as anti-imperial rebels. The first matters for attention, therefore, entailed obtaining a court mandate to remove their criminal status. The involvement of the emperor was also useful for the leaders of the antibakufu movement since it would emphasize the idea that the antibakufu faction was now fighting for a common cause: the restoration of imperial political power. In their view, a memorial sanctioned by the emperor offered the perfect opportunity to instill in the antibakufu supporters a sense of *son'nō*—reverence for the emperor—as well as a collective identity.

In 1862 Chōshū leaders successfully solicited Emperor Kōmei's approval to posthumously exonerate men who died for antibakufu causes. On August 2 of that year, Kōmei sent the bakufu an imperial message about his plan to memorialize "deaths in state affairs (*kokuji*)."[39] The message ordered the bakufu to provide the emperor with the names of the dead associated with the Ansei purges and all imperial loyalist deaths thereafter.[40] The bakufu had little choice but to comply with the emperor's order. Fourteenth shogun Iemochi gave permission to free all imperial loyalist prisoners, exonerated all those who had died, and granted permission to construct graves for them. Among those exonerated was Yoshida Shōin. Chōshū men requested this ritual largely to revive the name of Shōin, their revered teacher. But the event had even greater historical significance: It was the first memorial ritual initiated in the name of the emperor, it involved multiple domains, and those memorialized were officially acknowledged as deaths resulting from state affairs. Thus it can be considered the key event in the move to restore political power in the name of the emperor through the use of death rituals.

Kōmei himself officiated a *shōkon* ritual at the Reimeisha shrine at Mt. Ryōzen in Higashiyama, Kyoto, on December 24, 1862.[41] For the first time, men from multiple domains were memorialized together in the name of the emperor and recognized for their joint efforts to overthrow the bakufu.[42] This transformed the practice of memorialization into a tool for constructing a collective identity. The ritual also assigned a new meaning to the deaths: Not only were the men relieved of their criminal status, but they were also now heroes and martyrs who had sacrificed their lives for the imperial cause. This transformation closely parallels the myth construction in modern Europe but is firmly grounded in a Japanese narrative. In the following year, 1863, for the first time in Kyoto a physical structure was built exclusively for the *shōkon* ritual. Men from the Tsuwano domain constructed a small shrine inside the Yasaka Shrine grounds, situated at the foot of Ryōzen, where, on July 25, they collectively memorialized forty-six men. Immediately after the ritual, the shrine was relocated to the residence of Tsuwano leader Fukuba Bisei to conceal the event from pro-bakufu men. In 1931 the structure was transferred once again to Yasukuni Shrine, where it still exists on the grounds as the Motomiya, or original shrine.[43]

Chōshū rituals also took on a Shinto quality once the move toward restoration began. On May 25, 1864, members conducted a memorial at the Shiraishi residence, where the *kiheitai* (volunteer army comprised primarily of commoners; the *kiheitai* played a significant role in the restoration) would soon be established.[44] Loyalists from the Chōshū domain were in attendance along with Maki Izumi, the Kusunoki admirer and *son'nō jōi* advocate from Mito. For the first time for the Chōshū men, the rituals were conducted in the Shinto style. Prayers were offered not only for the dead but also for Kusunoki's success with *son'nō jōi*. For the first time the Chōshū idea of regularly memorializing dead comrades merged with the Mito idea of commemorating commendable deaths as gods in the Shinto tradition—and offering prayers for military success.

Back in their home domain, Chōshū also led the creation of physical structures for the rituals. In August 1865 Chōshū constructed a shrine at a site in Sakurayama (Shimonoseki), where memorial rituals continued to be held on a regular basis.[45] A permanent structure for the rituals provided a space dedicated to the memorialization of the soldiers' comrades: It would be useful not only for regular events but also as a visible marker, a constant reminder for the men of the importance of their political cause. During the previous month a law had been passed that required each county to build its own *shōkonsha,* or shrine for conducting memorial rituals.[46] By the end of 1865, fifteen such memorial sites were active in the Chōshū domain.[47] Unlike Yasukuni Shrine, gravelike stones with the names of the deceased now neatly stand behind the shrine. There are no bodies here, however, as they were cremated and the ashes buried at temples or battlefields. The stones are markers to which the spirits of the dead were to return. This idea of stone markers may seem distinct from the practice at Yasukuni Shrine. However, I suggest that the original plans included it quite likely as the "cemetery" proposed by Ōmura. Had the shopkeepers not protested the expansion of the shrine grounds, Yasukuni Shrine may have taken on an identity different from what it has today.

The Chōshū shrines were also educational. At the time of the restoration, many lower-ranked members of domains that were fighting on behalf of the emperor knew little about him. Moreover, the unification of the nation under the emperor's name was still a new idea. Some lacked access to even a part of the education that a child of a samurai received. In fact, in August 1863, in the midst of attacks by foreign battleships at Shimonoseki, Chōshū member Takasugi Shinsaku created the *kiheitai,* which enabled commoners to fight. Many soldiers thus maintained loyalty to their immediate leaders but were unaware of the larger cause of overthrowing the bakufu in the name of the emperor. To those fighting for the emperor and risking their lives, just as their deceased comrades had done, the memorial practice and physical presence of the *shōkonsha* buildings reinforced the message of an imperial cause. An iteration of Aizawa's 1834 proposal to annually commemorate Kusunoki's death is evident here: Men concluded their *shōkon* ceremonies by pledging to follow in the footsteps of their slain comrades and always followed the ceremony with military training.[48] In this sense, a *shōkonsha* was not merely a memorial site but also a place to which men pledged to return as spirits. For the commoners it held an educational purpose as well: They were conscripted to construct the local *shōkonsha.* Their involvement in building the shrine was a way to heighten their awareness of the idea that they were all fighting together for a cause.

The regular rituals also normalized two conditions that had recently been introduced along with the *shōkon* rituals: first, the idea that the domain, rather than the family member of the deceased, had authority over the memorialization process, and second, the attenuated distinction between shrines dedicated to gods and those dedicated to human spirits, given that the deceased were previously not considered gods.[49] The domain's authority over memorialization of the dead transferred the right to perform death rituals from the private entity of the family to a public one of the domain. This shift established the precedent for the Japanese state's control over the memorialization of war death in the later years.

Architects of the new government, which comprised primarily Chōshū men, developed this domain-based practice into a national one. In May 1868 the newly instituted government built a *shōkonsha* on Ryōzen to collectively commemorate imperial loyalists who had lost their lives in political struggles since 1853, as well as the soldiers of the Imperial Army killed at Toba-Fushimi, the first Battle of the Boshin War.[50] The Kyoto facility housed the graves of representative loyalist dead as well as several domain-specific shrines and was considered a central facility at the time. However, the practice of collective memorial was not limited to this site. For example, on June 2, 1868, less than two months after the bakufu relinquished Edo Castle, to collectively commemorate all deaths in the Imperial Army, the governor general of the Eastern Expedition Group (Tōseigun) held a large-scaled *shōkon* ceremony at Edo Castle rather than the newly constructed Higashiyama Shōkonsha. The ceremony was conducted in the very hall where negotiations to hand over the castle were held by the last shogun, Yoshinobu, thus highlighting the redemptive symbolism of the event: that the transfer of power occurred as a result of the lives lost. The official chronicle of Yasukuni Shrine points to this ritual as the beginning of the Tokyo Shōkonsha. Yet, it was not an official state ritual because it was a military memorial rite that happened to be conducted during the Eastern Expedition.[51] Nevertheless, this event, which took place in the same hall where Yoshinobu officially relinquished his right to political power, is significant for its symbolism and the specificity of its site. The multiplicity of sites at which memorials were conducted suggests, however, that the idea of collectively memorializing all imperial war dead at one site was not yet fully developed.

Memorial rituals continued in Kyoto as well. The spirits of 374 loyalist dead were memorialized at a Kyoto military training ground on July 10 and 11, 1868. Men also conducted memorial rites on the grounds where actual battles had taken place. But the situation changed on July 17, 1868, when Tokyo was designated the new capital. With the official relocation of Emperor Meiji from Kyoto to Tokyo in March 1869, the new government decided to construct a *shōkonsha* in Tokyo to replace the one in Higashiyama.[52]

WHO CAN BE ENSHRINED?

Chronologically, we have arrived at the moment when Ōmura Masujirō selected the site at Kudan. But before I discuss the development of the shrine, I want to address one more issue surrounding a characteristic of the *shōkon* practice at Yasukuni Shrine: the problem of selective memorialization. One major criticism of Yasukuni Shrine in recent decades is that it commemorates only particular kinds of deaths: mostly Japanese military deaths that resulted from wars of imperialism and, as outlined earlier, loyalist deaths that occurred during the restoration. This kind of selective memorialization has had further ramifications in the post–Asia-Pacific War period. Many bereaved family members have submitted requests to Yasukuni Shrine to have their loved ones enshrined, whereas others have demanded the removal of names from the shrine's register.[53] As I detail in chapter 5, the process of post-1945 memorialization includes the compilation of the names and other information about the deceased, which were often provided by the Japanese state. Although the head priest always makes the final decision in atypical cases, for example, the Class-A war criminals, a set of guidelines also helps determine the names for enshrinement. These guidelines have changed numerous times, even after 1945, sometimes resulting in enshrinement of those who had died decades earlier.[54] Nevertheless, enshrinement always followed the most current guidelines. When did this process of selective memorialization begin, and who determined the criteria by which the dead came to be enshrined?

The popular theory, namely, that antibakufu men started selective memorialization for political purposes during the restoration-related battles, may not be entirely accurate. Late Tokugawa memorial practices did become increasingly political, but there were no predetermined qualifications the deceased had to meet in order to be memorialized in a particular ritual. In fact, at times all of the deaths on both the imperial and the bakufu side were memorialized, as with the memorial that was ordered by the court and performed in October 1864 at Chion-in, a Pure Land temple in Kyoto.[55] Moreover, during the Boshin War, imperial loyalists often allowed the enemy dead to be memorialized. For example, imperial troops immediately consented to the burial and memorial of the pro-bakufu fighters who died in the Battle of Echigo-Koide in April 1868. Imperial loyalist leaders, who gave the consent, attended and participated in the memorial service.[56]

In principle, the concept of military enshrinement seems simple. In the case of Japan's wars of imperialism against foreign nations, the process was somewhat straightforward: Regardless of whether a military death on the field, a military death resulting from illness, or the death of a civilian who had proven affiliation with the military, it was not difficult to assess eligibility as long as a set of criteria was specified.[57] But matters were not as simple for restoration-related deaths. The process of restoration involved a variety of causes of death, for example, from a more or less straightforward death on the battlefield during the Boshin War to executions during the Ansei purges. In addition, the last years of the Tokugawa era saw shifting alliances between domains, which often made it difficult to determine which lives were lost while supporting the imperial cause. For example, the relationship between Chōshū and Satsuma, as well as Chōshū's perceived loyalty to the imperial court, both shifted dramatically in the last years of the Tokugawa period. Another case in point is the shifting alliance among the three domains of Aizu, Satsuma, and Chōshū. In August 1863, leaders of Aizu and Satsuma collaborated to drive the Chōshū powers out of Kyoto. In the

Kinmon incident of July 1864, Chōshū men attempted to recover their positions in Kyoto and became involved in an armed skirmish with Aizu men outside the imperial palace. As a result, Chōshū, which had always allied itself with the imperial court, was labeled an enemy of the court. In 1866, however, Chōshū established an alliance with Satsuma, thus transforming Aizu into a common enemy and restoring its relationship with the court.[58]

In such situations it can be difficult to determine who is eligible for an official, court-sanctioned memorial. Based on subsequent reinterpretation of late Tokugawa events, some men came to be eligible for enshrinement decades after death. It was not until the 1930s that Yasukuni Shrine formulated an official set of enshrinement criteria for those who had fallen in events associated with the restoration.[59] In other words, the origin of Yasukuni practice does not suggest a well-defined intention of posthumous discrimination. Rather, the focus was on the creation of a common, collective identity through memorial practice—a quality that I argue existed up to the end of the Asia-Pacific War.

POLITICAL USE OF DEATH: DEAD BODIES AND MEMORIAL PRACTICES

The idea to establish eligibility for memorialization and to use the practice of memorializing for political purposes thus developed gradually. At the outset, efforts were not focused exclusively on the spirits of the dead—the practice of Yasukuni Shrine—but on death rites in general, including proper burial of the bodies. And in later years, during Japan's wars of imperialism, the military took full control of not only the spirits of the war dead (through Yasukuni Shrine) but also their bodies as a way to exert power over those still alive. Although Yasukuni enshrinement often took center stage in the mass media, there were other, sometimes more elaborate procedures that dealt with the bodies. Local memorial services were also important. I detail these processes in later chapters. Here I want to highlight the presence of other kinds of practices surrounding war death.

Being under the jurisdiction of the military, it is not surprising that Yasukuni Shrine became a venue through which the military organized its dead. Particularly in the final years of the Asia-Pacific War, when retrieval of bodies from the battlefront was nearly impossible, this idea of mobilizing the spirits of the war dead became a useful replacement for rituals associated with bodies and ashes. At the same time, I suggest that memorial rituals at Yasukuni Shrine were only one component of a variety of practices that utilized death to promote militaristic nationalism and that such ideas gradually emerged during the restoration.

As we have seen in the discussion of the 1862 process of rehabilitating the posthumous status of men who were considered antibakufu, criminals and traitors (*kokuzoku*) were not eligible for typical death-related rites in Tokugawa Japan. As a case in point, I refer to Yoshida Shōin, who was executed in 1859 as a part of the Ansei purges, and follow Shōin's body to explore the use of dead bodies for political ends. On October 27, 1859, Shōin was beheaded in an Edo prison and thrown into a hole in the ground along with other executed criminals. On January 1, 1863, upon receiving permission from the bakufu, Takasugi Shinsaku led his men to unearth and transport Shōin's remains from the mass burial ground to open land in Tokyo that Chōshū owned.[60] Takasugi transformed the event into a spectacle. According to some accounts, the procession barged onto a Ueno bridge that was reserved exclusively for use by the shogun, viciously attacked the guards, and proceeded to cross the bridge. Kusaka Gensui, another of Shōin's followers, ordered the funeral rites to be conducted in the Shinto style. Takasugi read a poem that likened the landscape of the new gravesite to Shōin's hometown, where he had directed his school.[61] In 1882, followers constructed a Shinto shrine by the gravestone, thus elevating Shōin to the status of a god.

In the Shōin example, we see the dead—both the spirit and the physical remains—being utilized to make a political statement. Shōin's spirit was memorialized in an official ritual carried out by the emperor in Kyoto, thus signifying that the death was for an imperial cause. The spectacle that involved exhuming the remains and official reburial demonstrated that Shōin was not a criminal and further highlighted the mistake that the bakufu made in convicting him. The Kyoto ritual and the Tokyo spectacle together signified the determination of the Chōshū men to pursue the process of *jōi* in the name of the emperor—an action that Shōin himself had advocated. The procession that forced its way over the bridge reserved for the shogun—if it did indeed happen—symbolized the power of the imperial loyalists over the shogun. The rituals associated with Shōin's death were not conducted exclusively for the dead, for example, placating the potentially angry spirit of Shōin, but were transformed into practices that created new meanings for the living, both enemy and ally.

FORBIDDING PROPER BURIAL: AIZU DEATHS

Another significant instance during the restoration, when practices associated with death, burial, and memorial were highly politicized, was the Battle of Aizu, which took place around the castle town of Aizu-Wakamatsu and lasted from April 20–September 22, 1868.[62] I examine this battle in some detail because many death-related practices observed here—from the act of taking one's own life to the treatment of dead enemy bodies—are relevant for thinking about the perceived value of life as well as the use of death in ways that are associated with Yasukuni Shrine and, perhaps more important, why the shrine and the beliefs associated with it had such resonance in wartime Japan. A number of mass suicides took place during the battle, most famously the tragic deaths of the Shōnen Byakko-tai (the Boys White Tiger Corps). During and after the battle, the imperial troops—led by Chōshū—forbade the burial of Aizu dead. The subsequent Aizu struggle for proper burial of their people resulted in the fierce animosity between residents of two regions that persists today.[63] If Shōin's example presents a case study in posthumous restoration of honor through rituals involving the body and the spirit, incidents that occurred during the Battle of Aizu demonstrate the power to control people by denying proper burial and memorialization of their dead. Taken together, the two incidents provide a strong rationale for politicizing memorial practices, which took place alongside the development of criteria for enshrinement at Yasukuni Shrine.

The Battle of Aizu is one segment of the Boshin War. But by this point Edo Castle had already been seized by the imperial powers. Fighting persisted because pro-bakufu factions did not surrender upon the change of guard at the castle. The Battle of Ueno (May 15, 1868) took place a month after the castle fell, after which bakufu troops fled north to Aizu in order to merge with the pro-bakufu men in the northern domains. The people of Aizu had no chance of winning this battle. Aizu fighters initially outnumbered imperial troops approximately 7,000 to 3,000, but the emperor's men were equipped with better weapons. As a result of the constant exchange of fire with European fleets in the previous decade, Chōshū had been importing and utilizing armaments far superior to those owned by other domains, such as the Spencer repeating rifle and the Armstrong cannon.[64] Moreover, half of the Aizu troops were not trained soldiers but an ad hoc collection of farmers and merchants. Over the short period of time between August 23, when the imperial troops invaded the castle town of Aizu-Wakamatsu, and the fall of Tsuruga Castle on September 22, hundreds of corpses piled up in the castle town. I focus here on the treatment of these dead bodies.

The Aizu deaths were not limited to armed men or those killed by the enemy. When imperial troops entered Aizu-Wakamatsu, many Aizu residents rushed inside the castle walls, their last stronghold. However, numerous women and children chose to remain outside and take their own lives in order to avoid burdening the fighting men by getting in their way or consuming the limited supplies. The most spectacular of such mass suicides took place on August 23, 1868, inside the residence of Aizu elder Saigō Tanomo. Here, twenty-one family members, dressed in white, exchanged their last cups of sake, read their last poems, and stabbed themselves and each other.[65] Approximately 230 family members of Aizu fighters died in a similar manner on the same day.[66] Twice as many died in battle that day. Several hundred drowned while trying to escape by crossing the Aka River.[67] Many others took their own lives inside the castle. Some took a different path to their death: On August 25, at the Battle of Yanagi Bridge, some twenty women picked up their halberds (*naginata*) and charged the imperial troops.[68] In later decades, during Japan's wars of imperialism, many women reportedly killed their children and themselves so as not to emotionally burden their men as they went off to war. During the final years of the Asia-Pacific War, women began practicing with halberds and bamboo sticks to prepare for an Allied invasion. It is worth pointing out here that Aizu women did not need Yasukuni Shrine or the emperor to perform these actions, the impetus for which was instilled by Confucian teachings as well as their willingness to protect their hometown.

The imperial troops, which had swelled considerably by the end of July, broke through the castle walls on August 23. Aizu corpses piled up everywhere so quickly that many were thrown into old wells. According to an Aizu resident who was fifteen at the time of the battle, the imperial troops confiscated Aizu property, killed the elderly and children, raped some women, and captured many others who were kept at military bases and forced to have sex with the troops.[69] Parallels between imperial loyalist practices and Japanese atrocities in Nanjing decades later are notable. Some consider this brutality by Chōshū men retaliation for the Aizu residents' acts of betrayal earlier in the decade (i.e., the Kinmon incident and the coup of the previous year). The final attack on the castle was launched on September 15. Equipped with more than one hundred cannons, the imperial troops fired some twenty-seven hundred shots into the castle over the next twenty-four hours. Nevertheless, the Aizu continued to fight until September 22, when they finally surrendered by raising three white flags—sewn by women inside the castle from pieces of white cloth they had gathered—from the castle. Although the death toll on the imperial side was approximately three hundred, the Aizu suffered at least ten times that many losses.

Immediately following the Aizu surrender, the imperial troops began memorializing their own dead. Their site of choice was the Yūzū Temple in the castle town.[70] The first memorial stone—for twenty troops from the Ōgaki domain—was erected in October. By April 1869 a cemetery for imperial troops had been completed on the temple site. The construction of memorials for the imperial troops continued for another year. The last of the memorials—a Chōshū memorial for their fifteen troops—was completed in April 1870. Imperial loyalist deaths in Aizu were officially recognized by both the Aizu and the court in the subsequent years. In September 1870 prefectural governor Shijō Ryūhei conducted a *shōkon* ritual. During his northeastern tour in 1876, Meiji sent an imperial messenger to conduct a state-sponsored memorial service.[71]

The speedy construction of memorials and cemeteries for the imperial troops is not surprising given the history of memorial rituals conducted by Chōshū and their allied domains. Their treatment of the enemy (Aizu) dead, which may have been motivated by contempt, is a useful example of the political mobilization of dead bodies. The bodies of the Aizu dead were abandoned—left to rot throughout the battle. A diary entry by an Aizu resident in early September 1868 describes heaps of corpses, many headless, some with their stomachs slit open. Maggots oozed from the cuts. Wild animals feeding on the corpses further mutilated them.[72] But even after the castle's surrender, Aizu survivors were forbidden from burying their dead. Thus the imperial loyalists created a spectacle of the dead Aizu bodies. By denying the Aizu the right to bury and memorialize their dead, the imperial troops demonstrated their control over their defeated enemy.[73] The importance of taking care of their dead is demonstrated in the repeated attempts by the Aizu to obtain permission for burial and memorialization. In the remainder of this section I explore this idea of selective memorialization, of maintaining power over a group of people through the control of their dead.

Even after Aizu officially surrendered with a letter of apology for rebelling against the "emperor's military," the imperial troops forbade all rituals for appeasing the lost Aizu souls. The prohibition extended to the corpses: The bakufu dead were not permitted a burial. For many months, their bodies were left uncovered to rot on farms, in fields and mountains. Local residents made many attempts to bury their dead secretly, but the imperial troops stubbornly exhumed the remains and threw them back into the fields.[74] An account by an Aizu resident who made great efforts to bury and memorialize his former comrades exemplifies the situation: "The Western (imperial) troops forbade us to even touch any of the Eastern (Aizu and bakufu) dead. We were to be punished severely if we tampered with the bodies. Thus, no one ventured to bury the Eastern dead. The bodies became food for wild animals like foxes and raccoons, and wild birds like eagles and crows. The remaining parts further decayed, resulting in a sight so cruel that one could not even bear to see it."[75]

The situation was no better for the young members of the Byakko-tai, the famous auxiliary group of young men aged sixteen and seventeen, who committed mass suicide at the Iimori Mountain pass.[76] Like the others, their bodies were left scattered at the site of their death. Aizu residents had great respect for these highly trained young men and wished for their proper burial. In December 1868 Yoshida Saki, wife of Takizawa village chief Yoshida Isoji, had the bodies secretly buried at Myōkokuji, their family temple. But the imperial troops quickly discovered their action. Isoji was imprisoned (instead of Saki). The Byakko-tai bodies were unearthed and thrown into the fields once again.[77] The imperial loyalists permitted the reburial of the young men's bodies only after repeated pleas from surviving Aizu members. However, the reburial, which was conducted at the Iimori Mountain pass, was not official: It was conducted in the middle of the night with cooperation from villagers who were paid to transport the bodies. The Aizu were not given an opportunity to pay tribute to the young lives that were lost for what they considered a noble cause.

It is possible that the idea of selective memorialization developed through this process. For imperial loyalists, forbidding what the Aizu strongly desired (burial and memorialization of their dead) allowed them to exert control over the Aizu survivors. As the armed conflict between the imperial troops and the pro-bakufu faction was continuing at the time, imperial loyalists needed to maintain their demonstration of power over the Aizu survivors to prevent further uprisings. The more the Aizu survivors desired proper burial for the fallen, the more acutely they felt controlled by the imperial troops through their denial of proper burial.[78]

Aizu survivors continued to negotiate for the burial of bodies that were rotting in the fields. The imperial troops ultimately consented, but with restrictions that were even more stringent than those for the Byakko-tai burial. Since the dead, as members of the defeated side, were considered criminals, they were not to be buried on temple grounds. Moreover, their burial was to be conducted not by their family and friends but by the underclass (*hinin*), who suffered from social discrimination. Residents were forbidden to participate in the burial. The imperial loyalists proposed a riverbank site where executed prisoners had once been buried. Further negotiations enabled the Aizu to bury their dead on two local temple grounds, but the method of burial was to remain the same. In this manner, the Aizu survivors experienced a double deprivation: the loss of those who had fallen in battle and the denial of an opportunity to properly bury them.

Burial of the Aizu dead started on February 24, 1869, five months after the fall of the castle:

> Since the collection and burial of bodies took place in the midst of confusion following the fall of the castle, there was no proper equipment to transport the bodies. They wrapped the bodies in rough straw mats or placed them in bags made of woven straw and used door panels and even bathtubs for transportation. On the grounds of Amida Temple, they dug a round hole eight *ken* in diameter and several *ken* in depth [one *ken* is 1.8 meters, thus the hole was about fifteen meters in diameter and a few meters deep] and laid the bodies with their heads to the north on straw mats. They layered the bodies and the mats. The bodies piled up to several *shaku* [one *shaku* is approximately thirty centimeters] above the ground. They then transported the remaining bodies to Chōmeiji Temple for burial. They covered the pile of bodies on Amida Temple grounds with soil to construct a huge mound. They erected a marker on which was written "Spirits of Martyrs (*Jun'nan no rei*)" and constructed a small worship hall.[79]

All in all, 1,281 bodies were buried at Amida Temple, and more than one hundred were transported to Chōmeiji Temple.[80] The imperial loyalists, after making their inspection, disapproved the burial method at Amida and ordered the Aizu both to remove the marker that praised the dead as martyrs and to demolish the worship hall. Nearly ten years later, in August 1876, the Meiji government finally gave permission for the memorialization of bakufu dead throughout Japan.

The manner in which local residents were barred from participating in the burial process is emblematic of the imperial troops' demonstration of their authority over Aizu. The initial ban on burial forced the Aizu to viscerally acknowledge the cruelty of the imperial troops' treatment even after death: a constant reminder of the Aizu subjugation by the imperial troops. Furthermore, by permitting the bodies to be buried only by members of the underclass and thus erasing traces of dead bodies from fields and streets, the imperial troops silenced the Aizu from making further demands in relation to their dead. At the same time, however, the resulting absence of bodies robbed the Aizu of the opportunity to properly memorialize their dead.

Just as the collective memorialization of the imperial troops contributed to their construction of a singular identity, so the prohibition of burial obstructed the Aizu people's attempt to reestablish their collective identity after their defeat and consequently prevented future uprisings. Most Aizu burial requests were not initiated by family members of the dead but by locals who sought to exonerate their clan's status through proper burial of the dead. Through such burial, survivors sought to restore dignity to their collective identity as Aizu. By forbidding proper burial, the imperial troops were trying to prevent the Aizu from restoring their collective identity. During the Asia-Pacific War, the Japanese state took the role of memorial for the dead away from the immediate families of the casualties. Although it is not clear that the takeover was conducted for purposes similar to those of the imperial troops during the Battle of Aizu, the official treatment of war dead during Japan's later wars of imperialism (namely, memorial rituals for the bodies and enshrinement of spirits at Yasukuni) no doubt facilitated the sense of obligation and powerlessness that people felt toward the Japanese state.

THE SATSUMA REBELLION AND THE BIRTH OF YASUKUNI SHRINE

As we have seen, Yasukuni Shrine did not start out as a *jinja* (Shinto shrine) but as a *shōkonsha,* a term that can be literally translated as "a shrine to invite spirits." It initially had no official ties with Shintoism. The status of the memorial changed on June 4, 1879, when Grand Minister Sanjō Sanetomi issued a directive that announced the renaming of Tokyo Shōkonsha as Yasukuni Shrine. The document also designated Yasukuni Shrine as a Special Government Shrine (*bekkaku kanpeisha*).[81] This designation of the memorial as a Shinto shrine completes the first period in the history of Yasukuni Shrine. With the designation, the rituals and physical structures associated with the use of the war dead for political purposes were institutionalized. At the same time, the spirits of those enshrined became a permanent fixture in the shrine itself.

At the beginning of Meiji, numerous memorials for the imperial loyalist dead had already been constructed, situated mostly within the imperial loyalist domains.[82] In February 1874 the government ordered all such institutions to be renamed as *shōkonsha,* thus officially recognizing a network of restoration-related memorials throughout Japan. (This network was further institutionalized in 1939 with the designation of the shrines as *gokoku jinja,* or shrines to protect the nation.) In March 1874 the government announced financial support for the operation and maintenance of such memorials.[83] Tokyo Shōkonsha was the largest such memorial by far, yet at the time its status was no higher than that of the other shrines. In fact, only the dead from the Boshin War were enshrined in Tokyo at the time. The spirits of those who had fallen previously in restoration-related incidents were still memorialized in Kyoto.

On November 30, 1874, Hayashi Tomoyuki of the Ministry of the Interior proposed that the Kyoto spirits be transferred to Tokyo. However, the Grand Council of State did not give its consent. But on January 15, 1875, the council ordered the Ministry of the Interior to begin a comprehensive search for the names of and other relevant information about the men who had died in restoration-related incidents.[84] These men would not become enshrined in Tokyo until 1879, when the names of two men from the Yonezawa domain were added to the register.[85] But Hayashi's proposal is significant in that it marked the beginning of attempts to transform Tokyo Shōkonsha into a national institution. The desire for higher status was in part practical. Tokyo Shōkonsha had a serious lack of personnel at the time. As many as sixty-two men from patriotic groups were hired in November 1869 to take over administrative tasks, maintenance of the site, and performance of the ritual events; by 1872 the number was reduced to seven.[86] Naming the memorial was also a cause for concern. A *shōkonsha* was understood to be a site to which gods are temporarily invited from the heavens during rituals. It was not an appropriate designation for an institution where the spirits of the war dead permanently reside. This issue later became crucial for designating Tokyo Shōkonsha as Yasukuni Shrine.

The year 1874 saw two other important events at Tokyo Shōkonsha: Emperor Meiji's first visit and the memorial of those fallen in the Saga Rebellion of February 1874. Emperor Meiji visited the shrine for the first time during a festival on January 27, 1874. The young emperor paid tribute at the worship hall and observed a formal visit by his troops—the newly formed Imperial Army of commoner conscripts.[87] The following month, 192 of the new conscripts died in Saga while suppressing an uprising by a group of disgruntled former samurai. These men—the first casualties from the emperor's army—were enshrined at Tokyo Shōkonsha on August 27, 1874, as the first new additions since the creation of the shrine. The enshrinement ritual was performed at the newly prepared *shōkon saitei,* a site dedicated to inviting the spirits.[88]

The Saga Rebellion was the first of a series of armed skirmishes between former samurai and the new military. The shift of political power from the military control of the Tokugawa bakufu to a central government entailed many changes nationwide, including the reorganization of the entire country from domains to prefectures. Another significant change was the elimination of the status system, which hit the samurai class the hardest: They were forced to give up their right to wear swords, and their stipends were cut drastically. In January 1873 the new government inaugurated conscription, introducing and enforcing an entirely new concept of the Japanese military. These rapid reforms sparked uprisings by former samurai, the largest of which was the Satsuma Rebellion of 1877. Saigō Takamori led the revolt. He had resigned from the Meiji government and founded a private military academy in his hometown in Kagoshima, formerly Satsuma domain. On January 30, 1873, Saigō's army, supplemented by local dissenters, attacked government troops in the Kumamoto castle, only to be defeated by a large number of supplementary troops sent from Tokyo. By the time Saigō was killed on September 24, 1877, his army had suffered approximately twenty thousand fatalities. More than six thousand government soldiers were killed in the conflict.[89] Most of the government casualties were enshrined in Tokyo Shōkonsha on November 12, 1877.[90] Although Saigō had played a key role in the restoration, the dead on Saigō's side (including Saigō himself) were not enshrined because, having rebelled against the state, they were criminals. The Satsuma Rebellion was the last of the domestic disputes associated with the change of political power from the shogunate to the new Meiji government.

These rebellions, the last domestic battles of modern Japan, produced new military deaths: spirits that needed official enshrinement. Most of the imperial dead were enshrined in a ritual preceding a semiannual festival soon thereafter. But these additional deaths highlighted the need for a new function for Tokyo Shōkonsha—the continuous enshrinement of additional spirits. A structured and institutionalized ritual for memorial was desired, as well as official status for the *shōkonsha.* Army and navy personnel were administering ceremonies and events modeled on those of a typical Shinto shrine, with large semiannual festivals supplemented by midsized and small ones, as well as imperial events, including *yōhai*[91] ceremonies and the Tenchōsetsu[92] festival. But Tokyo Shōkonsha was not a Shinto shrine.

On October 24, 1878, the army sent a written request to the Grand Council of State asking permission to retain a regular priest to perform the rites at Tokyo Shōkonsha.[93] The Grand Council denied this request because Tokyo Shōkonsha was not an officially recognized Shinto shrine and did not qualify to retain a priest.[94] The army then made an inquiry to the ministries of the navy and the interior requesting the designation of Tokyo Shōkonsha as a Shinto shrine. The army representative argued that the presence of a regular priest was required inasmuch as it was a site where "spirits that died during noble battles for the nation reside permanently."[95] After several rounds of correspondence among officials of the army, navy, Ministry of the Interior, and the Grand Council of State, on June 4, 1879, all of the parties agreed to designate the shrine as a Special Government Shrine. They also decided that three ministries would share the responsibilities associated with the Tokyo Shōkonsha.[96] On the same day, Tokyo Shōkonsha was renamed Yasukuni Shrine.[97] On June 25 an imperial messenger arrived at the shrine in order to perform a ceremony to report the name change to the gods.[98] The army and the navy assumed sole control of the shrine in 1887.

Many scholars have analyzed the political aspects of designating Tokyo Shōkonsha as Yasukuni Shrine. For example, Murakami Shigeyoshi sees this transition as an attempt by the army to establish a hierarchy of *shōkonsha,* with the Tokyo Shōkonsha at the apex. Patriotism at the local level could be redirected to the state and the emperor by putting regional *shōkonsha* under state control. This would raise an awareness of an emperor-centered nationhood among regional residents, who still felt loyalty to their clans. According to Murakami, Tokyo Shōkonsha needed the official shrine status for this ideological purpose, and the army capitalized on the Satsuma Rebellion as an opportunity to put this system in place.[99] Shinto scholars disagree with Murakami. Sakamoto Koremaru, for example, points out that by July 1871 the domain system had been abolished in favor of prefectures.[100] Since regional *shōkonsha,* constructed with a domain's budget and previously supported by it, were neglected and had begun to physically deteriorate, the Meiji government took over the management and operation of regional *shōkonsha* in 1873 and 1874. The Shinto scholars also argue that the designation of Tokyo Shōkonsha as a shrine was not related to a hierarchical relationship between Yasukuni Shrine and regional *shōkonsha* since the regional institutions were not designated as shrines until 1936.[101]

Murakami's argument becomes less convincing when contextualized in the relationship between the Meiji government and Shinto in early Meiji. Beginning in 1868, the government had dropped its patronage of Buddhism and begun its official support of Shinto. But since Shinto was a cult of *kami* worship in the Tokugawa era, the relationship between Shinto and religion remained nebulous at this point. (This relationship would become one source of the postwar problems surrounding Yasukuni Shrine.) Nevertheless, the government made concerted efforts to institutionalize Shinto by assigning rankings to the shrines and organizing people into parishioners (*ujiko*) of shrines.[102] As Helen Hardacre illuminates in her study of State Shinto, the focal point (if any) for the government at this point in the campaign to popularize Shinto was Ise Shrine, already with strong ties to the imperial family.[103] Nonetheless, it is likely that both the military and the government saw the benefit in officially designating Shinto status to Tokyo Shōkonsha in order to raise the prestige of both Shinto and Shōkonsha.

The army's initial motive for shrine designation was to retain a regular priest. But this was not the most significant change that the memorial underwent when it was designated a shrine. According to Miyaji Naokazu, pioneering scholar of modern Shinto, the principal criteria of a Shinto shrine (*jinja*) is the permanent presence of the god's spirit within the structure.[104] Until the introduction of Buddhism in Japan, Shinto shrines were temporary structures, sometimes merely a small, square space demarcated by four sticks with a pillar in the center, on which the god was to descend during rituals. Sometimes natural objects such as a rock or a tree were considered to be the object into which gods descended. In each case, the gods were sent away after the ritual. When permanent shrines were introduced under the influence of Buddhist temples, it was understood that gods resided in the structures permanently.[105] Accordingly, the *shōkon* ceremony at Yasukuni does not include a ritual to send off the spirits after they are appeased. As the army requested, the spirits of the war dead were to reside permanently at Yasukuni. The names of the memorialized were deposited in the Reijibo Hōanden (hall for the enshrinement of registers), located behind the main shrine. The new status as a Special Government Shrine also indicated that those enshrined were loyal subjects, equivalent to the gods of Special Government Shrines throughout Japan, which included notables such as Kusunoki Masashige, Tokugawa Ieyasu, Toyotomi Hideyoshi, and Oda Nobunaga.[106]

It is not clear how the initial creators of Tokyo Shōkonsha conceptualized the building's relationship with the spirits of the fallen. By definition, *shōkonsha* is a shrine into which the spirits of the dead are invited. However, by the time the army requested Shinto shrine status, its interpretation of Tokyo Shōkonsha was that of a conventional Shinto shrine, where spirits resided permanently. The text of the army's request for a regular priest at Tokyo Shōkonsha argues that the site "is unlike a so-called *shōkonjō* [area designated for *shōkon* rituals], to which the spirits of the heavens are invited to receive an offering on occasion." The document continues that, if this were such a temporary residence for the gods, then "one custodian without a priest would suffice," but since it is "an important and eternal shrine where spirits who fought and died courageously for our nation since the Boshin [War] are enshrined, with four major festivals per year and four minor festivals per month," the employment of a regular priest was critical.[107]

As we have seen, the idea behind official memorialization of the war dead continued to develop during the first few years of its inception. The memorialization process assumed more or less its complete shape with the designation of Yasukuni Shrine as a Special Government Shrine, but enshrinement criteria continued to change. Perhaps more important, although the shrine quickly gained popularity as a site of entertainment after the permanent shrine was constructed, the general public, for the most part, remained unaware of the political motivation behind the monument. The character of Yasukuni Shrine would continue to change in succeeding decades, particularly with the onset of Japan's international wars of imperialism. Myths associated with war death were transformed into "Yasukuni the belief" during these conflicts.

TWO

INSTITUTIONALIZING JOY

Turning War into Spectacle at Yasukuni Shrine

Though she had hardly understood a word of what was being said, my master's eldest daughter had listened attentively while her mother and Cousin Yukie launched out upon their earnest discussion of the question of marriage. But suddenly, out of the blue, the little girl opened her mouth. "I," she announced, "would also like to get married." Though Yukie is herself so brimming with youthful ardor that she could well be expected to sympathize with Tonko's feelings, she was in fact struck dumb by such reckless lust. Mrs. Sneaze, however, took it all in her stride and, smiling at her daughter, simply asked, "To whom?"

"Well, shall I tell you? I want to marry Tokyo Shōkonsha. But I don't like crossing Suidō Bridge, so I'm wondering what to do."

Both Mrs. Sneaze and Yukie were distinctly taken aback by this unexpected declaration of an ambition to marry the shrine dedicated to the departed spirits of those who'd fallen in war for the sake of the fatherland. Words failed them, and all they could do was shake with laughter. They were still laughing when the second daughter said to her eldest sister. "So, you'd like to marry Tokyo Shōkonsha? Well, so would I. I'd love it. Let's both do just that. Come on. No? All right then, if you won't join me, I'll take a rickshaw and go get married by myself."

"Babu go, too," piped the smallest of my master's daughters. Indeed, such a triple marrying-off would suit him very well.

NATSUME SŌSEKI, I AM A CAT

A little girl in the novel *I Am a Cat*, by Natsume Sōseki, declares that she wants to get married at the Shōkonsha, and her younger sisters chime in, wanting the same.[1] This delightful episode takes place in the penultimate chapter of the serialized novel, originally published in the literary journal *Hototogisu* in April 1906. Due to its publication date—two and a half decades after the Tokyo Shōkonsha was renamed Yasukuni Shrine—it is possible that many readers did not know the shrine when it was officially named Tokyo Shōkonsha. But even at the time of publication, the name Tokyo Shōkonsha was familiar to many Tokyo residents, who continued to use it for many years after the Imperial Army officially changed its name and status. It is not surprising, then, that the little girls referred to the shrine by its former name. The girl's curious desire to marry the shrine is a brilliant play on words, which cannot be rendered in English. Tonko, the little girl, announces, "Watashi mo oyome ni ikitai na," which can be translated as "I would also like to get married." But here, the little girl clearly misunderstands the concept of *oyome ni iku* as going somewhere. (The verb *iku* can be literally translated as "to go.") Thus, she mistakes the act of going to a Shinto shrine to be married (*oyome ni iku*) with marrying the shrine itself.

I begin this chapter with this excerpt because the lighthearted exchange between the little girls serves as a lens through which we may observe the presence that Yasukuni Shrine had for Tokyo residents in its early decades. A driving question is what may have given rise to idea of marriage at (or to, in Tonko's mind) Shōkonsha in the mind of the little girl. This dialogue, of course, is fictional. But if Yasukuni Shrine had always been a highly politicized war memorial associated with the commemoration and aestheticization of war death, then why would a novelist create a connection between the institution and a wedding?[2] The larger questions I pose here are the following: What kind of a place was Yasukuni Shrine to the Tokyo residents in its earliest decades? For the ordinary Japanese, and by this, I mean those who were not in high government or military positions, when and how did Yasukuni Shrine take on the qualities that attract so much criticism today?

In the previous chapter I examined the beginnings of the shrine from the standpoint of its creators and the men who fought against the bakufu during the restoration. With the exception of the *kiheitai,* which was formed in 1863 as a volunteer army of commoners, the men in the imperial troops, who were eligible for enshrinement at Tokyo Shōkonsha if they died in the Boshin War, were career soldiers.[3] Those who fought, died, and were ultimately enshrined had no knowledge of the shrine when they departed for war. At that time, the rest of the population considered warfare as something completely irrelevant, as we saw with the Tokyoites gathering to observe the Battle of Ueno. This contrasts starkly with the situation during the Asia-Pacific War, when Yasukuni Shrine was central to the Japanese state's attempt to aestheticize war death. Thus, questions arise as to when and how the concept of Yasukuni enshrinement was popularized among the Japanese people and as to the role of the shrine grounds in this process.

In chapters 2 and 3, I cover the period between the early days of Tokyo Shōkonsha and the Russo-Japanese War years. I examine the development, dissemination, and popularization of what we have come to know as the Yasukuni ideology—the process through which "Yasukuni the belief" took on a shape not unlike George Mosse's Myth of the War Experience.[4] While the previous chapter examined the shrine from the viewpoint of its creators, this and the next two chapters concern the users. In this chapter I analyze the presence of "Yasukuni the site" in Tokyo: how the shrine grounds gained popularity with local residents and how the imperialist government's messages were disseminated through its events and facilities. In short, I examine the role of the shrine's physical space (Yasukuni the site) in popularizing Yasukuni the belief. For the Tokyoites in the earlier years, the site had a much stronger presence than the belief. In chapter 3 I examine the contemporaneous dissemination of the belief in regional Japan, where few people had access to Yasukuni the site.

Initially the shrine grounds in Tokyo had little religious or political significance for the Japanese people at large. It was well known as a venue for popular entertainment such as fireworks, sumo matches, vendors of food and trinkets, and freak shows. This atmosphere of Yasukuni Shrine was not unusual for sacred spaces at the time. Religion and entertainment were closely related in early modern Japan. Temples, in particular, incorporated entertainment facilities, in part for financial reasons, and also because many forms of entertainment were considered to be offerings to the gods and one's ancestors. The festive atmosphere at Yasukuni thus conformed to what its visitors expected at an urban shrine. It also offered the unexpected. To Tokyoites, many of the venues at Yasukuni Shrine—such as circuses, horse races, and a military museum—offered novelty, presented as what might have been characterized at the time as modern or Western. Yasukuni Shrine offered an enticing combination of the new and the familiar that was packaged as entertainment. Early visitors to the shrine grounds were typically drawn more by the diverse entertainment than by the shrine's religious or political significance. Many, in fact, were not aware of its political significance.

As Japan engaged in repeated episodes of armed conflict—first domestic but mostly international—militarism gradually became more prominent in Yasukuni events. During the wars against China (1894–1895) and Russia (1904–1905), the shrine's atmosphere was largely celebratory. Even during events associated with the enshrinement of the war dead, the commemoration of lives lost, a central component of Yasukuni Shrine, was downplayed. Popular consciousness associated the shrine more with celebrating military victory than with commemorating war casualties. The spatial practices performed by visitors at the time did not fully align with the main objective of the shrine's creators. Although the Army Ministry seemed intent on establishing an official, national memorial for the war dead, Tokyoites who frequented the shrine went there for the entertainment. Through participation in events, however, the visitors themselves—often unconsciously—became an integral part of the state-sanctioned narrative that came to celebrate the successes of the growing nation, which ensued from the loss of lives.

TOKYO SHŌKONSHA

As noted in the previous chapter, Yasukuni Shrine began as a group of temporary structures named Tokyo Shōkonsha, completed only two days prior to the start of its first memorial festival on June 27, 1869. There are not many sources pertaining to the shrine's earliest years. Excluding official documents compiled by officials of the shrine, records for this early period are limited primarily to published chronicles such as *Bukō nenpyō* (Chronicle of the Edo Period) and *Tōkyō shin hanjōki* (New Records of Tokyo Prosperity), brief entries in newspapers, and a handful of woodblock prints. I briefly return to Yasukuni Shrine's early years in order to look at its cultural representations as they give us some indications of the shrine's presence in popular imagination.

In July 1869 Kanda landowner Saitō Gesshin made an entry in *Bukō nenpyō*, his well-known Edo chronicle encompassing the years 1590 to 1873, which stated that the temporary structure was completed atop Kudan slope and listed its festival dates.[5] Gesshin failed to note the very first festival, but he went on to record the next event two months later: "On 22nd and 23rd (of September 1869) was a festival at the Shōkonsha in Kudan. Comedic dances (*dōke*), etc. took place in the neighborhood. There were many visitors."[6] There are several more entries, including a complaint about the expensive entrance fee for a mediocre circus show on the shrine site that took place on a cold day.[7] Some entries concern the festivals, whiles others refer to significant changes in the Kudan area. But since his chronicle ends in 1873, it does not include, for example, the visit of Emperor Meiji in January 1874. Moreover, with the exception of a brief description of the Shōkonsha as a war memorial in his initial entry, Gesshin highlights the festivals and other entertainment and does not refer to the shrine itself. Newspaper articles also focused on announcing events. It seems that there was little to report on in the early days of the shrine. In September 1875 the *Yomiuri* newspaper even featured an editorial by a Kanda resident, who lamented the lack of visitors on nonfestival days and recommended establishing commercial facilities on shrine grounds in order to increase the number of visitors.[8]

The subjects of Tokyo Shōkonsha and the Kudan slope also appeared in several early Meiji woodblock prints, yet with a peculiar absence. The print *Tōkyō Kudanzaka ue shōkonsha no zu* (Illustration of Shōkonsha atop Kudan Slope, Tokyo, c. 1871) is a case in point (see figure 1). It depicts the street outside the shrine busy with the comings and goings of people in a variety of attire from traditional kimonos to military uniforms and Western-style clothing. The impressive stone lantern at the shrine's main entrance gate—a cultural icon at the time—occupies the center of the print. But the shrine's presence is negligible: Only a sliver of its roof peeks above the clouds.[9] Similarly, other prints of Shōkonsha produced between 1869 and 1872 do not depict the shrine. Some include the wooden *torii* (gate) or the aforementioned stone lantern, but the shrine itself is absent or hinted at by the tip of its roof.[10] The representations of the Kudan area in these prints suggest the site's significance for local residents: They were aware of the site, but not as a shrine or war memorial. For Tokyoites, the shrine was a new *meisho*

FIGURE 1. *Tōkyō Kudanzaka ue shōkonsha no zu* (Illustration of Shōkonsha atop Kudan Slope, Tokyo), Risshō II, c. 1871. Used by permission of Yasukuni Shrine Yūshūkan Museum.

(famous site)—one of many that were emerging in and around the new capital at the time.

Despite the absence of the building itself from these early cultural representations, Tokyo Shōkonsha and the Kudan slope, with its spectacular view of Tokyo Bay, soon became an often-used subject in prints and other media. After the permanent structure was completed on May 7, 1872, the shrine gradually began to attract attention. Regardless of how the site was represented, its recognition at the time had little to do with its memorial aspect. Treatment of the dead had developed into a highly politicized act in the restoration years, as we saw in the previous chapter. Memorialization of the war dead was intended to build solidarity among loyalist domains during the Boshin battles; the imperialists' treatment of the casualties of the Battle of Aizu prevented Aizu residents from reclaiming their collective identity. This tradition was intended to continue at the Tokyo shrine. But the enshrined war dead held little political significance for typical residents (*shomin*) of Tokyo, the majority of Shōkonsha visitors. The Kudan site's character as a shrine was enhanced when the permanent structure was completed. Yet few visitors seemed to realize its memorial function or its difference from other Shinto shrines. In the early years of Meiji, entertainment figured prominently in Tokyo: The new government allowed numerous festivals and other events associated with shrines and temples as a way of appeasing Tokyo residents and easing their transition into a new social and political structure.[11] Yasukuni Shrine was one such venue. Visitors attended events hosted at the shrine as they would at many other shrines and temples in Tokyo in the early Meiji years. Thus, Shōkonsha (and later Yasukuni Shrine) was one of many locations for amusement in Tokyo. Tokyoites were not yet aware of the site's belief aspect, namely, its political implications.

State-sponsored events continued at Tokyo Shōkonsha after the completion of the new building. On January 27, 1874, Emperor Meiji visited the shrine for the first time during the annual festival commemorating the enshrinement of those who died in the Battle of Toba-Fushimi. This unprecedented visit, during which the emperor personally honored his fallen subjects, was meant to publicly demonstrate the tremendous value, honor, and significance of each life lost for the imperial cause. A concerted effort to enshrine the restoration fallen memorialized at various regional *shōkonsha* began in January 1875. In multiple rituals in the following years, the restoration fallen, along with those who died in subsequent military campaigns by the new state, including the Saga Rebellion (February 1874), the Taiwan

Expedition (April 1874), and the Ganghwa Incident (September 1875), were enshrined in Tokyo Shōkonsha.[12]

The list of armed conflicts and the ritual enshrinement of the casualties in the name of the emperor might suggest a military state that was rapidly developing under an imperial monarchy. The consolidation of all of the dead in Tokyo demonstrates the state's desire to transform the city into a new center of not only politics but also ritual. On the contrary, popular consciousness of the emperor was low in the early years of Meiji. Furthermore, pageantry showcasing the emperor to the people of Tokyo did not take place until 1889, after the emperor had moved into the newly constructed imperial palace immediately before the promulgation of the Meiji Constitution.[13] The central idea behind Yasukuni—the memorialization of the military dead—did not yet resonate with ordinary Japanese. The system of conscription was not well understood when it was launched in 1873, and, as I discuss in chapter 3, at first it affected only a few people. Despite this lack of recognition for its primary function, other factors led Tokyo Shōkonsha to rapidly become a famous and popular site.

YASUKUNI SHRINE AS A *MEISHO*

For most visitors, Yasukuni Shrine (Tokyo Shōkonsha) during its early years was a place for novel experiences. New types of entertainment—many of which were introduced from Europe—were often featured for the first time on the shrine grounds. On February 25, 1882, Yūshūkan, Japan's first military museum, opened to the north of the shrine. On February 5, 1893, the first bronze statue to be created by a Japanese artist was unveiled in the center of the outer garden (*gaien*). Events not yet familiar to the Japanese, such as circuses and horse races, coexisted with the traditional temple and shrine venues, including show tents, food stalls, Noh performances, sumo matches, and fireworks. The purpose of these events, however, was not the entertainment of nearby residents. Each event and facility introduced at Yasukuni Shrine had a military or a memorial objective. For example, sumo and fireworks had long been associated with memorializing the dead. And over time, the same kinds of events gradually took on an increasingly militarized quality. Visitors continued to enjoy the entertainment, at the same time becoming accustomed to its militaristic content. As Japan embarked on international warfare at the end of the nineteenth century, the shrine hosted celebrations to mark victories and to commemorate the military dead as heroes. Even though visitors may not have been fully cognizant of it, by viewing and participating in the militarized events, they were becoming participants in the national cause: imperialism. Through their spatial practices within Yasukuni Shrine grounds, where they took in the various war-themed amusements, the visitors were, at least on the surface, performing the role of good Japanese supporting their nation's imperial quests.

That the military museum was completed as early as 1882 demonstrates the importance of Yasukuni Shrine for the armed forces. The construction of the museum was directly associated with warfare: It was funded with money donated to the Imperial Army during the Satsuma Rebellion.[14] The initial objective of this museum is unclear. In fact, the display of objects seems to be only a part of the original function. Documents proposing the museum refer to the facility as a votive gallery (*emadō*), a common feature at Shinto shrines.[15] But an 1877 newspaper announcement of the museum's completion describes its functions as an assembly room, library, exhibit hall for paintings, and, finally, display space for weapons.[16] The museum's primary function was to educate the general public, and its original inventory suggests that the collection at the time of the opening differed markedly from the current one.[17] Yūshūkan today is filled with ephemera of war, including articles left behind by the deceased, such as letters and sketches from the front, uniforms, and other belongings. In the words of a curatorial staff member, it "enshrines the belongings of those men memorialized at Yasukuni."[18] But at first, paintings, documents, and weapons—most of which had little to do with the men enshrined—composed the museum's collection. Paintings included battle scenes and portraits.[19] Initially, the museum did not have enough material to fill all of the exhibition halls and resorted to loans of weapons from the Department of the Imperial Household.[20] The Army contracted Nakamaru Seijūro, a Western-style painter, to produce portraits of active generals at the rate of one per month. At the time, Yūshūkan was not a place for remembrance as it is today, nor was it geared toward commemoration of military deaths.

For the nearby residents, Yūshūkan was more notable as a component of Tokyo's modernizing urban fabric than as a military institution. The building was designed by Italian architect Giovanni Vicenzo Cappelletti, who came to Japan in 1876 to teach architecture at the Imperial School of Art as one of the "hired foreigners."[21] To the Japanese eye, the symmetrical, brick-clad design was completely Western: a two-story central tower flanked by single-story wings with smaller towers at each end. The slender pilasters ornamenting the three towers as well as their roofline gave the structure a fortresslike character. This addition to the shrine ground was a popular backdrop in Yasukuni-themed woodblock prints. Artists often juxtaposed kimono-clad women against the brick museum in the background. The museum was certainly a new and foreign introduction to both the shrine grounds and Tokyo, as buildings featuring Western-style architectural design were just beginning to be constructed in the city. Yūshūkan was the first military museum in Japan, as well as the second museum in the Western tradition. It opened just one year after the Imperial Museum at Ueno. Even the famed Rokumeikan (Deer Cry Pavilion)—the leading showpiece of modernized Japan, where French-style banquets were held for entertaining European dignitaries—was not yet built. It is also possible that Yūshūkan was conceived in part as a social space for the military, as it hosted dance parties for military officers in its early years.[22] Its function as a public museum was secondary: The exhibit space was open to the public only on Sundays. The visitors, then, most likely regarded the building as a fancy modern building for high-ranking people. It was not until 1904, with the addition of memorabilia from the Russo-Japanese War, that the museum opened its doors every day of the week.

It was not only as paintings in the museum building that notable military figures were celebrated. On February 5, 1893, a towering bronze statue was unveiled in the middle of the outer garden. It was a statue of Ōmura Masujirō, whom I introduced in chapter 1: the central figure in the founding of the Tokyo Shōkonsha. Ōmura himself did not live long enough to see the shrine flourish. As the vice minister of the Army Ministry, Ōmura was also the architect of a drastic restructuring of the Imperial Army, which he accomplished, in part, by replacing medieval weapons with modern ones. Consequently, he made enemies among the former samurai men, with their strong affinity to their class status as well as their swords: Ōmura was attacked by his dissenters on September 4, 1869, and died of his wounds later that year.

The statue took many years to complete. More than a decade after Ōmura's death, plans for the statue emerged at a memorial event on November 15, 1882. However, due to the amount of fund-raising and research needed to construct the first European-style monument in Japan—the sculptor studied in Europe for eighteen months—the statue was not completed until more than a decade later.[23] Nonetheless, the resulting monument was a greatly anticipated addition to the Yasukuni grounds. The Tokyo *Nichi-nichi* newspaper announced plans to erect the statue as early as

September 9, 1886. Work for the concrete foundation and the granite base started in August 1887, even before the sculptor left for Europe, and was completed in July 1888. The outer garden was packed with spectators on the day of the inauguration ceremony, which took place in February 1893, more than two decades after Ōmura's death.[24]

Atop a high, granite base in the middle of the outer garden, the bronze Ōmura stands with his left foot forward, a pair of binoculars in his left hand, and his gaze cast beyond the shrine grounds, across the entire city of Tokyo. The statue quickly became a popular icon among Tokyoites: It captured the attention of many cultural figures and became the choice subject matter of novels and woodblock prints (see figure 2).[25] Several writings on Ōmura were also published following statue's unveiling. The realistic three-dimensional representation of Ōmura sought to refresh the older generation's fading memories, demonstrate to the younger generation the importance of the Meiji Restoration, and commemorate Ōmura's groundbreaking modernization of the Imperial Army. In reality, however, Tokyoites most likely celebrated the statue for the novelty of its scale and form. Just like their interpretation of Yasukuni Shrine as a typical religious site filled with entertainment, the historical significance of Ōmura, the person, was lost to its viewers.

FIGURE 2. *Tōkyō meisho Kudanzaka Yasukuni Jinja no kei* (Scene from Yasukuni Shrine at Kudan Slope), Yousai Nobukatsu, 1899. Used by permission of Yasukuni Shrine Yūshūkan Museum.

ENTERTAINMENT, MILITARISM, RELIGION

The museum and the Ōmura statue were not the only draws to the shrine during its early years. Originally wider than it is now, what is today known as the outer garden (*gaien*) was once called the horse ground (*baba*). The area had already been named *baba* before the shrine was built since it was a training ground for bakufu infantry. But the term stuck due to the horse races that the shrine hosted regularly. The space was a popular park, known for the events held there. The shrine grounds were always packed during the spring and fall festivals. During these three-day celebrations, fireworks were displayed on the first night, followed by horse races on the second day, and a sumo tournament on the third.[26] Regular festival attractions such as vendors of sweets and snacks, games, and freak show tents (*misemono goya*) also contributed to the site's popularity. Artworks of the time suggest that the outer garden did not function as a shrine in the absence of the linear structure that exists today. Attractions at Yasukuni Shrine were similar to those typically offered at religious institutions in Tokugawa Japan, when religious spaces had strong ties with entertainment. Furthermore, early Meiji state regulations concerning venues offered at public spaces in Tokyo further influenced the popularity of Yasukuni events.

Western-style horse races, for example, were introduced to Japan in the late 1860s, when British residents of Yokohama's "foreigners' district" held horse races at a site in Negishi village that they rented from the Tokugawa bakufu.[27] But the races at Yasukuni Shrine, sponsored by the Military Horse Division of the Army Ministry, were the first to be hosted by the Japanese. These horse races took place at every regular and special festival, with as many as 268 horses competing in a single festival in 1896.[28] Prince Harunomiya Yoshihito (future Emperor Taisho) attended the races during the May and November festivals of 1887.[29] Horse racing, in the traditional Japanese style, was not an unusual feature at shrines. The most famous example is the annual horse race at the Kamo Shrine in Kyoto. But whereas traditional races had the horses run from the entrance of the outer garden straight up the main path (*sandō*), the events at Yasukuni were in the Western style, where horses raced on an oval track set around the Ōmura Masujirō statue. The traditional racers dressed in classical Japanese attire. But the Yasukuni horse races, in which men in military uniform competed, were a modern experience that allowed Tokyoites a glimpse of Western culture.[30] It also offered a very different kind of entertainment. The sharp curves of the track, necessitated by the shape and size of the space, resulted in frequent falls, adding to the excitement. Since viewing was free of charge, the shrine ground was always packed for the races. Some visitors even climbed the trees for a better view.[31] The stated purpose of these early horse races was to promote horsemanship in the interest of national defense. But materialism quickly infiltrated the races: Prizes were given to winners, and many spectators took to betting on the outcome.[32] Popular woodblocks of the time caricatured the events and often emphasized the boisterous and amusing atmosphere rather than militarism and horsemanship.

Circuses, or equestrian acrobatics, also became a fixture at Yasukuni grounds. A woodblock print titled *Shōkonsha keidai nai nite: Furansu daikyokuba* (French Acrobat Horses at Shōkonsha Grounds), a triptych of panels each approximately 36 centimeters by 24 centimeters, dated around 1871 and attributed to Hiroshige III, showcases horses and acrobats in Western and Japanese costumes executing a variety of poses and stunts. This peculiar set of images, on which the characters and their props float randomly over a tricolor background with no scenery to provide a context for these performers, is a depiction of the very first circus event at Yasukuni Shrine. According to Saitō Gesshin in *Bukō nenpyō,* "on October 26, 1871, a show of foreign men, women and horses took place at Shōkonsha grounds. It was a performance by a group named Soulie from France."[33] Gesshin was not impressed by the event: "[F]ew people in the audience. Highly priced for an uninteresting show. In addition, the day was short and getting cold."[34] But these events soon became a fixture at Yasukuni Shrine. Other shrines hosted circuses on their grounds, but Yasukuni circuses are well known for the literature they inspired, such as Kawabata Yasunari's "Shōkonsai ikkei (A View of the *Shōkon* Ritual)" and Yasuoka Shōtarō's "Sākasu no uma (The Circus Horse)."[35] Yasuoka, in particular, whose short story was based on his fascination with the circus while attending an elementary school close to the shrine, later wrote *Dai seikimatsu sākasu* (End-of-the-Century Circus), based on the diary of Takano Hironachi, a member of the first Japanese circus troupe to train in Europe.[36] Ashihara Eiryō, another student at a nearby school, was equally captivated by the Yasukuni circuses and later wrote an important book on the history of circuses in Japan.[37]

The nonlinear configuration of the outer shrine that I noted earlier is key to the perception of the shrine grounds in its early years. Horse races were discontinued after the festival of November 1898, and the outer garden came to be known as the "old horse ground" (*kyū-baba*). Before construction in 1919 of the large *torii,* which now stands at the eastern end of the outer garden and marks the main entrance to the shrine grounds, the space

FIGURE 3. *Yasukuni Jinja-zu* (Image of Yasukuni Shrine), 1896. Used by permission of Yasukuni Shrine Yūshūkan Museum.

typically functioned more as a park (*niwa* or *kōen*) than as a path to the shrine. Unlike today, the bronze Ōmura statue did not impose itself in the middle of the *sandō*, obstructing pedestrian traffic, but functioned as the focal point of an open public space that suggests a Western-style plaza (see figure 3). In a 1902 essay, Masaoka Shiki called this space "the garden of Yasukuni Shrine" and analyzed the entire compound as a combination of Western, Japanese, and Chinese styles. He recalled his initial encounter with Yasukuni Shrine in the 1880s, when, as a child, he "did not notice anything other than the white cedar trees planted in a row on the beautiful lawn," implying that he did not realize or care that it was a shrine.[38] Tayama Katai, whose father was enshrined at Yasukuni after the Satsuma Rebellion, titled the essay in which he describes his frequent childhood visits to the shrine "The Park at Kudan."[39] An 1880 publication also notes a flower garden (*hyakka no en*) and a lake with a fountain.[40] Ōmura's statue used to be enclosed by a fence, around which old cannons were placed as benches.[41] Modern novels such as *An Adopted Husband,* by

Futabatei Shimei, seat their protagonists on the cannon benches to evoke their pensive moods.[42] Yasukuni Shrine was the site of the first domestic exposition held in Japan.[43]

Thus an enormous gap existed between the creator's intentions for the site and the users' experiences of it. For its creators, Yasukuni Shrine was a national military memorial. For festival goers and everyday visitors to the outer garden, it was a place to play. In fact, the entertainment offered at the shrine was not unexpected for the visitors. The Ryōgoku temple Ekōin, built to pacify the dead from the Great Fire of Meireki (1657), often hosted sumo tournaments meant as "performance[s] to appease the souls" of those who were memorialized there.[44] The famous fireworks at Ryōgoku began in the early eighteenth century to calm the spirits of those who had died in Edo's many fires. Other kinds of entertainment presented at Yasukuni Shrine—those without any memorializing connotation such as acrobatic horse performances and freak shows—were also not out of character for a Shinto shrine. In the Tokugawa era, sacred sites were associated with public entertainment.[45] For example, Asakusa and Ryōgoku, Edo's two most popular amusement sites, were associated with the Sensōji and Ekōin temples, respectively.[46] In the case of Sensōji in Asakusa, an entertainment district was located adjacent to the temple grounds. The area became famous in the early twentieth century for its many modern features, such as the twelve-story Ryōunkaku tower, the Hanayashiki amusement park, panorama buildings, and movie theaters.[47] Behind Sensōji temple was Yoshiwara, the brothel district, relocated in 1657 from the current Ningyōchō area. A brothel district also adjoined Ryōgoku. Asakusa and Ryōgoku grew to be popular entertainment districts in their own right, but it was common practice for vendors and entertainers to open temporary businesses around temples, particularly for special occasions such as New Year's day or exhibitions of venerated Buddha icons (*kaichō*).[48] In some areas, the temples themselves operated amusement quarters. Inside the gates, temple grounds were landscaped into beautiful parks. This was in part an income-generating strategy for the temples. Fees paid by parishioners were the main source of their income. However, this source of income was limited because, under the *ujiko* (parishioner) system, only the residents of a designated district belonged to a temple and paid tribute. The commercial facilities attracted nonparishioner visitors and increased the temple's income through monetary offerings and sales of talismans.[49] In this context, it is not surprising that the visitors to Yasukuni Shrine had few to no reservations about enjoying the available entertainments.

Regulations initiated by the Meiji government that sought to alter the cultural landscape of Tokyo also indirectly affected the growing popularity of Yasukuni events. The relationship between entertainment and Tokyo urban spaces, including religious sites, started to change in early Meiji as the new government attempted to modernize the physical fabric of the new capital and "enlighten" its residents. The first major modification in 1873 followed examples from European urban planning: The government designated five areas around existing or former temples in Tokyo, including Ueno (Kan'eiji) and Asakusa (Sensōji), as official parkland.[50] Of the new parks regulated by the government, Ueno became the cultural showcase of the modern imperial capital. A part of Asakusa was transformed into a state park, and the remainder divided into seven districts.[51] Asakusa maintained its character as a site for entertainment, but businesses that the government deemed unacceptable were relegated to the Sixth District (Asakusa Rokku)—reserved for amusement—with higher taxes and restrictions on performances.[52]

In particular, the government focused on Ueno, the original candidate for Tokyo Shōkonsha, in their civilizing mission, which included new schools, museums, and libraries, as well as domestic industrial expositions (Naikoku Kangyō Hakurankai).[53] The construction of buildings that embody features of a modern nation, such as the museum of history (Daihakubutsukan, 1882), music hall (Hōgakudō, 1885), art museum (Nihon Bijutsu Kyōkai Reppinkan, 1888), and library (Teikoku Toshokan, 1906), followed one after the other in this area. A comparison between the imperial court's interest in Ueno and Yasukuni Shrine is revealing. Emperor Meiji attended every one of the industrial expositions, the opening ceremonies at Ueno Park (1876) and the zoo (1882), and horse races (1884). He was always present at Ueno events associated with the Sino-Japanese and Russo-Japanese wars.[54] By contrast, Meiji attended the festivals of the Yasukuni Shrine a total of only seven times during his forty-four-year reign. This contrasts with the popularly held impression of the close ties between Yasukuni and the imperial family. Even in the Showa era the emperor became a regular presence at Yasukuni festivals only in 1937, the middle of the Asia-Pacific War.[55] This suggests that the emperor's presence at Yasukuni was not emphasized until at least 1937.

New restrictions on the use of Tokyo's urban spaces also affected the popularity of Yasukuni Shrine. From the beginning, the Meiji government was intent on "civilizing" the people of Tokyo as residents of a modern capital, passing rules and regulations to restrict Edo customs that officials considered vulgar. These measures were meant not only to civilize Tokyo residents but also to reform them from bakufu followers to imperial subjects. For example, starting in 1870, a series of regulations was promulgated to control what the government considered Edo-style amusements in the capital. Between 1870 and 1891 a series of new regulations forbade the opening of shops and stalls in many places in Tokyo.[56] The Ishiki Kaii ordinance of 1872 restricted many activities central to street performance, such as opening new shops or performing without a permit; sumo performances between a man and a woman; pornographic shows or exhibitions of lewd images; and cross-dressing.[57] The display of persons with deformities, a popular feature of freak shows, was prohibited in 1873.

Despite its strong interest in civic reform and enlightenment in areas like Ueno and Asakusa, the government had little involvement in Yasukuni matters. Moreover, with its acquisition of the shrine in July 1869 and indifference to the government's reforms and enlightenment projects, the military (Heibushō) asked Tokyo to dissolve the government's control over Yasukuni grounds.[58] Thus, Yasukuni Shrine was not affected when the government issued a series of regulations affecting shrine and temple grounds, which, in principle, forbade the operation of *tokomise,* small shops and stands often used by vendors and street performers. Uprooted merchants and performers moved to less-regulated places, of which Yasukuni was one.[59] As a result, Yasukuni festivals came to be known for the number and variety of their attractions no longer available elsewhere in Tokyo.[60] In contrast to the cultural and imperial showcase of Ueno, which the Japanese government developed to symbolize the capital of modern Japan, Yasukuni Shrine continued to house forms of Edo-style popular amusements that the government was trying to eliminate in Tokyo. It established a solid presence in Tokyo's popular culture through its festivals and attractions, which had already been an important part of Tokyoite life since the Tokugawa period.

Yasukuni Shrine was thus not affected by the government's plan to modernize the imperial capital. Furthermore, despite their proximity to one another, little effort was made to establish a readily perceptible connection between the imperial court and Yasukuni Shrine. Between its inception in 1869 and the beginning of the Sino-Japanese War in 1894, Tokyo was vastly transformed. The emperor now resided in the Imperial Palace and made regular appearances before Tokyoites. The year 1889 saw two milestone events that demonstrated Japan's status as a modern nation: the promulgation of the Meiji Constitution and the convening of the Imperial Diet. Western-style architecture, often employed for government and educational facilities, dotted the cityscape. A national framework for children's education was set in

1872. At the same time, Yasukuni Shrine, which had started its modernizing process early on, seemed outside the state's attempts to civilize the city and its residents. Nevertheless, the shrine continued to be a *meisho*—a popular and famous site—in the capital city, albeit not for the role intended by its creators. Popular perceptions of Yasukuni Shrine gradually began to change in the following decades as a consequence of Japan's imperial wars, but it was not until the final years of the Asia-Pacific War that the shrine took on the ideologically charged qualities that we are familiar with today.

TURNING WAR INTO SPECTACLE AT YASUKUNI SHRINE

Japan's wars against China and Russia provided a key turning point for Yasukuni Shrine's presence in Tokyo. The shrine's prominence grew considerably, as did the presence of militarism. The records of monetary offerings and the number of entrants to Yūshūkan show an increase in the number of visitors to the shrine during these wars. Monetary offerings increased by 50 percent in both 1894 and 1895, during Japan's war against China. The number of visitors to Yūshūkan increased nearly sevenfold in 1894. Revenue from donations nearly doubled in both 1904 and 1905 in response to the Russo-Japanese War. Visitors to Yūshūkan increased from 4.25 million in 1903 to more than ten million in 1904 and remained in excess of ten million in 1905 and 1906.[61] Festivals increasingly incorporated themes of war and victory through installations of weapons and large-scale paintings of panoramic battle scenes. For example, Yūshūkan Museum, which had struggled to fill its exhibit halls when it opened its doors to the public in 1882, overflowed with spoils of war from Russia. In 1905 plans were announced to construct a second-floor addition to the museum to house the growing number of acquisitions.[62]

The shrine's increase in popularity was no doubt tied to Japan's military successes and their representations at the shrine but not necessarily to respect for the war dead, as I demonstrate later. For the most part, visitors continued to be attracted to the festivals because of the entertainment. But the combination of amusements and military success proved effective for promoting militarism, as visitors took in the spectacles in a celebratory mood. In addition, technological developments in both military armaments and visual culture rendered representations of war more spectacular. With each development on the front and in technology, the prominence of militarism at the festivals increased in terms of the scope of its content and the scale of its representation. Battlefield success and the resulting popular excitement increased revenue for the state and the shrine, which in turn funded more sophisticated and absorbing presentations of battlefield exploits.

Successful battles gave rise to new entertainment facilities on the shrine grounds. Kokkōkan, a panorama building that opened in 1902 as an annex to Yūshūkan Museum, was one such example. Panorama buildings, a European invention that offered the visitor a new kind of visual experience, were introduced to Japan in 1910 during the third Domestic Exposition in Ueno.[63] The outbreak of the Sino-Japanese War four years later ensured ample material for these facilities: scenes from the latest battles.[64] Panorama buildings proved particularly suitable for realistic presentation of battle scenes due to its ability to completely surround the viewer with three-dimensional renditions of battlefield scenery. Battle scenes were often accompanied by the sounds of cannons and gunfire, providing visitors both a visual and an acoustic experience. At the Nihon Panorama-kan in Asakusa the display changed periodically following the Japanese Army's exploits in Asia, displaying the Boxer Rebellion and the 1901 attack on the Tien-tsin castle, the third attack on Lüshun (Port Arthur) in 1905, followed by the Battle of the Japan Sea later that year. The presentation of the Battle of the Japan Sea even incorporated real water with machine-induced waves.[65] Packaged as spectacular entertainment, the battle-themed panorama displays were also meant to inform, educate, and instill a sense of pride in Japan's military prowess.

Given their popularity, in 1902 a proposal was submitted for a war-themed panorama exhibit at Yasukuni Shrine. Entrepreneur Murakami Tsuruzō suggested building a panorama building that would "educate visitors on the bravery of Japanese soldiers in the Sino-Japanese War and consequently promote patriotism and loyalty."[66] The result was Kokkōkan, a panorama building that opened during the festival of May 1902 as an annex to Yūshūkan at Gyūgabuchi, an adjacent site owned by Yasukuni Shrine. This new addition to Yasukuni proved a huge success, especially as the start of the Russo-Japanese War provided new themes to display. Kokkōkan functioned as an urban installation that both entertained and promoted militarism by obscuring miserable battlefield realities with a play of light. Soldiers were heroic in battle; new large-scale weaponry inspired awe. Panoramas, however, did not convey the horrific reality of war and the anguish of suffering and death.

The immediacy of the presentation, which stimulated multiple senses, was an entirely new experience for the visitors, who, until that point, had received news from the front through newspaper updates, sketches and prints, and the occasional photograph.[67] Novelist Edogawa Ranpo describes an experience of a battle-themed panorama building: "What an incredible illusion. Outside the panorama building, trains were running and vendor stalls were lined up. I could even see my own house beyond the stores. But those things completely disappeared once inside the panorama building, and I suddenly found myself in the midst of a vast Manchurian field expanding to the horizon. And a bloody battle too terrifying to look at was unfolding."[68] The panorama installations were active, the visitor's experience passive. Immediately upon entering the building, visitors found that their five senses were stripped of their freedom, and they had no choice but to take in the highly controlled sensory input. In the panorama building, visitors could vicariously experience the excitement of the battlefield while staying in the safety and comfort of this contrived setting. Japan's successful overseas campaigns, aided by their representations in visual media such as prints, paintings, and panorama buildings, sparked popular interest in battlefield exploits during and immediately after the Sino-Japanese War.

By the time Japan was fighting the Russo-Japanese War, technological advances had further transformed the visual representation of war. War photography that was used to a limited extent during the Sino-Japanese War became more common, and film was introduced. Theaters featuring newsreels gradually replaced panorama buildings. In Tokyo, key theaters, including Meijiza and Kabukiza, regularly screened footage from the battlefront.[69] Kokkōkan stayed in operation until early 1906, when the Tokyo City Railroad Company relocated the building approximately 15 feet to the southeast in order to accommodate a new railway. But what was to be a temporary closure turned into a permanent one due to the declining popularity.[70] The appeal of the panorama building waned with the rise of film, which quickly became the dominant medium for visual mass persuasion. Whether the viewing experience was through a panorama building or a film, however, the relationship between the viewer and the battlefield for the most part remained similar to that of the Battle of Ueno in the summer of 1868: Viewers could vicariously and safely experience the excitement of the battlefield. For the majority of visitors, battles remained spectacles and celebrations of victory, of nation, of imperialism. At that time, death played a minor role in the popular understanding of Japan's wars.

A NETWORK OF SPECTACLE

With the increase in frequency and scale of victory-related celebrations during the two wars, Yasukuni Shrine began to function as a key site in the visual network of war victory spectacles in Tokyo. The shrine became an integral part of a Tokyo-wide network of tools for war commemoration during these two wars, a network that mass media and technology later transformed into a nationwide one. In Tokyo, city-sponsored parades traveled to and from sites that included Yasukuni Shrine, Ueno Park, the plaza in front of the imperial palace, and other public spaces. Newspapers featured maps with parade schedules to assist readers in attending these events. Schools and other local organizations constructed triumphal arches, another popular European import that was adopted for Sino-Japanese war celebrations.[71] In the case of the Russo-Japanese War, victory celebrations at home started as early as August 10, 1904, a mere two days after Japan's surprise attack on the Russian Far East Fleet at Port Arthur, with thousands parading through Tokyo with flags and lanterns in hand.[72] Decorated trolley cars (*hana-densha*) traveled the streets of Tokyo for the first time during the Russo-Japanese War celebrations. On September 2, 1904, for example, the Tokyo Electric Railway Company (Tōkyō Densha Tetsudō Gaisha) and the Urban Railway Company (Shigai Tetsudō Gaisha) ran several trolleys decorated with flags and lights in honor of the victory at Luoyang.[73] Victory celebrations increased in size, intensity, and frequency with each military success. The tide of cheering people carrying lanterns and flags, along with the illuminated trolleys, created a network of spectacles across Tokyo. It connected the key sites associated with celebrations of Japan's imperialist nation building. During the Russo-Japanese War, the images of these spectacles, along with images from the battlefront, were reproduced and disseminated throughout Japan as prints and photographs.

Among the festivals that Yasukuni Shrine hosted, those of 1906 and 1907 were particularly notable for their grandeur and scale. In the spring of 1906 the most spectacular of these applauded Japan's victory over Russia. The shrine was a central component of the Tokyo-wide celebrations. Festivities began a day after the triumphal military review that engulfed the entire city of Tokyo on April 30. The next night a *shōkon* ritual was conducted at Yasukuni, followed by a special festival on the shrine grounds that lasted four days. For six consecutive nights, various areas of Tokyo were illuminated, boasting numerous spoils of war. At Yasukuni Shrine, two towers made of guns that were obtained from the Russian Army marked each side of the entrance. On one tower was the word *chūyū* (loyalty and bravery), and on the other *giretsu* (nobility of soul). Midway to Ōmura's statue, a triumphal arch was constructed and decorated with cedar branches bearing the words *kokkō hakki* (manifestation of national glory) and *kōi sen'yō* (enhancement of imperial prestige). All of the installations were illuminated at night. During the 1907 festival larger items confiscated from the Russian military, such as cannons and tanks, were on display at Yasukuni Shrine.[74] The emperor made an appearance for the May festival in both 1906 and 1907.

Although the main function of Yasukuni Shrine, according to its creators, was to serve as a memorial for military dead, the loss of lives received less attention. As I discuss in chapter 4, the ritual to call in the spirits of the dead for enshrinement became the central focus of the semiannual festivals in the last years of the Asia-Pacific War. However, while not as apparent to many visitors, Yasukuni Shrine regularly performed this ritual since its inception. Ever since the first *shōkon* ceremony on June 12, 1869, military dead were enshrined at Yasukuni in a ritual that took place on the night before the first festival day, and the two turn-of-the-century wars were no exception. For example, on December 8, 1894, *Jiji shinpō* newspaper listed the names of the 1,280 Sino-Japanese War dead to be enshrined during the upcoming special festival.[75] Several days later *Jiji* continued with lengthy reports on the three-day festival. But the only reference to the *shōkon* ceremony was the following sentence printed on December 17: "Yesterday the sixteenth, the loyal spirits (*chūkon*) of the army soldiers, who ran about exerting themselves for the sake of their nation, while tolerating the northern snows of the Liaotung Peninsula piercing their skins and the poisonous heat of Taiwan melting their bones, only to evaporate into battlefield dew, were enshrined at Yasukuni Shrine accompanied by a special festival."[76] Detailed depictions of entertainment, the visitors, and the emperor's visit on the second day occupy the remaining pages. It is likely that readers were left with the impression of an elaborate festival, one of many that simultaneously took place in Tokyo, rather than an event honoring war dead.

During the Russo-Japanese War, *izoku* (war-bereaved family members) were invited to visit Tokyo and attend the *shōkon* ritual. To reduce the expense of the trip to Tokyo they received discounts for railway tickets.[77] They also received permission from the Imperial Household Department to visit key imperial sites in Tokyo, including the detached imperial palaces in Hama and Akasaka, Shinjuku Imperial Park, and the imperial museum and zoo in Ueno.[78] Also during the Russo-Japanese War, the military had started compiling photo albums of the festival.[79] As I discuss in chapter 4, these albums were sent to the *izoku* families at a later date as another tool to disseminate the beliefs associated with Yasukuni enshrinement. Nevertheless, according to *Jiji shinpō*, for the *shōkon* ceremony of December 1895, only 130 bereaved families visited the shrine in response to 1,004 invitations, while, at the same time, the shrine grounds were packed with people viewing the sumo matches, fireworks, military bands, and other entertainment.[80] Even the immediate families of the fallen were not interested enough to make the trip to Tokyo to attend this ritual, which was supposed to have been the highest honor that a Japanese could receive. The description of the *shōkon* ceremony in the *Jiji shinpō* increased to a paragraph in 1905, when the Russo-Japanese War deaths were memorialized, but, as I discuss in chapter 4, this is still unremarkable when compared to the coverage of the Asia-Pacific War years.[81]

As the new nation was taking shape with the completion of the new Imperial Palace (1888), the convening of the Imperial Diet (1889), and the promulgation of the Meiji Constitution (1889) and the Imperial Rescript on Education (1890), observance rituals involving the emperor and his subjects who died in war also acquired more formal characteristics.[82] Informal amusement at Yasukuni festivals changed to more structured and institutional activities, while maintaining the quality of entertainment. Events at the festivals took on a more militaristic tone. The rambunctious horse races and lively circuses were gradually replaced with the military museum and battle scenes presented in the panorama buildings. From the Sino-Japanese War to the Russo-Japanese War, Yasukuni Shrine steadily evolved into a state military institution.

But despite the shift in the tone of the Yasukuni festivals from popular to military and the incorporation of lessons associated with the festival into the elementary school curriculum, public perception of and behavior regarding Yasukuni enshrinement remained undisciplined. According to newspaper editorials from 1895, few festival visitors showed the proper military spirit and respect, and some even ridiculed the battered weapons on display from the Sino-Japanese War.[83] Even after the Russo-Japanese War, some families of the war dead gave away their tickets to worship at Yasukuni or sold them to neighbors rather than attend themselves.[84] Similar trends appear in the pattern of participation in the national ceremonies, often mandated to promote patriotism and reverence for the emperor. While the majority followed the prescribed activities for national ceremonies, few participated solely on their own initiative. For example, schools lured students to ceremonial readings on national holidays by distributing sweets and combining the events with exhibitions, music festivals, or athletic meets.[85] Local governments needed to distribute official notices instructing residents to fly the national flag, take a day off from work, or hold local observances.[86] But even though the entertainment on the Yasukuni grounds successfully attracted Tokyoites to the shrine events, the visitors did not necessarily subscribe to the beliefs these activities were promoting. Furthermore, the majority of Japanese people lacked easy access to the shrine and had even less appreciation for this national memorial. Nevertheless, celebrations in Tokyo and Yasukuni Shrine, with large numbers of participants, created a visual image of an entire nation fully endorsing Japan's imperialist endeavors. And this is the image that has been preserved to shape the Japanese collective memory. Through their actions the participants—visitors to Yasukuni festivals and revelers at the victory celebrations—were transforming themselves into full subjects of imperial Japan whether or not they were aware of the fact.

THREE

NETWORKS OF GRIEF AND PRIDE

Yasukuni Shrine in Regional Japan

> During the [Sino-Japanese] war, we elementary school children received the honor of attending the funeral of a fallen soldier, along with the mayor, the district headman, and other volunteers. Because the soldier was from a poor family of a devastated part of town, townspeople did not try to hide their discontent that the town awarded him such an impressive ceremony.
>
> *JOURNALIST UBUKATA TOSHIRŌ, PERSONAL RECOLLECTION*

During the Sino-Japanese and Russo-Japanese wars, Yasukuni Shrine, utilizing the latest technology, transformed itself from a popular *meisho* into a military-themed entertainment site that offered sensational representations of battlefront triumphs. It was a space for celebration: of war, of national strength, and of modernity and technology. Together with enhancements to its physical presence, such as the museum and the panorama building, as well as the spectacles and festivals the shrine hosted, the prominence of the Tokyo memorial grew. But most Japanese did not visit it. Unless one lived in central Tokyo, the shrine was not easily accessible. Unlike the Tokyoites depicted in the previous chapter, residents elsewhere in Japan did not frequent the shrine. How did they become familiar with the beliefs associated with Yasukuni Shrine? Or, to put it more precisely, in what ways—other than through cultural representations of the events hosted on and around the shrine grounds—did the Japanese come to understand the ideas of death and memorialization associated with Yasukuni Shrine?

In this chapter I explore the gradual institutionalization of regional death rituals. An examination of rural Japan—areas far away from Tokyo in particular—is crucial for understanding the widespread and growing recognition of Yasukuni Shrine. For the most part, men enshrined there as a result of Japan's earlier wars had never set foot in Tokyo. Family members of most military dead had only mediated knowledge of the shrine. And yet, by the time of the Asia-Pacific War, the myth of Yasukuni enshrinement was widely known throughout Japan, if not yet fully accepted by all. Drawing on examples from outside Tokyo, I want to explore here the process through which people without easy access to the shrine came to understand Yasukuni enshrinement. The previous chapter deals with the development of "Yasukuni the belief" through "Yasukuni the site"; this chapter examines the belief in the absence of access to the site.

In this period we also see the beginnings of a nationwide network that disseminated ideals associated with the emperor and Yasukuni Shrine to all of Japan: an ideological network that utilized a range of tools from conscription and funerals to victory celebrations and school rituals, with which all Japanese—regardless of where they lived—had an obligatory relationship. This network became more institutionalized in later decades through the construction of *gokoku jinja* (nation-protecting shrines) and war memorials and through organized visits to Yasukuni Shrine by bereaved family members. Live radio programming enabled some rituals to take place simultaneously throughout the Japanese empire, further reinforcing the network (chapter 4). Yasukuni Shrine was central to this network. At the same time, I want to emphasize that the shrine was only one part of a larger system in which mass media, education, and rituals played key roles. My intention here is not to downplay the role of Yasukuni Shrine in imperial Japan but to highlight other actors without which the idea of honorable war death would not have taken root as powerfully as it did.

I begin with two contrasting episodes from journalist Ubukata Toshirō's memoir, *Meiji Taishō kenbunshi* (Observations of Meiji and Taisho Life) in order to provide a glimpse into life in rural Japan at the turn of the century. The first scene is the epigraph that opens this chapter: a town funeral for a soldier during the Sino-Japanese War (1894–1895).[1] Ubukata remembers the townspeople's discontent upon observing the elaborate funeral for a son of a poor family, for which numerous people, including town dignitaries and elementary school children like Ubukata, were present. The second episode took place about a decade later: a similar funeral for a soldier from another poor family, killed in the Russo-Japanese War (1904–1905). This time, he recalls, the attendees whispered enviously to each other that the deceased would "now become a god at Kudan (Yasukuni Shrine)."[2] Ubukata, a fierce critic of Japanese militarism, was expressing his disdain for this quick shift in public opinion. Nonetheless, these two excerpts together demonstrate a dramatic shift in popular consciousness in response to the two wars. In just a decade, the perceived status of the war casualty was transformed: The dead soldier was no longer just another dead person who was not worthy of the ceremony accorded to him; he had now attained a position of reverence and envy. By the time of the Russo-Japanese War, more people were also aware of the idea that the war dead became gods at Yasukuni Shrine.

The impressive ceremony that Ubukata mentions was not unusual at the time. Funerals for the military dead were typically planned and carried out by the town or the village, partially funded by residents' donations. Schoolchildren and members of various local associations attended, sometimes resulting in thousands present for the funeral of a single low-ranking soldier. Prefectural governments often directed mayors and village heads to submit a detailed report of the funeral: a requirement that pressured the local administrators to host events that were as grand as possible.[3] These ceremonies can be considered the local equivalent of the multiday festivals at Yasukuni Shrine that followed the *shōkon* rituals. The practice taught participants that war death should be publicly recognized and, further, should be an occasion for commemoration and even celebration rather than mourning. However, as indicated by Ubukata's narrative, not everyone approved of the grandeur of these ceremonies. The idea of reverence for the war dead took hold at an uneven pace throughout Japan. Ubukata's story takes place in Numata City, Gunma Prefecture, almost one hundred miles north of Tokyo. Even though Ubukata and his neighbors could not yet understand the state-constructed significance of war death at the time of the Sino-Japanese War, writer and educator Lafcadio Hearn (Koizumi Yakumo) encountered a quite different situation. One of Hearn's former students, en route to fight in the Sino-Japanese War, asserted not only that was he proud to fight but also that he intended to die for the emperor. The student reassured his astounded teacher that he would be respected and worshipped by all Japanese people after his death. He recalled a visit to a local shrine with fellow conscripts, during which the group silently contemplated the likelihood of being enshrined there as gods (just as at Yasukuni Shrine).[4] These contrasting episodes related by Ubukata and Hearn do not represent the full spectrum of popular belief at the time.[5] Many would continue to express dissent or indifference toward the Yasukuni system of enshrinement even in the later years.

This chapter examines attitudes toward war and war death in regional Japan primarily during the years of the Sino-Japanese and the Russo-Japanese wars. For example, the elaborate funeral ceremony that Ubukata recalled was central to propagating support at home for imperialist wars. Funerals were not the only opportunity. Structured events from military-related ones (e.g., victory celebrations; sending troops off and welcoming them home; local funerals) to those that honored the emperor (e.g., recitation of the Imperial Rescript on Education, celebration of imperial holidays, and paying tribute to the imperial portrait) gradually instilled in participants the idea of proudly dying for emperor and nation. General changes in death rituals, precipitated by the arrival of modernization in regional Japan and the resulting structural changes in the family, also affected the ways that people perceived war death. The shift in awareness is not uniform, as I have suggested with the contrasting examples of Ubukata and Hearn, but steadily spread to all of Japan. During this period the state established the social infrastructure needed to support a militarized nation, namely, conscription, education, public events, the legal system, and so on. Chapter 4 takes up how this structure was further institutionalized during the Asia-Pacific War.

CONSCRIPTION: BECOMING A SOLDIER IN MODERN JAPAN

For a soldier in the Imperial Japanese Army or Navy, war death was the route to "becom[ing] the god at Kudan."[6] Conscription, the system of securing these soldiers that were to die for imperial Japan, was introduced in 1873, shortly after the completion of Tokyo Shōkonsha.[7] Conscription was by far the most significant step in the process of militarizing the young nation. The system not only maintained a supply of young men in training but also allowed the state to gather and collect detailed information on every male Japanese.[8] Most important, it was meant to instill in all Japanese males the sense of their obligation to serve the emperor and the nation as a soldier and possibly die in the process. The importance of having and raising healthy sons eligible for conscription was inculcated among Japanese girls and women. Even the mundane process of paperwork required of every Japanese male became a rite of passage: It was a reminder that being male meant it was necessary to consider the possibility of dying for Japan. Yasukuni Shrine, then, always loomed in the background.

The conscription process was designed to motivate boys and young men to become model citizens by maintaining a healthy body as well as a good academic and social standing. The state categorized all twenty-year-old men into five ranks based on a health and fitness examination.[9] Unless one was assigned to the fifth rank, created for those who were ill and needed to retake the examination, a man's ranking did not change throughout his life. Fitness ranking thus constructed an ideal male image: A patriotic Japanese male was in the top two ranks and physically eligible for conscription. Only 15 percent of the examinees enjoyed the honor of earning the highest rank.[10] This ranking method transformed the process of becoming a soldier from one based on birth to one based on effort; it also brought soldiers admiration and respect.[11] This creation and instilling of desire to fulfill a state-imposed obligation continued throughout the history of Imperial Japan: Men wanted to achieve the highest rank in the physical exam even though that increased the probability of military service and war death; schools wished to become eligible for the imperial portrait; local governments aspired to obtain permission to build war memorials. Similarly, the education system instilled in young men the desire for enshrinement at Yasukuni Shrine.

The primary goal of conscription is to meet a need for military personnel. But at the outset, the lottery process ensured that one's probability of being conscripted was quite low.[12] In 1893, the year before the start of the Sino-Japanese War, the lottery selected approximately 20,000 out of the 120,000 eligible men, about a 17 percent chance of conscription. In 1902, the probability rose to 47 percent and to 66 percent in 1910.[13] Those not conscripted into the military were nevertheless incorporated into the new system, which ranked all adult males according to their physical qualities. In fact, all men between the ages of seventeen and forty were registered for conscription purposes.[14] The required information on each man, which was compiled at the village level, consisted of not only the aforementioned physical qualities but also academic and criminal records, neighborhood reputation, and the family's financial data, including taxes paid, real estate owned, and household income.[15] The information also allowed the state to regard the entire male population as potential fighters for Japan. But more important, for the male population, the process of documenting and submitting information was meant to foster a sense of obligation to the state. Even if men were not conscripted into the military at age twenty, the possibility always remained. This sense of awareness would grow and increasingly tie into awareness of Yasukuni Shrine as Japan experienced more military conflicts.

CELEBRATING WAR IN RURAL JAPAN

Although the idea of becoming a soldier slowly gained acceptance after conscription began, the system was not conceptually tied to Yasukuni Shrine in the minds of most. In the absence of warfare, serving in the military did not necessarily signify fighting in battles or, perhaps more important, dying.

It was not until the Sino-Japanese War that the general public first became aware of the fact that conscripted men would be sent to fight and die in battle. The concept of fighting another country was foreign to many Japanese. For example, when the Sino-Japanese War started in July 1894, twelve-year-old Ubukata Toshirō felt extremely confused. He did not understand why his country and China needed to be at war. Writing as an adult, he recalled that, even as a child, he was aware of China's positive cultural influence on his life: Beautiful artworks from China were in his house; every night his father taught him to read classical Chinese literature; the characters he learned every day at school came from the Chinese language. This confusion was shared with many others in Japan at the time. How then did the general public come to understand the concept of international warfare?

Ubukata's childhood experience is useful here.[16] Once the war started, anti-China sentiments quickly engulfed the boy's life. Various aspects of his day, from classroom education and games with friends to news and entertainment, explained why the war was justified and even necessary. Popular culture quickly shifted to incorporate the theme of war. Woodblock prints depicted courageous Japanese soldiers defeating Chinese troops. In these visual representations, the Japanese soldier was always presented as a tall, dignified man, clad in a Western-style uniform, whereas the Chinese counterpart was shorter, cowardly looking, and dressed in traditional garb. Japanese troops always managed to easily rout their Chinese opponents.[17] In comedic theater, Sino-Japanese War–themed features were simple but popular. On stage, a few Japanese soldiers would fight a large army of Chinese men and always beat their foe with ease. In tears, the Chinese soldiers would apologize and then, following the Japanese soldiers' orders, engage in silly acts and songs.[18] Toys and games featuring the Sino-Japanese War theme were also popular. Similar images ornamented everyday objects such as rice bowls and plates.[19] In all of such renditions, courageous and righteous Japan was at war with the cowardly and corrupt China for the sake of Asia. These kinds of visual representations instructed the general public, uninitiated to the concept of imperialism, on the legitimacy of Japan's wars.

Japan's victories in the ongoing battles also made these jingoistic narratives convincing. The news traveled fast through various media. The young Ubukata was sent out many times a day by his mother to check the latest news posted on the bulletin board at the police station. Every update reported another Japanese victory, he recalls, and people were ecstatic.[20] By the time of the Russo-Japanese War, newspapers began to play a key role in the dissemination of information from the front. Even in rural areas, mailmen delivered extras by train to town halls, villages, and temples. Family members of soldiers gathered every day at their local temple to have the cleric read the newspaper to them.[21] Such group readings of newspapers and bulletin boards also promoted a collective experience of joy and pride as subjects of the empire.

Reports in the mass media conveyed the grandeur and excitement of local celebrations. The following excerpt from the *San'in* newspaper describes an event in April 1895 celebrating Japan's victory over China at a town in Shimane Prefecture:

> At Hiranuma Town, Tatenui District, numerous people, including town residents, civil servants, and school children of various grades, climbed atop Mount Atago hailing the flag of the rising sun from eight in the morning. The townspeople, organized in twenty-one neighborhood associations, all shouted *banzai* to the Empire of Japan and the Japanese people. At the Atago Shrine, the mayor delivered a speech and school principals offered congratulatory addresses. . . . Later, all twenty-one groups gathered at flag-adorned houses and held receptions for military families. After dark, the groups hung lanterns throughout the city, marched to the Izumo Shrine, where they offered supplication for the prosperity of the imperial authority and prayed for the safety of the troops.[22]

The excerpt depicts a town filled with energy and excitement, proud of the military accomplishments of their local men, and ecstatic about their nation's prospects. But a careful reading of the passage reveals that participants in the events presented here are not individuals but parts of organized groups such as schools, businesses, and neighborhood associations.[23] Participation in these events was neither voluntary nor spontaneous. Each participant was compelled to partake in the activities and often required to pay for equipment such as flags and lanterns.[24] But to the casual reader, the event appears to have been a joyful celebration by willing participants. Furthermore, these representations in the mass media became the lasting image—rather than fleeting moments of discontent experienced by some of the participants—which gradually became institutionalized as the official memory of Japan at war.

Reports of celebrations and other public events were not the only way that the mass media conveyed an image of an entire nation wholly invested in the national cause. During the Russo-Japanese War, newspapers reported on episodes that exemplified the ultimate sacrifice for the nation.

For example, the *Yomiuri* newspaper reported in March 1904 that a sixty-four-year-old woman had taken her own life to lessen the burden on her daughter-in-law, who, in the absence of her husband, worked without sleep to feed their two young children.[25] Men reportedly divorced their wives before going to the front so that they could fight without reservation.[26] Mothers killed themselves so that their sons could go to the front without worrying about them.[27] Also in March 1904 a father sent a tablet of unvarnished wood to his enlisted son with a letter instructing him to "come back as this tablet" (i.e., to die on the battlefront).[28] Stories of widowed men killing their children upon enlistment also appeared in print around this time.[29] The significance here is not so much the veracity of these incidents, although it is possible that fathers made a desperate decision so their children would not be left alone to suffer and starve, but rather that they circulated as commendable tales, as models for readers. Such episodes later became a staple of mass media reports during the Asia-Pacific War: If the duty of a Japanese male was to fight and die for the emperor, the ultimate sacrifice possible for women and children was to enable men to perform their duties even if it cost them their lives.

Despite these narratives, support for Japan's wars—or, more specifically, for participating in Japan's wars—did not grow steadily during these years. In agricultural communities families that lost the main breadwinner to the war often struggled to maintain their land. Even when the men returned home, some refused to go back to their previous farming lives. Others suffered from war trauma, became warped by their neighbors' adulation, or turned to alcohol and violence. Excluding these extreme situations, the financial burden of taxes, war bonds, and donations sometimes resulted in discontent with state policy. The mainstream media, however, rarely reported such negative sentiments, particularly when they happened on an individual basis.

MOURNING DEATH AT THE LOCAL LEVEL

I opened this chapter with references to two public funerals in a Gunma town. Funerals played a key role in presenting to rural Japan the importance of fighting in and dying at war. These funerals were not private events planned by the deceased's family. They were official commemorations, organized and executed by town and village associations, town representatives, and military support groups. During the Sino-Japanese War, public funerals required consent from the deceased's family. But by the time of the

Russo-Japanese War, public funerals were mandatory, and families no longer were allowed to conduct their own rituals.[30] For example, in Sakai City, Osaka, the local association of military affairs (*heiji-kai*) conducted both Shinto and Buddhist memorial rites for all of the city's war dead, including those who died of illness while in service.[31]

However, when compared to the last years of the Asia-Pacific War—the years that are most closely associated with enshrinement at Yasukuni Shrine—loss of life during Japan's wars at the turn of the century did not have the same significance. In rural Japan, commemorative towers (*gaisen kinenhi*) often had an equally dominant presence as memorial structures.[32] This also parallels the presentation of war on the Yasukuni Shrine grounds, where the presence of lives lost was overshadowed by victory celebrations. One obvious reason is the relatively small number of war deaths. During the Sino-Japanese War, for example, war death was something that happened to other people in the community: Of the entire population, the percentage of all war-related deaths of conscripts was about 0.03.[33] For most of the families that lost fathers, husbands, and sons at war, the importance of their loss to the nation was not registered. The death toll rose dramatically during the Russo-Japanese War, when nearly every village lost a man.[34] But as I note in the previous chapter, the conceptual tie between war death and Yasukuni Shrine was not yet explicit.

At the same time, popular attitudes toward warfare in general were changing. Wars of imperialism were presented to the Japanese populace in ways that led people to believe they were a positive experience. Some families worried about the fate of their conscripted loved one, and others suffered the loss of their breadwinner, but the vast majority regarded war as a cause for celebration. We see here, too, a parallel between Tokyo and rural Japan. In Tokyo, numerous people visited Yasukuni Shrine to enjoy the entertainment, served with an increasing slant toward militarism, but few attended the *shōkon* rituals. Although war death was still understated at the festivals both in and outside Tokyo, war victory was certainly recognized and celebrated everywhere.

These funerals continued to take on a commemorative structure. Some records show temporary triumphal arches and fireworks during public funerals conducted on elementary school grounds during World War I.[35] Food associated with celebration, including red rice with beans (*sekihan*) and red and white sweet dumplings (*kōhaku manjū*) were typically distributed.[36] Rituals no longer involved the home of the deceased but were relocated to public places such as a schoolyard or a town hall. Memorial events were changed from the traditional evening funeral to noontime rites in order to accommodate a larger number of people and to make the experience more uplifting. Some remember funeral processions being as magnificent as victory parades.[37] The events were simultaneously individualized and mass produced. Local associations such as the Association of Reservists printed and circulated instructional handouts about the ceremony's procedures. According to these handouts, the program included many commemorative features such as a chorus of schoolchildren, a memorial address by a dignitary, and a display of the deceased's photograph. The memorial address was usually preprinted, so that the reader could merely insert the name and rank of the deceased. Words such as the "state" and "emperor" appeared numerous times in the address, as did "Yasukuni Shrine." Military songs and *banzai* choruses usually concluded the occasions. Crying at funerals also began to be discouraged around this time.[38]

By taking part in these events and acting as a collective, going through the motions of celebrations together, the participants consciously and unconsciously became an integral part of the nationally sanctioned narrative. The speeches delivered by town officials and school principals, peppered with key words such as "emperor," "honor," "sacrifice," and "Yasukuni Shrine," gradually inculcated the participants with the idea of proudly dying for the nation. Group participation at the local level instilled respect for war death and the sense of being a part of a larger cause, while references to Yasukuni Shrine during these rituals emphasized the importance of the monument and reinforced the conceptual ties between local events and the Tokyo institution. Thus tenets of Japanese imperialism took hold in participants' minds through repeated action, viewing similar performances, and being viewed by others.

WAR, THE EMPEROR, AND YASUKUNI SHRINE IN SCHOOLS

In addition to rituals, popular culture, and mass media, the educational system was instrumental in propagating Japanese imperialism in the emperor's name among inhabitants of regional Japan. For young Japanese, elementary school education was central to the indoctrination of these values. Knowledge of the emperor was just as important as that of Yasukuni Shrine in order for ideas about ultimate sacrifice to take root. Accordingly, instruction on the topic of the emperor took place alongside lessons on Yasukuni Shrine. All lessons associated with these two concepts were presented with an emphasis on producing desire and gratitude. The distribution of the imperial portrait is a perfect case in point: Although the state ordered schools to receive and carefully maintain the photographs, the task, as mentioned earlier, was presented as something for each school to aspire to and be grateful to achieve.[39] In this sense, there is an important parallel between practices involving receipt and maintenance of the imperial portrait and the act of serving in the military (or even being grateful for having a son, a father, or a husband who died in the military for the emperor, as discussed in chapter 4). Furthermore, the portrait and the rituals associated with it, along with classroom education, strengthened the conceptual ties between the imperial institution and Yasukuni Shrine. These experiences reinforced children's understanding of what they were supposed to do (i.e., obediently follow their teachers' rules, no matter how absurd they seemed) and what they were supposed to believe in—that the emperor was the god that they must respect and sacrifice themselves for if necessary. This process of constructing and instilling expectations, as well as creating obedient subjects who respond to these expectations often willingly and with gratitude, resulted in the idea of "institutionalized grief," which I introduce in chapter 4.

In the classroom, Yasukuni Shrine and the emperor were fundamental to instilling the concept of honorable war death in students. This process was gradual, as was the increase in the military presence in Yasukuni Shrine or the grandeur of local funerals. Classroom instruction was deliberate and systematic. As Japan's modern system of education developed alongside Japanese imperialism, classroom activities and textbooks became the optimal instrument with which to instill state ideologies in the minds of young Japanese. The Elementary School Order of 1886, which required government authorization of all textbooks used in elementary schools, for the first time regulated the curriculum and instructional materials. In 1904 the shrine was included in the first edition of the national textbooks.[40] For example, the 1904 edition of the fifth-grade Japanese language reader gave a detailed historical and descriptive account of the shrine, including its history as Tokyo Shōkonsha, details of those enshrined, and key structures on the grounds, such as the statue of Ōmura Masujirō and the Yūshūkan Museum. The idea of following in the footsteps of the war dead was already firmly established in the 1910 edition. The fourth-grade ethics reader, for example, introduces Yasukuni Shrine as follows:

> Yasukuni Shrine is located on top of the Kudan Hill. Enshrined here are those people who lost their lives fighting for this country. An imperial

> messenger visits the spring and fall festivals, and the Emperor and the Empress themselves sometimes visit the special festivals (*rinji taisai*). These loyal warriors have come to be memorialized with special care through these ceremonies due to the Emperor's kind intentions. We must remember the depth of the Emperor's blessings and devote ourselves to our country, following [the example set by] the people who are enshrined here.[41]

That is, as early as 1910, children were taught that enshrinement in Yasukuni Shrine was the highest honor they could achieve: one that merited personal visits by the emperor. The third and fourth sentences of the passage explain that those who demonstrated their loyalty by dying while fighting for the nation would be rewarded by the emperor's visits, an honor that is obtained only through death. The last sentence of the passage instructs children to follow those enshrined at Yasukuni—in other words, honor associated with war death was already instilled in the minds of elementary schoolchildren through the myth and symbolism of Yasukuni Shrine. The shrine appeared in almost all editions of state-authorized ethics and language readers, usually in the third or the fourth chapter, so that the lesson on Yasukuni would coincide with the shrine's spring festival in late April.

During the wars against China and Russia, schools also began to introduce concepts associated with memorializing the military dead in contexts outside the classroom. Under instruction from the local government, elementary schools incorporated war-related events into their curriculum, including sending off troops to the front and welcoming them home, offering prayers for victory at local shrines, celebrating war victories, and, perhaps the most important, attending funeral rites of the war dead, as Ubukata had. From the 1910s on, school trips increasingly involved visits to Shinto shrines, not only local ones but also prominent shrines such as Ise, Meiji, and Yasukuni.[42] Rituals involving worshipping Yasukuni Shrine from afar on annual festival days started in the late Meiji period, and the practice was mandated by the Ministry of Education beginning with the special festival of May 1938.[43] Mandatory education was designed so that the children, who had never been to Tokyo, would consider Yasukuni Shrine an integral presence in their lives. Even though the shrine was but one useful component of a larger system of instruction, all of which were intended to transform people into obedient and loyal subjects of imperial Japan, its symbolism was certainly potent: It simultaneously reaffirmed the importance of both the emperor and the war dead and augmented the social position of the latter by honoring their special relationship to the emperor.

DEATH RITUALS AND MODERN FAMILY STRUCTURE

Classroom education and participation in public events were integral to the dissemination of ideas around Japan's emperor-centered expansionism. But activities such as the celebration of military victories and imperial expansion, as well as the commemoration of the lives lost in the process, do not immediately translate into an acceptance of Yasukuni Shrine's role in relation to war death: that one was to serve the emperor even if it meant death with enshrinement at Yasukuni as a reward and that the Japanese state rather than the deceased's family assumed the role of memorializing such losses. However, the Japanese people had little choice in this matter. Unless one acquired an exempt status, a conscript had to fight during wartime. And if the conscript died at war, a funeral would be conducted by the local administration, and his spirit would be enshrined at Yasukuni Shrine. While not everyone embraced this idea, a great number of Japanese at least acknowledged the fact of the process. For many, Yasukuni enshrinement became a prescribed outcome of war death even if it was not motivation for fighting and dying at war.

In the process of familiarizing the Japanese people with the idea of Yasukuni enshrinement, we again see the use of current customs for the invention of tradition. One method involved strategic application to the Yasukuni myth of folk beliefs about death and the afterlife, as well as the communal rituals and festivals associated with them. Another tradition incorporated into the state-sponsored rites of military death was the *ie* (family lineage) system, a concept central to death-related rituals, particularly in rural Japan. The traditional *ie* system functioned around the *senzo,* the founding male ancestor of each family's patriline, and the *ie* occupied a central place in death-related practices.[44] This ancestor was the only person that needed to be memorialized each year. Other family members received Buddhist memorial services on specific dates and years after death for a period of thirty-three to fifty years, depending on local custom. After the set number of years, their spirits were considered to have lost their identity and merged with the spirit of the original ancestor. The ancestor was considered as the family god, who would prevent natural disasters and bring luck and happiness. Families annually conducted rites to call back the spirits of ancestors, entertain them with food and music, and finally send them off again so that they would continue to protect the living and bring good fortune.

During Japan's imperial era, the nation appropriated the system such that all Japanese were to rally around the emperor as the founding father of the nation instead of the *senzo* as the founding ancestor of the family.[45] This cooption of family ritual took place with relative ease, as the outflow of the young workforce from rural villages to the metropolis in the early twentieth century weakened the *ie* unit. With the establishment of Yasukuni Shrine, the god of Yasukuni (spirits of the war dead) gradually took on the role of maintaining peace for Japan. Instead of the ancestor protecting the family, the Yasukuni god was to protect the nation. Events at Yasukuni are comparable to the ancestral rituals: The semiannual festivals that took place following the *shōkon* rituals are meant to be offerings of entertainment for the enshrined spirits; the traditional attractions such as sumo and fireworks were to appease the spirits. The newer military-themed venues, including the museum, panorama building, and other temporary installations, were not only to celebrate victory but also to commemorate war death.

Many conceptual parallels exist between ancestor worship by *ie* members and Yasukuni enshrinement. Ancestors were memorialized by their offspring as a demonstration of gratitude for their hard work in establishing the *ie* and for being a protector god of the household; in imperial Japan, the spirits of the men who died for the emperor came to receive tribute for protecting the nation. The rituals associated with ancestor worship helped maintain a sense of unity among the *ie* members; local public memorials and their conceptual ties to Yasukuni Shrine promoted national identity. The mortuary tablet of the ancestor was considered extremely important, and family members were taught to protect it at any cost: just as the state later told each school principal to protect the imperial portrait from damage at all costs.[46] The key structural difference between the traditional rituals and the Yasukuni festivals is how they end: In the ancestral rituals, the spirits are sent back to where they normally dwell; at Yasukuni Shrine, the spirits are not free to depart after the festivals. The spirits of the war dead are held hostage by the state in Yasukuni Shrine (as the mother in the opening epigraph to the Introduction lamented).

The state's takeover of memorialization processes made sense in the context of the changes brought about by modernization and wars of imperialism, particularly for regional Japan. The traditional structure of the family memorial was declining, and increasing numbers of men, who were supposed to maintain the family patriline, were losing their lives at war. As young men began dying at war, more parents were faced with conducting death rituals for their children. This created a demand for a new form of memorial, particularly in regions where it was taboo for parents to attend their child's funeral. Yasukuni Shrine and other public memorial practices quickly replaced both losses. The nation (*kokka*) gradually came to substitute for the family (*ie*) in war death–related practices. Memorialization of the dead by the nation instead of the *ie* transformed the conventional respect for the ancestral dead into a cult of worshipping the war dead. For the Japanese, the significant deaths were no longer familial. They were national: Those people had lost their lives to establish and later to "protect" the nation. Supporters of this cult of remembrance increased and eventually surpassed the familial form of remembrance as the numbers of honored war dead increased, with the Russo-Japanese War marking the turning point. At this time the modern Japanese state fully appropriated this broadly shared, albeit waning, notion of ancestral worship.

The shift of the family unit from *ie* to the nation was undertaken on a structural level as well. In October 1908 the government initiated its regional improvement movement (*chihō kairyō undō*), which reorganized local organizations such as youth groups (*seinendan*) into state-controlled bodies, including schools, associations of reservists, and morality groups (*hōtokukai*), thus introducing systems of rule within people's everyday life. According to cultural anthropologist Kawamura Kunimitsu, these groups reinforced two concepts for their members: the family-state (*kazoku kokka*) and ancestor worship.[47] Kawamura defines the *family-state* as a system that posits the nation as an extension of the *ie* system, in which the relationship between the emperor and his subjects parallels that between the ancestor and his descendants. Just as descendants were taught to demonstrate loyalty and filial piety to the ancestor according to the Confucian tradition, so the emperor's subjects were required to show the same qualities to the emperor.[48] Along with the concept of the family-state, the concept of ancestor worship was highlighted in order to enforce the worship of Amaterasu Ōmikami, considered the mythological ancestor-god of the imperial family.[49]

Along with the deterioration of the *ie* as a concept, the structure of each household also altered in modern Japan. The introduction of the family register system (*koseki seido*) in the early Meiji period reduced the family unit to one household with one head (*ko-nushi*). Through the register, the head of the household was positioned just below the village or town headman (rather than the ancestor), thus incorporated at the very bottom of the administrative hierarchy while the emperor resided at the top.[50]

This reorganization eliminated the ancestor as the object of worship and replaced him with the emperor as the head of the expanded *ie* system. Instead of *ie* members worshipping their common ancestor, each household was to worship the emperor in appreciation for creating and maintaining their larger unit: the nation-state. Instead of the *ie* head conducting funeral rites to allow the newly dead to join the ancestor and all other family members that were dead, the state was to conduct the *shōkon* ritual to have the newly dead join all others at Yasukuni Shrine. The Yasukuni ritual, limited to the military dead, thus created a hierarchy among the dead.

Issued in October 1890, the Imperial Rescript on Education (Kyōiku Chokugo), which schoolchildren were required to cite from memory, also contributed to the reinforcement of the family-state concept. A handbook for teachers, the *Commentary on the Rescript* (Chokugo engi, 1891), accompanied the short rescript. The commentary's interpretation of the rescript demonstrates the connection between the family and the state, which the government advocated in relation to the emperor system. For example, the phrase "be filial to your parents" in the rescript was supplemented by a lengthy sixteen-page commentary fundamental to the appropriation of the family unit by the nation-state: "Just as you are at once a subject of his majesty and the offspring of your parents, the state is an expansion of the family unit. A command of the head of the state is no different from a benevolent order by the parents of a family. Therefore, if the Emperor calls upon all you subjects to rise to an occasion, you must listen attentively with deep gratitude, as you would toward your honored father and affectionate mother."[51]

In education, the philosophy of the family-state was incorporated into the second edition (1910) of the national textbooks.[52] In the ethics textbooks in particular, concepts such as "freedom," "progress of society," "competition," and "trust," used in the first edition (1904), were replaced with lessons such as "founding the nation (*kenkoku*)," "the glory of the national polity (*kokutai no seika*)," "maintaining the prosperity of the imperial throne (*kōun fuyoku*)," and "loyalty to the emperor and piety to the ancestor (*chūkō icchi*)."[53] In the second edition, the analogy between the family unit and the nation-state was more apparent, particularly in the ethics textbooks. For example, the seventh-grade ethics textbook taught the following: "Our country, based on the family system, forms one large household with the emperor as its head. We, the people, revere the Imperial throne, succeeded in an eternally unbroken line, with the sentiments of veneration that a child has for its parents. In view of this, loyalty to the throne and filial piety cannot be separated."[54] Although textbooks took a turn toward liberalism in the third edition (1918), published during the so-called Taisho democracy period, themes associated with the family-state returned more explicitly in the fourth and fifth editions (1933, 1941).

The modern *ie* system also had a significant legal dimension. The Meiji Civil Law (Meiji Minpō, 1898) stipulated that each family maintain a single surname. The wife was to "marry in" to the husband's family by taking his surname. Law scholar Hozumi Yatsuka, who played a central role in writing the law, argued that "the national polity of [the Japanese] state is based on the *ie* system. The state is an extension of the family, and the family is a component of the state."[55] Hozumi also reasoned that, since the same gods are the ancestors of the emperor and the Japanese people, the act of pledging loyalty to the emperor represents a pledge of allegiance to the spirit of the gods. Hence, the *ie* system, which originally had no genealogical relationship to Yasukuni Shrine or the ancestral gods of the emperor, became incorporated into the emperor system. This incorporation merged the emperor and his people by appropriating a version of ancestor worship at Yasukuni Shrine. The Confucian respect for the ancestor or the family elder was reconfigured as utmost respect for the emperor. With the status of the emperor as the founding father of Japan consolidated, the act of dying at war (for the emperor to protect the country he created) came to be acknowledged as the highest achievement for a Japanese man. Through this series of transformations, Yasukuni enshrinement replaced ancestral worship, and the state created a structured system to commemorate the dead locally and nationally and thereby consolidate the Myth of the War Experience.

INVENTION OF THE *EIREI*

I conclude this chapter with an examination of the term *eirei*, or heroic spirits, which refers to the spirits enshrined at Yasukuni Shrine. *Eirei* consistently appeared in news reports of the war dead and in speeches and eulogies at public ceremonies. While the word *gunshin* (military god) was sometimes used during the Asia-Pacific War to refer to men who died a particularly heroic death ("the Nine Gods of War," who perished at Pearl Harbor, for example), *eirei* most commonly referred to the typical war dead. But this usage is a modern invention. According to ethnologist Tanakamaru Katsuhiko, the word *eirei*, which today is always associated with the war dead, was not originally used in that context. Dictionaries from the Meiji and early Showa periods, for example, define the word as the spirit of a great or superior man.[56] Newspapers used terms such as "war dead" (*senshi no mono*) and "spirits" (*reikon*) to report deaths during the Satsuma Rebellion and the Sino-Japanese War. By the time of the Asia-Pacific War, however, all of the spirits at Yasukuni Shrine were referred to as *eirei*. This invented term further transformed the nature of the war dead by eliminating individuality and transforming individuals into an anonymous collective. As I explain later, it also exonerated the war dead from any wrongdoing they may have conducted during their lives. Today, *eirei* is a representative term that refers to the spirits enshrined at Yasukuni Shrine, as can be seen in the booklet series *Eirei no koto no ha* (The Last Words of the Heroic Spirits), compiled, edited and published by the shrine office. In this section I also introduce the issue of war responsibility, which I explore in chapters 5 and 6. I broach the postwar topic of war responsibility here because it is an important topic that underlies the discussion of the Asia-Pacific War in chapter 4.

The word *eirei* appeared for the first time in the *Kokumin shinpō* newspaper on May 3, 1907, in an article reporting a Yasukuni ceremony after the Russo-Japanese War. Several newspaper articles use the word in 1910, all in relation to those who had died in the war against Russia. But Tanakamaru, who has surveyed the usage of the word, argues that these earlier uses did not equate *eirei* with war dead (the persons) but praised the actions or personal qualities of those who had died.[57] The first time that the word *eirei* was used to refer exclusively to the war dead was in the introduction to *Yasukuni Jinjashi* (Chronicle of Yasukuni Shrine), published in 1911, in which Navy Minister Saitō Kan writes: "To construct a shrine for the *eirei* who demonstrated great achievements for the nation and to conduct ceremonies for them to praise their deeds and respect their virtue are fine customs that our country has practiced since antiquity."[58] Here, the word *eirei* has become synonymous with "war dead" rather than a description of the deceased. Tanakamaru also notes, however, that the main text of the chronicle or other Shinto-related documents does not include *eirei* until the 1930s and concludes that its use was promoted by the military or the media rather than Shinto shrines.[59] Over time, the status of *eirei* came to embody values beyond heroism, tragedy, or war death. Those who died in war came to be considered *eirei* regardless of their actions. Every *eirei* was remembered as noble, kind to his parents, hard working, and a good student. *Eirei* was a useful word for the purpose of obtaining popular support for wars since it was considered the highest praise for the common soldier. The *eirei* was honored not only at funeral rites and festivals. The household of an *eirei* received a wooden plaque—inscribed with the words *homare no ie* (house of honor) for army dead and *isao no ie* (house of merit) for navy dead—to hang by the front door, signifying that a man of the house had died at war. Children were instructed to tip their hat or bow when passing by. The connection of the *eirei* to the household alludes to the idea that the *eirei* was supposed to become the household's main breadwinner and eventually someone to be worshipped as an ancestor.[60] But since, instead of working for the *ie,* the *eirei* had died serving the emperor, he was worthy of respect not only from immediate family members but also from members of the new expanded family, which encompassed all of Japan. Thus, the system of Yasukuni Shrine was to be understood as an expanded and nationalized form of ancestor worship.

Of course, not everyone agreed that every war casualty was a good person worthy of respect. In 1921 political philosopher Yoshino Sakuzō, for example, delivered a scathing critique of the idea that everyone who died at war was a noble soul: "I know a fellow who, while working as a shop clerk, stole money and ran away. He later died at war and is now honored as a god at Yasukuni Shrine. This system, which allows anyone to become a god as long as he dies at war, whether he was a libertine or good-for-nothing while alive, cannot be satisfactory for our ethical ideal."[61] Yoshino's commentary met with fierce criticism from readers. Although many—particularly intellectuals—shared his sentiments, most Japanese did not agree with him, not openly at least. But whether they agreed or not, most did not question how it was possible that anyone, regardless of their lifetime deeds, could become a god. How did this "system" work? According to ethnologist Orikuchi Shinobu, the *shōkon* ritual is key to this process. Orikuchi explains that the spirits, which are "wandering through faraway mountains, fields, oceans, and rivers, are called in and enshrined [at Yasukuni] as evidently pure spirits" that would "become gods after three years' time."[62] Orikuchi uses the phrase *akiraka ni kiyoi* for "evidently pure." The choice of the word *kiyoi* suggests that the spirits are also cleansed in the process of enshrinement. The spirits at Yasukuni Shrine, then, have been cleansed of past wrongdoings, including those committed before the war and the killings and other atrocities committed during the war.

The invention of the *eirei* contributes to Japan's difficulties in resolving its war responsibilities. According to the logic of enshrinement of the war dead at Yasukuni as *eirei,* as a god that had sacrificed his life for Japan, guilt could no longer be attributed to the war dead. Included at Yasukuni Shrine today are those found guilty of war crimes during the Tokyo war crimes tribunals and other trials in the months following the war's end. If we subscribe to the belief that the spirits are cleansed in the enshrinement process, those honored at Yasukuni, even the Class-A war criminals, are no longer guilty of war crimes. When then Prime Minister Hosokawa Morihiro referred to Japan's "war of aggression (*shinryaku sensō*)" during his speech on August 15, 1993, Itagaki Tadashi, then head of the Japan Association of Bereaved Families, protested that the prime minister had "desecrated the *eirei*."[63] An acknowledgment of Japan's war responsibilities is not possible according to this logic since it would require recognition of the crimes that the *eirei* committed while alive, which, in turn, would diminish or invalidate the status of the *eirei* as impeccably honorable.

In addition to being cleansed of all acts performed prior to war death, the spirits, once enshrined as *eirei,* lose their individuality. They become a collective ancestor of the Japanese state: the ancestor that sacrificed to establish and protect the family, which is Japan. All military-related war dead, from the foot soldier and the civilian supporter to the commander, have become part of a collective that is defined through the belief in Yasukuni Shrine as propagated by the wartime state. Responsibility for individual crimes, including those during war, no longer exists for the enshrined war dead. Even the Class-A war criminals are no longer individual men culpable for the crimes they committed. The *eirei* system, which created a collective out of all war dead, enables many to point their finger at Yasukuni Shrine—the shrine itself rather than the individuals enshrined there—as the culprit of Japan's wartime aggression. However, it was the presence of a system of practices and beliefs, including Yasukuni Shrine, death rituals, and a variety of media, that fostered the widespread acceptance of *eirei* throughout Japanese society.

FOUR

INSTITUTIONALIZING GRIEF

Yasukuni Shrine and Total War

> The night that the white palanquin entered Yasukuni Shrine, I was just so thankful . . . so thankful.
>
> *A MOTHER'S COMMENT DURING A GROUP DISCUSSION AFTER A YASUKUNI ENSHRINEMENT RITUAL*

> I truly had a hard time with that broadcast. You see, the ceremony is conducted in pitch dark. And there'd be tormented screams like "Murderer!" "Give me back my child!" coming from the bereaved families that lined both sides of the main approach. The military police were at a loss as these people had just lost a close family member. But I had to make sure that the microphone would not pick up these voices. That was really tough.
>
> *NHK RADIO ANNOUNCER RECOUNTING HIS EXPERIENCE DURING A LIVE BROADCAST OF THE YASUKUNI ENSHRINEMENT RITUAL*

At 10:20 p.m. on September 18, 1931, dynamite planted by Japan's Kwantung Army exploded at a segment of the Southern Manchurian Railway near Mukden. This episode—referred to at the time in Japan as the "Manchurian Incident (Manshū Jihen)"—launched the Asia-Pacific War: the extended military conflict that Japan fought for the next fifteen years. From 1937 on, it was a total war that required new kinds of support from the home front. It demanded not only the production and supply of weapons and other resources for the military but also—and perhaps more importantly—emotional readiness: readiness of men to engage in warfare and of women to support the men at any cost to themselves. The willingness to sacrifice everything, including one's own life, was inextricable from emotional readiness.

This chapter examines the construction of emotional readiness on the home front: readiness to send a loved one off to war with the understanding that he most likely will not come back; readiness to accept loss with pride and gratitude. I refer to this process as the institutionalization of grief. We saw, in chapters 2 and 3, the institutionalization of joy. Organized groups transformed public rituals, celebrations, and even funerals into spectacles. People who previously were mere spectators became participants through collective activities: singing military songs, shouting *banzai* choruses, and parading in victory celebrations. The institutionalization of grief involved similar practices. Institutions such as elementary schools, neighborhood associations, local veterans' groups, and women's organizations created public displays out of each occasion associated with grief—from receiving the death notice and ashes of the fallen, to taking part in funerals, memorial practices, and, finally, enshrinement of the deceased's spirit at Yasukuni Shrine. Involvement in these organized communal activities instructed the participants in socially acceptable or appropriate emotional responses to personal moments of grief. A new way of marking death was conceived through this institutionalization of grief: a value system that favored pride and gratitude over sadness and sorrow; a value system that sought to define an exalted meaning for war death. Through narratives of public and private grief the mass media reproduced, propagated, and instructed readers in acceptable emotional responses to such loss. This chapter's first epigraph is one such example: A mother who had just attended the enshrinement ritual of her only son expresses gratitude rather than sadness.[1] The Myth of the War Experience, which initially emerged from modern Japan's earlier wars, appears to have been fully established and accepted by this time.[2]

At the same time, however, not everyone subscribed to these forms of emotional responses. Some went through the prescribed motions to avoid conflict or social censure. Others expressed their sadness and anger in private. Still others were arrested for public expressions of dissent. But media reports and other printed narratives during the war rarely related demonstrations of discontent, sorrow, and anguish. The radio announcer in the second epigraph recounts one such experience: In the midst of the enshrinement ritual, where all in attendance were supposedly grateful that their loved ones were becoming the god of Yasukuni, some family members vociferously accused the Japanese state and the shrine of murder.[3] But just as the microphone eluded their screams of grief, so both self-censorship and censored media representations created an image that all of Japan was united in its "Yasukuni the belief": the idea that war death in a family was an occasion for pride and joy. This censored or repressed image later shaped the collective memory of wartime Japan as it relates to Yasukuni Shrine—the collective memory that provides the strong foundation of "Yasukuni the issue." I suggest the importance of acknowledging the presence of counternarratives and, further, of paying attention to the complex process by means of which the censored images were created. One of my aims here is to complicate the relationship between Yasukuni Shrine and what is popularly understood as the Japanese experience of the Asia-Pacific War: one that reinforces the narrative of victimhood.

This chapter is organized around the fate of an ordinary army private, Kurokawa Umekichi, a twenty-year-old from Kanagawa Prefecture who enlisted in December 1933 and died six months later due to injuries sustained during service. I trace Umekichi's journey through objects left behind. These 420 objects and documents associated with his military service, his death, the return of his ashes, local memorial services, and Yasukuni enshrinement have been stored in a custom-made cedar box and preserved first by his father and later by his younger brother.[4] At the time of Umekichi's death, less than three years into the fifteen-year war, all death-related practices, including cremation and memorial at the battlefront, as well as the reception and memorialization of his ashes back home, received extraordinary care and attention. At the same time, even in the early years of the war, the institutionalization of grief was firmly established in the postdeath practices, including public rituals and their representations in the mass media. To give a fuller picture of the cultural practices associated with military death during the Asia-Pacific War period, I juxtapose Umekichi's journey with similar episodes from later years of the war compiled from various media sources and material produced by Yasukuni Shrine. In particular, I consult an official itinerary for a family visit to a Yasukuni enshrinement in April 1940: a detailed document that informed bereaved families of the schedule of events that would take place in association with the *shōkon* ritual for their loved one. Due to the lack of time and resources, the death rituals of many who died in the later years of the war were more truncated than those of Umekichi. But as I demonstrate later, death-related practices on the home front continued to be a vital part of the institutionalization of grief.

A striking feature of the war's later years, especially after the start of the all-out war against China in July 1937, is the use of mass media and public spectacle to create an impression that, regardless of the tremendous number of lives lost, every Japanese military death received personalized acknowledgment. Thus, the impression was that the state and the military accounted for and tended to each and every one of the hundreds of thousands of Japanese who lost their lives each year. I examine the use of the news media and photographs to record, disseminate, and publicize the thoroughness of the treatment accorded to the bodies (the return of the ashes from the front) and the spirits (Yasukuni enshrinement) of the war dead. Family attendance at the *shōkon* rituals, which memorialized the spirit of the dead at Yasukuni Shrine, received particular media attention. In reality, only a fraction of the bereaved family members were able to attend these *shōkon* rituals during the Asia-Pacific War years. But technology and media allowed all of these families throughout the Japanese empire to experience the rituals vicariously. The mass media also created an impression that participation in the ritual was imminent for all who had experienced a war death in their family. Similarly, making a spectacle of returning the ashes of the dead from the battlefront was meant to demonstrate the care and consideration the state and the military accorded each military death. These presentations, along with photographic reproductions in the mass media, also reinforced the message that war death was the highest honor a Japanese male could achieve; that death at war was acknowledged and appreciated by the state and should be accepted by the family with pride, not sorrow.

THE "HONORABLE DEATH" OF ARMY PRIVATE KUROKAWA UMEKICHI

Kurokawa Umekichi enlisted in the Imperial Japanese Army in late 1933, the early stages of the war. Japan's view of the military conflict in northern China at the time was overwhelmingly positive, as its military had achieved a series of victories, and the death toll had not climbed to the unfathomable magnitude that it did in the later years. The mass media constantly conveyed, through newspaper articles, photographs, and newsreels, success stories of Japanese troops helping the development of Japan's puppet-state, Manchukuo.[5] Celebration of war expanded into and invigorated popular culture. Umekichi's experience was typical for a man who enlisted during the early years of the war. He received a grand, celebratory send-off with banners decorating the front door of his family's home, an official speech by the head of the neighborhood association, and a parade beyond the local train station and as far as the gate to his regiment. And after his death, too, the military treated his body and remains with great care.

Immediately after enlistment, Umekichi was stationed in Dunhua, China. After six months of training, he was assigned to guard the Kyōhaku Academy, a local school for young Japanese immigrants to Manchukuo. On June 7, 1934, six days after the completion of his training, Umekichi, along with fourteen other men from his unit, took off on a multiday supply transport mission. Two days into the trip, local bandits ambushed the group, and Umekichi and four other soldiers were killed. The surviving unit members cremated the bodies on site the same day. The five men's ashes were flown back to Dunhua on June 18 and, after a brief tribute, temporarily entrusted to the Dunhua branch of Higashi Honganji Temple. On June 28 a portion of their ashes was buried at Goryō-gaoka, a cemetery inside the Kyōhaku Academy. Another portion was interred in a local war memorial. A wake was held on July 10, exactly one month after their death. The following day, Umekichi's unit held a dignified memorial at the temple for the five men. The remaining ashes were divided into two portions: One was buried at the temple, and the other was sent to the home of each deceased soldier in a box of unvarnished wood wrapped in white cloth. By this point, Umekichi's and his comrades' ashes had already received multiple memorial services. The box with Umekichi's ashes left the Dunhua temple on July 12, 1934, and traveled to the port city of Dalian via Hsinking (capital of Manchukuo) and Mukden (present-day Shenyang). A sergeant from Umekichi's unit was charged with supervising transportation. The trajectory of this trip is well recorded. The sergeant carefully noted the details of the journey, including not only the route but, more notably, the kinds of people who welcomed the remains at various points during the trip.[6]

The homeward journey of dead soldiers' ashes was institutionalized into a spectacle during the Asia-Pacific War. Unvarnished wood boxes wrapped in white cloth were a familiar sight throughout Japan. These boxes were, in fact, meant to be visible to the public; they were typically transported from the front by returning troops, who paraded back to their local posts just as they had done when they left for the front. But the parade was often significantly smaller since many men who had marched off were now replaced by wooden boxes wrapped in white cloth and hung around the necks of the surviving soldiers.[7] The boxes were called *kotsubako,* or ash box, and were traditionally used to carry the urn holding the deceased's ashes.

The journey of Umekichi's *kotsubako* created spectacles along its route even before leaving Manchuria. According to the transportation log, fifty-three names were recorded in association with his wake and send-off in Hsinking, the capital of Manchukuo on July 13. On July 14, Umekichi's *kotsubako* arrived in Mukden, where another sizable memorial service was held. Personal names were not recorded for this event, but the log notes that dozens of people were present. On July 15 the ashes traveled by train to Dalian. Representatives of local women's groups and other associations welcomed the arrival of the ashes and paid tribute at stations along the way. Umekichi and his comrades received another memorial service at Dalian, with "hundreds of schoolchildren and citizens" in attendance.[8] According to the log, many made offerings of flowers, sweets, and lanterns at the services. The log documents the extent to which the military mobilized Japanese residents in Manchuria to participate in the war effort.

On July 16 the box embarked by boat at Dalian and were shipped from there to Kobe, Japan. En route to his hometown, Umekichi's *kotsubako* received similar tributes. Among the objects preserved by his family are numerous business cards that traveled home with him. The cards were left by people who greeted his ashes at various stops in Japan. The majority of the cards belonged to members of various veteran's associations, as well as the Patriotic Women's Group (Aikoku Fujinkai) and the Women's Group for National Defense (Kokubō Fujinkai), two leading women's organizations that mobilized housewives for homefront support activities.[9] The cards are grouped by city and prefecture, and we find that Umekichi's ashes stopped briefly in at least ten locations between Kobe and his hometown. Large numbers of people gathered at each stop to pay tribute to Umekichi's *kotsubako* and to present offerings of flowers and sweets. The objects left behind thus attest to a series of elaborate commemorations at multiple locations that had no prior association with the deceased. But most of the attendees did not participate in these events voluntarily. As we know, Umekichi was an army private from a small town in Kanagawa. But his ashes received a hero's welcome at all of these places because the crowds in attendance were organized by the women's groups, veterans associations, and elementary schools. Most of those gathered had been forced to attend as members of these organized groups. The military also sent detailed schedules and instructions in advance, with the expectation that crowds would be mobilized.[10] The result was a well-orchestrated and an intensely experienced display of appreciation for Umekichi's sacrifice and achievement.

Umekichi was the first war dead from his small hometown. The town's annual summer festival was canceled in deference to the events marking the return of Umekichi's *kotsubako* and his funeral. The mayor accompanied Umekichi's parents to receive the *kotsubako* at Kamakura Station on July 20. Two days later, his hometown hosted an elaborate Buddhist-style funeral at the Kanazawa elementary school. Newspapers reported that the procession that transported Umekichi's ashes from the local temple to the school stretched for more than one kilometer. Neighbors recalled that the funeral lasted at least three days. Surviving documents suggest the Kurokawa residence received guests for more than a week. Local newspapers report several thousand people in attendance at the funeral. Notable figures sent funeral offerings, including the emperor and empress, the army minister, the chief of staff, and other military leaders.

YASUKUNI SHRINE DURING THE ASIA-PACIFIC WAR

The town's funeral was not Umekichi's final memorial service. Several memorial events for a single military casualty were not uncommon during the early years of the war. Furthermore, memorial sites for the dead were not restricted to one location or a single religious tradition. In fact, in modern Japan the military dead typically received multiple memorial rituals.[11] Many towns and villages conducted their own public memorial service, usually in the Buddhist style. Some held Shinto-style services at the prefectural *gokoku jinja* (literally, "nation-protecting shrines"; as prefectural versions of Yasukuni Shrine, these were incorporated into a nationwide hierarchical network of shrines and memorials with Yasukuni at the top).[12] The family of the deceased often conducted a private funeral in accordance with their own religious beliefs, as they also did for other family members. Most families also followed the Buddhist tradition of memorializing the deceased individuals at their family altar (*butsudan*). Beginning in the late 1930s, many cities, towns, and villages constructed a *chūreitō,* a communal memorial built according to a single design guideline, on which the names of the dead were engraved and into which personal effects such as nail clippings and locks of hair were deposited.[13]

The most notable memorial service for imperial Japan's military dead was the *shōkon* ritual at Yasukuni Shrine. Umekichi was a part of the forty-ninth collective enshrinement ritual, conducted in April 1935, to commemorate 813 war deaths that occurred in Manchuria.[14] A *shōkon* ritual was scheduled for April 26, followed by a special festival (*rinji taisai*) and a regular festival (*rei taisai*) on the thirtieth.[15] In early April, Umekichi's family received a large brown envelope from the Army Ministry's Committee for Yasukuni Shrine Special Festival. Among other documents in the envelope was a smaller white envelope containing a formal notice of Umekichi's Yasukuni enshrinement: a rectangular card with gold edging and a gold cherry blossom stamped on the top center. At the time of Umekichi's enshrinement, up to three family members were eligible to participate in the *shōkon* ritual and associated events.[16] Following instructions provided by the military, Umekichi's father, Tomizō, mother, Aki, and younger brother Kikuzō traveled to Tokyo using the discounted train tickets and a subsidy of fifteen yen provided by the Patriotic Comfort Association (Aikoku Jippei Kai). The family stayed at the Military Hall (Gunjin Kaikan) in Tokyo, where they remained until the thirtieth. They participated in various events organized by the military and visited several sites in Tokyo. This elaborate trip accompanying a family member's war death provided more than an opportunity to participate in the memorial ritual. As I illustrate later, the trip encompassed a much larger agenda not only for the family that attended the ritual but also for all Japanese families who had already sent a member to war or were about to do so.

As soon as the details of the enshrinement ceremony were determined, the families of the war dead were sent an invitation to it. They also received a detailed itinerary of their visit. Umekichi's family received a sheet of paper with a five-day schedule with events inside the shrine grounds as well as visits to the Ken'anfu Hall,[17] Shinjuku Imperial Garden, and Meiji Shrine. Families' visits grew in size and number of events in the following years as the number of death toll rose. In April 1940, for example, the itinerary was a seven-page booklet (see figure 4). The 1940 event involved a much larger number of families than that for Umekichi's memorial, and its itinerary is a well-choreographed schedule of 12,802 bereaved families divided into 128 groups of approximately one hundred families each.[18] (Since two people per deceased soldier were invited in 1940, we can assume that approximately twenty-five thousand people were scheduled to attend this event.) According to this itinerary, registration for the families started on April 20 and continued until noon of April 23 at the Yasukuni Shrine grounds and the Imperial Guard Grounds, both atop Kudan Hill. Families registered with the shrine upon their arrival in Tokyo and continued to follow the schedule provided.

I will return to Umekichi's journey, as well as that of the family that received the April 1940 itinerary, to describe what a typical *shōkon* ritual would have been like. But first I refer to other sources that suggest what bereaved families experienced during their visit to the grounds of Yasukuni Shrine. The discussion of Yasukuni Shrine in chapter 2 ended with the Russo-Japanese War. Many additions and changes had been made to the shrine by the time of Umekichi's enshrinement. The Great Kantō earthquake of September 1, 1923, destroyed the shrine office and Cappelletti's museum. Furthermore, the shrine's declining prestige in the decades following the Russo-Japanese War led to institutional changes. In fact, documents suggest that Yasukuni Shrine diminished in popularity after all of the war dead from the Russo-Japanese War were enshrined. In an effort to continue

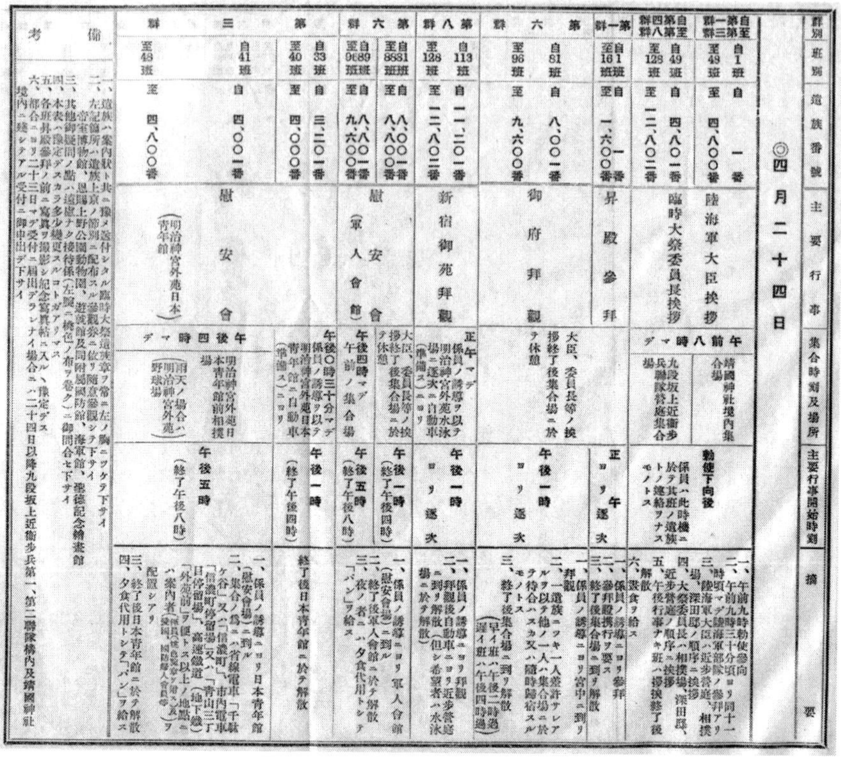

FIGURE 4. Schedule for the war-bereaved families' visit to Yasukuni Shrine, April 1940 (author's collection).

attracting visitors to the semiannual festivals, the Yasukuni management drafted a proposal around 1922 to designate regular shrine festival days as annual holidays.[19] According to the proposal, "despite the vast number of spirits enshrined with potential for increasing indefinitely in the future," visitors to the shrine were limited to members of the military. The general public showed little interest in the shrine during those years. The proposal further lamented the lack of visits by the prime minister.[20]

War brought nonmilitary visitors back to the shrine. Efforts to transform festival days into national holidays failed, but the increasing number of war deaths in Manchuria redirected popular attention to Yasukuni Shrine. New structures on the shrine grounds also appealed to the visitors. In October 1931 the heavily damaged Yūshūkan building was replaced by a new building designed by the prominent architect Itō Chūta.[21] He also drew up plans for two other additions: a stone *torii* at the south entrance of the outer garden (1933) and the shrine gate for the inner garden (1934), a commanding presence with two heavy wooden doors, each embellished with enormous golden chrysanthemum seals. A memorial hall for the fiftieth anniversary of the promulgation of the Imperial Mandate for the Military was added in 1933. A new shrine office was completed in 1934. The increasing number of Japanese casualties in Manchuria also brought about a change to the shrine grounds. According to the *Asahi* newspaper, a small shrine was added to the Yasukuni grounds in November 1931 to accommodate the increasing length of time between death and enshrinement. Spirits of the war dead were to be placed here temporarily until their official enshrinement during the semiannual festivals.[22]

As in previous wars, the new Yūshūkan Museum dynamically reported and celebrated Japanese military achievements. The newly built museum building did not resemble Cappelletti's fortresslike brick structure. Consonant with the rapidly intensifying nationalist milieu, it featured a modern rendition of a Japanese castle, echoing the theme of a military museum. The museum's first floor prominently featured the years of the Meiji Restoration and celebrated the imperial nation, which was indebted to the sacrifices of those enshrined at Yasukuni Shrine. Periods of Japanese history prior to the Meiji era were relegated to the second floor. Of the ten rooms on the first floor, the first five (rooms 11 to 15) were dedicated to previous wars of the modern period, from the Meiji Restoration to World War I. Displays in the remaining five rooms were dedicated to the ongoing "incident" and were updated continuously. Room 16, dedicated to the Manchurian Incident, displayed articles left behind by the fallen Japanese troops, commemorative items from events at home in support of the war, and weapons and uniforms taken from China as spoils of war. Room 17 contained weapons from Taiwan and the southern islands. Room 18 was dedicated to contemporary naval weaponry, room 19 to weapons used on land, and room 20 to aerial weapons. The main feature of the museum was the two-story central atrium, where large-scale military hardware, including tanks and airplanes, were exhibited and around which the smaller exhibit rooms were located.[23] When the museum reopened in 1931, most of the items on display showcased Japan's military technology and achievements—a trend consistent with the museum's earlier objective of using objects to educate visitors about recent military achievements. But with the intensification of the Asia-Pacific War, a new trend at the museum took hold, namely, an emphasis on personal items and mementos of the war dead, which is evident at the museum today.[24]

Additional war-themed displays outside Yūshūkan were available in 1935, when the Kurokawa family was visiting Tokyo. Beginning in 1932, Yūshūkan held two-week-long special exhibits in an annex building on a regular basis. These exhibits were free of charge and showcased items related to the "China Incident," including spoils of war, items left behind by the fallen soldiers, and commemorative gifts for exemplary members of the home front. Items on display were updated regularly in order to "provide an accurate description of the Incident and to show the activities of our soldiers."[25] Special exhibitions were also held in the annex on Army Day (March 10), Navy Day (May 27), and the anniversary of the Japanese military (November 28). For example, nearly thirty thousand people visited the annex on the morning of April 25, 1932, the day of the forty-seventh *shōkon* ceremony, which enshrined the victims of the Manchurian Incident.[26]

At the time of the Kurokawa family's visit, another exhibit space, dedicated to Japan's ongoing battles, was—in the tradition of the panorama building from the Russo-Japanese War years—designed to captivate the audience with technological sophistication: the National Defense Hall (Kokubōkan), which opened in 1934.[27] The objective of this new addition was to enable visitors to gain an understanding of the "true meaning of national defense (*kokubō no hongi*)" through various representations of the latest military technology.[28] Evidence indicates, however, that the Kokubōkan was a simulated military environment that allowed visitors to vicariously observe and participate in warfare.

Kokubōkan no longer exists. The building was renamed Yasukuni Hall (Yasukuni Kaikan) during the Allied occupation and currently houses a visitor's lounge on the first floor and a library on the second. Literature associated with Yasukuni Shrine mentions the facility only in passing.[29] Yet its wartime exhibits are documented along with numerous (grainy) photographs in a booklet published by the Yūshūkan Museum in 1934.[30] According to the booklet, exhibits were dedicated to the ongoing war and, with the exception of one room dedicated to the home front, each room featured new military technology such as chemical weapons, laser telephones (*kōsen denwa*), and machine guns. Most of the exhibits were experiential in nature. The cockpit of an actual heavy bomber was displayed in the exhibit titled "Bombing from an Airplane (*Kijō yori suru bakugeki*)." The visitor entered the exhibit and was allowed to sit at the controls in the cockpit for a simulated flight at an altitude of one thousand meters and speed of 180 kilometers per hour. The illusion was accomplished by means of a device positioned several feet below the floor. A large piece of cloth painted with a landscape moved in a loop to give the "pilot" a sense of altitude and speed. A push of a button in the cockpit produced a flash of light on the landscape, simulating the detonation of a bomb. The cockpit was also equipped with a machine gun, which the visitor could swivel to simulate its operation. In the Gas Experience Room (Gasu taikenshitsu), the visitor donned a gas mask and walked into a room filled with tear gas. In the Indoor Shooting and Contemporary Warfare Diorama Room the visitor could "shoot freely at targets such as human figures, tanks, and planes in flight and acquire shooting skills as a kind of hobby."[31] Some of the activities, including the gas room and the operation of remote-control model tanks, required the supervision of museum personnel.[32] Whenever it was available, the latest technology was incorporated to enhance the visitor's experience. For the fall festival of 1939, for example, several exhibits incorporated sound effects using the Filmon endless sound belt, a technological innovation that allowed the continuous playing of prerecorded sound by utilizing a looped audiotape approximately thirteen meters long.[33] While the panorama buildings promoted wars of imperialism by allowing viewers to vicariously observe realistic representations of battlefields, these installations presented an overwhelmingly positive view of the ongoing warfare through the lure of technology. Such exhibits most likely targeted young boys to intensify their interest in the military.[34]

It was not only inside these buildings that visitors could admire the accomplishments of the ongoing war. For every special festival during the Asia-Pacific War, additional war-related exhibits were mounted on the shrine grounds. The spatial configuration of the shrine, however, was different from that for festivals of the previous wars. At this point, the intended approach was linear—as it is today. The space was fully configured as a shrine, unlike its park-like atmosphere in earlier years, suggesting that the religious and commemorative aspects of the space had been strengthened. A trip down the main approach to the worship hall and back could be considered a pilgrimage. But during these festivals the trip was nothing like a typical pilgrimage to a religious institution. Large battlefield dioramas with three-dimensional, life-sized figures of Japanese troops lined the main approach of the outer shrine (see figure 5). The exhibits were newly created for each festival. They often represented the latest feats of the Japanese military, functioning as a source of news about the war and propagating militarism. For example, a diorama approximately ninety meters long was created for the festival of April 1942, portraying a scene of Pearl Harbor on December 8, 1941, using material donated by the Imperial Navy.[35]

FIGURE 5. Families viewing exhibits in the outer garden of Yasukuni Shrine (*Yasukuni Jinja rinji taisai shashinchō*, April 1940).

With the monumental scale and technological splendor of the exhibits, the shrine grounds increasingly took on an atmosphere of an elaborate festival celebrating Japan's militarism. Thus, for local visitors the Yasukuni festivals were an updated and militarized rendering of the Meiji festivals with circuses and horse races, at least until attacks on the Japanese homeland became a real possibility.[36] For the bereaved families, however, the war-themed exhibits may have had an additional function. Life-sized representations promoted a sense of the enormity of both the Japanese cause and the military success; at the same time, the displays helped families of the war dead to appreciate the national significance of their loss.

THE *SHŌKON* RITUAL

The main event for bereaved families was the *shōkon* ritual. For the Kurokawa family, it took place on their second night in Tokyo. Approximately twenty-four hundred bereaved family members gathered from around the country. For the ritual, which commenced at eight, they were instructed to be sitting at designated places on the shrine grounds by seven in the evening. In attendance were members and representatives of the military units associated with the war dead being enshrined, as well as representatives from all military divisions throughout Japan and officer training schools in Tokyo. Head priest Kamo Momoki officiated at the ceremony in the presence of ten priests. The ritual concluded when a wooden box, into which the spirits were believed to have gathered, was purified and transported on a palanquin into the main shrine.[37]

Starting in 1869, *shōkon* rituals were conducted as needed just before the regular spring and fall festivals. The ritual itself traditionally took place at two o'clock in the morning but was moved up to the evening beginning with the annual festival of May 1911. Even during the extended peacetime in the 1920s, several enshrinements were conducted for war dead from World War I and the Siberian Intervention (1918–1922). After the start of the armed conflict in China, *shōkon* practice recommenced in earnest at the forty-sixth ceremony, which preceded the spring festival in 1932. The rituals took place annually until 1937 and twice a year thereafter. When the all-out war began in China that year, the death toll quickly increased. In the fall of 1938 the number of those enshrined was more than ten thousand, and this number increased throughout the rest of the war. As the number of war dead to be enshrined grew, the number of invitations extended to family members was reduced to two per family.

I now turn to the April 23, 1940, *shōkon* ritual to give a more detailed picture based on the itinerary, the official photo album, and newspaper articles. Families were expected to spend the entire day of the ritual on the shrine grounds. According to the itinerary, the morning and early afternoon were dedicated to viewing the "incident-related exhibition" in the outer garden. Families were instructed to gather at designated locations in and around the shrine as early as three in the afternoon. From there, officials directed them to their assigned seating area. Photographs of the event show that their seating area was not limited to the shrine grounds but extended along residential streets immediately outside the shrine. The families were dressed in formal attire and were seated huddled together in rows on thin mats laid directly on the ground (see figure 6). Military personnel sat in front of the seated families. All in attendance were to be seated by 6:30 p.m., and they were expected to remain in their places until 10 p.m. In lieu of dinner, they were given a piece of bread to eat while waiting.

Family members began seating themselves around four in the afternoon, awaiting the start of the ritual.[38] According to the *Yomiuri* newspaper's report the following morning, approximately twenty-five thousand people attended, which suggests that the families of almost all of those enshrined were present.[39] Bonfires were lit on the *shōkon* grounds around 7 p.m. Thirty minutes later, government and military personnel entered and took their places on folding chairs under tents. Following the performance of the song "Umi yukaba" by the Imperial Navy band, the head priest stood in front of

FIGURE 6. Families during the *shōkon* ritual (*Yasukuni Jinja rinji taisai shashinchō*, April 1940).

FIGURE 7. *Shōkon* ritual (*Yasukuni Jinja rinji taisai shashinchō*, April 1940).

the small shrine at the innermost area of the *shōkon* grounds and conducted rituals to call in the spirits of the military dead so that they could be appeased and cleansed (see figure 7). During this ritual, 12,799 spirits were called into the shrine to be commemorated as god. It was understood that all of the spirits to be enshrined that evening were gathered in a small chest of unvarnished wood (*karahitsu*) that was placed in the small shrine.[40] Accompanied by *koto* music and the navy band, the head priest made offerings and paid tribute in the direction of the Imperial Palace. Representatives from the government and the military also presented offerings. The head priest then stepped out of the *shōkon* grounds and carried the offerings to the main shrine. When he returned, all of the music stopped as he placed the chest containing the spirits in a cedar palanquin wrapped in white silk.[41] The music then resumed, and a procession of priests carried the palanquin to the main shrine. Instead of going directly into the main shrine, the procession traveled out of the shrine grounds through the north gate, meandered through the adjacent streets, alongside which families sat, and finally reentered the main entrance at the east end, where they proceed along the main approach to the shrine building. Family members bade farewell to their fathers, sons, brothers, and husbands as the palanquin procession passed by. An *Asahi* newspaper article describes sobs whirling like the wind above the family members, the sound of hands clapping, and white handkerchiefs waving farewell in the dark.[42] Coins thrown by the families—monetary offerings for the Yasukuni god—showered the palanquin.[43] After the spirits were placed in the main shrine, all of the lights in the shrine grounds were lit for the first time. The ritual ended with a performance by the military band at exactly ten o'clock.

BEREAVED FAMILIES IN TOKYO

As mentioned earlier, the Kurokawa family and other families invited to the *shōkon* ritual received a package that included tickets to various facilities in Tokyo. Among the Yasukuni-related documents preserved by Kikuzō is an envelope that had contained such tickets. The inventory lists the following: free passes for Tokyo city trams; certificates for visits to the Ken'anfu Hall and Shinjuku Imperial Garden; entrance tickets for the Imperial Museum, Yūshūkan Museum, National Defense Hall, and the Ueno Zoo; tickets to the entertainment in the Yasukuni outer gardens; and entrance tickets to various entertainment facilities in Tokyo. Remaining in the envelope are tickets to some of the facilities listed, as well as the Hanayashiki amusement park in Asakusa.[44]

Various activities were also planned for the family who traveled to Tokyo in April 1940 (the original owner of the itinerary in my possession). In the morning after the *shōkon* ritual, all of the families attended speeches by the army and navy ministers. Thereafter, schedules were arranged according to the group the family was assigned to: well-choreographed planning had as many as five different events for the families occurring simultaneously (see figure 8). The itinerary has handwritten check marks above certain activities—presumably made by the original owner of the itinerary. I follow this person's activities to present a typical family's Tokyo experience.

In the late morning of April 24, after the speeches, the family reported to the Meiji Jingū swimming pool, where they were driven to the Shinjuku Imperial Garden. They presumably used their certificate to enter the beautifully landscaped gardens. On April 25 was the emperor's visit. The family reported to a designated location by 7:30 a.m. and sat in their assigned area as they had for the *shōkon* ritual. The emperor made his brief visit at 10 a.m. The front page of the evening edition of *Asahi* newspaper that day featured a photograph of the emperor in his military uniform, decorated with medals, saber in his left hand, and hat in his right. The grand chamberlain, the Minister of the Imperial Household, and the emperor's chief aide-de-camp,

FIGURE 8. Families touring Tokyo sites (*Yasukuni Jinja rinji taisai shashinchō*, April 1940).

among others, escorted him. Accompanied by the *kimigayo* performance by the military band, the emperor proceeded into the main shrine at 10:10, paid tribute to the *eirei* at 10:15, when a siren wailed to mark the precise moment of his tribute, and departed the shrine at 10:17.[45] No events were scheduled for the family following the emperor's visit that day.

On the morning of April 26, one of the family members visited the Ken'anfu.[46] On April 27, the family attended shows at the Japan Youth Hall. On the morning of April 28, the family entered the main shrine to pay their final tribute to the spirit of the deceased, who, by that point, had been transformed into god ("highly anticipated meeting [*ureshii taimen*]," according to the *Asahi* newspaper). The main shrine visit was packaged with the taking of commemorative photographs with their assigned groups (see figure 9). All 128 group photographs are included in a photo album that was sent later to the families.

The albums were produced for many of the special festivals, although their thickness varied from year to year.[47] The 1935 album, produced for the festival during which Umekichi was enshrined, is relatively slim, with forty-six leaves with photographs printed on one side. A list of the military dead enshrined follows the photographs. The April 1940 album is about 1.5 inches thick and has 113 leaves of photographs along with pages that list the names of those enshrined. The albums typically follow the families' journey, starting with their arrival at Tokyo Station.[48] They show families at registration desks, entering the Yūshūkan Museum, and viewing the displays in the outer garden. The *shōkon* ritual is covered in detail: a close-up of the shrine where the ritual was performed; photographs of military officials seated in folding chairs under tents; many more of the *izoku* crowded on mats. The photograph of the head priest performing the ritual was usually taken from behind. Most of the albums also include the palanquin processing in the darkness through the crowd of families. Albums for events at which the emperor appeared include photographs of him and the empress immediately following scenes from the *shōkon* ritual, forging a connection between the most sacred ritual and the imperial visit. The emperor, however, never visited during the ritual itself. The remaining pages cover the families' activities: men and women entering the main shrine, groups of families visiting other sites on their Tokyo itinerary. The album also includes snapshots of the entertainment at places on their itinerary, such as the Kabukiza theater and the Military Hall.

Details about the origin and production of these albums are unclear. Ethnologist Tanakamaru Katsuhiko, for example, discusses an April 1942

FIGURE 9. Group photograph of the families of war dead (*Yasukuni Jinja rinji taisai shashinchō*, April 1940).

photo album in a chapter of his posthumous book, which explores modern military death. He notes that "there is no preface or commentary, and it is not possible to know the objective or the particulars of its production."[49] It is clear, however, that the albums were distributed to the bereaved families.[50] The idea of distributing one album per deceased individual is astounding, particularly in the later years, when more than twenty thousand dead were being enshrined at each event. But the implications of the albums spread far beyond the immediate family. Families, on receiving the albums when back home, most likely circulated them in the community and in neighborhood or women's associations, as was the practice with mass-market magazines and other publications at the time, along with stories of their trip.

These photo albums and their communal viewing became especially meaningful in the final years of the war, for not everyone who had lost a family member was awarded a trip to Tokyo. To be more precise, the vast majority were not. Enshrinement at Yasukuni Shrine was a multistep process that included the compilation of detailed paperwork as well as the formal blessings of the emperor. Consequently, the enshrinement rate of the Asia-Pacific War deaths at the end of the war was a little more than10 percent. That is, of the 2,319,994 deaths from that war currently enshrined at Yasukuni, the rituals were completed for only 251,135 as of August 1945.[51] Between death and enshrinement was a long delay, which increased as the number of war dead rose. Umekichi's spirit was enshrined in the first ritual that followed his death. But the enshrinement of the so-called Greater East Asia War (1941–1945) dead began in earnest only in April 1944.[52] Families typically had to wait several years before they were invited to Tokyo to participate in the enshrinement of their loved one. The photo album, then, provided families-in-waiting a vicarious experience of the *shōkon* ritual and associated events until they could attend themselves.

The viewing experience would have been an opportunity to demonstrate patriotism and to witness and express the appropriate emotional response to a war death. It provided an opportunity for the albums' owners to show the photographs and tell their stories with pride; those gathered around would listen and respond with respect for the man who had just fulfilled the most honorable duty to the nation. It was also an opportunity to create a community of members who not only censored their own comments but also kept a close watch on the words and behaviors of others. This form of mutual surveillance further encourages self-censorship. Thus the group performs, willingly or in response to the gaze of others, an institutionalized response to grief demonstrated through pride, gratitude, and respect rather than sorrow. This kind of communal practice, whether in the context of informal gatherings of neighbors or meetings of established organizations such as women's associations, played a key role in propagating fanatic forms of nationalism and militarism.

THE FATE OF THE DEAD BODIES

Umekichi died at a time when each military death was given individual attention. The number of war dead was still small enough for sufficient time and resources to be available for the performance of Umekichi's cremation and memorial rituals close to the battlefield. This came to an end as battles intensified in the Pacific theater and hundreds and thousands of Japanese troops died in short periods of time. Entire units were decimated; planeloads of troops crashed; ships sank along with their entire crews. At this rate, the war casualties could no longer be attended to individually. Moreover, the dead bodies were far from Japan.

Through its treatment of the bodies and cremated ashes, the Japanese military used the distance between the site of death and the home of the deceased to promote patriotism, institutionalize grief, and aestheticize war death and sacrifice. As we saw with Umekichi's journey, during the early years of the war the return of the ashes from the battlefront served as an occasion for a new kind of spectacle that culminated in public funerals. In the later years of the Asia-Pacific War, as it became increasingly impossible to transport the material remains (ashes) of the war dead, the Yasukuni rituals, with their focus on spirits, were further highlighted. When the death rate drastically increased, making timely enshrinement at Yasukuni Shrine impossible in the final years of the war, the mass media created an image of imminent enshrinement.

All along the Japanese military was aware of the problem of managing dead bodies on faraway battlefields. The military devised regulations and continually revised them as it attempted to streamline its treatment of the fallen. But as I explain later, this process of streamlining also proved effective for tightening the military's control over its living and dead troops—and by extension over their family members. The careful treatment of Umekichi and other war dead was in part driven by the military's need to demonstrate its authority over the people.

According to historian Harada Keiichi, who conducted an extensive study of military life and death in modern Japan, from the outset the regulations frequently changed.[53] Initially, before major international armed conflicts, the military focused on exercising control over the method of and the location for burying its dead. In 1869 the newly established Military Ministry (Hyōbu-shō) ordered that, when a soldier died from illness, the body would be buried in a temple near the location of death and a sum of ten *ryō* provided to the family.[54] At the time, soldiers were given a Shinto-style ritual, and their bodies buried without cremation. Two years later discussions began on the selection of sites dedicated to military burial, and several military cemeteries were established in the following years. In December 1873, shortly after the start of conscription, the Army Ministry, which, together with the Navy Ministry, replaced the Military Ministry in 1872, announced that, unless a family member requested otherwise within two days of death, all noncommissioned officers (*kashikan*) and privates (*heisotsu*) who died while on active duty, both at war and in peacetime, would be buried in their local army cemetery.[55] In 1886 the army added a provision allowing the family to request a reburial within six months of death.

The likelihood of families retrieving dead bodies or ashes diminished considerably during wartime. Burial regulations became more specific during the Sino-Japanese War, when both the army and the navy established regulations for wartime burial.[56] For example, the army stipulated that the corpse was to be buried in an "army burial ground, shared cemetery, or other selected site. Depending on the circumstances, cremation and collective burial are permitted."[57] "Other selected site" most likely referred to battlefields. In August 1897 the army announced that both army and navy personnel were to be buried in military cemeteries. According to this new ordinance, families were required to wait ten or more years after the soldier's death before requesting a reburial. In other words, if a conscripted soldier were to die on active duty, his family was denied its customary death-related rituals for at least a decade.[58] Death-related rituals, previously held locally and privately by the family, were thus taken over by the military, which maintained full custody of the men even after death. This model of military control remained in force throughout the Asia-Pacific War years, with modifications that enabled the families to believe that the military was giving the utmost care to their lost loved ones.

With the start of international warfare, the military began to regulate management of the dead in order to ensure that ashes and important mementos be returned from overseas battlefields. During the Russo-Japanese War, the army established its Regulations for Battlefield Cleaning and Burial of the Dead (Army Notice 100, May 30, 1904).[59] According to this notice, a "battlefield cleaning troop" (*senjō sōji-tai*) was to be organized in each unit immediately following a battle. Their job was to search for the dead and the wounded, as well as their belongings.[60] Cremation methods differed according to the rank of the deceased. When individual cremation of all of the dead was not feasible due to battlefield circumstances, noncommissioned officers and privates could be collectively cremated after locks of hair were cut off each body to be sent back home. Even in these cases, all higher-ranking personnel were to be cremated individually. The military also conducted *shōkon* ceremonies on site. For example, in his study of five hundred letters sent home during the Russo-Japanese War, Ōe Shinobu notes that an auxiliary soldier, Matsuzaki Yonosuke, who, upon arrival in Lüshun after the ceasefire, wrote home about an elaborate ceremony for the fallen that involved fifteen Buddhist priests from the head temple.[61] Battlefield *shōkon* ceremonies at the time consisted of a formal Shinto ritual followed by an informal Buddhist one. In fact, General Nogi himself conducted the formal Shinto-style portion of this ceremony, which took place on January 14, 1905, two weeks after Russia's surrender. These rituals on the front were opportunities for the surviving men to witness the treatment they would receive if they were to die: Their spirits would be memorialized at Yasukuni Shrine, whereas their bodies would be cremated by the hands of their unit members.

According to the original plan, battlefield burial was considered a temporary measure, and all of the remains of the fallen were to be transported back home, where they would be buried in their local military cemeteries. Notices requesting reburial as well as permission for reburial remain, but no record exists on the actual reburial procedure. Due to the unprecedented number of combat deaths during the war against Russia, official reburial of the dead does not seem to have been realistic.[62] The majority of the ashes remained buried close to the battlefields. This practice from Japan's earlier wars would change completely during the Asia-Pacific War, when the ashes of the fallen were transported back home, allowing the family to bury the dead in their family grave. This new system of homecoming did not just benefit the family. It also empowered the military with symbolic control of its men even after their death and robbed the family members of the opportunity to perform the full death rituals, which included the viewing of the dead body before cremation for a final farewell. More important, the spectacle created by the homecoming of the ashes would emphasize the significance of dying for Japan at war. While Yasukuni Shrine is singled out today for taking over the death rituals of the fallen and consequently robbing the family members of opportunities for proper memorial services, these practices of the Japanese military demonstrate that Yasukuni rituals constituted only one part of the postdeath procedures. Rituals and spectacles associated with the return of the ashes, along with their representation in the popular media, played a key role in the institutionalization of grief, which functioned to promote positive attitudes about dying for one's country. Yasukuni Shrine played a central role in death rituals in the last years of the Asia-Pacific War in part, because the excessive number of war casualties and the resulting difficulties in the management of corpses highlighted the convenience made possible by the spiritual transaction at the shrine.

Umekichi's ashes returned in a box of unvarnished wood wrapped in white cloth. Numerous other families received similar boxes in the years during and immediately following the Asia-Pacific War. It was understood that these boxes contained the actual ashes of their loved ones, who were cremated on the battlefield where they died. In many cases, they did, as was the case with Umekichi. But as the war intensified, so did the difficulty of battlefield cremation. Ashes came to be replaced by locks of hair, teeth, and other portable, nonperishable body parts, sometimes stored in safety by its owner before his death or otherwise retrieved from the corpse by his comrades.[63] For deaths that occurred while troops were far from their base, the surviving members had to hold on to the ashes and other mementos until they arrived at a site from which these items could be sent to Japan. But it was not uncommon for the men who carried their comrades' mementos to be killed as well. In the more disastrous battles of later years, starting with the Battle of Guadalcanal (August 1942–February 1943), retrieval of even the smallest body parts was no longer possible, as mutilated corpses quickly piled up on the battlefields. In fact, for the near-naked corpses in the tattered remains of their uniforms, the only identification possible was as Japanese troops.[64] In many instances, bodies were lost to the Pacific Ocean along with the ship or plane that had been carrying them. Nevertheless, the war dead typically returned to their family as a wooden box.

What, then, did these boxes typically contain? Ono Eiko, winner of a 2004 speech contest for Chiran (Kagoshima town known as a former *tokkō* base), remembers that a small stone was inside the box instead of her father's ashes.[65] In many cases, the box that family members of the deceased received contained a piece of paper, a rock from the battlefield, or a handful of sand in place of ashes. Recipients typically placed the box on their family altar and later in the family grave. Even during the war, it was well known that some, if not almost all, of the boxes did not contain the ashes or a piece of bone of the deceased. Although some families were infuriated by this, most chose to treat the box as if it contained the actual remains of their loved ones. In the case of a Shizuoka family whose son had drowned while being transported to a southern island, a piece of paper was found inside the box that was returned in lieu of the son. The family added to the box the lock of hair and nail clippings that he had left with them prior to his departure and conducted a traditional Buddhist funeral as if the box contained the son's actual ashes.[66]

The presence of a handful of sand or a rock from the battlefield was sometimes a result of sincere intentions. Bereaved family members of troops in the 29th Infantry Regiment who lost their lives on Guadalcanal Island received a note written by Commander Ōshima Mamoru along with the handful of sand in the boxes. The note explained the significance of the sand. I summarize it here to give a picture of the battlefield situation on the southern islands. First of all, the surviving troops found it difficult to cremate the dead bodies since smoke resulting from cremation would alert enemy planes of their location. Moreover, whatever small amounts of ashes they were able to obtain were lost when the soldiers who were carrying them were themselves killed. The surviving troops agreed that the spirits of the war dead descended to the beach on the island, gathered some sand, and conducted a *shōkon* ceremony. As was the case in the Russo-Japanese War instance that I noted earlier, the commanding officer conducted a Shintō ritual, followed by the Buddhist chaplain's recitation of the sutra. They then divided the sand by the number of fallen, placed a small amount in individual boxes, and sent the boxes to the family members.[67]

Additional correspondence about the dead depended on the circumstances and the rank of the deceased and might help the family accept the death of the father, the son, the brother, or the husband. The military was unlikely to supply extra information and material unless the deceased was a high-ranking officer prior to his death. For most casualties, the delivery of a telegram or a postcard followed by a box wrapped in white cloth completed the military's obligation.[68] Many did not learn of the death or receive the box until after Japan's surrender. Unable to acknowledge the death of their loved one, family members often sought further details about the death. Some fortunate families were able to hear about their sons' and husbands' final moments, mostly from their fellow soldiers, who often sought out the families of their fallen comrades to deliver the mementos. But most never received any concrete information about the death. Even today, close to seven decades after the war, many family members of Japanese war dead still travel to former battlefield sites in Southeast Asia looking for remains.[69]

Many consider the encounter with whatever parts of the dead body may still remain the best opportunity available to them today.

Through Yasukuni enshrinement, the military tended to the spirits of the war dead. These spirits, thought to have separated from the body at death, were called into the shrine during the semiannual rituals that took place prior to enshrinement. The spirits remained at the shrine instead of returning home. But the spirits were not the military's only focus. The narrative of Umekichi's heroic homecoming illustrates the weight of the military's concern to enable proper treatment of the dead. But the practice of posthumous homecoming symbolized the state's rather than the family's ownership of the body. The structure of the nation-state, in which people became loyal subjects of the emperor, was maintained even after one's death. Just as the body mattered to the family, or perhaps *because* the body mattered to the family, it, too, mattered to the military, which regulated the disposition of dead bodies. By controlling the fate of both the body and the spirit of the war dead, the military demonstrated its authority over its men. It also exerted authority over the family of the war dead by controlling the ways in which the bodies were or were not returned to them in a manner reminiscent of the imperial troops' denial of Aizu burial (see chapter 1). For a society in which the living maintain a close relationship with the dead, the treatment of the latter strongly affected the relations among the former. Even the heroic return of Umekichi's remains can be considered, along with the enshrinement of his spirit at Yasukuni, as a display of the state's control of its military personnel.[70]

REPORTS OF LOSS IN THE MASS MEDIA

Umekichi's death was reported in local newspapers as early as June 13, 1934. *Yokosuka bōeki shinpō*, for example, headlined the news of his death as "My Son's Death, Which I Have Offered to the Emperor: The Emotional Tears of Father, Tomizō" and reported that the father was "joyful at heart for the son, whose death [he is] proud of," while smiling through tears.[71] *Tōkyō nichi nichi* newspaper reported that Tomizō said, "It is at least a consolation that my son has died for the nation."[72] The local press continued to follow the story of Umekichi's war death. On July 22 and 23 newspapers reported on the town's elaborate funeral for Umekichi. On April 2, 1935, newspapers announced Umekichi's Yasukuni enshrinement. The elements in the local press's narrative are familiar: A young man loses his life at war, the family is proud of his contribution to the national cause, and his death is acknowledged, appreciated, and commemorated both locally and nationally.

During the Asia-Pacific War, newspapers, along with other forms of mass media, contributed to the construction of the image of a home front that fully supported the war effort. As Louise Young details, the latest technology, along with the collaboration between the media and the military, enabled almost immediate reportage of battlefront news back home. War was profitable for the press, and thus the press heavily invested in covering it.[73] Readers enthusiastically followed Japan's military successes, actual ones in the early years and fabricated ones near the end of the war. However, many readers considered the fate of the men sent away from their own community to be even more important. Regional newspapers closely followed the fates of local men as they were sent off to the battlefield, particularly in the early years of the Asia-Pacific War. The "heroic" war dead and their subsequent memorial activities were always covered in detail. The purpose of media reports on local deaths was not simply to disseminate information. By following the journey of the local war dead, media reports also instructed the readers in the importance of publicly commemorating war death.

Newspaper articles also informed readers of and provided guidance on the protocol associated with commemorating war deaths. I present here an example from Niigata chronicled by historian Yano Keiichi.[74] In November 1931 *Niigata* newspaper began following the homecoming of the first local war dead: four men from Niigata City who had died in Manchuria. As the date of the public memorial approached, articles began directing the residents to fly the *hinomaru* flag with a black ribbon. The same paper also announced a detailed schedule of events, starting with the arrival of the ashes at Niigata Station, followed by military parades to the homes of the deceased and then to the municipal memorial. The publication of this information implied that the readers were expected to participate in these events. Newspapers also reported on the memorial service the following day with ample details and photographs of a crowd numbering more than twelve thousand. These papers followed up the next spring with reports on the Yasukuni enshrinement of the local dead. Thus, media coverage helped mobilize the public to participate in the memorial process both in person and vicariously.

Newspapers and mass-market magazines also focused their coverage on the bereaved families. The widows, parents, and younger siblings typically responded to interviews describing the deceased in terms appropriate for an *eirei,* such as caring, loyal, and brave, while depicting their own emotions as grateful and proud. Such coverage was also instructive. The reports indirectly coached readers not only on the behaviors proper for a bereaved family but also on the appropriate emotions they should experience. The media were thus a powerful tool in institutionalizing grief and propagating expectations regarding the behaviors and emotions suitable for grieving war death. Narratives of families conforming to the new conventions for war death bereavement prepared other families to respond in a like manner as the need arose. In the quoted comments, bereaved family members usually exhibited pride and gratitude along with sadness, as did Umekichi's father (quoted earlier). Such comments were often, but not always, a sincere expression of the grieving family's emotions.

There were also instances when the media, in the absence of publishable quotes, fabricated typical and fitting quotes.[75] In *Imōtotachi no kagaribi* (A Beacon by the Younger Sisters), a compilation of the memoirs of women who lost their older brothers during the Asia-Pacific War, one woman recalls the period immediately after her older brother's death. Her local newspaper reported the death with a photograph of the four siblings taken prior to the brother's departure. A statement attributed to her accompanied the photograph: "This is an honor. I will work as hard as my brother in homeland defense." According to the woman, however, she had not spoken to anyone for quite some time after her brother's death, and she did not even know how the newspaper obtained the photograph.[76] By reading reports of other families' reactions to their loss, people knew what was expected of them. Thus, families typically spoke in that manner. As Jonathan Abel points out, the goal of censorship in wartime Japan was to cultivate an internal censor in all imperial subjects so that censorship would no longer be required.[77] Activities in these systems of mutual surveillance nurtured self-censorship. By continuing to comment in an acceptable and expected manner, bereaved families displayed and propagated the proper response to grief. Once published, these comments remained on record and in collective memory.

In addition to reporting on the festivals, newspapers provided programming information on live radio coverage of the *shōkon* ritual, which began on April 25, 1932. The NHK broadcasting service transmitted *shōkon* ceremonies live not only in Japan and its colonies but also in Japanese-occupied Manchuria and Shanghai.[78] During festivals at which the emperor made his appearance, listeners had another opportunity to participate in a collective ritual throughout the Japanese empire. At the exact time the emperor was scheduled to pay tribute at Yasukuni (10:15 a.m.), the whole country came to a halt to observe a minute of silence.[79] Through this broadcast, all imperial subjects had an opportunity to vicariously, yet collectively, experience the intimate ritual that was taking place in Tokyo. This shared experience—one that historian Hara Takeshi calls "rule by time (*jikan shihai*)"—created a virtual community centered around Yasukuni Shrine and the emperor and encompassing the entire Japanese empire.[80]

CREATING *BIDAN* FOR EVERYONE

Ritual activities and festival events at Yasukuni Shrine varied little over the years. A case in point is the live radio coverage of the *shōkon* rituals by an NHK announcer. Although live radio gave the impression that the announcer was describing what he was watching, in reality, the announcer was just reading a script.[81] That is, he timed the reading to synchronize with what was taking place on the shrine grounds. With the music and other sounds in the background, the generic prose could seem authentic to off-site listeners. Despite changes and updates to the installations in the Yasukuni-owned museums and the outer garden, these texts were always about the ongoing war. Outer-garden panoramas were about events on the battlefield; museum exhibits were about weapons and personal possessions of the deceased; and the rituals memorialized the war dead. Each event was a variation on a theme. Differences were so slight that a lengthy script could be written ahead of time even for the most important component of the event.

Producers of mass media were acutely aware of this problem. To maintain readers' interest in the semiannual events throughout the war years, newspapers featured personal stories collected from the bereaved festival attendees. On the first day of the April 1942 festival, for example, *Asahi* newspaper introduced three visitors to Yasukuni as representatives of "faithful devotion to the *eirei* (*eirei ni sasagu sekisei*)": a father who fell ill during his trip from Fukuoka and died upon arrival in Tokyo (his wife vowed to pay tribute for both of them); a wealthy war widow who donated fifty yen for every festival in accordance with her deceased husband's wishes; a younger brother of a deceased soldier who collected money from his classmates to donate to the shrine.[82] The personal stories offered much-needed variation to repetitious articles about enshrinement and at the same time continued to instruct readers on proper patriotic behavior on the home front.

A favorite of the *Asahi* newspaper was the annual "orphans' visit"[83] to Yasukuni Shrine, which started in August 1939 and was sponsored by the Soldiers' Relief Association (Gunjin Engo Kai).[84] That year, the *Asahi* followed the children from August 3, when the first child arrived in Tokyo, until

August 6, when they were finally able to "meet" their fathers in the inner shrine. Similar reportage continued every year with a focus on several children with backgrounds of interest. *Asahi* also featured children at other times. On January 31, 1932, for example, the paper introduced fifteen boys and girls aged eight to fifteen, who visited the shrine every morning at six o'clock. The article featured the children's photograph and commended the youngsters for praying every day for good weather for the soldiers fighting in Manchuria, as well as for a Japanese victory.

The orphans' visits to Yasukuni, like those of *shōkon* participants, were officially recorded in photo albums. According to the 1939 album, 1,301 sixth-graders representing every prefecture as well as Korea and Sakhalin gathered in Tokyo for three days in August. The highlight of the visit was on Sunday, August 6, when they received gifts from the empress at the Military Hall and visited Yasukuni Shrine, Yūshūkan, the National Defense Hall, the Navy Hall, Meiji Shrine and its treasure hall, the outer garden of Meiji Shrine, and the picture gallery (Kaiga-kan). Due to the large number of participants, worship at the Yasukuni Shrine took place in two groups. Each group lined up in the gravel courtyard between the inner shrine and the worship hall and received purification from a priest. One boy and one girl, representing the group, ascended into the inner shrine and made the *tamagushi* (sprig of a sacred tree) offering while the rest of the group prayed with their heads down. Forty-eight buses were mobilized for the tour of Tokyo sites to follow. In the gathering at the Military Hall that night, military officials made speeches, assuring the children that their fathers had become the god of Yasukuni, regardless of their social status or military rank at the time of their death.[85]

Newspaper stories about mothers and wives of the deceased were also popular. For example, in September 1939 *Asahi* newspaper featured a meeting on Yasukuni grounds of a soldier and the mother of his deceased comrade. After his comrade's death, the soldier regularly wrote to the mother from the front.[86] A mother interviewed at the fall 1941 event was quoted as feeling grateful and honored to be invited to the ceremony for the second time—a year before, for her eldest son, and this time for her third son.[87] Widows were also introduced in articles. These human-interest stories featuring dedicated family members were called "*bidan*" (beautiful stories, or praiseworthy anecdotes) and were a media favorite throughout the war.[88]

As the death toll began increasing in the mid-1930s, Yasukuni Shrine became a staple for articles in mass-market magazines. For example, *Shufu no tomo* (Housewife's Companion), the most popular women's magazine at the time, regularly featured articles on Yasukuni Shrine. Rare cases of female enshrinement at Yasukuni were always covered in detail. In May 1938, for example, the magazine published an article on three nurses who were enshrined in Yasukuni, detailing the heroic death of each.[89] A popular format in *Shufu no tomo* was group discussions (*taidan*) among women in the magazine's target demographic. For example, the May 1939 issue showcased a discussion among five young mothers whose husbands had died before the birth of their children. On the first two pages was a photograph of the five women with young children in their arms, against a background illustration easily identifiable as Yasukuni Shrine by the large *torii* and Ōmura's statue. A young widow responds to a sympathetic comment about the loss of her husband: "It cannot be helped as it is for the nation, for Japan. I am happy that my husband died for the emperor." Another recalls her husband telling her not to worry since his spirit will live on at Yasukuni after his body dies.[90] In the next issue (June 1939) was a discussion among elderly widows that took place immediately following the *shōkon* ritual; their only—and unmarried—child had died at war. The elderly mothers, who were now alone and without family, expressed awe and gratitude in response to their experience. Here is an excerpt that conveys the tone:

> MORIKAWA YUKI: The night that the white palanquin entered Yasukuni Shrine, I was just so thankful . . . so thankful.
>
> MURAI YOKI: It is all the fine doings of the emperor. It is too good to be true.
>
> NAKAMURA SHIGE: Yes, we all cried.
>
> TAKAI HINA: Tears of happiness. We cried tears of happiness.
>
> NAKAMURA: I am just so grateful that folks like us were given children that could serve the emperor.

The mothers proceeded to talk about the beauty of the imperial garden, which they had just visited (by virtue of their sons' death), likening it to paradise.[91]

This mothers' dialogue is well known. It has been cited in various critiques of Yasukuni Shrine ever since literary critic Hashikawa Bunzō reproduced the passage in his 1974 article "The Establishment and Transformation of Yasukuni Philosophy (*Yasukuni shisō no seiritsu to hen'yō*)."[92] For Hashikawa, the discussion was "the most exemplary representation of Yasukuni belief." Takahashi Tetsuya disagrees with Hashikawa's reading. He reintroduced the dialogue in his 2005 bestseller, *Yasukuni mondai* (The Yasukuni Issue), quoting earlier parts of the dialogue, in which the mothers express sadness and loneliness, to demonstrate an emotional shift.[93] For example, Morikawa Yuki, quoted in the preceding extract as being thankful, says earlier in the discussion that "I understand that my child is already gone. But when I see a healthy soldier, I cannot help thinking perhaps he is alive somewhere just like that man. Since I am by myself, I end up complaining, in the evenings especially. I know it's shameful, but as a parent, I think of how wonderful my son was. But whenever I have such a thought, I quickly remind myself what an honorable deed he has done. I can then smile with all my heart."[94]

For Takahashi, the problem of Yasukuni Shrine is that it functions as what he calls an "alchemy of emotions (*kanjō no renkin jutsu*)," which replaces grief and sadness with a feeling of honor and gratitude by assigning a new significance to death.[95] Takahashi explains that this is precisely what had happened as Morikawa demonstrated an emotional transition from sadness to gratitude. For her, the topic of Yasukuni Shrine represented the honorable deed her son had performed. The unbearable sadness was thus replaced by joy, supported by phrases such as "honorable death for the sake of the country" and "having a son who could be of use to the emperor."

COUNTERNARRATIVES

For me, the juxtaposition of Morikawa's comments represents not a replacement of grief with honor but a wide range of honest emotions that a grieving person might experience. It is the oscillation between sincere sadness and the kind of appropriate response that one had been conditioned to have through activities and media representations such as those I have outlined. I would further argue that this is the range of emotions commonly expected of someone coping with a major loss: wavering between allowing oneself to be consumed by immense grief and attempting to identify and grasp some positive outcome or benefit. A similar range of emotions can be observed in the printed responses of Umekichi's father. The local newspaper *Yokosuka bōei shinpō* reported Umekichi's father as saying, "Since I had already offered my son to the emperor [when I sent him off to the front], I am truly pleased to have him die."[96] This seems to be the typical response expected of a patriotic Japanese subject during wartime. But according to another newspaper, *Tōkyō nichi nichi shinbun,* Umekichi's father, having experienced the death of two young sons before Umekichi, became hysterical with sadness and yet stated that he was "at least consoled by the fact that he died for the country."[97] Umekichi's brother Kikuzō, eleven years old at the time, remembers differently. According to Kikuzō, his father, upon receiving the notice of Umekichi's death, tore apart scrolls dedicated to the gods while screaming in distress that there are "no gods or buddhas in this world."[98]

The printed comments by the elderly mothers and Umekichi's father were in part a result of the self-censorship that took place when bereaved family members talked to the media. Producers of mass media also practiced self-censorship. Years after the Asia-Pacific War, a veteran announcer of the Japanese national network NHK recalled his toughest wartime assignment as a live radio broadcaster during *shōkon* ceremonies at Yasukuni. I reproduce here the quote that I introduced in the epigraph: "I truly had a hard time with that broadcast. You see, the ceremony is conducted in pitch dark. And there'd be tormented screams like 'Murderer!' 'Give me back my child!' coming from the bereaved families that lined both sides of the main approach. The military police were at a loss as these people had just lost a close family member. But I had to make sure that the microphone would not pick up those voices. That was really tough."[99]

For the radio audience, the erasure of dissenting voices from the official broadcast rendered them absent. In the official narrative, family members in attendance at the *shōkon* ritual were proud and grateful. But ethnographer Orikuchi Shinobu remembers hearing sobs as well as clapping and joyous voices when he attended the April 1943 ritual.[100] The emotions of the bereaved families were not uniform; the motives behind the emotions exhibited were varied. Some attendees were perhaps truly happy and proud, whereas others like the elderly mother oscillated between pride and loneliness. Those who felt only sad or angry probably did not attend the ceremony. The radio representation of the *shōkon* ritual—highly manipulated by the state network personnel—constructed a scenario that reinforced the image that all Japanese supported the current militarist state.

This image—a literal representation of the wartime slogan "one million hearts beating as one"—still shapes the Japanese collective memory not only as wartime state propaganda but also as the wartime norm. But many accounts also reject the pro-war propaganda. Wartime police records contain numerous reports of ordinary Japanese arrested for making antiwar statements or comments that did not revere the emperor. In January 1942, merely a month after the glorious reports of the Pearl Harbor attack, a fifty-one-year-old male was arrested for repeatedly uttering as follows in public: "I received notice that my son died in Singapore. It might be for the country as they say, but as a parent, I cannot help crying."[101] That same month, a man was arrested in a Hokkaidō bar for making statements such as "Even if I am conscripted, I will not die for the emperor."[102] In March 1942, when newspapers were reporting consecutive victories by the Japanese military on a daily basis, a man was arrested for arguing that "Japan started a large-scale war with the United States, but there is no way that such a small country can win."[103] But such voices of dissent were almost always silenced and never publicized by the mass media.

Dissent was not always vocalized. Also in 1942, graffiti on a wall of a Tokyo subway station read: "Peace should not be bloody."[104] Many antiwar graffiti were found on public bathroom walls: "Stop the war, we have no rice," "Stop the war, give us back our freedom."[105] Many other reported graffiti were critical of the emperor and the imperial family and questioned the validity of the emperor system. But these graffiti, too, were quickly erased, preserved only as police documents. The public narrative that can be gathered from mass media and other approved publications did not even hint at the presence of such sentiments.

Since these voices were typically silenced during the war, apart from police records, they can be heard only through venues such as oral history interviews. Cultural anthropologist Kitamura Riko points out the difficulties of interviewing people about wartime experiences, as the outcome often depends on the questions asked or how they are framed. For example, a Mr. Sugamaru, born in 1911, did not go to war because he did not pass the health examination. Asked how he felt, he initially responded that he was distressed because he was not able to fulfill his obligation; he believed that joining the military was something to be grateful for. When Kitamura repeated the same question after two hours of interviewing, Sugamaru responded, "Well, you know, we'd talked about joining the military as something to be proud of, but in reality, no one wanted to go."[106] Here the respondent had worked through his past and untangled his emotions in order to distinguish the memories of his personal emotions from what he had been conditioned to believe. Many of the village practices that Kitamura documented were subversive. Villagers recalled climbing a mountain to pray, outwardly for Japan's victory but in reality so that their sons would not be drafted. Others constructed hidden meanings for everyday practices such as shouts of *banzai*. In some villages, when these shouts were used to send soldiers off to war, they were tacitly understood to signify "come back safely" rather than "long live the emperor."[107] Other anthropologists have collected memories of attempts to fail the health exam and of prayers and talismans that were meant to prevent injuries and death on the battlefield.

As was the case with the disparity between Umekichi's father's response to local media and his cry of distress inside his home, most Japanese succeeded in suppressing their emotions in public. They typically responded to social expectations, which included participating in military-related events, particularly those associated with honoring the dead. Participation in such events offered opportunities to practice and perform an acceptable form of patriotism. These practices and performances became further normalized through their repetition at events associated with the homecoming of the ashes and memorializing of the dead, as well as celebrations and commemorations of reported military successes. Disseminating representations of such events through the mass media further reinforced the image that all imperial subjects were fighting as one. For some, participation in these events gradually indoctrinated them in the official narrative of the state: a narrative that declared the Asia-Pacific War a holy war, that celebrated Emperor Hirohito as the living manifestation of god, and that encouraged young men to die at war. For those who were born during the war, this was the only narrative they knew. Many did not have more complete information for contextualizing their experience. With the passage of time, however, these complex relationships with Japan's Myth of the War Experience were gradually simplified into a narrative of victimhood. The presence of Yasukuni Shrine as the principal party accountable certainly facilitated this process.

During the final years of the war, Yasukuni Shrine continued to hold *shōkon* rituals and regular festivals regardless of the deteriorating living conditions in Tokyo. During the spring festival of 1942—less than a week after the first air raid that damaged parts of Tokyo—police cautioned visitors and nearby residents not to mistake the light and sound of ceremonial fireworks for air raids.[108] Fireworks, battle-scene dioramas, and flower arrangements showcased inside the inner shrine were prohibited during the fall festival of 1944.[109] Sumo matches, however, took place even in April 1945 in the midst of air raids. Despite the sober atmosphere resulting from the prohibition on vendors and show tents, sizable crowds attended each festival.

In the very last years of the war the military demonstrated concern for the attendees' safety during the *shōkon* ceremonies. By the spring of 1944, only one family member per deceased soldier was permitted to participate. The elderly, women, and children were advised not to attend. Because of the apprehension about air raids, family members were lodged outside Tokyo. In the fall of 1944 family attendance at the *shōkon* ceremony was strongly discouraged. Instead, regional ceremonies took place at *gokoku* shrines throughout Japan, during which family members listened to the radio broadcast of the Yasukuni ritual and worshipped Yasukuni Shrine from afar.[110]

Early in the morning of March 10, 1945, 325 Allied B-29 bombers were mobilized to drop nearly eighteen hundred tons of incendiary bombs on Tokyo. More than a third of the city was decimated; in excess of one hundred thousand people were killed. Two more raids occurred in mid-April, when an incendiary bomb struck the shrine grounds near the main shrine. Although the military prohibited family members from attending, Yasukuni Shrine's spring *shōkon* ritual took place as scheduled.[111] The sixty-sixth *shōkon* ceremony, which was held in the evening of April 24, was interrupted many times by air raids. Only army and navy officials participated. During the ceremony, the officials were relocated to air raid shelters several times, while the two chief priests, Ikeda Ryōhachi and Fujita Katsushige, remained at the *shōkon* grounds.[112] Nonetheless, the spirits of 37,053 fallen were merged into the Yasukuni god at the end of the evening. A special festival took place the following day. The emperor and the empress visited separately, on April 28 and May 5, respectively.[113] This was the last *shōkon* ritual of Imperial Japan.

FIVE

WHO HAS THE RIGHT TO MOURN?

Politics of Enshrinement at Yasukuni Shrine

> This is a terribly difficult issue. [My opinion, outlined here,] might be interpreted as overly sensitive to the current conditions or as thankless or immoral. But, as a result of a thorough consideration of the various factors involved, I have decided to make the following proposal. My proposal is to respectfully request the abolition of Yasukuni Shrine.
>
> *ISHIBASHI TANZAN*

> If it is true that Yasukuni Shrine is the core of State Shinto and the source of a misguided nationalism, what we must abolish is the system called State Shinto and not Yasukuni Shrine. We advocate complete freedom of religion. All those who died for their country should be enshrined in Yasukuni Shrine regardless of their religious beliefs.
>
> *FATHER BRUNO BITTER,* MAKKĀSĀ NO NAMIDA: BRŪNO BITTERU SHINPU NI KIKU

Less than two months after Japan's defeat, journalist and politician Ishibashi Tanzan began his proposal for the future of Yasukuni Shrine with a thoughtful yet bold recommendation: Shut it down.[1] Ishibashi considered multiple factors, including the difficulties associated with the impending enshrinement of countless war dead and the incompatibility of rushed enshrinement with the stated ideal of Yasukuni Shrine.[2] He further maintained that enshrining military leaders as national heroes should not be approved in light of the international political climate following Japan's defeat. While arguing for the shrine's closure, Ishibashi was also aware of the difficulty of carrying out such an act. "The termination of Yasukuni is not as simple as the closing down of one shrine," he acknowledged.[3] He was concerned about the political implications of the proposed closure. That is, messages propagated during the war that justified Japan's wars of imperialism would not be eliminated simply by closing the physical and institutional structure of the shrine. In other words, Ishibashi was arguing that Japan's war responsibilities would not end with the elimination of "Yasukuni the site."

In the proposal, Ishibashi referred to the statement by Prime Minister Higashikuni Naruhiko, "one hundred million to repent together (*ichioku sōzange*)"—a phrase that would have a lasting impact on the ways in which the Japanese would consider the Asia-Pacific War.[4] While agreeing that all Japanese were responsible, Ishibashi considered this statement to be problematic. For in this scenario, political and military leaders and civilians, including young children, were assumed to be equally responsible. He maintained that, despite the fact that all Japanese were responsible, they should be assigned different degrees of liability. The central question implied in Ishibashi's commentary on Yasukuni Shrine remains relevant today. Under such circumstances, should all Japanese war dead be venerated as *eirei* at Yasukuni Shrine? Abolishing the shrine following Ishibashi's recommendation might have circumvented such issues for the time being.

Ishibashi was not alone in his predicament. The physical presence of Yasukuni Shrine and prefectural *gokoku jinja,* as well as the wartime structure of Shintoism as a national belief, were the key concerns of the Supreme Commander of the Allied Powers (SCAP) members who arrived in Japan on August 28, 1945. After lengthy deliberations and consultations with Japanese religious scholars, on December 15, 1945, the occupation forces issued the Shinto Directive, which separated the Japanese state from Shinto, thus dismantling what came to be known in the postwar years as State Shinto.[5] The directive was later incorporated into the new Japanese Constitution as Article 20, which guaranteed religious freedom to all and prohibited the state from participating in religious activities. Debate ensued on the fate of shrines that were closely tied to the Japanese state. However, SCAP members eventually agreed to preserve them on the condition that the Japanese state terminated its support. After deliberations over the fate of Yasukuni Shrine, including suggestions about changing its name and transforming the site into an amusement park, authorities agreed to privatize it.[6]

Termination of state support has had a profound impact on Yasukuni Shrine and the war-bereaved military families (*izoku*), namely, the spouses and close relatives of those enshrined at Yasukuni.[7] The effect on the shrine was twofold: First, it no longer was supported by public funds; second, termination of its ties with the state significantly altered the shrine's symbolism. For war-bereaved military families, it suggested that the Japanese state no longer officially recognized the death of their loved ones. The postwar history of Yasukuni Shrine is thus replete with attempts by various interest groups to reestablish the connection between the shrine and the Japanese state.[8] Two organizations in particular, the Liberal Democratic Party (LDP)—the majority ruling party for the most of the postwar years since 1955—and the Japan Association for the Bereaved Families of the War Dead (Nihon Izokukai; hereafter Izokukai) are central to these attempts.[9] Consequently, they are also the key to what is known today as the "Yasukuni issue."[10]

In the 1960s and 1970s the LDP, backed by the Izokukai, made five attempts to pass the Yasukuni Shrine Bill (Yasukuni Jinja Hōan), which would have restored state support of the shrine. All five attempts failed, but the gesture signaled to the war-bereaved military families that the LDP was committed to restoring the shrine's ties with the Japanese state. At the same time, the controversy over the Shrine Bill placed Yasukuni Shrine in the spotlight for the first time during the postwar era, which ushered in a period of public scrutiny of visits to the shrine by prime ministers and other government officials.[11] Until 1985 such controversies were primarily a domestic concern. But on August 15, 1985, the fortieth anniversary of the end of the Asia-Pacific War, Prime Minister Nakasone Yasuhiro's official visit to the shrine made headlines both inside and outside Japan. The official status of his visit was demonstrated when he signed the guest register with his tittle, used public funds to pay for offerings, and stated that he had made the visit in his official capacity as prime minister. Reported alongside news about the prime minister's visit was information that was nearly seven years old in 1985. Namely, during the Yasukuni fall festival of 1978, head priest Matsudaira Nagayoshi quietly enshrined fourteen men who were convicted of Class-A war crimes at the Tokyo War Crimes Tribunal.[12] Taken aback by the intense international criticism of his visit, Nakasone subsequently distanced himself from Yasukuni Shrine.

Since this incident, most prime ministers have attempted a balancing act by avoiding the August date and taking an ambiguous position on the status of their visits. Consequently, by the 1990s the so-called Yasukuni issue seemed to have subsided. But this changed in the first decade of the twenty-first century, when Koizumi Junichiro seriously strained Japan's relations with other Asian nations by his repeated visits to Yasukuni and comments on Yasukuni worship. The so-called performances by the flamboyant prime minister resulted in renewed attention to the shrine that quickly developed into larger discussions associated not only with the prime minister's visits to the shrine but also with issues ranging from Japan's war crimes and lack of reparations to how history is being taught in Japanese middle schools. These wide-ranging discussions also brought to light the fact that Yasukuni Shrine neither requests nor obtains permission from family members to enshrine the war dead. Koizumi's actions ultimately led to lawsuits as well as a proposal to build a new national memorial that would replace Yasukuni.

Although all components of "Yasukuni the issue" are closely intertwined, in this chapter I detail lawsuits pursuing the removal of names of the war dead from the Yasukuni register. In particular, I examine a recent case filed by Okinawans at the Naha District Court in March 2008 (deliberations concluded in October 2010), suing for the removal of civilian names from the register. Okinawa presents a fascinating case study as the only Japanese site that was invaded and became US territory until 1972. Furthermore, many civilian casualties in Okinawa, some of which are included in the Yasukuni register, were caused by the Japanese military. Many Okinawans thus resent the fact that their families are enshrined collectively with the Japanese military, which not only failed to protect them but, even worse, also turned against and killed civilians. At the same time, Okinawan families also have relatives who died as members of the armed forces. The lawsuit against Yasukuni Shrine demonstrates these Okinawans' attempt to negotiate complex emotions arising from conflicting attitudes about and experiences of the Japanese military. Testimony for the lawsuit reveals their turbulent emotions with regard to war death and Yasukuni Shrine.

In what follows, I also touch on demands by Taiwanese and Koreans for the removal of their citizens' names from the Yasukuni register. As Japanese colonial subjects during the Asia-Pacific War, Taiwanese and Korean men were forced to join the Japanese military. Consequently, many non-Japanese war dead were enshrined at Yasukuni without their families' knowledge or consent. Korean and Taiwanese nationals filed lawsuits with the support of Japanese sympathizers. The plaintiffs have not yet won in court but are continuing their appeal through venues such as books and documentary films.[13] These former colonial subjects argue that they cannot bear the knowledge that their loved ones are commemorated by their former colonizers. Furthermore, that they are enshrined together with perpetrators of Japanese imperialism (i.e., Japanese who died during the colonization of Taiwan and Korea during the early twentieth century), is an affront. At the same time, however, the groups have conflicting positions on Japan and Yasukuni Shrine, contradictions that are more prominent among the Taiwanese, for whom the Yasukuni issue is intertwined with domestic politics.

Lawsuits filed in Japanese courts are not limited to those by Okinawans and non-Japanese nationals. Mainland Japanese have also filed cases to have the names of their family members removed for political, religious, and other reasons.[14] Most of the cases I cover in this chapter, such as the former colonial subjects and Okinawans, are anomalies in that the plaintiffs have maintained particular kinds of relationships with the Japanese state both during the Asia-Pacific War and at present. But I find these cases useful for examining issues of war memorialization. Deliberations on these cases raise the following question, among others: Who has the legal right to memorialize the dead and to mourn their loss, especially in a society where one death can be memorialized multiple times at multiple places? Until 1945 the Japanese state sought to exercise sole authority over both the bodies and the spirits of the war dead. In the absence of such control, who now should have the authority to memorialize the dead? Furthermore, does memorialization by another party legally infringe on a bereaved family's experience of mourning?

One central criticism of Yasukuni Shrine concerns its role of commemoration (*kenshō suru*). But most modern states commemorate their war dead in ways that are partly in the service of promoting national identity. Terminology thus plays a key role in how to negotiate memories of the war dead in Japan. Three terms, *irei, tsuitō,* and *kenshō,* which can be rendered in English as memorial, mourning, and commemoration, respectively, are typically used to distinguish attitudes of the living toward the dead.[15] However, other terms add semantic and emotional nuance, including *chinkon* (placating of the spirit), *aitō* (similar to *tsuitō* but perhaps with a stronger connotation of sorrow or lament), *kuyō* (derived from the Sanskrit term *pūjanā* and suggesting the presence of an offering), and *jōrei* (cleansing of the spirit).[16]

As historian Akazawa Shirō points out, the recent controversies often emerge because of the gap between how politicians explain their visits to Yasukuni (for example, Koizumi repeatedly described his visits as an act of *tsuitō*) and how critics refer to them (typically as *kenshō*).[17] In particular, "commemoration" (*kenshō*), which is a normative modifier for remembrance activities for the military dead in many societies, has now taken on a complex quality in Japan due to its recent history. Commemorating the military dead, in the case of Japan, is considered an act of affirmation of the Asia-Pacific War. Recognizing the complexities of terminology, the plaintiffs in the lawsuits argued that families had the right to "freedom of mourning" (*tsuitō no jiyū*), that is, the right of families to prevent unwanted parties from participating in the mourning process, especially when they consider the outside party's act as commemoration. However, the judicial system could respond only within the legal framework of "freedom of religion." Accordingly, the court ruled that the constitutional right to freedom of religion gives institutions, including Yasukuni Shrine, the right to engage freely in an act of mourning. An analysis of these lawsuits reveals the complex ways that modern war death is recognized in Japan.

YASUKUNI SHRINE IN NONMILITARIZED JAPAN

Many of the political issues currently associated with Yasukuni Shrine are rooted in the changes that the shrine and the war-bereaved families faced in the immediate postwar period. As a result of SCAP's focused deliberations, Yasukuni Shrine escaped demolition by transforming itself into a private religious entity (religious juridical person).[18] But all of the issues that were examined during the occupation period remained, along with the physical structure of the shrine. Nonetheless, for several decades after the war the political implications of the shrine attracted little public attention. Rituals and festivals continued to take place in the postwar years to complete the enshrinement of the Asia-Pacific War dead. The relationship between the shrine and the state and with the imperial institution quickly resumed, at least superficially. Even though prime ministers had mostly stayed away from the shrine during the occupation, Yoshida Shigeru—accompanied by cabinet representatives—made the first of his regular visits on October 18, 1951.[19] On October 16, 1952, during the first festival in postoccupation Japan, Emperor Hirohito visited Yasukuni Shrine for the first time since November 1945. He received a warm and grateful welcome by approximately three thousand war-bereaved military family members and five thousand other visitors. The evening edition of major newspapers published photographs of people sitting on the ground in their formal attire, as they had done during wartime imperial visits. Some raised their arms into the air, presumably shouting *banzai* to the emperor, while others were waving. The *Yomiuri* newspaper reported, however, that the general visitors included young children and women in their aprons, suggesting a more casual atmosphere.[20] The *Yomiuri* newspaper also featured a photograph of the emperor waving back to the crowd, silk hat in hand.[21] These key visits suggest a seamless continuation from the war years.

On the surface, then, interventions by the occupation forces, including the new constitution and the Shinto Directive, seemed to have little impact on the operations of Yasukuni Shrine and its relationship with war-bereaved families. But the termination of state support foretold financial difficulties for the shrine.[22] Another key intervention by the SCAP received less attention in relation to the political issues surrounding Yasukuni Shrine: the February 1946 decision to terminate pensions and other financial support for members of the military and the war bereaved, with the exception of support for veterans with disabilities. Families whose main provider was among the war dead were the hardest hit by this measure. Mothers were left to raise young children alone and without financial support.

Nihon Izokukai, the group associated with LDP and the Yasukuni issue, was established in response to the SCAP termination of pensions. In late 1947 war-bereaved families in need of a support system established the Japan League for the Welfare of War-Bereaved Families (Nihon Izoku Kōsei Renmei), which worked out of an office inside the Yasukuni Shrine grounds.[23] Persistent lobbying by the Japan League resulted in the War-Injured and War-Bereaved Families Relief Act (Senshōbyōsha Senbotsusha Izoku-tō Engohō; hereafter Engohō) established on April 30, 1952. It was passed two days after the end of the Allied occupation and guaranteed pensions for war-bereaved families.[24] In 1953 the Japan League became a juridical foundation under the name Nihon Izokukai.[25] However, even the members were not always familiar with the history and operations of the foundation. For the bereaved families, motives to join Izokukai were sometimes as simple as an opportunity for regular visits to Yasukuni Shrine.[26] Others mistakenly believed that membership in Izokukai was necessary to receive a pension.[27] Moreover, Izokukai was not the only organization for the war-bereaved families.[28]

One further aspect of Engohō is relevant here. In order to receive a pension, war-bereaved families needed to submit paperwork to the Ministry of Welfare (Kōseishō), the antecedent of the current Ministry of Health, Labor, and Welfare (Kōsei Rōdōshō).[29] Basic information on the deceased, such as name, age, and hometown, was required, as well as location and cause of death and rank at the time of death. The ministry thus was able to compile a vast amount of data on military-related deaths from the Asia-Pacific War. This information soon became valuable for Yasukuni Shrine since it included the details necessary to complete the enshrinement process for the deceased. Engohō, which was established to support war-bereaved families during the immediate postwar years, became a resource for Yasukuni Shrine's efforts to enshrine a multitude of deaths from the Asia-Pacific War.

POSTWAR ENSHRINEMENT OF ASIA-PACIFIC WAR DEATHS

Almost all of the military-related dead from the Asia-Pacific War were enshrined after the war. As I mentioned in chapter 4, only about 10 percent of the military deaths had received the *shōkon* ritual at Yasukuni Shrine when Japan surrendered to the Allied Forces on September 2, 1945. Thus, the spirits of more than two million war dead had not yet transformed into the Yasukuni god. The postwar enshrinement of these war casualties was possible only with the assistance of the Demobilization Ministry. This collaboration is central to the political issues associated with the shrine today.

In theory, the spirits of all outstanding dead were gathered at Yasukuni Shrine in the fall of 1945, although they were not formally enshrined at that time. The following discussion outlines this curious process. The Army Ministry took the initiative for enshrining the outstanding war dead and drafted a proposal on September 21.[30] The ministry proposed two separate events: a special fall festival to collectively enshrine all military deaths and a separate memorial festival for both military and civilian deaths to take place outside the shrine. The proposed collective enshrinement would not be a conventional *shōkon* ritual since the names of the deceased to be enshrined had not yet been identified. But the army maintained the importance of this ritual as the final service of the military. For this ritual, the army suggested the inclusion of not only the dead who were active military personnel and workers at military factories but also those who took their own lives at the end of the war and civilians whose deaths were caused by the enemy.

The army's proposal to conduct such unconventional memorial services was not well received by the other concerned parties. The Navy Ministry agreed to the enshrinement of military personnel and workers at military factories but not of suicides and civilians, and it did not respond to the suggestion of a combined festival outside the shrine.[31] Shrine authorities refused to enshrine persons of unknown numbers and names but refrained from commenting on the fate of nonmilitary personnel or on the combined memorial festival.[32] The Imperial Household Department's suggestion resolved the conflict: Conduct a memorial festival for the outstanding military deaths on the shrine grounds and plan for a formal enshrinement in the future once the names and other information of the deceased were identified.[33] Furthermore, instead of a combined memorial festival that included civilians, the Imperial Household Department suggested that the event that would take place outside the shrine involve only civilian casualties. It also considered it appropriate to request that the emperor attend the civilian memorial.[34]

The collective Yasukuni memorial for the outstanding military deaths took place at 6:00 p.m., November 19, 1945. Attendance of bereaved family members was limited, and, unlike at the previous ceremonies, there were no state-sponsored invitations with a travel subsidy. According to the shrine's chronicle, only forty-one bereaved families attended the *shōkon* ritual on the nineteenth. The next day, despite several attractions, including a Noh performance, a play at a temporary stage set up by the lake, flower arrangements, and some vendor stalls, the festival did not draw the usual crowds. Although it is noted that 1,092 members of war-bereaved families paid tribute on this occasion, it is not clear whether they were the families of the newly enshrined.[35] The shrine's chronicle notes that all of the shrine gates were closed at 7:00 p.m. since the festival traffic had stopped. The total number of visitors was approximately thirty thousand. The following day, the gates were closed at 5:00 p.m. due to poor attendance.[36] The emperor made an appearance on November 20 and remained on the shrine grounds for approximately five minutes.[37] There is no record or media report of an event outside the shrine for civilian deaths.

Another reason for the low attendance was the secrecy behind the *shōkon* ritual. The festival coincided with a period when SCAP personnel were deliberating the fate of the shrine. The event was planned to minimize negative reaction from SCAP. Religious scholar Kishimoto Hideo, who was acting as an adviser to the SCAP Religious Division, took pains to limit publicity as well as military presence during the ceremony.[38] A newspaper advertisement of the ceremony was quickly withdrawn as a result.[39] Members of the military were strongly advised not to appear in uniform. A special *shōkon* ritual took place the following day under the watchful eyes of Kenneth Dyke (Civil Information and Education Section, SCAP), William Kenneth Bunce (Chief of Religious and Cultural Resources Divisions, SCAP), and George Warp (deputy chief, Religious Division, SCAP). The emperor appeared in his civilian clothing and paid tribute along with Prime Minister Shidehara, army and navy personnel, and bereaved family members. That same day, the Japanese cabinet agreed to a policy that terminated state sponsorship of Yasukuni Shrine.[40]

The key difference between this ritual and the wartime *shōkon* rites was that the spirits of the dead did not become a god. Names and other details of the deceased were not inscribed in the register at this time, which, according to the shrine, is the process that signifies the merging of the spirits into the Yasukuni god. The spirits invited to the *shōkon* grounds on November 19 were placed together in the main shrine, apart from the god of

Yasukuni, to await formal enshrinement until all relevant information was gathered.[41] Another reason for postponing enshrinement, particularly for those who died in the final year of the war, was as follows: Yasukuni Shrine maintained that, according to Shinto tradition, spirits of the dead could not be transformed into god until one full year had passed after death.[42]

In order to properly enshrine these spirits, Yasukuni personnel quickly began the process of compiling the necessary information. For the April 1946 festival, a total of 26,887 names were identified and added to the register, and their spirits were merged with the god of Yasukuni.[43] Women from the imperial household often helped inscribe the names and information on the register.[44] Enshrinement continued in the following years in the same manner, with one or two rituals taking place every year. The number of enshrinements per ritual varied, with more than a quarter million enshrined in the fall of 1957.[45]

Proper enshrinement of the outstanding two million proved to be a daunting task. Diet meeting transcripts included in *A New Compilation of Materials on the Yasukuni Shrine Problems* (*Shinpen Yasukuni Jinja mondai shiryōshū*), compiled and published by the National Diet Library in 2007, record repeated discussions on expediting enshrinement. The problems were twofold: the extensive labor needed to compile the information necessary for proper enshrinement and the high price of the entire operation. Initially, municipalities were instructed to compile the information for all local military dead who met enshrinement criteria and send it to Yasukuni Shrine via the Demobilization Ministry.[46] Shrine personnel then informed the family of the deceased.[47] Unlike the wartime enshrinement process, the emperor's acknowledgment was eliminated. This procedure, however, proved excessive for local administrations, which were already overwhelmed by the demands of postwar rehabilitation. In order to alleviate the burden on these local offices, the Demobilization Ministry soon decided to take over the task.[48] According to the summary provided in the Diet meeting transcripts, "It is impossible for other parties to complete this task since the investigation can be conducted only in association with reparation duties." In addition, the job was considered the ministry's moral obligation to the military dead, "who made the ultimate sacrifice during the war."[49]

During the occupation, the parties involved attempted to comply with the directive from the SCAP, which prohibited the ministries from actively cooperating with the shrine. For example, rather than directly supplying the names of the war dead to the shrine, an agreement was made on August 2, 1948, for the shrine to borrow from the Ministry of Welfare a copy of its official bulletin, which presumably had current information about the deceased.[50] The situation changed, however, with the end of the occupation and the establishment of Engohō, which allowed war-bereaved families to apply for a pension. The shrine and the ministry were no longer under SCAP's supervision; the application to the Ministry of Welfare by war-bereaved families included all information necessary for Yasukuni enshrinement. The ministry personnel assessed the documents and compiled the names of qualified pension recipients. The shrine then requested the information from the ministry, and the ministry responded in accordance with administrative routine. Many families never received notice of enshrinement, however. Diet transcripts suggest that both the shrine personnel and the lawmakers assumed that families wanted their loved ones to be enshrined, and therefore it did not matter how the shrine acquired the needed information. Moreover, families were never notified that the information they offered to receive their pension was transferred to Yasukuni Shrine.

Transference of the Engohō information led to arguably the most important component of the Yasukuni issue—enshrinement of war criminals. Through Engohō, families of men that were executed for war crimes as well as those who died in incarceration became eligible for a pension.[51] For example, families of Class-A war criminals who were executed or died at Sugamo Prison qualified. Their inclusion on the Ministry of Welfare's list meant that their names would be delivered to Yasukuni Shrine along with those of all other military dead.

A review of the Diet proceedings relevant to Yasukuni enshrinement suggests that in the early postwar decades, lawmakers were intent on completing the enshrinement of the war dead and notifying the families of the procedure. Discussions surface repeatedly on the need to complete the process in order not only to satisfy the families but also to demonstrate proper respect for those who sacrificed their lives for the state. Many lawmakers considered the completion of enshrinement a state responsibility. The documents included in the collection released by the National Diet Library have caused controversies in recent years as they leave a paper trail proving that the Ministry of Welfare was providing information to Yasukuni Shrine for enshrinement of the war dead. But the documents are also valuable in highlighting the social milieu of the time, at least with regard to the Diet sessions. The language in the Diet transcripts into the 1950s and 1960s differs very little from that of the wartime years. The military dead were *eirei,* who needed to be honored by proper enshrinement, after which they would be transformed into a god. Yasukuni Shrine was equivalent to a national memorial that needed to recognize all of Japan's military dead. Little regard was given to the constitutionality of even the process of holding these discussions under Article 20 in the early postwar decades.

Enshrinement-related documents end in April 1985 with a letter from Yasukuni Shrine requesting the names of military-related casualties that occurred after the San Francisco Peace Treaty.[52] No response is recorded. With the passage of time, the word *eirei* appeared less frequently in the Diet proceedings, although it was still used into the 1970s. Discussions shifted to more controversial topics: the enshrinement of war criminals and requests to remove names from the Yasukuni register. But such arguments circle around Article 20 of the constitution, which guarantees freedom of religion and prevents the state from engaging in religious activity. Since the constitution prohibits the state from interfering with activities of Yasukuni Shrine, little could be said during Diet sessions in relation to problems associated with the shrine's refusal to remove names from the register. Article 20, which was meant to guarantee freedom of religion to everyone, in these circumstances protected Yasukuni Shrine from the government. It later became an obstacle for plaintiffs suing the shrine for the removal of names on religious and political grounds.

PROTESTS AGAINST YASUKUNI ENSHRINEMENT

Legal cases directly dealing with Yasukuni enshrinement did not begin until the twenty-first century. However, appeals to Yasukuni Shrine for removal of names began in the 1960s. This section thus begins with an outline of earlier appeals and related lawsuits as background for the later cases. The earliest documented appeal occurred on September 5, 1968, when Christian priest Tsunoda Saburō visited Yasukuni Shrine to request that the names of his two older brothers be removed from the shrine register. The shrine responded two weeks later: "[We] cannot complete the request due to the objectives and the tradition we have upheld since the shrine's establishment."[53] The following year, on August 15, 1969, Tsunoda returned to the shrine with eleven members of the Association for War-Bereaved Christian Families, which he had joined earlier that year, to request the removal of nine names (including those of his brothers). The response they received from head priest Ikeda Ryōhachi was similar to what Tsunoda had received the previous year: "Since Yasukuni Shrine was built following the imperial order of Meiji to 'establish an institution where every war death would be memorialized and which would be forever respected by the Japanese people,' we cannot accept requests by relatives and other third parties to either enshrine or not enshrine a particular individual."[54]

Christians were not the only group who attempted to have names removed for religious reasons. Buddhist war-bereaved families began protesting in the 1980s as members of Shinshū Izokukai. Established on January 22, 1986, this was the first Buddhist association formed in response to Nakasone's visit on August 15 of the previous year.[55] Yasukuni head priests always responded that they could not remove names due to the shrine's mission and tradition.

In the meantime, lawsuits associated with the so-called Yasukuni issue were being filed in regional courts. In 1971 a city official in Tsu City, Mie Prefecture, sued the mayor for allocating public funds to a groundbreaking ceremony conducted by a Shinto priest for a municipal government building. The Supreme Court dismissed the case in 1977 on the grounds that the ceremony could be considered more of a tradition than a religious activity.[56] In 1972 residents of Iwate Prefecture sued the prefectural assembly, which had submitted a written statement to the state appealing for official worship at Yasukuni Shrine and the use of public funds for offerings to the shrine. In the late 1980s, citizens groups in Ehime Prefecture sued the prefectural governor for using public funds as offering money to the prefectural *gokoku jinja* and Yasukuni Shrine.[57] These two cases were ultimately ruled unconstitutional.[58] Another lawsuit is relevant here. In 1979 Nakaya Yasuko, a Christian widow of a Self-Defense Forces (SDF) member who died on duty, sued the SDF Yamaguchi District Communication Division and the SDF Veterans Association of Yamaguchi prefecture for violating Article 20 of the Japanese Constitution (freedom of religion). The defendants had enshrined the deceased in the Yamaguchi prefectural *gokoku jinja* without the plaintiff's permission. Nakaya won the first deliberation at the Yamaguchi District Court but lost in the Supreme Court on June 1, 1988.[59] Although these cases did not directly involve families of those enshrined at Yasukuni, they set a precedent for using legal means to protest against Yasukuni Shrine in particular and ties between Shinto and the state in general.

The war-bereaved families' collective interest in using legal means to appeal to the shrine became apparent during the premiership of Koizumi Junichiro (April 26, 2001–September 26, 2006). When Koizumi announced his candidacy as a representative of the Liberal Democratic Party on April 11, 2001, Izokukai had been pressuring the LDP to resume prime ministers' visits to Yasukuni Shrine. No prime minister had visited Yasukuni Shrine since Hashimoto Ryūtarō's visit on his birthday, July 29, 1996. In mid-April, Koizumi publicly promised Izokukai that if he became prime minister, he would make official visits to Yasukuni Shrine. On May 10, 2001, at a House of Representatives session, he made a public announcement that he planned to visit Yasukuni Shrine on the upcoming August 15.[60] The first lawsuits were thus not specifically about the removal of names; rather, they condemned Koizumi for making public visits to Yasukuni Shrine. But the issue of enshrinement without family approval was highlighted as a part of the legal proceedings that concerned Article 20 of the constitution. The proceedings problematized the process of gathering information for the enshrinement, during which the Ministry of Welfare provided data that had been compiled for Engohō purposes with regard to the shrine.

Even before Koizumi's first visit, Korean nationals sought legal recourse. A little less than 1 percent of those enshrined at Yasukuni (21,181) are Korean.[61] The fact that there are Korean and Taiwanese nationals enshrined at Yasukuni became public knowledge as early as April 1978, when the shrine caused an uproar by sending enshrinement announcements to a number of Taiwanese war-bereaved families. At the time, several Taiwanese families protested the enshrinement and requested the removal of the names, but the movement was short lived.[62] Koizumi's publicized stance toward Yasukuni Shrine revived the issue of colonial enshrinement. In June 2001 a group of Korean war-bereaved families filed a suit against the Japanese state in the Tokyo District Court. As a part of their demand for compensation, the plaintiffs pressured the state to withdraw from Yasukuni Shrine their relatives' "notice of war dead (*senbotsusha tsūchi*)" (the document that provides information about the deceased that is necessary for enshrinement).[63] This was not a straightforward demand for the removal of names. But without this information, Yasukuni Shrine would not have been able to enshrine these people. Therefore, if the information were to be taken away from the shrine, it could be argued that the names should no longer be included in its register.

That summer, Koizumi visited Yasukuni Shrine on August 13, not only disappointing the Izokukai members who wanted him to visit on the fifteenth but also generating intense contempt among the critics. The visit resulted in six separate lawsuits against the Japanese state, Koizumi, and Yasukuni Shrine in district courts in Osaka, Matsuyama, Fukuoka, Tokyo, Chiba, and Okinawa. Plaintiffs included war-bereaved families from Korea, Taiwan, and Okinawa. The focus of the case was the constitutionality of Koizumi's recent visit. But the discussion of the relationship between state and religion also raised the issue of Yasukuni enshrinement without the consent of the deceased person's family. The plaintiffs asserted that enshrinement would not have occurred had the state not assisted the shrine by providing information.

The lawsuits also reveal the plaintiffs' narratives of victimhood. In many instances these narratives are complicated by the aggressive acts of the Japanese military, of which many Japanese war-bereaved were cognizant. For example, the testimony by a son of a soldier who died of illness in New Guinea in January 1944 conveys the father's complicated position: "To honor and appreciate the dead, who was a victim of the state and who was forced to die as a perpetrator in a war of aggression, as a heroic spirit is an abuse of the dead to justify the state's war crimes and to evade its responsibility for them. It is to doubly obliterate the dead."[64] In this testimony, the son acknowledges Japan's role as the aggressor in the war. At the same time, however, having been forced to fight and carry out war crimes, as well as having been enshrined against his will to justify Japan's war crimes, the father remains a victim of the state. In this scenario the Japanese state is the only party evading responsibility. Many maintain the stance that the wartime state was responsible, and the people were not only innocent parties but also the victims of the state. This position is based on a stark divide between the state and its people: The state is the perpetrator and the people are the victims; there are no gray areas in between. But this clear division between victim and perpetrator is not sustainable in an all-out war. This complex relationship that war-bereaved families perceive between their deceased loved ones and their role in the Asia-Pacific War is explored further in the Okinawan case given later.

Many war-bereaved Japanese passionately support Yasukuni Shrine, such as the widow referred to in the Introduction, who felt as though her body were being shredded to pieces upon hearing criticisms of the shrine. Koizumi hoped to appeal to people such as this woman with his pledges regarding Yasukuni Shrine. In the face of the legal challenges, Koizumi made a bold statement by visiting the shrine for the spring festival on April 21, 2002. He ensured publicity of his visit by alerting the media in advance and lingering at the shrine site for about an hour while waiting for more media to arrive before paying his tribute.[65] When asked to comment on the lawsuits filed against him, he responded, "There are strange people (*okashii hito*) out there. It's ridiculous."[66] His cavalier comment led to a civil suit in Osaka, in which plaintiffs demanded an apology and monetary compensation for defamation.[67]

Koizumi's comment was certainly thoughtless. But his words, which demonstrate his unwillingness to understand others, are worth considering as they can serve as a lesson in thinking about war responsibility. Takahashi Tetsuya, for example, notes that the concept of responsibility denotes a willingness to respond to others. He says this to motivate the younger generation in Japan to respond to the voices from the rest of Asia.[68] His point is certainly valid, important, and necessary. Yet, I want to suggest that there is another group of people to whom Yasukuni critics ought to respond to: war-bereaved families who rely on the shrine to help understand and bear their loss. Suggesting that the emotions of war-bereaved persons who support Yasukuni Shrine are based on the "alchemy" that the shrine had played on them takes away the real experience and the memory that these people maintain.[69] The voices of many war-bereaved persons demonstrate the emotional support they derive from the belief that their loved ones are at Yasukuni Shrine. Their perspectives are as valid as those that accuse the shrine of manipulation. My goal here is to examine the complex ways that experiences and emotions are remembered. Aspects of the controversy surrounding Yasukuni Shrine highlight this complexity. There is not one collective Japanese memory of the Asia-Pacific War; there is not a single correct way to remember the Asia-Pacific War.

Koizumi's actions generated popular interest in Yasukuni Shrine. Visitors to the memorial increased dramatically; books and articles on the Yasukuni issue proliferated. The opening of a renovated and expanded Yūshūkan Museum in July 2002 contributed to this increased interest. Mass media dubbed the renewed attention the "Koizumi effect (Koizumi *kōka*)." Opponents waited two years to prevail. In April 2004 the Fukuoka District Court ruled that Koizumi's visit was unconstitutional.

THE EMOTIONAL ISSUE VERSUS THE LEGAL ISSUE

A month after the Fukuoka decision, on May 13, 2004, the Osaka District Court rejected a case against Koizumi, Yasukuni Shrine, and the Japanese state.[70] The deliberation of this case demonstrates the difficulties associated with lawsuits based on intangible criteria such as impressions and emotions. For example, the plaintiffs for the case argued that prime ministers' visits to Yasukuni Shrine give an impression that the shrine is of exceptional rank when compared to other Shinto shrines. It also gives an "impression to the society (*seken ippan no fun'iki*)" that one must not criticize Yasukuni Shrine's doctrine, which glorifies war. Therefore, the visits contain a component of coercion that violates religious freedom. They further elaborated on the "impression to society" as follows: "This 'impression to society' sanctifies imperial ideology and hereditary emperors. This is a notion that is incompatible with democracy. [The 'impression'] also approves the 'Yasukuni ideology (Yasukuni *shisō*),' which glorifies the act of dying at war for the emperor and the state. We must not overlook the fact that [the 'impression'] is strongly supported by political authorities that seek to promote this ideology."[71]

The plaintiffs argued that the function of Koizumi's visits was to steer them toward a particular religion: a Yasukuni brand of Shintoism that they considered closely aligned with the pre-1945 State Shinto. They argued that, by justifying his action with the statement "It is natural to visit Yasukuni Shrine to mourn for those who sacrificed their lives for their nation," Koizumi was forcing people to visualize a spiritual act of "mourning for those who sacrificed [their lives] for their nation." His actions thus coerced people from Japan and beyond to accept the belief that it is natural to pay tribute to the war dead who are enshrined at Yasukuni Shrine.[72]

The judges accepted Koizumi's argument that the visit was personal because it was motivated by his own spiritual beliefs and was not based on a cabinet decision. At the same time, the court acknowledged the social influence of actions by a person with such high status. That is, a prime minister's actions can have a much stronger and wider impact than an ordinary person's (*ippan shijin*); thus, depending on the nature of the action, it is necessary to consider its social implications. Having clarified the social influence of a prime minister's acts, the judges examined each of Koizumi's actions during his visits, including the vehicles he traveled in, public statements, signatures in the registry, and donations. Of his individual actions, only his use of an official car and being accompanied by his secretary could be construed as public actions. However, both were deemed as sometimes being necessary for the private business of a prime minister. Thus, the judges ruled that Koizumi's visits were private in nature and dismissed the case.[73]

The plaintiffs appealed to the Osaka District Higher Court on September 30, 2005.[74] The plaintiffs' demand for monetary compensation was dismissed, but the comments that accompanied the ruling made headlines. The judges cited the Fukuoka case as a precedent and ruled that Koizumi's visits to Yasukuni were unconstitutional. The mainstream press, including the *Asahi* and *Mainichi* newspapers, applauded the decision. This trend overshadowed reporting on the actual ruling against the plaintiffs, who sought monetary compensation for emotional suffering. Conservative outlets such as the *Sankei* newspaper criticized the judgment as inconsistent with other rulings on religion and the state. In particular, *Sankei* compared this case to the groundbreaking Supreme Court decision in the 1977 Tsu case, in which the court ruled that state support of Shinto-related rituals was constitutional. In the meantime, Koizumi's visits continued: He would visit the shrine three more times during his tenure as prime minister.[75]

TAIWAN AND KOREA: LEGACIES OF THE COLONIAL PAST

Approximately 120 Korean and Taiwanese nationals were among the 639 plaintiffs in the first Osaka case (2001). Most were relatives of those who died as colonial subjects conscripted by the Japanese military during the Asia-Pacific War. The experience of Japanese colonialism makes the enshrinement of Koreans and Taiwanese in Yasukuni Shrine even more complicated and problematic for non-Japanese war-bereaved persons than for Japanese. For example, for Korean families the presence of relatives on the Yasukuni register perpetuates Japan's colonial legacy. During the first hearing at Osaka District Court on February 22, 2002, a Korean plaintiff pleaded: "What right does Yasukuni Shrine have? Whose permission did they get to make our compatriots into *eirei?* They force our family to work for them even after death. Please give us back our compatriots."[76] This statement highlights the military's control of the war deaths of former colonial subjects through Yasukuni Shrine. Furthermore, the anger expressed by the plaintiffs echoes repeated pleas by the Aizu people for permission to properly bury their dead.[77] From the Korean plaintiff's perspective, Yasukuni Shrine, and by extension the Japanese state, still maintains control over Korean nationals today through the spirits of their dead.

In the second case in Osaka, the Taiwanese plaintiffs argued that the inclusion of their relatives suggested that they agreed with Japan's waging of war.[78] The Taiwanese case is even more complicated than the Korean case because the attitudes of Taiwanese nationals toward Japan in general, and Yasukuni Shrine in particular, are starkly divided along political party lines. Parties that belong to the Pan-Green Coalition favor Taiwanese independence from the Republic of China. They promote a positive view of their colonial past under Japanese rule as a way to emphasize a history that is independent of Chinese influence. Thus, members of parties in this coalition support Yasukuni Shrine.[79] Members of the Pan-Blue Coalition, on the other hand, desire a Chinese nationalist identity and are highly critical of the Japanese colonial legacy. In addition, Japanese occupation was particularly harsh for Taiwanese aborigines, exemplified by the brutal response of Japanese troops to the Wushe Uprising in 1930.

Among the Taiwanese plaintiffs in the February 2003 case was the high-profile Gaojin Su-mei (Ciwas Ali), a member of the Atayal Tribe, legislator in the Taiwanese government at the time, and former film actor. As an independent, Gaojin usually aligns herself with the People First Party, which belongs to the Pan-Blue Coalition. Gaojin noted that even though she has not identified any relatives enshrined at Yasukuni, she joined the lawsuit as a part of her fight for aboriginal rights.[80] On June 14, 2005, she led a group of Taiwanese aborigines and attempted to conduct a ritual on the Yasukuni Shrine grounds to remove the spirits of their people from the shrine. Due to right-wing protests, the group canceled the ritual and instead conducted a press conference in front of Lawyer's Hall (Bengoshi Kaikan) in Kasumigaseki, where they also sung a traditional song for spirit retrieval.[81] In response to the decision of the Osaka High Court, which ruled that Koizumi's visits were unconstitutional, Gaojin commented that they were not concerned with the constitutionality issue. "[Whether Koizumi's actions are] constitutional or not is an issue for the Japanese," she argued. "We are not invested in that. Our focus is for Japan to reflect on its past and to apologize and compensate for its actions. We also want Yasukuni Shrine to return to us the spirits of our ancestors enshrined there."[82]

Earlier I mentioned the relationship between the documents that the war-bereaved military families filed for funds under Engohō and Yasukuni enshrinement. Taiwanese and Korean nationals did not qualify for a pension, so they did not compile any documents with the information necessary for enshrinement.[83] If Yasukuni Shrine personnel had conducted its postwar enshrinement based on Engohō documents, how were they able to include the names of Taiwanese and Korean military dead? Transcripts of Diet sessions reveal that there was strong interest in enshrining the colonial dead. Among the heated debates on ways to precipitate enshrinement (during which the possibility of assistance from the Japanese state was often mentioned), the topic of Taiwanese and Korean enshrinement occasionally surfaced. For example, during a session on April 12, 1962, Minister of State and Welfare Nadao Hirokichi noted, "I understand they [former colonial subjects] have not been enshrined." In response, House of Representatives member Ukeda Shinkichi argued that "[w]hether they are Koreans or Taiwanese today, they were members of the Japanese army when they died. How can we allow the fact that these *eirei,* who were Japanese soldiers at the time, are not enshrined at Yasukuni today?"[84] The language used in such discussions suggests that the enshrinement of former colonial subjects did not necessarily have the political motivation of symbolizing colonial power but rather emerged from a strong sense of obligation to enshrine all who died during the war.

It is also clear, however, that Korean, Taiwanese, and Chinese opponents view Yasukuni Shrine as the symbol of Japanese wartime aggression. State support of Yasukuni Shrine is conflated, in these cases, with Japan's refusal to accept full responsibility for and compensate victims of its wartime aggression. This position, I would argue, is a conflation of the issue and the site. The removal of names is an act that should be demanded of Yasukuni Shrine, although given the status of Yasukuni Shrine as a private and religious institution, a lawsuit may or may not be the most efficacious strategy. At the same time, complaints against Japan's wartime actions in these countries should not be directed only against Yasukuni Shrine. The focus on Yasukuni Shrine, even with regard to issues of war crimes, obscures that the fact that the root of the problem is Japan's inadequate attempts at reconciliation.

COMMEMORATION VERSUS MOURNING

The first legal action focused solely on the removal of names from the Yasukuni register occurred in the spring of 2007, when a group of war-bereaved families filed a suit in the Osaka District Court. Prior to filing, the group requested in writing and in person that the shrine remove specific names from the register. Yasukuni Shrine rejected all of the requests. The plaintiffs' main argument neatly follows what Takahashi Tetsuya emphasizes as the main problem with Yasukuni Shrine: the difference between commemoration and mourning. As an expert witness at one of the hearings, Takahashi argued that the shrine's function is commemoration (*kenshō*) rather than mourning (*tsuitō*). According to him, those enshrined were forced to participate in an act that also involved a call to follow in the footsteps of those enshrined. State acknowledgment of Yasukuni enshrinement, then, signified Japan's intent for future rearmament.[85]

For the plaintiffs, commemorating the war dead was a wrongful act. They argued that their relatives died a "dog's death (*inu-jini*)" and that they died without good cause. From their perspective, the Japanese state forced innocent civilians into the military and compelled them to commit atrocities, while not supplying enough provisions for survival in many cases. They took issue with the expression "sincere gratitude," often used in discussion of those enshrined at Yasukuni, and demanded an apology from the state for forcing their relatives to participate in a wrongful war. "I cannot comprehend why being killed would be considered a great deed," noted a Buddhist priest whose uncle drowned when a transport ship sank in the fall of 1944. He believes that this idea resulted from a kind of mind control that was in place during wartime.[86] Some see their family members as both victim and aggressor. For example, Nishiyama Seiichi's father died of wounds sustained in China. He suspects that his father wounded and killed Chinese people. For him, his father was a perpetrator in a war of aggression. But at the same time, he was a victim who was killed in war.[87] Here, too, the demand was for an apology rather than commemoration.

For the plaintiffs, commemoration of the war dead leads to the glorification of war and ultimately, a resurgence of militarism in Japan. Many people think that Yasukuni Shrine continued to commemorate war death in order to produce more people who would die for Japan.[88] Furthermore, many believe that Yasukuni Shrine has no right to retain control over the spirits of their relatives or to use them for propaganda. The plaintiffs argued that the shrine and the Japanese state must relinquish control over the spirits of their deceased family members because they opposed the state's use of their loved ones for the purposes of propaganda.

On February 26, 2009, the court rejected every appeal by the plaintiffs. In the judges' view the plaintiffs did not have a right to deny enshrinement of their family members and the damage the plaintiffs suffered was merely "emotions of displeasure." Moreover, they ruled that there was no evidence of coercion or violation of human rights in the shrine's act of enshrinement without permission.[89] While pointing out that "it is desirable as a social courtesy to obtain an agreement or consent from the family member when someone other than a family member of the deceased conducts an act of mourning etc.," the court added that the family members of the deceased "did not have a right or legal interest to exclusively remember or memorialize the deceased and to reject such actions by others."[90] Furthermore, the court emphasized, Yasukuni Shrine was operating within its own right to freedom of religion: "The act of enshrinement itself is an extremely abstract and conceptual one that involves the deification of gods. As such, it is an act that can be considered as freedom of religion. We did not observe a conflict of interests with others."[91]

It is possible to construe the act of enshrinement as abstract and conceptual. No physical artifacts are involved in the act of enshrinement. If one does not subscribe to the belief that enshrinement collectively deifies the spirits of the war dead, it is possible to argue that there are no spirits at Yasukuni Shrine and that the shrine holds no power over the deceased or their families.

It is also possible to argue that things such as *eirei* do not exist and to ridicule the idea that, after enshrinement, all of the spirits are merged into one deity. Additionally, one could argue that, after enshrinement, it is impossible to remove a specific individual.[92] At the same time, however, the problem of names on the register remains. Journalist Tanaka Nobumasa argues that even though the act of enshrinement may be an abstract one for the shrine, it is not for the bereaved families, who are distressed that their loved one—not an abstract concept—is being commemorated as *eirei*.[93] Tanaka further maintains that the shrine uses the spirits of the deceased in its activities. "Throughout the year, Yasukuni Shrine hosts various festivals of differing scales in order to revere and console (*hōi suru*) the approximately 2,466,000 gods enshrined here."[94] The constitution protects the right of both the individual and the shrine to exercise the right to freedom of religion. Its interpretation does not resolve cases in which two parties are in conflict over their right to religious freedom. Moreover, Tanaka contends that the shrine uses names of individuals without their consent (although the names are never made public) in the expression of its religious beliefs. The different ways in which the various parties respond to Yasukuni enshrinement demonstrate the variety of emotions and interpretations attached to the institution. The incompatibility between these opinions generates animosity both within Japan and abroad. Indeed, they are political issues. At the same time, for the families and others involved, they are more than political issues. Thus, first steps toward resolution are to conceptualize the differences and to formulate ways to negotiate them. These steps require a measure of detachment from entrenched political stances, recognizing that pain underpins both positions and empathizing with the pain of the opposing side.

OKINAWA: THE PROBLEM OF CIVILIAN *EIREI*

I now turn to the Okinawa court case to examine another consequence of the collaboration between the Ministry of Welfare and Yasukuni Shrine: civilian *eirei* who were enshrined in the absence of any association with the Japanese military. On October 26, 2010, Naha District Court rejected a suit filed by five Okinawans against Yasukuni Shrine and the Japanese state. Titled "We will not forgive collective enshrinement from Okinawa (Okinawa *gōshi gattin naran soshō*)" and filed on March 19, 2008, this case demanded that the names of the plaintiffs' relatives be removed from Yasukuni's register and that a payment of one hundred thousand yen be made to each plaintiff in compensation for pain and suffering.[95] The court rejected both demands.[96]

Among the ten names that the plaintiffs demanded be removed from the register were those of seven civilians who were enshrined as *jun-gunzoku* (secondary affiliates of the military).[97] More than half of the 103,565 Okinawan names registered at Yasukuni Shrine as *eirei* of the Asia-Pacific War are those of civilians. Indeed, Yasukuni Shrine emphasizes the fact that it enshrines the deaths not only of Japanese military personnel but also of those who died in war, such as nurses, students who were mobilized for the war effort, and people who were affiliated with the military.[98] The Okinawan case is remarkable, however, because of the disproportionately large number of civilians who were enshrined and because of the presence on the register of people who obviously were not affiliated with the military, including infants and elderly persons.[99] How had this happened? The deification of Okinawan civilians was also a result of Engohō. When it was established on April 30, 1952, Engohō was not applied to Okinawa. But as a result of lobbying by the Association of Ryūkyū Bereaved Families, the government made Okinawa eligible for Engohō in August 1953.[100] Since Okinawa was the only prefecture to experience an Allied land invasion, Engohō was further expanded in May 1958 to include Okinawan civilians who cooperated with or assisted the Japanese military.[101] If a civilian assisted the military in one or more of twenty categories of "war cooperation and war participation" designated by the Ministry of Welfare, the individual was eligible for a pension. Categories included obvious ones such as "participation in direct combat" and "transportation of ammunition, supplies, and injured troops," as well as items that allow for wider interpretation, such as "provision of food items," "offering shelter," "collective suicide," "death due to suspicion of spying," and "acting as a guide." Names of and relevant information about those applicable were entered into the War Dead Questionnaire (*senbotsusha chōsa hyō*). Just like all of the other documents filed in prefectures when a war-bereaved military family applied for a pension, the Okinawan documents were submitted to the Ministry of Welfare and then sent to Yasukuni Shrine.

The expanded Engohō was a valuable system for the Okinawans, who struggled tremendously in the immediate postwar years to rebuild their lives. Numerous residents therefore applied for a pension. Many believed that they could not have raised their children without it.[102] The application process, however, often resulted in retelling and forging personal narratives to make the applicant eligible for the funds. For example, one woman submitted an application detailing her experience of losing two young children when the house they evacuated to was hit by enemy fire. The city clerk advised her to revise her narrative. "People at the Ministry of Welfare are not going to qualify you for funding with this [narrative]. You should write that you evacuated to a cave . . . and that you left the cave when the Japanese military requested you hand over the cave for their operation. You should write that your children died less than twenty-four hours later."[103] The clerk was advising the applicant to construct a narrative in which her children died in the service of the military. The rewriting of the narrative transformed her children from victims of enemy fire to patriots who sacrificed their lives for the cause of the nation.

Such rewriting of the past to qualify for financial support was common practice for postwar Okinawans. These revisions did not occur only in instances in which civilians died due to enemy attacks but also in many civilian deaths in Okinawa that had resulted from heartless operations by the Japanese military. The Ministry of Welfare staff closely inspected these applications and returned the paperwork to the Okinawan municipalities if they determined that the narrative merely demonstrated a kind of passive cooperation (*shōkyokuteki na kyōryoku*). Even at the ministry level, the staff suggested ways to rewrite the document so that the applicant could become eligible for the financial compensation. The following is one such comment attached to a returned application:

> The request for condolence money for a battle supporter (*sentō kyōryokusha*) listed on the attached document was returned from the Division of Inspection. It is assumed from the circumstances of the battle, however, that the deceased did not merely engage in the items listed but also participated in activities included in the "list of eye-witnessed accounts (*gen'nin shōmei jikō ran*)." If the death did indeed result from such active battle support (*sekkyokuteki sentō kyōryoku*), a document by an eyewitness is necessary. It is believed that multiple people would have observed activities such as those included in the list of eye-witnessed accounts at the time. If so, please make the appropriate arrangements.[104]

This comment, while rejecting the application as inadequate, clearly instructs the applicant on specific ways to revise it. The "list of eye-witnessed accounts" refers to the twenty categories of civilian "war cooperation and war participation" mentioned earlier. Many Okinawans who were chased out of the caves where they were hiding were advised to report that they offered their evacuation site to the Japanese military. In many instances, it was the city clerk (as in the case mentioned earlier) or members of the Prefectural

Association of War-Bereaved Families (Ken Izoku Rengōkai) who advised the residents to modify their account to make themselves eligible for the fund. But such acts of kindness resulted in a gross misrepresentation of the civilian experience in Okinawa during wartime. While the Association of War-Bereaved Families considered Engohō as compensation by the state, the forging of the narratives resulted in the transformation of Okinawan civilians into cooperators with the Japanese military.[105] This process resulted in the enshrinement of 55,724 civilians at Yasukuni.

These revisions, while allowing monetary relief for the Okinawans, also left feelings of contempt. "Since I lost my left leg in the war, I am entitled to compensation," said one Okinawan whose left leg was amputated when he was ten years old as a result of a wound he sustained during the war. He applied to the relief fund and qualified by testifying that he had once given a piece of a potato to a Japanese soldier. His documents listed his cooperation as "supplying of provisions." He was unable to come to terms with the idea that he had assisted the military, however. "Engohō's categorizing of a civilian as a [military] supporter aestheticizes warfare," he argued.[106]

The process of crafting a narrative to earn eligibility for Engohō compensation created obstacles to remembering the actual experiences of civilians in Okinawa during the war. As we have seen, many revised their narratives in order to qualify for the compensation. But many others refused and did not receive state compensation. Even though they acted on principle, the experience left them with contempt for not only the Japanese state but also for neighbors who fabricated testimonies and received financial assistance. Whether a family received funds or not created a dual structure among the survivors that produced difficulties among Okinawans to maintain a collective memory of their experience.[107] The revised narratives also enabled the Japanese state to legitimize civilian deaths. According to the official narrative of the Japanese state, these Okinawans died courageously while assisting the military and therefore were recognized by the state through the Engohō, which treated them as equal to military dead.

OFFICIAL HISTORY, CIVILIAN EXPERIENCE, REVISED TESTIMONY

The number of civilian deaths from air raids and naval artillery attacks for all of Japan (excluding Okinawa) is approximately three hundred thousand.[108] But the civilian death toll for Okinawa is close to one hundred thousand in spite of Tokyo's prior knowledge of the Allied invasion plans.

Several factors account for this high civilian death toll. First, civilians were mobilized to assist in the construction of *tokkō* air bases into the last months of the war, and most were unable to evacuate. Approximately 490,000 civilians were trapped on the islands when the Allies landed on March 23, 1945. Further, Tokyo mandated a prolonged battle for Okinawa and ordered the military to seize supplies from civilians. Strategies for Okinawa also eliminated the distinction between military and civilian whenever convenient. Tokyo ordered the "unification of military, government, and people (*gun-kan-min kyōzei kyōshi no ittaika*)." Okinawa's colonial history (the Ryūkyū kingdom was forcefully incorporated into Japan as Okinawa Prefecture in 1879) also affected the military's treatment of Okinawans generally. As historian Ishihara Masaie demonstrates, the Japanese military historically was advised to be particularly wary of Okinawan conscripts as they were ignorant of concepts such as the imperial family and national polity; were lazy, slow, and selfish; lacked integrity; made a habit of stealing; and had low morals.[109]

A large proportion of the one hundred thousand civilian deaths resulted from what is referred to as "mass suicides (*shūdan jiketsu*)."[110] According to the official history of Okinawa, compiled by the Japanese Ministry of Defense, the mass suicides occurred "due to the [residents'] strong belief in the idea of 'all one hundred million as special forces (*ichioku sō tokkō*),' which resulted in their reluctance to surrender to the enemy even as noncombatants."[111] The official history thus presents the tragedy as a consequence of the Okinawan civilians' strong belief in the state ideology, which encouraged death over surrender. But the mass suicides that the official history described as the "noble spirit of sacrifice" were in fact murders of family and friends enforced by the military. Okinawan civilian casualties also resulted from not only enemy fire and willing self-sacrifice but also heinous actions by the Japanese military. According to civilian testimonies, the Japanese troops tortured and killed numerous Okinawans who were suspected of spying for the Allied forces. Japanese troops killed many more in order to steal their supplies or appropriate their hiding places. In short, the term "mass suicide" is a euphemism for Japanese troops' killings of Okinawans.[112]

Similar discrepancies exist for all twenty categories of "cooperation and participation." For example, the category "offering of the shelters" was the euphemism for death due to "exposure to bombardment, machine gun attacks, or gasoline fire" conducted by Japanese troops to take shelters away from the civilians.[113] Such occurrences were particularly common in the heavily attacked southern areas, where lack of access to a shelter was a death sentence. But bereaved family members were instructed to revise the incident in a narrative that suggests that the victim willingly cooperated with the military, evacuated the shelter, and was fatally wounded by enemy fire while searching for other protection.[114] "Offering of food" was a result of pillaging by the soldiers, who did not receive sufficient provisions from the mainland. The reason offered for the accusations of civilian spying is that these persons died to maintain military secrets. (But in fact, they were killed by the military.)[115] The noble civilian "suicides" were, in reality, forced deaths. Numerous testimonies from Okinawa narrate the experience of families and neighbors sitting in a circle, each holding a hand grenade and being coerced by the neighborhood group leader to kill themselves with it. Other accounts by civilians relate that they had witnessed their mothers killing their younger siblings and that the mothers intended to take their own lives after first putting their children to death. The killing of family members, neighbors, and friends in response to the instructions and commands of the Japanese military was also rewritten as "voluntary deaths for the country *(junkoku shi)*."[116] Testimonials documented in Engohō applications belie these tragedies, however. For example, the prevalence of the phrase "mass suicide" rather than "forced mass death (*kyōsei shūdan shi*)" obfuscates the reality of the Okinawan experience.

Thus, contempt for the Japanese military and the state is much stronger in Okinawa than in the rest of Japan. Many Okinawans who encountered Japanese troops during battle regard the military as the enemy for having killed Okinawan civilians and also having forced them to kill themselves. Others, whose family members died as Japanese troops, consider the Japanese military as the institution that forced their loved one to fight and, as a result, to die, only to have their names added to the Yasukuni register. This contempt for the military is compounded by the general mistrust of mainland Japan and by Okinawa's prolonged occupation by the US military, whose policy was to treat Okinawans as non-Japanese.[117]

In spite of this widespread contempt, visits to Yasukuni Shrine resumed shortly after trips from the rest of Japan, with the first postwar group visit taking place on October 14, 1953. Thereafter, groups of Okinawans visited twice a year for the semiannual festivals and, from 1955 on, three times a year, with the addition of summer visits. Okinawa's relationship with Yasukuni Shrine was the same as that of other prefectures. Documents with the names of the deceased to be enshrined traveled from the prefectural government to the shrine. Bereaved family members received a subsidy for travel. According to a Diet transcript on May 23, 1956, a leader of an Okinawan battlefield tourism group testified that "[The Okinawan people] seem to strongly desire the enshrinement of their loved ones at Yasukuni Shrine. Bereaved families have already participated in group tours of 30 or 50 people to pay tribute to Yasukuni Shrine."[118] The Okinawa Area Headquarters of the Association to Support Yasukuni Shrine (Yasukuni Jinja Hōsankai Okinawa Chihō Honbu) opened in October 1957. Personnel from Yasukuni Shrine, alongside representatives of the Japanese state, attended a prefectural memorial service in January 1958.[119] The main hall of Okinawa Gokoku Jinja burned down during the war; its reconstruction was completed in April 1959.[120]

The relationship between Okinawans and Yasukuni Shrine in the immediate postwar years suggests that not all Okinawans held the state or the shrine in contempt. As with the rest of Japan, the surviving family members' feelings about the shrine are as varied as their war experience (were they willing participants, or were they forced to comply?) and their postwar experience (did they come to believe that they were deceived by the government?). Both collective and personal memories of the war also vary based on individual experiences and are further reshaped through official narratives constructed after the war, as well as the creation of personal narratives for Engohō. But Okinawans' colonial and postcolonial experiences added variation and specific emphases in the emotional content of their war memories, further complicating their relationship to the wartime past. For some Okinawans, seeking legal redress is an attempt to hold the Japanese state responsible for the brutality of their war experiences.

THE COURT CASE: A PROCESS OF MOURNING OR PERSONAL POLITICS?

In the "We will not forgive" case, the plaintiffs faulted the shrine for including the names of their family members in the register without their consent and for refusing to comply with their requests for removal of the names. They also sued the Japanese state for violating Article 20, item 3, and Article 89 of the constitution by providing information and financial support for enshrinement without the consent of the deceased's family.[121] They further argued that the shrine and the state violated personal rights such as "freedom of mourning" (*tsuitō no jiyū*), resulting in emotional damage. The plaintiffs had made prior requests to the shrine. For example, on September 4 and November 13, 2007, leader Kawabata Kōzen had requested that the shrine remove the names of his mother, Kawabata Ushi, and his older brother, Kawabata Kōei. The tone of the shrine's response was more strident than it had been in responses to requests made in the preceding decades (quoted earlier): "[T]he shrine does not obtain permission from family members prior to enshrinement. Yasukuni Shrine is entitled to freedom of religion and will not respond to the request for removal of names."[122] The other plaintiffs received the same response to their requests.

Plaintiffs argued that "freedom of mourning" is a personal right. According to the plaintiffs, freedom of mourning should include the freedom of "spiritual work such as the method by which to memorialize a close relative without disruptions from others."[123] They maintained that the shrine was violating this freedom by enshrining their family members without consent, by continuing to reject requests for the removal of the names, and by preventing them from remembering their losses in peace. As victims of the Battle of Okinawa, they argued, they could not bear the thought of their family being honored as *eirei* who served Japan by providing assistance to the former Japanese military, an institution that they considered the perpetrator of violence and injustice against them.[124] Finally, they argued that the enshrinement of Okinawan victims as *eirei* aestheticizes militarism, thus opening the possibility of future rearmament, a position similar to those presented in the Korean and Taiwanese cases discussed earlier.[125] For the plaintiffs, the act of mourning the dead was personal. Thus the enshrinement of their loved ones at the shrine, an institution that shared nothing in common with them, was an act that tremendously disturbed their freedom to memorialize their loved ones.

The defendant (shrine) maintained that the case had no legal standing since the "register is one component of the enshrinement process (*gōshi*), which is a religious act [conducted by the shrine]. Acts such as entering names in the register and making decisions about whether or not to obtain permission from family members are issues that are concerned with the shrine's religious doctrine." The defense argued that the plaintiffs' intent was to obtain a judicial ruling on the doctrine of the shrine and that the erasure of names of the enshrined deities from the shrine register was "a deplorable act that should never be committed against the holy deities."[126] They maintained that the suit should be dropped in order to guarantee freedom of religion. They further insisted that the shrine did not violate the plaintiffs' freedom of religion because the only contact it had with the bereaved family was to notify them of the enshrinement of the dead. The shrine "never forced the plaintiff to participate in the religious activities, rites or events that they conduct, nor do they prohibit, restrict, pressure or interfere with the religious beliefs and actions based on such beliefs."[127]

The court ruled against the shrine's demand that the case be dropped. But the judge's ruling was in favor of the shrine. Namely, although the plaintiffs' emotional distress was reasonable, it would be a violation of the shrine's right to freedom of religion to rule that the defense had infringed on the plaintiffs' legal right due to incompatible beliefs.[128] Thus, the court maintained that if it can be ruled that the shrine violated the Okinawans' freedom of religion through the shrine's religious act (enshrinement of the deceased), then it can also be argued that the Okinawans would be violating the shrine's freedom of religion by interfering with its religious act. The ruling also rejected the plaintiffs' complaint against the Japanese state by accepting the state's insistence that supplying names and information to the shrine was a routine act performed by the government in response to a legitimate request.[129] The plaintiffs accused the court of making a "ruling that covers up the state's crime of glorifying war."[130]

These rulings illustrate the difficulties of using a legal framework to argue a case that can be construed as primarily an emotional one. In these cases the judges used legal reasoning to decide whether the shrine, the Japanese state, or Koizumi had violated the constitution. The rulings on the separation of state and religion, which some courts found Koizumi to have violated, is more straightforward than those on the right to freedom of religion, which matters the most in cases concerning *izoku* opposition to Yasukuni enshrinement. In adhering to the constitution, the court maintained that the right to freedom of religion must be guaranteed to all Japanese, including individuals and religious organizations.[131] However, as a result, all of the parties were left feeling deprived of their freedom.

In the discussion of these court cases, my intention is not to identify problems with the legal procedure. Rather, I am interested in the plaintiffs' personal testimonies. In many cases, their understanding of the significance of Yasukuni enshrinement is what mattered most to them. In the Okinawan case, the plaintiffs opposed the idea that enshrinement of their family members signified that they willingly cooperated with the Japanese military, when in fact they considered themselves victims of the military.[132] In the Korean and Taiwanese cases, the plaintiffs took issue with the idea that their military dead continued to be imprisoned and controlled by Japanese militarism, and, by extension, the living, too, were under Japanese control. The absence of information on the deceased's religious and political beliefs about enshrinement further complicates many of these cases. For example, in the Yamaguchi Self-Defense Forces case, the judge challenged the validity of the widow's using her Christian beliefs to argue her case, given that her deceased husband was not a believer.

Some bereaved families that participate in the lawsuits acknowledge that their enshrined family member probably anticipated Yasukuni enshrinement but insist that if they had lived on into the postwar years, they would have changed their minds. One Buddhist plaintiff contended that Yasukuni took away the Shin belief from his father and his brother. For him, the process of trying to remove them from Yasukuni meant not only deleting their names from the shrine's register but, at the same time, helping to restore their right to freedom of religion.[133] Another plaintiff talked about what his uncle might have become had he lived: "If my uncle had survived, there would been opportunities and possibilities for him to grasp the cruelty of the war that he was forced to collaborate in. But that opportunity has been taken away from him forever."[134]

Many argue that those who support Yasukuni are blinded by the persistent ideology of the wartime state and that they are conditioned by the "emotional alchemy." Sugahara Ryūken, a Buddhist plaintiff who observed Nakasone's visit to Yasukuni Shrine, expressed his disbelief when witnessing other bereaved family members welcoming Nakasone with applause. He argued that since the dead are victims of the state, it is an "inversion (*tōsaku*)" for their families to welcome the prime minister. According to Sugahara, this is because the bereaved families, along with the majority of Japanese, are imprisoned in a "cell named Yasukuni (*Yasukuni no ori*)" without being aware of that fact.[135] In his writing, he refers to this episode to question the bereaved families: "The war dead were forced to sacrifice their lives for the state's selfishness. How can the families allow such a deceitful act?"[136] He repeatedly but unsuccessfully requested the removal of his father's name from Yasukuni. He was infuriated when one deputy priest told him that his father might be pleased about his enshrinement.[137]

While those active in bringing cases against Yasukuni Shrine are justified in pursuing the removal of the names of their family members, they overreach when they criticize the feelings of other bereaved families. Is there only one way to grieve? If Yasukuni's critics demand freedom of religion or of memorial for themselves, should the same right not be protected for others? It is possible that, for many families left behind, the commemorative aspect of Yasukuni enshrinement—the idea that the death was for a cause—facilitated their process of mourning. The issue of Yasukuni is tremendously complex because it is also about memorializing lives lost in a wrongful war. It is a difficult issue to resolve because Yasukuni Shrine is not only a political and legal problem but also a war memorial. Here again, it is important to separate the issues. Japan as a nation and the Japanese as a people are responsible for negotiating a form of reconciliation that is acceptable to the nations and the peoples that they victimized. In the process, it is useful to understand the role Yasukuni Shrine played to promote a collective identity among the wartime Japanese, one that mobilized them for all-out war. At the same time, focusing on Yasukuni Shrine alone obstructs the process of reconciliation. For Yasukuni's opponents, the shrine justifies Japanese people's unwillingness to be held accountable for their nation's wartime actions. For if the people truly were deceived by the shrine, they are not responsible for acting on postwar reparations.

When discussing its postwar history, Yasukuni Shrine refers to Father Bruno Bitter, a Vatican envoy to Japan whom the SCAP had consulted when deliberating on the fate of the shrine. According to the shrine's history, Bitter heroically saved the shrine from demolition by arguing that every nation has the right to memorialize those who fell for a national cause. However, the shrine's statement omits the sentence I quoted in the epigraph: "If it is true that Yasukuni Shrine is the core of State Shinto and the source of a misguided nationalism, what we must abolish is the system called State Shinto and not Yasukuni Shrine."[138] Bitter optimistically believed that Yasukuni Shrine could be freed from State Shinto, with which it was intricately intertwined. Yet the connection between Yasukuni Shrine and State Shinto remains strongly present in the minds of the war bereaved regardless of whether they are opposed to the enshrinement of their family members.

SIX

MOBILIZING MEMORIES

Postmemorial Conservatism at Yasukuni Today

It is
a way of life that constitutes the core of
the existence of Yasukuni.
The numerous *eirei,* who,
since the upheaval that marked the end of the Edo period,
sacrificed their own lives
in order to protect
the independence and dignity of Japan.
Why are the *eirei* noble?
Why is it necessary
for all Japanese
who live today
to understand and respond to
the noble spirit of the *eirei?*

MITAMA O TSUGU MONO *(FILM)*

The film *Mitama o tsugu mono* (To Carry On the Spirit of the War Dead, 2008), the source of this chapter's epigraph, is screened four times a day at the Yūshūkan Museum.[1] As the epigraph's final question suggests, the film emphasizes *eirei* (heroic spirit), a concept invented in the early twentieth century to confer nobility on Japanese military dead (see chapter 3). However, the film's treatment of *eirei* attempts to update the concept for the generations born after 1945, whose connections with the Asia-Pacific War are different from those of the preceding generations. Thus, the film is an important tool for familiarizing postwar generations with the brand of nationalism propagated through Yasukuni Shrine until 1945 and for garnering ideological and financial support for the shrine. The film, however, includes little material from the war years. Instead, it features a seemingly irrelevant item, coffee, which is introduced to forge a positive connection between

Japanese wartime presence in the South Pacific, the sacrifices the *eirei* made during that war, and coffee that Japanese youth (like those presumably in the audience) can enjoy today. By extension, many other contemporary commodities available in Japan today and, moreover, the peace and prosperity that Japanese currently enjoy, are made possible by *eirei*'s wartime sacrifices. I discuss the film in more detail later, but this chapter as a whole examines the ways that beliefs associated with Yasukuni Shrine, exemplified by the term *eirei,* have been repackaged and re-presented in recent years. The film *Mitama o tsugu mono* is one such example. I am interested in the ways that these recent representations attempt to influence the way in which the Asia-Pacific War is remembered today.[2]

Yasukuni Shrine is not alone in the effort to preserve memories of the war. The passage of time since 1945 motivates various groups to engage in activities to preserve and communicate wartime memories, from recording oral history narratives and mounting museum exhibits, to hosting websites and mailing lists.[3] Many of these efforts had begun as early as the 1970s, and the venues offer a range of positions vis-à-vis Japan's role in the Asia-Pacific War—from a revisionist narrative that presents Japan as the savior of East Asia from Western imperialism, to a narrative of victimhood in which Japanese wartime leaders are war criminals and civilians their victims. But, as I argue later, many of the latest repackaging efforts are motivated by concerns other than the preservation of memories.

The concept of postmemory is useful in thinking through the recent representations of war in cultural productions. In recent decades, bearers of Asia-Pacific War memories have shifted from the generation that comprised soldiers and civilians during the war to "postmemory generations," that is, those born after the event (after 1945 in this case) and who have therefore never directly experienced the trauma of an all-out war. However, the postmemory generations are deeply affected by the original event (the Asia-Pacific War). According to Holocaust scholar Marianne Hirsch, who coined the term "postmemory" in her examination of Holocaust memories, members of these generations have grown up "dominated by narratives that preceded their birth, whose own belated stories are evacuated by the stories of the previous generation, [which were] shaped by traumatic events that can be neither understood nor recreated."[4] They inherited the trauma of the previous generation through the environment in which they grew up, via everyday conversations, mass media, visual culture, and education. Mediated by representations, the transmission of memories is neither fully accurate nor complete (as is the case with any relaying of memories). Furthermore, inherited memories of trauma are not comparable to the immediate experience of trauma. But this legacy is significant for certain communities such as the children of Holocaust survivors, whom Hirsch discusses, and children of Asia-Pacific War survivors, whom I discuss in this chapter, since, as I will argue, the inherited trauma can be much more complex and thus sometimes more difficult to negotiate.[5]

In considering memories of the Asia-Pacific War today, it is important to take into account the specificity of time and place, that is, changes that occur with the generational shift, as well as the particularities of the Japanese case. A useful and rich area of inquiry on themes associated with the war experience is the increasingly active production and promotion of cultural works in fields such as literature and visual media. Scholarship on the preservation and representation of Holocaust memories, with its abundance of sophisticated analyses of relevant themes, is useful for analyzing postmemory cultural productions in Japan.[6] While I draw on ideas from Holocaust scholars, I am mindful of the enormous differences between the two situations, which make a direct comparison of Japanese and Jewish experiences both impossible and irresponsible. Nevertheless, theoretical ideas on memory transmission developed by Holocaust scholars are relevant for thinking through the Japanese case.

Much of the more recent cultural production in Japan demonstrates a trend distinct from production associated with Holocaust memories. In Japan one focus is on the creation of a revisionist narrative—the kind that we encounter on the Yasukuni Shrine grounds. Instead of engaging with issues of war responsibility or investigating the reasons for Japan's engagement in an extended military conflict that lasted nearly fifteen years, many of these narratives attempt to reimagine an idealized past, which is eerily reminiscent of the state's propaganda during the war years. According to these narratives, the Japanese war against the Allied powers was for the protection of the homeland. Some go as far as to argue that Japan did not invade East and Southeast Asia as part of an imperialistic war of aggression but rather was attempting to liberate Asian nations from Western imperialism. Furthermore, the peace and prosperity enjoyed not only by Japan but also by other East and Southeast Asian nations would not have been possible without the tremendous suffering and sacrifice of the Japanese during the war years. Such revisionist history, with its roots in wartime state propaganda, has existed since 1945, particularly at Yasukuni Shrine. But I have seen an audience that is increasingly receptive to such narratives in recent decades. For some time now, the intended audience of these narratives has been the postmemory generations; more recently, the authors of these narratives increasingly belong to the postmemory generations.

Not surprisingly, events hosted at Yasukuni Shrine and the exhibits mounted at the recently renovated Yūshūkan Museum now cater to an audience distinctly different from that during wartime and the immediate postwar years. Yūshūkan, in particular, has been completely reinvented as a site to educate postmemory generations in revisionist history. The key actor in these new creations is the Yasukuni Jinja Sūkei Hōsankai (Association for the Support and Reverence of Yasukuni Shrine; hereafter Hōsankai), established in 1998 on the occasion of Yasukuni Shrine's 130th anniversary.[7] A brainchild of then head priest Yuzawa Tadashi and former Imperial Army lieutenant colonel Yamauchi Toyoasa, Hōsankai was to function as a formal support system for the shrine, which, by then, was struggling financially with a decrease in the number of war-bereaved families. Hōsankai has played a key role in the recent initiatives at the shrine to encourage the postwar generation to learn and participate in revisionist history, from the 2002 renovation of Yūshūkan Museum to the creation of associations and events targeting the young. These initiatives are examined in this chapter.

The revisionist trend demonstrated in the Yūshūkan narrative is not part of Japan's mainstream today, but undoubtedly it is finding an ever more receptive audience. The contingency groups associated with the institution, most of whom have experienced the war in some capacity (Izokukai is one important group), have become a key factor in the curatorial decisions made in these exhibition halls. But the trend among the younger audience warrants further examination. One explanation is curatorial strategies that cater to the younger audience, but the relationship between postmemory and trauma is also useful for better understanding this shift. This trend among postmemorial generations is characterized by a need for conservative and redemptive discourse not only to overcome their inherited past but also to evade the issue of war responsibility, which is intertwined with traumatic memories. My aim in analyzing the narratives presented at these institutions is not to critique the narratives for their historical inaccuracies but rather to explore the reasons for their appeal—for both the producers and the audiences.

TRAUMA AND RECOVERY

Before presenting my analysis of the spaces and representations of war, I first address the desire of the postmemory generations to reconstruct, through museum exhibits and other cultural productions, the past that they have not experienced. Theories on trauma are useful here, given that the postmemory generations inherit their previous generation's trauma. Studies and analyses of posttraumatic stress disorder (PTSD) and the process of recovery offer insights into the kind of memory work the younger generation encounters.[8]

Psychotherapist Judith Herman has explained the path to recovery from trauma as a process for victim/survivor to reconstruct the self. This process typically includes working through, or remastering of the traumatized memory. The survivor must transform the traumatized memory—which consists of disjointed fragments—into a coherent narrative that can be told to, and be understood by, others. The production of a coherent narrative allows the survivor to objectify the event and create a sense of distance—a distance that is both temporal and spatial—from the experience. Establishing the event as separate from the current self enables the survivor to mourn the losses experienced in the trauma and, ultimately, to work through the event. This is not an easy process, in part because of the difficulty associated with piecing together fragmented memories of the event and the impossibility of representing and communicating the experience of trauma through language or other means.[9]

The application of trauma theory to postmemory generations raises an interesting problem: What happens in the process of recovery when the trauma is not one's own but is inherited? How does one overcome a trauma that has no well-defined origin, structure, or clear end? This is where attempts to rebuild the past can be useful: that is, rebuilding a tangible past with finite temporal and spatial boundaries that can be acknowledged and eventually overcome. Historian Dominick LaCapra offers insights into this process of rebuilding an unexperienced past. In addressing the process of overcoming significant historical trauma, LaCapra points out the importance of distinguishing between two kinds of conditions in which the object of desire is not present: absence and loss.[10] "Absence" refers to the condition where the object of desire was never present, whereas "loss" indicates the object was present at some point in time. The distinction between the two is important in understanding trauma and recovery since the process of working through a traumatic experience involves reestablishing the self in spite of the loss. In the case of war, the loss may be either concrete (anything from people and objects) or abstract (a sense of security or happiness, for example). Working through and overcoming the trauma of war enables survivors to reestablish their lives without what was lost. For postmemory generations, however, the loss experienced by the parents and grandparents was never a part of their own concrete past. Although it is possible and necessary for the overcoming process to work through, come to terms with, and help one restructure oneself around loss, it is never possible to overcome the nonpresence of something that never existed. In other words, it is never possible to overcome an absence. To me, such an act of rebuilding one's past using inherited memory and recreating the loss is an attempt by postmemory generations to overcome their trauma.

Some members of the Holocaust postmemory generations developed original ways of rebuilding. For artist Shimon Attie, for example, efforts at rebuilding resulted in a series of projections in a Jewish quarter of Berlin. Attie collected local archival photographs taken prior to the Holocaust, identified the exact location at which they were taken, and projected them onto the spot, allowing the images to fill in the void.[11] Another photographer, David Levinthal, created Nazi pageantry using collected vintage German figurines and photographed them to make representations that were his "only historical reality."[12] A number of artists toured and photographed concentration camps, which have virtually no trace of the tragedies that occurred there; others captured images of their own Holocaust-themed interventions in their daily "lifescapes."[13] The creation of an imagined past in ways that can be visualized can function as the first step in the process of coming to terms with a postmemorial trauma.

In discussing postmemorial responses to the Holocaust, James Young explains the creator's motive as a desire to incorporate into the work the "truth of how [the postmemory generations] came to know the Holocaust."[14] Young points out an important component of the postmemorial attempt to come to terms with unexperienced past. But from the perspective of trauma and recovery, that is only part of the motive. More important, it seems to me, is their need to recreate and take ownership of this inherited past that was never a part of their own experience. The graphic novel *Maus* by Art Spiegelman, a child of Holocaust survivors, is useful for understanding this need.[15] A key plot of *Maus* is Spiegelman's relationship to the haunting presence of his older brother, Richieu, whom he never met; Richieu died in the Holocaust, and his parents have never ceased mourning him. Spiegelman's trauma, then, does not involve his own experience of the Holocaust but his having grown up with survivor parents, who remain traumatized by their Holocaust experiences. In order to overcome this postmemorial trauma, Spiegelman first needs to understand the original trauma (that of his parents) and then to deconstruct the inherited one so that he can retell it as his own narrative. The latter process might involve reconstructing the vicarious postmemorial experience in order to contextualize it within the parents' trauma. The development and creation of *Maus* involved Spiegelman interviewing his father about his Holocaust experience as a way for Art, the son, to rebuild the traumatized past—not just his parents' trauma, which he had never experienced, but also his own.[16]

Ideas and findings from Holocaust studies are useful in helping us think through ways in which Japanese postmemory generations have had to grapple with their heritage. But it is unsettling that theories related to Holocaust victims can be useful for our consideration of the Japanese war experience. Like the children of Holocaust survivors, many Japanese born to parents who experienced the Asia-Pacific War in some capacity grew up in an environment similar to what Marianne Hirsch describes: one that is shaped by memories of their parents' experience as well as by cultural productions aimed at preserving memories of Japan at war. And whereas the children of people who experienced the war (whom I call the first postmemory generation) were often surrounded by the traumatic memories, the succeeding generations (second postmemory generation) in Japan were exposed not so much to the memories themselves but to debates about Japan's war responsibilities. Their inherited memories are thus not uniform. Nevertheless, victim consciousness often dominates both kinds of memories. Since the carriers of the memories are, in their mind, victims, theories of Holocaust memories ironically become useful for analysis of the Japanese case.

While a comparison of the structural similarities between the Japanese case studies that I cover and the Holocaust examples that I have outlined is useful in reflecting on ways that trauma is experienced, remembered, and passed on, the Japanese examples of recent war-related cultural productions are distinctly different from the Holocaust case studies in two ways. First, the Japanese examples are typically not on the level of personal trauma and recovery (as was the case with Attie and Spiegelman) but strive for acceptance as a collective memory and are presented through media with possibilities for a wide audience (e.g., textbooks, museum exhibits) and a variety of visual media, including films and comic books. Second, they have increasingly shifted toward rebuilding an idealized past (what I refer to as revisionist history) than maintaining memories of their past. Representative examples here are Fujioka Nobukatsu's Association for Advancement of Unbiased View of History and graphic novels, such as those by Kobayashi Yoshinori.[17] These two differences result from the gap between the victim consciousness that Japanese feel in general and the perpetrator role that Japan played during the war.

The current management regards Yasukuni Shrine as a cornerstone of peace since the peace and prosperity that are enjoyed by Japan today are the result of sacrifices endured by the previous generations (those enshrined at Yasukuni). Accordingly, to offer tribute to Yasukuni Shrine is to show gratitude for their sacrifices.[18] What we see here are attempts to reconceptualize "Yasukuni the site" and construct a new "Yasukuni the belief" that is tailored to the generations born decades after 1945. The goal is the dissolution of "Yasukuni the issue," which can occur only if enough people embrace the new belief.

In the previous chapter I discussed the postwar termination of state support for Yasukuni Shrine and its effects on the enshrinement process. The shrine's identity shift from a national war memorial to a shrine for peace is another consequence of its privatization. Yasukuni Shrine's main source of postwar funding is donations from members of Izokukai.[19] With those generations diminishing in numbers in recent decades, Yasukuni Shrine needs a conceptual makeover to cultivate a new following that will support the institution financially. The shrine administration has put forth a variety of initiatives to engage the postmemory generations in its activities in recent decades. Its motivation is to increase the number of younger supporters and to seize a moment when the conservative faction of Japanese society is gaining ground.

YŪSHŪKAN AS A MUSEUM FOR PEACE

Here I turn to Yūshūkan to examine attempts by the shrine management to popularize its revisionist history through the museum exhibit. Nowhere is the Yasukuni brand of modern Japanese history more apparent than in the post-2002 Yūshūkan. The museum's current exhibit narrates the imperialist history of modern Japan as the story of Japan protecting and liberating the rest of Asia from Western imperialism. In addition to its original postwar role as the repository of mementos that belonged to those enshrined at Yasukuni, Yūshūkan today prides itself on being an educational facility that teaches the younger generation the "true history" of modern Japan.[20] At the same time, the fact that the presentation of a revisionist narrative resulted in an increase in visitors suggests the presence of an audience that is already somewhat receptive.[21]

Hōsankai managed the Yūshūkan renovation project along with other "peace education" initiatives with a view to solidifying a new generation of supporters, particularly from the second postmemory generation. In today's Japanese society, which has long renounced war, the highlighting of virtues associated with war death demands creativity. Hōsankai's message, imparted through the museum, also subscribes to the cornerstone-of-peace concept with a focus on the *eirei* as those who worked to establish this. For example, the message featured on their official website in June 2013 by their president, Ōgi Chikage, urges visitors to contemplate the *eirei,* their experiences and the reason they fought, since otherwise the Japanese "will not be able to reflect upon the progress of Japan—a nation that has developed into one of the key global economic powers—or to appreciate the tranquility and peace we are able to enjoy today."[22] The appreciation for the work of one's predecessors harkens back to the ethical values represented by the *eirei* in wartime Japan. Previously, the Japanese people were to appreciate the sacrifices of the *eirei* for protecting Japan in wartime. Today, they are to be grateful for the peace and prosperity the war brought to Japan. By forging a connection between the war and today, the Hōsankai narrative seeks to renew the value of *eirei* for contemporary society.

The group's founding objectives lament the contemporary situation, in which Japanese society does not demonstrate the proper measure of gratitude to *eirei:* "Propagating such knowledge as the spirit of *eirei* and the vestige of their sacrifice and dedication will contribute to the improvement of the spiritual decline observed today, as it will nurture a sense of gratitude toward the previous generations. It will also function as an educational role in the reacknowledgment of the traditions and the ethical spirit of our country."[23] The group considers its mission to be the ethical education of current and future generations—one that emphasizes reverence for the war dead and equates reverence with spirituality, a doctrine that is very similar to what was propagated nationally during wartime. Since its inception, Hōsankai has hosted symposia and a lecture series, with speakers ranging from university professors and lawyers, to conservative journalist-celebrities such as Sakurai Yoshiko, as well as other figures of nationalist interest, including the parents of Yokota Megumi (victim of much-publicized North Korean abductions in 1964). In addition to the Friends of the Yūshūkan Museum and initiatives for elementary schoolchildren—two programs that target the younger generation, which I briefly discuss later—the Hōsankai has also opened a youth branch (Asanagi) for those between eighteen and forty years of age.[24] Through its two branches (eastern and western Japan), the group coordinates its own lecture series and other activities (such as the cleaning of the shrine grounds, including Yasukuni and prefectural *gokoku jinja*, as well as the Imperial Palace Plaza), which are typically categorized as "voluntary service work (*hōshi katsudō*)." The Yūshūkan renovation, with a focus on education, fits squarely into the Hōsankai's objectives, along with its other activities.

The new Yūshūkan, planned with the blessings and support of the Hōsankai, is markedly different from its former presence both before and after 1945. As I discussed in chapters 2 and 4, Yūshūkan Museum was an integral part of Yasukuni Shrine from its inception in 1882 to September 1945, when the SCAP ordered its closure. The building was then leased to the Fukoku Life Insurance Company between 1946 and 1980. Its rental provided income for Yasukuni Shrine after it became a private religious corporation on February 1, 1946.[25] In April 1961 Yasukuni reopened an abridged display, "Treasures and Articles of the Deceased (Hōbutsu Ihin-kan)," using the second floor of the former National Defense Hall (renamed Yasukuni Hall after the war), the experiential museum I introduced in chapter 4.[26] When Yūshūkan finally reopened to the public as a museum in July 1986, however, the display bore little resemblance to its predecessor.[27] Although utilizing the same space in the main museum building, which at the time of its closure in 1945 so prominently promoted a Japan that was both modern and grounded in tradition, cosmopolitan and ultranationalist, the newly opened museum was but a shadow of its glorious past. The first postwar museum offered a chronological display of objects associated with Japan's modern wars, but without a coherent narrative.[28] The highlight of the exhibit shifted from representations of Japan's military might, such as spoils of war and weapons featuring the latest technology, to mementos that belonged to the war dead. The museum boasted an average of more than ten thousand visitors per month in the initial years, but by the time I first visited in the summer of 1998, visitors were few and far between.[29] Inside an ill-lit and rather dusty series of rooms, uniforms, small-scale weapons, and other mementos occupied old-fashioned display cases.

After the war, the main objective of Yūshūkan became education. According to the first postwar curator, Itō Yoshiyuki, the museum was conceived as an educational facility to promote the idea that Yasukuni Shrine is directly associated with the foundation of peace and prosperity in postwar Japan, where visitors could acquire adequate information for a "correct understanding (*tadashii ninshiki*) of the gods honored at Yasukuni."[30] When the newly renovated and expanded Yūshūkan opened its doors in 2002, the museum had nearly doubled its exhibit space; the number of rooms had increased from fourteen to twenty. A marked change was the exhibit style, which featured methodologies that reflect the newest trend in history museum exhibits. Colorful, large-scale panels present narrative accounts of modern Japanese foreign relations complete with charts, maps, and photographs. The panels also provide summaries in English.[31] The renovation utilized the services of academics and a professional production company. Researchers of military history at the National Institute for Defense Studies (Bōeishō Bōei Kenkyūjo) compiled the information for the historical narrative printed on exhibit panels. Planning and design company Nomura Kōgei planned the exhibit space, following the general direction of the shrine priests.[32] The two focal points for developing the exhibit were educating the public on Japanese military history during the modern period and memorializing and honoring the spirits enshrined. Yasukuni supporters contend that since all of the political controversies surrounding the shrine stem from a lack of understanding of Japan's modern wars, education of the visitors through its museum is an important mission for the shrine.[33]

THE "TRUE HISTORY" OF JAPAN AT YŪSHŪKAN MUSEUM

The presentation of the narrative in a history museum setting—complete with photographs, objects, and panels filled with information—lends legitimacy and authenticity to the Yasukuni version of history.[34] A visitor to the museum enters through a new two-story glass atrium attached to the eastern end of the symmetrical 1931 building. Immediately inside is a large airy entrance hall that features a refurbished Zero fighter plane, a locomotive, and a tank, among other large items. The text describing these objects is telling. For example, the label for the locomotive simply reads "Model C56-31 locomotive." Further information follows in smaller text: "This is a locomotive that was produced in our nation and actively utilized in the 'Thai-Burma Railway,' which connected Thailand and Burma during the Great East Asian War. In the postwar period, it played an active role in regional development as a part of the Thailand National Railway."[35] The text gives no indication either of why Japan was building a railway in the area or of the brutal violence the Japanese military inflicted on the local people and Allied prisoners during its construction. This revisionist tone is consistent throughout the museum. As writer Zushi Minoru summarizes in his unofficial guidebook to the museum, the text in the exhibit is consistent in its message: All wars conducted in the name of the emperor are just wars.[36]

The exhibit proper begins on the second floor, where the visitor arrives via an escalator that overlooks the large-scale exhibits in the entrance hall. The escalator experience is that of ascending, with visitors literally lifted into the airy space toward light that filters through a large window at the top.[37] The light creates a halo around a small statue that stands in front of a glass panel. The statue is simply titled "Statue of a soldier (*Heishi no zō*)."[38] Etched on the glass panel behind it is a poem by the third-century-BC Chinese philosopher Xunzi, which is offered as the description of the museum's namesake: "Travel far and learn from noble people in order to become a man of virtue." Next to the exhibit entrance are two theaters, in which films produced by Yasukuni, including *Mitama o tsugu mono,* referred to at the beginning of this chapter, are screened daily.

The first two exhibit rooms situate the origin of the Yasukuni narrative in the spirit of the warrior. Room 1, "The spirit of the warrior," is dimly lit and features a glass case containing a replica of the marshal's sword (*gensuitō*) in the center, said to have been used by the emperor's guards in the Heian era. Scrolls with calligraphy of classical poems on the theme of noble war deaths hang from the ceiling. Particularly of note is a composition by Nara-period (710–794) poet Ōtomo no Yakamochi, titled "Umi yuka ba," which became the lyrics for one of the most popular military songs during the Asia-Pacific War.[39] The presentation suggests that the spirit of the warrior is the true Japanese spirit. If Room 1 is a philosophical representation of the warrior spirit, Room 2 presents it with objects and narratives from Japan's premodern wars. Featured here are mythical figures such as Emperor Jimmu and Yamato Takeru, as well as historical individuals, including Kusunoki Masashige and Oda Nobunaga. Almost all of the objects on display are military related, as the objective here is to establish the importance of warfare (a civilized and noble war) to nation building as a concept that has been an integral part of Japan's history since ancient times.

In Room 3, the narrative jumps to the modern period, beginning with the encroaching of Western powers on Asia in the mid-eighteenth century. The first wall text depicts the whole of Asia in danger and frames all of Japan's modern wars as resistance to Western imperialism for the sake of Asia rather than the reality of Japan's efforts to also establish itself as an imperial power in Asia. The theme of Asia's resistance to the West is consistent throughout the exhibits. In the following rooms, for example, visitors learn that Japan's earlier wars against China (1894–1895) and Russia (1904–1905) were conducted for the sake of Korea rather than to pursue Japan's imperial ambitions. The start of Japan's military aggression against China in 1931, for example, is portrayed as an attempt to support the Chinese Nationalist government in its civil war against the Communist Party, led at the time by Chiang Kai-shek, and not because Japan wanted to control territory in northern China because of its abundant natural resources. The innocuous name China Incident (Shina Jihen) is used for the undeclared, all-out war against China that was triggered by a skirmish between Japanese and Chinese troops at the Marco Polo Bridge outside Beijing on July 7, 1937. The invasion and occupation of cities such as Nanjing "resulted in peace and happiness in the city," and the atrocities in the city, in which hundreds of thousands of people were brutally murdered, are described as the "identification of the Chinese troops in civilian disguise."[40]

The narrative on the second floor extends to the end of the 1930s so that the entire first floor can be dedicated to the five-year period that Imperial Japan used to call (and conservatives still refer to as) the Greater East Asia War (Daitōa Sensō: December 8, 1941–August 15, 1945). Most of the rooms are composed of a combination of colorful, freestanding explanatory panels; glass display cases that feature uniforms, tools, and weapons that belonged to the deceased; newspaper clippings; and archival documents. The curatorial style of two rooms, however, differs from that of the others. Room 7, "Panorama Hall of the Russo-Japanese War (Nichiro Sensō Panorama-kan)," and Room 9, "Shōkon ceremony grounds (Shōkon Saitei)," offer audiovisual experiences complete with background music and special lighting effects. Room 7 (Panorama Hall) is loosely modeled after the panorama building, a popular war-themed entertainment venue at the beginning of the twentieth century (see chapter 2). Inside the room, the blasting music of "Battleship March (Gunkan Māchi)" is augmented by intermittent cannon blasts and a rousing narrative that starts with "And [thus] Japan stood up (*Nihon wa tachi agatta*)!" On entering the room through a miniature replica of a triumphal arch—a popular commemorative feature of the Russo-Japanese War period—the visitor encounters sixteen minipillars of translucent glass, on which photographs of major military figures are etched along with their rank and accomplishments. Projected on the wall behind the pillars are grainy, monochrome film clips of battle scenes. Although curated along the same principle that features reproductions, the quiet of Room 9 (Shōkon ceremony grounds) contrasts with Panorama Hall. In the center of the dimmed room is a lit-up replica of the palanquin used for the *shōkon* ceremony. To one side of the palanquin is a miniature reproduction of the *shōkon* procession: Priests carry the palanquin toward the shrine building. Recordings of live radio broadcasts of the ceremony play in the background. In a glass case along one wall are items that visiting bereaved family members would have received, such as the invitation card, schedule of events, and tickets. Enlarged photographs of families waiting for the procession cover other walls.[41] While these two rooms offer a contrasting impression to the visitor, the presentation style is similar, as are the visitors' reactions. These two rooms lack the aura of authenticity provided by the actual objects, photographs, and documents associated with those memorialized at the shrine, which are the strength of the Yūshūkan exhibit.[42] Visitors show markedly less interest in the displays in these two rooms than in those in the other rooms, which prominently feature objects that record the scars of war.

Objects, photographs, and documents are key to the narrative presented on the first floor, where the first five rooms introduce the historical context (Greater East Asia War 1–5), and the last four are dedicated to the "Gods of Yasukuni." The narrative portraying Asia as the victim of Western imperialism continues here. For example, Japan attacked Pearl Harbor because it was facing an unreasonable encroachment by the ABCD (America, Britain, China, and the Dutch) forces, not because it did not want to accept Allied demands to pull its troops out of China and Southeast Asia. The narrative presented in this section is consistent with that for the previous wars: Japan is fighting for Asia; Japan is a peace-loving nation whose people were willing to sacrifice not just for their own sake but also for the well-being of the rest of Asia. *Sen-nin bari*[43] and other similar objects demonstrating homefront support, blood-stained flags, and documents featuring wartime slogans and newspaper headlines serve as material evidence to support the narrative presented in the rooms.

One distinct characteristic of the Greater East Asia War section is the focus on individuals. The first example is the "Nine Gods" from Pearl Harbor: the young men who charged to their deaths in the midget submarine mission that preceded the attack from the air.[44] Nine photographs are displayed along with telegrams reporting the success of the mission and newspaper pages with headlines such as "Declaration of War against Tyrants America and Britain."[45] Photographs of the fallen are arranged throughout the display cases along with mementos such as pieces of clothing, weapons, and other items used at the battlefront, as well as handwritten letters sent home. Objects such as caps, notebooks, or flags may have little significance if displayed independently. However, clustered together with a photograph of their deceased owner, along with a short description of his achievements or of how his young life abruptly ended, and an item that records a personal trace of the dead (handwritten letter, diary, last note, etc.), the objects create a powerful and emotional narrative that invites the viewer to identify with the deceased. The practice of viewing these items together encourages the viewer to identify, empathize with, and feel gratitude for these young men and their sacrifices.

The final rooms, named "Gods of Yasukuni," provide a moving experience that make the last and possibly a lasting impression on visitors. Entire walls of each room are completely covered with hundreds of monochrome photographs depicting uniformed faces of the fallen. Each photograph is supplemented with basic and telling information: rank and name (with the suffix *mikoto* to signify their god status), date of birth, location of death, and their home prefecture. Although the date of death is not provided, their birth years suggest how young they were when their lives ended. Freestanding in the middle of the rooms are glass cases containing belongings of the deceased, which encourage viewers to identify with the "gods." Among the objects are several dolls of women in kimonos. The dolls were donated by family members of these young men, who never had a chance to marry. These miniature brides are believed to become wives of the unmarried military dead in the afterlife.[46] In the last "Gods of Yasukuni" room, several areas of the wall panels remain open—as if to encourage those not already mounted to find their way to their final resting place on the walls of Yūshūkan among their fellow *eirei*.[47] Inconspicuously interspersed among the rows of portraits are three photographs of Class-A war criminals, including Tōjō Hideki.

The central atrium, situated between rooms 18 and 19 of the original museum building, showcases large weapons. (Room 19 is a part of the "Gods of Yasukuni" series, but the atmosphere here is markedly different: Although photographs and mementos are on display, the room's distinct feature is the row of high-backed chairs lined up in front of a desk along one wall, where visitors are invited to write down their thoughts in the notebooks provided by the museum.) Notable large-scale weapons include Ōka, a glider plane equipped with an armor-piercing bomb, and Kaiten, a manned torpedo that was used to attack enemy ships underwater. These weapons were a product of desperation in the final years of the war, when little material was available to manufacture legitimate weapons and when human life was considered to be the only viable replacement for the heavy metals required to build fighter planes and battleships, of which Japan no longer had enough. While accompanying panels provide only the technical specifications of these weapons, the way the viewing experience is framed firmly situates these missions within the Yasukuni ideology: that the men who operated these weapons willingly and proudly performed their duty. The thoughts of the more educated *tokkō* pilots—their doubts about the war in general, their knowledge that it was impossible for Japan as a nation to have a meaningful outcome from this war, their resolve to go on the mission for their family—find no place in this exhibit.[48]

The "Gods of Yasukuni" rooms and the central atrium displaying the *tokkō* weapons provide an emotional climax to the museum experience set up by the first fifteen rooms. By the time visitors arrive at these last rooms, they will have seen that Japan has, at least in the modern period, always fought heroically against Western imperialism, not just for the sake of Japan but also, or perhaps more importantly, for the well-being of East and Southeast Asia. In the process, Japan always followed the path dictated by the spirit of the warrior, as presented in the first two exhibit rooms. Early efforts at technological development yielded a series of "successful interventions" geared toward Asian safety and stability, including the "independence" of Korea and the establishment of a multiethnic paradise (i.e., Manchukuo, the Japanese puppet state in Manchuria). A turning of the tide in the 1940s produced an increasing number of young deaths, representative examples of which were showcased in the "Greater East Asia War" rooms and conform to the narrative of a nation proudly sacrificing for the good of East Asia. In the final rooms visitors are surrounded by visual testimony of the history they witnessed in the previous rooms in the form of countless photographic portraits. In the central atrium, visitors encounter the weaponry that aided these soldiers in their courageous final moments.

The last stop in the museum visit is the gift shop, at the corner of the entrance hall. Merchandise available ranges from plastic model kits of fighter planes and battleships, replicas of items from the Japanese military, including hats, flags, and prepackaged food consumed during war by military personnel, CDs of battle hymns and other patriotic songs, and other merchandise and toys from the 1930s and '40s that are not directly related to the war. The selection of books is extensive, ranging from writings by Fujioka Nobukatsu and his cohorts, Kobayashi Yoshinori's graphic novels, collections of the last words of the *eirei* (*Eirei no kotonoha* series), and a wide variety of revisionist history books. Also available are reprints of wartime elementary-school textbooks. The war-themed products here are firmly situated in an atmosphere of nostalgia. Taken in the context of contemporaneous objects such as dolls and tops, the replicas and reprints take on an innocuous quality that evokes nostalgia for the wartime generation and the younger generation's fascination with things retro.[49] I return to this theme of nostalgia later on.

CULTIVATING YOUNGER GENERATIONS OF SUPPORTERS

The renovation initially succeeded in increasing the number of visitors, but museum attendance soon leveled off at around a quarter million visitors a year. The generational composition shifted, however, fulfilling the shrine's key objective in renovating the museum. Prior to the renovation the majority of visitors were war-bereaved families and veterans, who traveled from faraway prefectures on organized tours for official worship at the shrine.[50] Visitors to the renovated museum appear to be mostly of the postwar generation. According to Iki Hiroshi, a curatorial staff member at Yūshūkan, whom I interviewed in 2005, the museum also often receives formal and informal visits from groups of schoolchildren. Iki emphasized the importance of teaching the history of modern warfare, which is not adequately covered in schools except to relay the message that "Japan did bad things at war."[51]

The desire of the shrine authorities to cultivate a larger number of supporters from the postwar generation is also apparent in the architectural design of the 2002 addition to the museum. Unlike the quasi-traditional design of the original structure, the glass and steel addition creates a distinctly modern atmosphere. Three designs were considered for the new wing.[52] The first featured an addition in the same style as Itō Chūta's design; the second a warehouselike design with a brick finish; and the third, the glass and steel structure that was ultimately selected. The design, which bears no resemblance to any of the existing structures in the Yasukuni compound, was not popular with some of the Hōsankai constituencies. One member, for example, engaged in a lengthy, written exchange with the shrine representatives protesting the selected design. The shrine management responded by emphasizing the importance of appealing to the younger generation. Yasukuni's chief of general affairs (*sōmu buchō*), who drafted the response, also noted that the design's openness allowed glimpses of the exhibits and activities within the museum building to serve as an invitation to passersby.[53] The more compelling reason, however, seems to have been the design's potential to showcase the Zero fighter plane and make it visible from the outside to entice young men to enter the building.[54]

The museum also attempts to attract the younger generation by producing and screening feature films. These, too, have narratives in line with the Yasukuni discourse and portray present-day accounts rather than storylines from the 1930s and '40s so that they will better resonate with visitors in their teens and early twenties—the second postmemory generation. On September 1, 2008, Yūshūkan's main theater began screening Yasukuni's most recent film production, *Mitama o tsugu mono*. It is a romantic drama that features protagonist Ishibashi Takanobu, an unemployed twenty-five-year-old college graduate with no particular goal in life: a situation that resonates with many Japanese of his generation. Depicted as an angry and unmotivated young man at the beginning of the film, Takanobu is particularly irritated at his father, a *kigyō senshi* (corporate warrior) whose life revolves around a successful career that sometimes advances at the expense of others. Living in the same household is his paternal grandmother, who is at once a war widow (she lost both her husband and her brother in Papua New Guinea in the last years of the Asia-Pacific War) and a military affiliate survivor (she served as a military nurse). The film thus attempts to represent stereotypes of the three generations that make up the visitor profile of the museum, with hopes of appealing to viewers of all ages and to encourage dialogue among them.[55]

The film follows Takanobu as he encounters Yasukuni and the concept of *eirei* through his girlfriend, Manami. War enters the narrative very slowly, gradually familiarizing the viewer with the concept along with the protagonist. Early segments of the film deal more with issues that might interest Takanobu's generation, such as friendship, romance, family relations, and job prospects or the lack thereof. About a third of the way into the narrative, Takanobu begins to apprentice under Manami's uncle Yasaki Masato, a manual roaster of coffee beans. In conversations with Yasaki, Takanobu learns about the source of the beans in Papua New Guinea, and both Takanobu and viewers are alerted to the relationship between coffee beans and the Asia-Pacific War. Here, coffee symbolizes the fruits of Japan's engagement in the fifteen-year war. According to the film's narrative, coffee production is possible today in Papua New Guinea because Japan liberated the island from Western imperialism during the Asia-Pacific War. Through his interactions with Yasaki, who sternly trains him to become a qualified coffee roaster, and Manami, who works at an institution for people with disabilities, Takanobu begins to respect his grandparents' generation for the sacrifices they made in the war. The film connects the lifestyles of Manami (working to help those who are weak) and Yasaki (continuing to work for the sake of the people of Papua New Guinea, whom Japan had liberated) to the principle of the *eirei,* those young men who sacrificed their own lives for the good of Japan. In short, the two are living a lifestyle of *eirei* in today's context. Takanobu ultimately vows to live selflessly and to follow, in concept, the way of the *eirei*.

In an interview on Channel Sakura, a conservative satellite television network founded in 2004, director Matsuda Takeyuki discussed his goal for the film: stressing the importance of a selfless relationship with others, as that would allow the Japanese to become the kind of people who would be supported by the spirit of the *eirei*.[56] The presence of three generations in the film (grandmother, father, and son) was a way not only to appeal to audiences of all generations but also to create a link between Yasukuni and future generations.[57] The film instructs viewers not only to appreciate the sacrifices made by the *eirei* but also to strive to become selfless human beings willing to make sacrifices (like the *eirei* enshrined at Yasukuni). The film thus evangelizes the belief system that centers on a concept that can be called the way of the *eirei*.

Networks of Yasukuni supporters also look to the younger generation. To mark the grand opening of the renovated exhibit, Hōsankai established the Association for the Friends of the Yūshūkan (Yūshūkan Tomo no Kai), which provides incentives and privileges similar to the Hōsankai at a more affordable membership fee for people twenty-five years of age or younger.[58] For an annual fee of one thousand yen (Hōsankai's annual fee is three thousand yen), members have free entry to the museum (typically eight hundred yen per visit for an adult) and are invited to attend symposia, study groups, and nature camps geared to themes associated with Yasukuni. In 2004, as a part of the association, Yasukuni initiated programs for elementary schoolchildren and their parents, who are also members of the postmemory generation, to participate in. Events for the younger cohort include gatherings for Girls' Festival (Hina Matsuri, March 3), Children's Day (May 5), and Tanabata Festival (July 7).[59] In 2010, for example, approximately four hundred parents and children gathered at Yasukuni for the Tanabata Festival on July 11, the first Sunday after July 7. The children wrote down their wishes on pieces of paper, which they carried to the main shrine, where they received purification and participated in offering a prayer for good health and academic success. After attaching their prayer papers to large bamboo branches on the shrine grounds in accordance with the Tanabata Festival tradition, the group viewed "Family Concert of Singing Pirates (Utau Kaizokudan Famirii Konsāto)" and competed in a "quiz rally" in the museum.[60] The newsletter of the Hōsankai concludes its report on the event with the wish that, by participating in such events associated with traditional Japanese culture, "the children will learn about the honorable spirits of the *eirei* and the correct modern history of Japan."[61] The relationship between the singing pirates and the honorable spirits of the *eirei* was not apparent from the newsletter.

These new initiatives build on existing narratives that target the young generation. "Poppo," a white pigeon, is one such example. During a child–parent gathering on February 27, 2011, to celebrate Girls' Festival, participants viewed "Poppo-Chan Visits Yasukuni (Poppo-chan no Yasukuni Mairi)," a film designed for a young audience. In the film, Poppo the pigeon introduces the shrine and its associated beliefs using simple yet persuasive language.[62] Poppo represents the approximately three hundred white pigeons that are bred on the grounds of Yasukuni. According to the shrine's website, only one out of every ten thousand pigeons is pure white in color—representing peace—suggesting that these symbols of peace naturally chose Yasukuni grounds as their home.[63] While the Poppo video was introduced in recent years, a cartoon version of the white pigeon has long been a staple of Yasukuni Shrine. Pamphlets available at the shrine feature Poppo explaining, in simple language and with phonetic guidance for kanji characters, the significance of Yasukuni and the gods enshrined there. The material is presented in comic-book style with a question-and-answer format, and the knowledgeable Poppo answers the children's questions about the history of the shrine, the meaning of the word "Yasukuni," and the god of Yasukuni.[64] Poppo encourages the young readers to visit Yasukuni in order to demonstrate their gratitude for the god that has protected the peace and independence of Japan and also to pledge to become upstanding human beings (*rippa na hito*).[65] Here again, a good person is someone who shows appreciation for the *eirei*.

The Poppo pamphlet is also available in English, Chinese, and Hangul translations. These versions do not always accurately reflect the Japanese version, however. For example, the Japanese pamphlet refers to the war criminals as "one thousand and several hundred people whose lives were mercilessly taken when they were unilaterally accused as war criminals in the perfunctory trial conducted by the Allied forces that fought against Japan" and whom Yasukuni Shrine refers to as "Showa martyrs (Shōwa *junansha*)."[66] The English version, however, merely refers to them as "people who were labeled war criminals and executed after having been tried by the Allies." Such differences are also evident in the translations of the Yūshūkan exhibit's text.

MITAMA MATSURI: CONFLATING THE TRADITION AND IDEOLOGY

The grand opening of the newly renovated Yūshūkan took place on July 13, 2002, to coincide with the opening day of Mitama Matsuri, the four-day festival that is a major annual event at Yasukuni Shrine.[67] Here again, narratives of the past are revised to seamlessly connect with the present and the future. At first glance, Mitama Matsuri is a typical summer shrine festival. More than two hundred vendor stalls selling snacks and trinkets line the approach to the shrine, barkers stand in front of old-fashioned freak shows inviting visitors to enter, and people clad in summer kimonos participate in the traditional *bon* dance around the temporary wooden stage that encloses the Ōmura statue. Some three hundred thousand people, mostly high school and college students, visit the shrine for the festival each year.[68] The festivities take place in an atmosphere that is markedly different from the politically charged mood only a month later on August 15, the day when Japan observes the anniversary of its defeat in the Asia-Pacific War. At night, the shrine is packed with young couples who stroll up and down the approach, which is brightly lit by rows of thirty thousand yellow votive lanterns,[69] stopping now and then to check out the vendor stalls (see figure 10). Approximately fifty kinds of shows, both traditional and contemporary, take place on the Noh stage on the shrine grounds during the festival days. Little indication of militarism is present, save for some elderly men (presumably veterans) in military uniforms and the occasional singing of war-themed songs.

Mitama Matsuri is a postwar invention. It began in 1947 at the initiative of a young priest, Sakamoto Sadao, who approached the renowned ethnologist Yanagita Kunio with the idea of honoring the spirits memorialized at Yasukuni by reviving certain aspects of the semiannual festival of prewar days. According to an official shrine publication, Yanagita wholeheartedly agreed, noting that "the memorialization of the *mitama* is an extremely important activity that would contribute to world peace.[70] The festival should be joyful and refined (*hanayaka de fūryū*)." The publication continues: "With the support of bereaved family members and veterans' associations, the first Mitama Matsuri, which took place for four days from July 13 in

FIGURE 10. Visitors to Yasukuni Shrine grounds during Mitama Matsuri, July 2014 (author photograph).

the 22nd year of Showa (1947), was a huge success. The festival, which takes place under bright lantern lights, increased in scale every year and is now reminiscent of the *shōkon* festivals from the earlier years, which boasted horse races and fireworks."[71] Just as the festivities succeeded in attracting Tokyoites to the newly established Tokyo Shōkonsha in 1869, so Mitama Matsuri contributed to the postwar reinvention of Yasukuni as a military memorial to an institution promoting peace.

The use of space here is notable. Unlike earlier festivals but similar to the wartime celebrations, Mitama Matsuri maintains the spatial practices of a Shinto shrine. Regardless of the attractions situated along the approach and throughout the shrine grounds, the intended flow of traffic is linear. A typical visit to the festival involves a stroll through the main *torii* and up the approach with the worship hall as the destination—a pattern of traffic identical to that followed by shrine visitors at nonfestival times, where the main objective is to offer a prayer to the gods. After paying tribute at the worship hall the festival-goer might wander deeper into the shrine grounds to take in the entertainment at the Noh stage or visit the Yūshūkan Museum but most likely will return via the main approach and through the *torii*—just like a visitor on a day without special events. This spatial practice, which reinforces the festival-goer's acknowledgment of the space as a Shinto shrine, emphasizes perception of the site as a religious institution for peace, where one's participatory role involves offering a prayer to the gods that protect the nation. Through their own spatial practice, the festival-goers become participants in the postwar version of Yasukuni discourse by creating a spectacle in which they, at least on the surface, comply with shrine conventions that involve a prayer for peace at the worship hall, preferably in the Shinto style of bowing twice, clapping one's hands twice, and bowing once more. By observing and being observed by others acting in a similar manner in this space, visitors reinforce, through a kind of mutual surveillance, the innocuous presence of the site as a shrine dedicated to peace, which Yasukuni supporters wish to endorse.[72] In this context of mutual surveillance, the objective of the visit does not matter since all visitors ostensibly conform to the formal practices expected at a Shinto shrine (linear traffic pattern and properly offering prayer at the worship hall).[73] Just as wartime Yasukuni festivals transformed Tokyoites into practitioners of the kind of nationalism the Japanese state endorsed through the shrine, current festivals incorporate visitors into Yasukuni's presentation of itself as a typical Shinto shrine.

Festival entertainments obscure the politicized nature of the space by highlighting the qualities of a typical Shinto shrine. Present here, too, is an evocation of nostalgia. This invented festival maintains an impression of being a tradition by offering the attractions associated with summer festivals at typical Shinto shrines. Some of the seemingly traditional venues also harken back to the earlier days of Yasukuni Shrine. For example, Mitama Matsuri is well known for its freak shows (*misemono goya*), which are reminiscent of the vulgar entertainment that attracted many Tokyoites in its early history.[74] The central location of the shrine also attracts many visitors. Thus Yasukuni's presence on these four summer nights has little in common with what occurs less than a month later and fuels tension between Japan and the rest of East Asia, as well as among the various political constituencies in Japan.

VICTIMS, PERPETRATORS, RESPONSIBILITY

The significance of the transmission and transformation of war memory in the Japanese case is manifold. Japan's defeat in 1945 was a conclusion to a military conflict that lasted a total of fifteen years and resulted in approximately 2.5 million military and civilian deaths. The massive loss of life and resources was compounded by Japan's defeat as well as difficulties associated with the allocation of accountability. Ongoing debates in the postwar decades have not yet reached a consensus in the social realm on who was the responsible party—the emperor, the Japanese government, or the people at large—or on how to address the issues of reparation (who were the victims? The Japanese state, the Japanese people, the East Asian nations that Japan invaded, or the Allied troops that the Japanese military killed or injured?). The debates associated with Yasukuni Shrine focus largely on whether the Japanese state and/or the Class-A war criminals are responsible for war crimes. In conjunction with this debate it is important to consider the problem of those who need to shoulder the burden of (post)war responsibility, namely, the generations born after 1945, who hold the majority of key positions in society. These generations for the most part are reluctant to accept responsibility for the Asia-Pacific War even when many do accept the notion that the Japanese government and military committed war crimes. As a whole, then, the prevailing voice is the narrative of victimhood: Although wartime Japan was responsible, the individuals alive today are not. In the rest of this chapter, I use the concept of postmemory to briefly explore the possibility that the dominance of this narrative of victimhood should not be attributed only to political explanations and that the unwillingness of the younger generations to assume responsibility for Japan's wartime past can also be understood by employing a theoretical interpretation of trauma and memory.

The postmemory generations in Japan inherited two types of "past" to overcome. The first past is similar to the Holocaust postmemory experience: the suffering and losses of their parents' generation, which have become ingrained in the younger generations through their upbringing and environment. This is the absent trauma that postmemory generations need to rebuild in order to work through it. But the rebuilding process is complicated in Japan due to the presence of another kind of past that needs to be worked through: that of war responsibility. Many members of the generation that lived through the war attempted to evade this issue by allocating blame to the wartime government and the military. This is the "narrative of victimhood" that I presented in the Introduction—a narrative that sharply distinguishes between victim and perpetrator; a narrative that argues that the Japanese people were the victims of their own government and thus bear no responsibility for the crimes committed during war.

Yet the crimes have remained unresolved for nearly seven decades. Inadequate war reparations to the rest of Asia and the resulting international tension make the postwar generations feel that they are unfairly being held responsible for the crimes committed by the previous generation. As a general trend, this feeling of unfairness intensifies the further removed one is generationally from the war experience. The primary trauma for second postmemory generations in particular, then, is not the experience of the war itself or even of growing up surrounded by the experiences of the previous generation but is that of living in the never-ending postwar of Japan's defeat and of being burdened with the task of making reparations for past injustices.

One response to this inherited responsibility is the argument against the need to be accountable for something that happened before one was born. An example of this school of thought is the public comment in 1995 by Takaichi Sanae, at the time a member of the Lower House. Born in 1961, Takaichi argued that she was under no obligation to contemplate (*hansei suru*) Japan's war responsibility since she was not alive at the time of the war.[75] Takaichi's statement drew a variety of responses. Liberal media outlets, including *Asahi* newspaper, condemned her point of view as deplorable (*totemo kanashii*).[76] At the same time, many Japanese people of her generation, including those who acknowledge Japan's wartime crimes, admitted to having similar sentiments.[77] This latter response suggests a trend more complex than that of a generation refusing responsibility for something that happened before they were born. Those who acknowledge Japan's war crimes feel that the Japanese state has an obligation to pay for its wartime injustices but feel no individual responsibility for the war crimes.

The concept of "postwar responsibility" offers some possibilities for addressing the reactionary trend.[78] This concept is concerned not so much with accepting responsibility for the war and its associated crimes as it is with the postwar responses. The "responsibility" in this approach is therefore not for the acts committed during the war but for ending the international discord resulting from unresolved issues of the war, which can be achieved only through reconciliation. The issue remains of who is responsible and why, and scholars differ on this point. Renowned historian and activist Ienaga Saburō argues for collective responsibility that transcends experience or generational group: Given that the postwar generations have benefited from the peace and prosperity built on the Japanese war experience, it is necessary for all Japanese to bear responsibility.[79] Others argue that responsibility is not based on nationality but should be founded on a critical assessment and understanding of Japan's imperial past. That is, the postwar generations should not be forced to inherit war responsibility without rational reasoning or acceptable explanation.[80] The implication here is that if one responsibly learns and thinks about the past, the need for inheriting war responsibility will become obvious. Many scholars have actively and often transnationally contributed to the discourse on Japan's war responsibility in recent years. However, the concept of the people's responsibility has yet to take hold among the general public in Japan.[81]

The revisionist history that I present through Yasukuni Shrine and Yūshūkan are attractive because it absolves the postmemory generation of war responsibility (since there were no crimes or wrongdoings to account for in the first place). Following LaCapra, I argue that the postmemory generations in Japan have been attempting to recreate versions of the past in order to convert their absences into losses. But in the case of such Japanese revisionist narrative, the past that has been recreated is structured in a way that absolves Japan of any kind of responsibility for its actions in the 1930s and '40s. In this revisionist narrative, the past does not require the second kind of overcoming in the form of reparations. In this scenario, Japan has no obligation to address the issue because it never existed. Such revisionist scenarios simultaneously satisfy the need to convert absence to loss by rebuilding something lost and, at the same time, allow a political reinterpretation of the past to fill the void left by the absence of the past, thus absolving the postwar Japanese of responsibility for deeds committed by their nation before they were born.

In the representations offered by Yasukuni Shrine and other mnemonic sites, memories of the Asia-Pacific War continue to be caught between competing interpretations of the past. The generation that experienced the war often seeks a redemptive interpretation of its losses (i.e., those lives were not lost in vain). Some align with the revisionist narrative offered at Yasukuni; others cater to the narrative of victimhood presented at venues such as the Shōwakan Museum.[82] Yūshūkan Museum seeks to attract those who were born decades after the war and who struggle with the idea of war responsibility. Regardless of the narrative, through the physicality of the spaces and the objects displayed within them, these sites of memory have a tendency to solidify a particular kind of war memory.

History tends to be distorted to varying degrees in these spaces, most often through omission. At the same time, what is presented in these spaces and through other forms of media can offer useful lessons for postmemory generations who desire a better grasp of the controversial past. Rather than criticizing versions of the past that do not align with what the viewer considers to be true, exploring the reasons that institutions portray the past in specific ways can offer productive lessons. Multiplicity in representations of the past provides future generations with an important record of the ways that different interest groups interpret the past. A constructive analysis explores the reasons for the existence of competing narratives. A productive approach to Yasukuni Shrine is one that attempts to understand why its versions of history were constructed in the first place.

EPILOGUE
CONTESTING MEMORIES

Yasukuni Shrine as a Countermonument

> As a child I greatly admired the men of the tokkōtai. I don't doubt that their spirit of loyalty and patriotism was true, and I would never want to defame or criticize them. Wartime education was very thorough. It led us to firmly believe that fighting and dying for the emperor was the most honorable deed that we could do.
>
> *A FORMER* GUNKOKU SHŌNEN *(AUGUST 19, 2002)*

> But, you know, nobody believed that we would be honored as gods after we died. I did think that when I die, I could become food for the fish in the coral waters or compost for the jungle trees. I never heard of anyone courageously shouting "long live the emperor" when they died. What I heard instead were accounts of men whispering "Mother" or "Sister" with their last breaths. If they had had the energy to shout for the emperor, they would not have starved to death!
>
> *A SEVENTY-SEVEN-YEAR-OLD VETERAN (MAY 28, 2002)*

On November 29, 2003, under the main *torii* of Yasukuni Shrine, I met up with a group of people ranging in age from a teenage girl to a veteran in his eighties. It was an off-line meeting of a Japanese mailing list that I had been participating in for several years. The main objective of the meeting was to take a tour, led by a list member, of the Yasukuni Shrine grounds and the Yūshūkan Museum. In this short epilogue, I briefly describe this tour as a starting point for ways to think about the shrine's future. Rather than demolishing the shrine or creating an alternative national war memorial to divert attention away from the shrine, creative uses of the shrine grounds can generate opportunities for actively and critically thinking about the issues from Japan's imperialist past with a focus on Yasukuni Shrine as a key institution of modern Japan. I also briefly discuss some of the mailing list participants in order to further complicate the generational structure I introduced in chapter 6 by dividing the "survivor generation" into two: people who experienced the war as adults and the generation of *gunkoku shōnen* (literally, "boys of a militant nation," i.e., men and women who were part of the national school system, which was established in April 1941).[1] The Asia-Pacific War experience differed greatly depending on the age and the location of the survivor. Furthermore, how memory is shaped also differs based on experiences not only during the war but also in the years following the war. And as I demonstrate throughout the book, Yasukuni Shrine is not, and more importantly, never was, a univocal institution for the Japanese: To some it portrays an inexcusably distorted view of the past; for others, its representation of military death helped them through the difficult postwar years.

The mailing list, "No-More War: Mailing List for Maintaining Memories of War Experiences," was initiated by the late Nishiha Kiyoshi (1933–2010), a self-proclaimed former *gunkoku shōnen* who wished to create a virtual space where participants of all ages could talk about Japanese experiences of the Asia-Pacific War.[2] The list member conducting the tour that day was Hasegawa Jun'ichi, four years Nishiha's junior and a retired Shinjuku district assemblyman. After retiring from the public position in 1999 and until his second retirement to his father's hometown, Kanazawa, in 2010, Hasegawa engaged in peace-promotion activities as the president of the Shinjuku Peace Committee and an organizing member of the "Group to Walk the War Ruins of Tokyo [Tōkyō no Sensō Iseki o Arukukai]."[3] Nishiha, in particular, was an outspoken critic of the wartime state and education and frequently voiced his thoughts through his mailing list and other activities.[4] His messages were in many ways similar to those of the writers of his generation, such as Yamanaka Hisashi, a prolific author who writes about childhood experiences in the final years of the Asia-Pacific War and publishes thorough documentation of the war years.[5] Many Japanese of this generation, who attended the national schools as young children and were educated in a curriculum that revolved around the idea of the emperor as god and Japan as a god's nation, experienced a strong sense of betrayal by authority figures, including the government, teachers, and adults in general, with the news of Japan's defeat in the Asia-Pacific War. Their narrative—that they were thoroughly indoctrinated by the wartime state and therefore that not only those in their generation but also all Japanese, with the exception of the wartime leaders, are victims—has been persistent enough to become the mainstream voice in Japan today. The mailing list generally took this tone as well.

I participated in the tour several times, each tour led by a different volunteer, beginning in fall 2003 and most recently in March 2012. With Hasegawa no longer based in Tokyo, a middle-school history teacher or a graduate student of modern Japanese history typically conducts the tours. This Yasukuni Shrine tour is not officially approved by the shrine.[6] Its objective is to "examine the shrine grounds and the museum exhibits from the perspective of Asia as a peaceful community and to think about the problems of Yasukuni Shrine."[7] The guides thus attempt to use the shrine grounds, its monuments, and the museum exhibits as tools to discuss what they consider the "true" history of Yasukuni Shrine, namely, the history of the shrine as the culprit that coerced millions of Japanese to participate in a destructive and self-destructive militarism. This attempt, then, is a use of the shrine grounds as what James Young has coined a "countermonument": a monument that is meant to be self-critical and challenges the very premise of its own being.[8] In his discussions of countermonuments, Young was examining a new kind of artist-designed monuments in Germany (Holocaust memorials for the most part), which challenged the conventional premise of monuments—to commemorate historical events—and attempted to push viewers to think critically about the past. Young was also critiquing the process of monument construction, which, in his opinion, takes away the task of remembrance upon completion. "In shouldering the memory work," he argues, "monuments may relieve the viewers of their memory burden."[9] The Yasukuni guides do not have to construct their own countermonument; they appropriate the space of the shrine itself in order to narrate an anti-Yasukuni version of history. At the same time, both the supporters and opponents of Yasukuni Shrine are allowing the shrine to take over their memory work: Regardless of whether it represents the brave sacrifices the 2.6 million enshrined there made to create a peaceful Japan or symbolizes Japan's past aggressions and desires for future remilitarization, Yasukuni Shrine seems to have only one, correct meaning for each interest group. My insistence throughout this book is that the shrine has had varying and often shifting meanings to the Japanese over the years and that the shifts reflect larger trends in society. Even today it is a site to remember family and friends for some; for others it is a symbol of Japan's military aggressions. It therefore can have new implications and different roles in the future by producing novel meanings and spaces, as I discuss in the Introduction.

Highlights of the shrine tour include various spoils of war and large items donated by Japanese corporations. Rather than boast of Japan's imperial victories, the spoils of war now stand—for the purposes of the tour—as proof of Japan's aggressive imperialism. The donations, such as the stone *torii* at the south entrance and the impressive main shrine gate, demonstrate the large corporations' complicity with the shrine. Most of the items examined on the tour are meant to demonstrate ways that Yasukuni Shrine exercised and, more importantly, still promotes emperor-centered imperialism. For example, the tour always stops at the pair of large stone lanterns outside the main shrine gate. Eight copper panels etched with scenes from key moments of the Imperial Navy (left side facing the gate) and the Imperial Army (right side) encircle the base of each lantern. The traces of dried concrete at the edges of some panels, according to the tour guides, are proof of the shrine authorities' defiance of the city of Tokyo in the postwar period. In February 1947, cognizant of the occupation forces, the Tokyo City Department of Education and the Security Department of the Metropolitan Police Department instructed the shrine to remove these panels. The panels still remain because shrine authorities, instead of removing the panels, covered them with concrete, which they removed at the end of the occupation. According to the tour guides, the panels also reveal the shrine's continued insistence on glorifying Japan's military past.

The most important stop on the tour of the inner grounds is the two small shrines hidden behind tall trees to the left of the worship hall. One is the Motomiya, the original shrine, which I introduced in chapter 1. The other, the Chinreisha, or "spirit-pacifying shrine," is the focus here. According to the shrine's website, this small memorial was "built in 1965 to console the souls of everyone who died in wars that were fought anywhere in the world."[10] It thus seems to be a place for everyone who was not eligible for inclusion in the majestic structure next door and provides the tour guides an opportunity to emphasize the selectivity and politics of Yasukuni Shrine's memorialization process. The Chinreisha was conceived by then head priest Tsukuba Fujimaro after he returned from his travels in Europe, accompanying members of the Peace Mission of Religionists for the Prohibition of Nuclear Weapons (Kakuheiki Kinshi Shūkyōsha Heiwa Shisetsu-dan). The shrine's official narrative is that through his trip Tsukuba came to realize the importance of universally memorializing all war dead. Historian Hata Ikuhiko has suggested that Tsukuba, who was strongly opposed to the enshrinement of Class-A war criminals, may have conceived of this shrine as a resting place for their spirits.[11] But for the tour, the main point of this memorial is its size and location. It is a small, simple shrine tucked away in the woods, out of sight, and does not even have a *torii*. Until 2006, an iron fence prevented visitors from approaching it. The tour guide also emphasizes that its year of completion, 1965, was when Izokukai and the Association of Shinto Shrines were attempting to reinstate state support for Yasukuni Shrine.[12] Thus, in the narrative of this tour, the Chinreisha was constructed to direct attention away from the fact that Yasukuni Shrine is a political space that commemorates only selected people in an attempt to secure state support for itself.

The tour of the Yūshūkan Museum for the most part consists of a close reading of representative wall texts to highlight the one-sided representation of historical events. The selected depictions not only situate Japan as the victim of Western imperialism but also ignore Japan's aggression against its colonial subjects. Although the wall texts are written in both Japanese and English, not all of the information is available in English. This suggests the shrine's attempt to present a message for international visitors that differs from what it tells Japanese visitors. The tour often ends in the central atrium, where larger items are on display, including the Ōka, a *tokkō* glider, hanging from the ceiling, and Kaiten, the manned midget submarine that was designed to collide with enemy ships. The midget sub seats only one person and has no windows. It is operated by relying on visual information obtained through a periscope. It is a "moving coffin in which men were shut in alive," the guide emphatically tells the audience. Constructed during the final years of the war, the tank on display appears to have been built with inadequate materials that could not have protected the man inside. All of the displays are interpreted to support the argument that the Japanese government did not value human life and that Yasukuni Shrine justified reckless decision making by military leaders.

The argument presented throughout the tour posits the Japanese people as victims of their wartime state. This view coincides with the epilogue's first epigraph. The quote is from an e-mail by a list member, who was born in 1933 and indoctrinated as a young boy by the national school system, which was established in 1941. Many of his generation firmly believed the nationalistic lessons they learned in school, one of which was that the emperor was god. And many felt an intensely painful sense of betrayal at the end of the war. Unlike the postmemory generations, which tend to embrace the ultraconservative argument that Japan fought a war of self-defense, members of the former *gunkoku shōnen* generation are, for the most part, extremely critical of the wartime state. They strongly oppose the presence of Yasukuni Shrine and Yūshūkan on the grounds that they reinforce the official wartime narrative, which presents the Asia-Pacific War as a battle to liberate Asia from Western imperialism. Theirs are the voices that most Yasukuni opponents are familiar with. But, as I have argued throughout the book, these voices, which cast the political and military leaders as the perpetrators and the rest of Japan as victims and fault Yasukuni Shrine for Japan's problematic relationship with its wartime past, interfere with the work of coming to terms with the past. This stems from the ease with which critics conflate Japan's war crimes with Yasukuni Shrine. According to this scenario, Yasukuni Shrine becomes the scapegoat. It then is simply a matter of pointing a finger at Yasukuni Shrine as the wrongdoer.

The second epigraph, however, presents a starkly different view. Here, the author is aware that he will not become a god even if he dies at war. Further, he argues that those around him have also never really believed in the ideology propagated by Yasukuni Shrine. How do we reconcile these competing voices? The author of the second epigraph was seventy-seven years old when he wrote the message to the list. Thus, he was born around 1925. Many Japanese of his and older generations did not receive the intensely nationalistic education of the *gunkoku shōnen* generation. They did not go to war because they believed that they needed to die for the emperor and that they would be rewarded with a god status. They went to protect their homeland and their family. For many, enshrinement at Yasukuni Shrine was an inevitable outcome, not the motivating factor. It is said that many promised each other that they would meet at Yasukuni (i.e., after they were killed). If these words indeed were spoken, for many they were an expression of comradeship. But for the most part, the men of this generation, who served in the military and survived to return home, did not talk or write about their experiences. By the time some began to voice their thoughts decades later, many of their generation had died. Although this generation has provided narratives and representations of their war experience, they are less prominent than those about the *gunkoku shōnen* experience. The availability of such narratives today also affects the shaping of war memories.

The use of the shrine for the presentation of a counternarrative is not only an innovative use of the shrine grounds but also a relevant factor in accessing and understanding competing historical interpretations. But the currently prevailing counternarrative, with its focus on Yasukuni Shrine as culpable for the Asia-Pacific War, reinforces the positing of a simplistic dichotomy of victim and perpetrator. There are a variety of ways to push the discussion further to include questions of what it means to be a victim, to be deceived, to be responsible for being a part of something without fully understanding the implications—all in the context of an all-out war. These are useful discussions for thinking about ways to move forward with issues of war responsibility and reconciliation, on both domestic and international levels.

The physical presence of Yasukuni Shrine, as well as the memory of events that transpired there, should stand as a testimony to the variety of Japanese war experiences over time. Furthermore, the competing narratives of wartime Japan, whether personal experiences or larger issues of the roles the Japanese people or the state played in the war, do not have to be used as evidence for one side to condemn the other. Rather, the narratives can serve as lessons for working through the past. Both recognizing and exploring the reasons behind shifts in the prevalence of the kind of memory expressed by the first epigraph, in preference to the kind of memory expressed by the second, help us think about the structure of memory and the relationship between memory and time, between memory and space. Just as media and institutions, including Yasukuni Shrine, variously functioned as institutions of memory keeping in wartime Japan—the kind of memory examined here—postwar publications and museums associated with war memory are now developing into institutions that will similarly shape the memory of postwar Japan for future generations. Instead of a monument to be demolished or ignored because it imparted imperialistic messages during the Asia-Pacific War, Yasukuni Shrine can serve as a reminder of the tumultuous history of modern Japan, facilitate debate on the ways in which the war is remembered over time, and, in particular, become a reminder of the ongoing need to examine the concept of postwar responsibility (*sengo sekinin*) as it applies to past, present, and future generations.

NOTES

ABBREVIATIONS USED IN THE NOTES

FSHSG	Fukoku Seimei Hoken Sōgō Gaisha
KKT	Kokuritsu Kokkai Toshokan Chōsa Oyobi Rippō Kōsakyoku
NDC	Naha District Court
ODC	Osaka District Court
OHC	Osaka High Court
TDC	Tokyo District Court
THHI	Tōkyō Hyakunenshi Henshū Iinkai
YJ	Yasukuni Jinja
YJY	Yasukuni Jinja Yūshūkan
YSSSKI	Yomiuri Shinbun Sensō Sekinin Kenshō Iinkai

INTRODUCTION

1. When the Japanese speak of *sensō* (war) without naming a specific war, they are usually referring to some or all of the battles that involved Japanese military forces from the Japanese invasion of China to the end of World War II (1931–1945). Earlier wars, including the Seinan War, Sino-Japanese War, Russo-Japanese War, and World War I, are normally referred to by name.

The term "Pacific War" (Taiheiyō Sensō), coined by the occupation forces as an alternative to the official Japanese term, "Greater East Asian War" (Daitōa Sensō), semantically fails to encompass the invasions in East Asia. Cultural critic Tsurumi Shunsuke proposed using the term "Fifteen-Year War" (Jūgonen Sensō) in order to include the Japanese aggression in China (1986, 124). More recently, Japan scholars tend to use the term "Asia-Pacific War" (Ajia Taiheiyō Sensō) to refer to Japan's battles on both the East Asian and the Pacific fronts. The term initially covered only the years 1941 to 1945 but has come to refer to 1937 and sometimes goes as far back as 1931. In this book I use "Asia-Pacific War" to cover the entire period of Japan's military engagement from September 1931 to August 1945. For earlier naming of the Asia-Pacific War, see Kisaka (1993).

2. A recording of the song is included on the CD-ROM accompanying Ogawa (2006).

3. Ōe S. (1984, 188).

4. Kokumin Kayō, a daily program on the public radio network, aired from April 1936 to February 1941 as a way to promote patriotism through music. The program continued until August 1945 as Kokumin Gasshō (National Chorus).

5. All military-related deaths in modern Japan were collectively merged into the god of Yasukuni during enshrinement rituals that took place once or twice a year. See chapter 4 for a detailed description of the rituals.

6. Ōe S. (1984, 187–190).

7. Fourteen Class-A war criminals, including the seven that were executed, five that died while serving their sentences, and two that died before the final trial, were quietly enshrined in the fall of 1978. See chapter 5 for details about the enshrinement.

8. Besides Ōe's work, representative scholarship in Japanese on Yasukuni Shrine include Murakami (1974), Zushi (2003), Takahashi (2005c), and Akazawa (2005). Examples of edited volumes on the topic that incorporate voices from inside and outside Japan include Nakano and Jōchi Daigaku 21 Seiki COE Puroguramu (2006), and Kawakami et al. (2006). Journalist Tanaka Nobumasa has written numerous works on topics associated with Yasukuni enshrinement. For English works, see Breen (2008).

Most Japanese scholarly and journalistic works on the shrine are driven by their strong support or criticism of the institution. The supportive stance is taken by Shinto scholars, members or supporters of the Japan Association for the Bereaved Families of the War Dead (Nihon Izokukai), and most members of the LDP. The critical position is maintained by political liberals and liberal intellectuals. Because of their political motivations, these writers often oversimplify issues in order to deliver a more persuasive polemics.

Officials of Yasukuni Shrine try to distance the institution from political debates and accuse the LDP of using it as a political tool. Shrine officials were especially critical after LDP members attempted to remove the names of the Class-A war criminals from the shrine's register. In an interview with journalist Itō Tasumi (1987), then head priest Jin'no condemned the LDP and the Izokukai for demanding the removal of the names so that prime ministers would be able to make official visits to the shrine.

9. For an example of a scholarly analysis of the controversies associated with the memorial, see Sturken (1991).

10. On the significance of commemorating death for the construction and strengthening of national identities, see Gillis (1994) and Mosse (1990). For a collection of more recent studies that examine changing trends in the culture of commemoration, see Homans (2000). In Japan, the Research Center for Memorial and Remembrance (Irei to Tsuitō Kenkyūkai) at Kokugakuin University Centre for the Promotion of Excellence in Research and Education has conducted a series of symposia on the topic. Their research is available in three edited collections: Kokugakuin Daigaku Kenkyū Kaihatsu Suishin Sentaa (2008, 2010, 2013).

11. Since the Japanese language typically does not differentiate between singular and plural, it is tricky to discern how the gods at Yasukuni are counted. In response to postwar requests for removal of names from the register, shrine officials have described that the "god" of Yasukuni is singular although it comprises the spirits of approximately 2.6 million war dead. Shrine officials use an analogy by way of explanation: Once the spirit of a dead person is formally enshrined, it merges with the others into a single god, just as multiple candle flames merge into one. In addition to this many-souled singular god, there exists another god for the two members of the imperial family that are also enshrined there. Yasukuni Shrine refers to each "god" as *za* (a seat). It is important to note here, however, there is no mention of this many-souled singular god in the prewar literature produced by Yasukuni Shrine (see, for example, Kamo, 1911b). It is thus possible to speculate that the idea of the many-souled singular god was invented by the Yasukuni officials in the postwar period to deny requests for disenshrinement.

The Japanese terms used to refer to the individual gods include *gun-shin* (military god), *gokoku-shin* (nation-protector god), and *eirei* (honorable spirits). I discuss the term *eirei* further in chapter 3.

12. Religion was not conceptualized as a generalized phenomenon in pre-Meiji Japan. Thus, the introduction of Shinto was not understood in the sense of "modern Christocentric notions of religion" Hardacre (1989, 18–19).

13. Ōe S. (1984, 190).

14. The Council of Worshipers' Representatives, made up of ten people selected from financial circles and members of Nippon Izokukai (the Japan War-Bereaved Families Association), meets several times annually to decide matters concerning the shrine's management and operation. Yatabe Masaomi, the president of Jinja Honchō (Association of Shinto Shrines), made news in 2006 by becoming a member of the Council of Worshipers' Representatives (*Kyōdō Tsūshin,* October 25, 2006).

15. Until 1945 the military was in control of the events hosted at the shrine. In the postwar years, successive head priests were responsible for making policies on issues such as the Class-A war criminals' enshrinement and the small, supplementary shrine for all of the war dead.

16. The plan to build a new national memorial stalled in 2002 but remains under consideration as one of the few possible solutions to the Yasukuni issue. At the national

memorial service on August 15, 2008, for example, Kōno Yōhei, speaker of the House of Representatives, appealed for a renewal of the process of planning a nonreligious national memorial (*Mainichi shinbun,* August 15, 2008, evening edition). For overviews and analyses of plans and debates surrounding the new national memorial, see Tanaka (2003b), Kokusai Shūkyō Kenkyūjo (2004), and Yamamoto J. (2010).

17. Some argue that the destruction of architecture signifies not just the demolition of a physical structure but also the eradication of its associated cultural meanings. Such arguments are made in the context of the deliberate destruction of enemies' cultural heritage in an attempt to erase history. I am pointing out the problematic nature of deliberately destroying one's own cultural heritage in order to erase inconvenient histories. See Bevan (2006).

18. Examples of studies on the relationship between memory and war memorials include J. Young (1993), Sherman (1999), Winter (1995), Kosher (2000), and Gillis (1994).

19. Yasukuni Shrine is more than a war memorial, and its political nature requires careful consideration. As historian Akazawa Shirō (2005, 2) notes, a key issue surrounding Yasukuni Shrine is whether the monument should have national significance. My objective here is to highlight other kinds of meanings associated with the shrine as a means of appreciating the site's complex relationship with efforts to come to terms with Japan's wartime past.

20. English translation published in 1980. (Halbwachs 1980, 128–157).

21. Theorists have since expanded on Halbwachs' ideas to incorporate the impact of modernity and postmodernity. See, for example, Nora (1989) and Huyssen (1995). For an overview of recent studies on memory, see Olick and Robbins (1998).

22. Halbwachs (1980, 141).

23. Ibid., 154. The city of Hiroshima has proposed several similar ideas for the transformation of its image, hoping to deemphasize its atomic past by demolishing buildings damaged by the atomic bomb. Yoneyama (1999, 43–82).

24. Nora (1989, 7). See also Winter (1995).

25. For an overview of modernist and postmodernist trends in spatial theory, see Harvey (1989, 211–239).

26. Halbwachs (1980, 140).

27. Lefebvre (1991).

28. Foucault (1993) and Lefebvre (1991).

29. My analysis of Yasukuni as a site draws on Lefebvre's theorization of space.

30. Written testimony by Iwasaki Masuko, submitted at the Osaka District Court on April 19, 2002 (Takahashi T. 2005c, 13).

31. Takahashi T. (2005c, 43–45).

32. Gluck (1992, 12–13).

33. Representations of Japanese history in the Yūshūkan Museum are discussed in chapter 6.

34. The word *eirei* was newly appropriated in the early twentieth century to refer specifically to the war dead. This term is examined in more detail in chapter 3.

35. The lack of concern for life apparently not only gave rise to battle tactics that resulted in high casualty rates but also influenced broader strategies that failed to factor in the need to supply soldiers at the front, which led to widespread starvation among Japanese troops. For example, historian Fujiwara Akira (2001) argues that more than 60 percent of Japanese military deaths were due to starvation.

36. For example, Irie Yōko, born in 1935, describes the elementary school system of her generation as "mind control" (2000). Children's author Yamanaka Hisashi, born in 1931, has written extensively on childhood experiences during the war, in part fueled by his contempt for teachers who were engaged in strict imperialist education. After the war they quickly turned to favor American democracy without offering any explanation to their students. Yamanaka's writings are compiled into numerous books, including the six-volume series *Bokura shōkokumin*. Yamanaka (1974–1981). Similarly, throughout the war years readers were fed misinformation by newspapers and other forms of mass media, which collaborated with and were strictly censored by the military. See, for example, L. Young (1998), Yomiuri Shinbun Sensō Sekinin Kenshō Iinkai (2006), and Abel (2012).

37. Adorno (1986).

38. For the social circumstances of Japan during the Allied occupation and the reception of the new constitution, see Dower (1999).

39. Yoshida Y. (1995, 54–55).

40. Adorno (1986, 155).

41. The best-known collection of soldiers' writings, *Listen to the Voices from the Sea,* is a compilation of letters written by student soldiers during the Asia-Pacific War (Nihon Senbotsu Gakusei Kinenkai [Japan Memorial Society for the Students Killed in War], also known as the Wadatsumi Society). Rynn and Quinn (2000) have translated a selection into English. Historian Ōe Shinobu (1988) analyzed some five hundred letters written home during the Russo-Japanese War and notes that in most cases the writer does not refer to the emperor. Emiko Ohnuki-Tierney (2006) also analyzes selected diary entries by student soldiers.

42. This poll was taken before the emperor declared himself human (*ningen sengen*) on January 1, 1946. In the poll, 30 percent felt regret, grief, or sorrow, and 23 percent experienced surprise, shock, and perplexity, while 22 percent felt relief or happiness. Yoshimi Y. (1987, 262).

43. Kitamura (1999).

44. Foucault (1977, 140).

45. Maruyama M. (1969, 84–132).

46. Ibid., 128–129. Here, Maruyama is not referring to Yasukuni Shrine in particular but to the general concept of modern Shintoism, with the emperor at the zenith, who is being revered merely because he is at the top.

47. For analyses of the Tokyo War Crimes Tribunal in English, see Totani (2008) and Minear (1972).

48. Gluck (2009, 97).

49. Lecture delivered on August 15, 1998, at a gathering of the Japan Association for Memorializing Fallen Students (Nihon Senbotsu Gakusei Kinenkai). The transcript is published as "'Sengo sekinin' saikō," in Takahashi T. (2005b, 24–64).

50. The term "postwar responsibility" came into usage in the 1970s, but it has been mobilized since the 1990s, leading to a flurry of publications that use the phrase to explore new ideas to overcome the postwar impasse. For recent discussions on postwar responsibility, see, for example, Ōnuma (2007), Awaya et al. (1994), Taguchi (1996), Takahashi T. (2005b), and Kōketsu (2009). An anonymous reviewer noted that the earliest work with the term *sengo sekinin* in its title was published in 1971 by theologian and veteran Watanabe Nobuo. However, this book is a collection of essays that were published in the journal *Fukuin to sekai* (The Gospel and the World) on Watanabe's war experience and postwar activism, including essays opposing the passage of the Yasukuni Shrine Bill. However, the book's ideas on postwar responsibility are not in conformity with those that have been discussed since the mid-1990s.

51. Valid criticisms have been made of the concept of postwar responsibility. Historian Akazawa Shirō (1989), for example, apprehends the potential for being unclear or insufficiently specific about what one must be responsible for. But I believe that, when considered together with the idea of postmemory, the concept of postwar responsibility is useful. See chapter 6 for further discussions of postwar responsibility and postmemory.

52. YSSSKI (2006, vol. 1, 208–209).

53. Ibid., 208.

54. For a detailed account of Japanese life immediately after the war, see Dower (1999).

55. Cited in Yoshida Y. (1995, 108).

56. Breen (2008, 156).

57. Ienaga (1987, 337–341).

58. Igarashi (2000, 13).

59. See, for example, Harootunian (1999b, 145).

60. *Mainichi* (newspaper), June 21, 2011. The Itami quote is from Ōe K. (1971). I would like to thank Aaron Gerow for posting the newspaper article on Facebook.

61. For a discussion of postmemory, see Hirsch (1996).

62. J. Young (1993).

CHAPTER 1: MOBILIZING DEATH

Epigraph. Kido Takayoshi (1983), entry dated January 15, 1860.

1. Kido (1983, 184–185).

2. Ikeda (1967). Archival documents associated with the construction of Tokyo Shōkonsha are available in the first chapter of the one-hundred-year history compiled by Yasukuni Shrine (YJ 1983–1984, vol. 1, 1–75).

3. Recollection of Kamo Mizuho, the second head priest of Yasukuni Shrine (Murata 1919, 286). Architectural historian Suzuki Hiroyuki credits Ōmura as one of the few people in the history of modern Japan who was capable of urban planning with a long-term view. In addition to his proposal for the urban transformation of the Kudan area, Ōmura predicted, at a time when the land prices of former daimyo residences throughout Tokyo had fallen drastically with the political transition from Edo to Meiji, that the value of the Kudan land would soon rise. Fifty years after Ōmura's prediction, land prices in Tokyo increased to as much as sixty thousand times their original value in areas such as Nihonbash (Suzuki H. 1996, 1–2).

4. The map is included in YJ (1983–1984, vol. 1, 40–41).

5. Diary entry dated June 26, 1869. Kido (1983, 248–249).

6. The temporary structures were situated not at the current shrine location but in the middle of what is today the outer garden (Ikeda 1967, 56).

7. Details of this first festival are included in ibid. (56–58).

8. The permanent structure, completed in 1872, consisted of only the inner shrine in *shinmei* style. The worship hall and corridors connecting the two buildings were not constructed until 1901. The inner shrine was dismantled and refurbished in 1989 for the 120th anniversary of the shrine.

The ceremonies fell on the dates of the four battles that decided the Imperial Army's victory in the Boshin War: January 3 (Battle of Toba-Fushimi), May 15 (Battle of Ueno), May 18 (the Fall of Hakodate), and September 22 (the Fall of Aizu). The two May dates were combined into a single festival. (YJ 1983–1984, vol. 1, 387).

9. For information on early operations of the shrine, including its budget and relationship to the court, see Sakamoto (1984).

10. *Yūbin hōchi shinbun* (monthly), June 1872, italics added. The event that took place in May was reported in June since this was the newspaper's first edition.

11. Aoki K. (2004, 10).

12. Mosse (1990).

13. Ibid., 5–7.

14. Ibid., 70–73.

15. See Hobsbawm and Ranger (1983) and Fujitani (1998b).

16. Representative scholarship on Yasukuni Shrine that includes a summary of its early history includes Murakami (1974), Ōe S. (1984), and Akazawa (2005). A summary in English is available in Breen, "Introduction," in Breen (2008, 1–21). Most of the recent works draw on Murakami and Ōe S. for the shrine's early history.

17. Rituals, from funeral rites to various memorial milestones in the months and years following death, were designed to allow the living to respond to the desires of the dead and, at the same time, establish a boundary between the living and the dead. Even though they were understood as ways to signify to the dead that they now

belonged in a world separate from that of the living, for the living, in fact, they served as a process of mourning (Namihira 2004). This is not an exclusively Japanese practice: As Robert Pogue Harrison notes in his discussion of Western thoughts on death, "[t]he dead like to stay close to the living . . . To realize their fate and become truly dead they must first be made to disappear. It is only because their bodies have a place to go that their souls or images or words may attain an afterlife of sorts among the living" (Harrison 2003, 1).

18. Namihira (2004, 77–79).

19. Nishimura (2006, 56–57). Many other religious scholars and folklorists have written on the medieval practice. See, for example, Gorai (1994, 90), Tamamuro (1963, 79–82), and Sakurai (1984, 9). Sakurai notes that, after the mid-twelfth century, the spirits of the war dead became easier to appease since those engaged in warfare accepted death as the outcome of battle. In fact, the war dead, when appeased appropriately, were considered capable of bringing good fortune to the living.

20. Shinto scholars also have pointed out that, since belief in *goryō shinkō* cannot be observed in the late Tokugawa practices that developed into the *shōkon* ritual of Yasukuni Shrine, the medieval practice could not have been the origins of Yasukuni belief. Tsuda T. (2002).

21. Ōe S. (1984, 120–122). See also Murakami (1974).

22. Ōe references a work by ethnographer Sakurai Tokutarō, *Reikon kan no keifu,* to make this point. Ōe S. (1984, 120–122).

23. For studies on the political use of the dead outside Japan, see, for example, Verdery (1999), Rév (2005), and Ballinger (2003).

24. Nihon Shiseki Kyōkai (1916).

25. Ibid. (vol. 2, 425–426).

26. Prior to the Tokugawa period, the Mōri family, the leader of the domain, was a daimyo of significance, with vast land holdings in the strategic areas of present-day Hiroshima. But when Tokugawa Ieyasu took power, he banished the Mōri family to the western end of the island in retribution for Mōri Terumoto's role in the Battle of Sekigahara, the decisive battle that enabled Ieyasu to seize power. The Mōris had held a grudge against Tokugawa ever since.

27. Ichisaka (2008, 59).

28. For a closer analysis of the text, see Wakabayashi (1986) and Harootunian (1970).

29. When repeating the names of historical Japanese figures, I choose either the first or the last, whichever is more commonly used in Japanese literature to refer to the person.

30. For an English translation of *Taiheiki,* see McCullough (2003).

31. Known today through popular-culture renditions of "Mito Kōmon," Mito Mitsukuni also supervised the creation of *Dai Nihonshi,* a version of Japanese history that legitimizes the Southern Court, an alternate court that Emperor Go-daigo established in Yoshino after fleeing Kyoto in the Nan-boku-chō period. The *Dai Nihonshi*

allows the Kusunoki narrative to be the triumphant one: Kusunoki sacrificed his life for the sake of Go-daigo, who continued his imperial rule from the Southern Court.

32. Kobayashi and Terunuma (1969, 40–43).

33. Ibid., 45–47.

34. On April 23, 1862, imperial loyalists gathered at Teradaya inn in Kyoto to plot a revolt to seize control of the Imperial Palace, only to be placated by Satsuma elder Shimazu Hisamitsu. Nine loyalists died as a result.

35. Kobayashi and Terunuma (1969, 48).

36. Shōin was placed under house arrest for smuggling his way onto an American ship and attempting to travel abroad without proper documents while on probation. After being sent back home, he started a private school for young, low-level samurai and other disciples.

37. There was a belief that the Mōri family was distantly related to the son of the fifty-first emperor, Heizei. Theories also claimed that the Mōri family was related to Kusunoki (Ichisaka 2008, 56–57, 62–63).

38. In 1858, bakufu elder Ii Naosuke led the Ansei purges, in which he attempted to eliminate the loyalists who opposed his political stance, including his handling of the shogunal succession and the signing of the U.S.–Japan Treaty of Friendship and Commerce. A number of men were executed or died in imprisonment; others received punishment ranging from exile to loss of land holdings. Antibakufu men retaliated by attacking and killing Ii on March 3, 1860, in the Sakurada Gate incident.

39. "Deaths in state affairs" is a term subsequently used in reference to qualifications for Yasukuni enshrinement.

40. An excerpt of the relevant section of this imperial order is available in Kobayashi and Terunuma (1969, 30–31).

41. Reimeisha was a shrine founded in 1823 for the purpose of holding funerals (ibid., 55–56). For a detailed account of this memorial service, including the names of attendees and the prayer offered during the ritual, see Katō T. (1967).

42. The men were later enshrined at Yasukuni around 1889 (Kobayashi and Terunuma 1969, 31).

43. Tsuda T. (2002).

44. In attendance at the first Chōshū ritual was Maki Izumi and members of the Kōmyōji faction, a radical *jōi* group that had conducted the first armed attack against foreigners (an American commercial fleet) on May 10, 1864. Attacks against foreign fleets continued in the following weeks. Attacks by U.S. and French battleships resulted in the first Japanese casualties on June 1 and 5 of that year. Thus the start of the *shōkon* coincided with Japan's military demonstration of *jōi*. Tsuda T. (2002, 131).

45. The Sakurayama shrine compound included a site for tomb stonelike pillars. However, partly for practical reasons, body parts or ashes were not buried here: Since the bodies of those who died in battle were buried close to the battlefield, the collective memorial for *kiheitai* could be a site only for spirits. This model was used for regional shrines, as well as for Tokyo Shōkonsha and, later, Yasukuni Shrine.

46. *Shūtei bōchō kaitenshi* 7. Cited in Ichisaka (2008, 128–129).

47. Nihon Shiseki Kyōkai (1916, vol. 1, 182–184), YJ (1973, 5–11).

48. Ōkawa (1980, 78).

49. Tsuda T. (2002, 144).

50. Murakami (1984, 19–22).

51. Hata I. (2010, 25).

52. The official documents of the imperial army were issued while the emperor's relocation was being planned (exact date unknown), and orders were given to research and create a list of all the war dead since the Battle of Toba-Fushimi and to submit the list to Jingikan of Tokyo. The earliest record of construction activity at Tokyo Shōkonsha is Kido Takayoshi's diary entry for March 15, 1869.

53. For example, family members of medical students killed by the atomic bomb while studying at Nagasaki Medical University requested their enshrinement. Nishimura (2003).

54. Hata I. (2010).

55. Kobayashi and Terunuma (1969, 34).

56. Imai Akihiko speculates that this was because Matsushiro and Iiyama, the imperialist clans that were in charge, were sympathetic due to their geographical proximity (Imai 2005, 75).

57. These criteria also changed over time. For example, deaths due to illness were not initially included in Yasukuni Shrine. And as I demonstrate in chapter 5, criteria for civilian affiliates were determined in the postwar period.

58. In addition, Saigō Takamori, who played a central role as a commander of the imperial loyalist army, is not memorialized at Yasukuni Shrine, as he later rebelled against the imperial government in the Seinan War.

59. Hata I. (2010, 17).

60. This land was designated for emergency purposes. Takasugi Shinsaku chose the site due to its resemblance to Shōin's hometown. Currently, Shōin Shrine occupies the site (Ichisaka 2008, 83).

61. Ibid., 84.

62. June 10 to November 6, 1868, according to the Gregorian calendar.

63. In 1987, for example, representatives in Hagi City, present-day Chōsū, sent a request to the city of Aizu-Wakamatsu for a reconciliation to commemorate the 120th anniversary of the Boshin War. Aizu representatives declined, citing citizen protest. *Asahi shinbun* (Tokyo), September 26, 1987, morning edition.

64. Morioka and Imai (1982, 4)

65. Gōda (1995, 100–103).

66. Morioka and Imai (1982, 4).

67. Imai (2005, 31).

68. Not all women took their own lives. Many fought with whatever weapons were available. Others participated in activities such as extinguishing fires inside the castle. For the fate of Aizu women during the Battle of Aizu, see Adachi (1981).

69. Yamakawa Kenjirō, ed., *Aizu Boshin senshi,* cited in Hoshi (1990, 67).

70. Yūzū Temple is a Pure Land Buddhist temple in present-day Ōmach, Aizu Wakamatsu (Imai 2002, 252).

71. Morioka and Imai (1982, 10). For Meiji's tours, see, for example, Fujitani (1998b).

72. Dated September 2, 1868 (Hoshi 1990, 69).

73. Burial, or cremation and burial, is a modern practice. In medieval times, dead bodies were deliberately left out in the open so that they would weather away and disappear. It was believed that, as soon as the rotting body disappeared completely, the spirit would be purified. The quickest method of purifying the spirit was to expose the dead body to the elements or submerge it in water (Gorai 1994, 13).

74. Imai (2005, 43).

75. Machiya Mondo, "Meiji Boshin junansha no rei hōshi no yurai," from Miyazaki Tomihachi, cited in Imai (2002, 253).

76. Members of the Byakko-tai had been called in to help prevent the imperialists from approaching the castle. Failing to do so, they retreated into the mountains. The next morning, twenty of the young men who had reached the Iimori Mountain pass witnessed Tsuruga Castle surrounded by flames. Mistakenly believing that their castle had fallen, they took their lives with their own swords amid a fierce storm. Only one member, Iinuma Teikichi, a fifteen-year-old who had lied about his age in order to join the Byakkotai, survived (Imai 2002, 247–248).

77. According to Imai Akihiko, sources note that four bodies were transported to Myōkokuji and others buried at Iimori Mountain. Yoshida was later released when it became apparent that the burial was conducted at his personal request rather than by an official order from the Aizu.

78. Similarly, it can be argued that, in later decades, the modern military extended its power over family members by controlling the bodies of the military dead. I return to this idea in chapter 4.

79. Machiya Mondo, "Meiji Boshin junansha no rei hōshi no yurai," from Miyazaki Tomihachi, cited in Imai (2002, 258–259).

80. Amida Temple was originally a high-ranking temple of the Pure Land sect, but it was left devastated as a result of two fires. Chōmeiji Temple was the site of an especially fierce battle between the Aizu and the imperialist troops. Historians Morioka Kiyomi and Imai Hiroshi speculate that the imperialists consented to burial at these two temples because of their unfavorable conditions (Morioka and Imai 1982, 8).

81. The designation Special Government Shrine was an early Meiji invention, elevating the status of shrines dedicated to persons who loyally served the emperor in one way or another. The "god" to whom these Special Government Shrines was dedicated ranged from Fujiwara no Kamatari of the seventh century, to Sanjō Sanetomi, who was a member of the Kuroda Cabinet (1888–1889). Some of the shrines were built centuries earlier and were designated as such only in the early Meiji. Others were built anew as Special Government Shrines in the early Meiji. Most shrines established

their designations in the early Meiji. Kitabatake Shrine, the latest to be designated, received its ranking in the Showa era.

82. According to *Yasukuni Jinja shi*, a history of Yasukuni Shrine compiled by then head priest Kamo Momoki, as many as 105 memorials for the imperial loyalist dead were constructed between 1865 and 1870 (Kamo 1911b).

83. The previous year, the government announced that all *shōkonsha* land was exempt from taxes and that it would sponsor all rituals and maintenance related to the shrines (Kobayashi and Terunuma 1969, 65–68).

84. YJ (1987, 113).

85. In 1883 eighty men from Tosa were added. The largest addition occurred in 1888, when 601 men from Chōshū and five from Tosa were enshrined (YJ 1973, 38, 42, 46).

86. Mihashi (1986, 87).

87. YJ (1973, 28).

88. Ibid., 29.

89. Gordon (2009, 85–87).

90. In 1877, at the eighth collective enshrinement, 6,505 were enshrined; 160 in 1878; and 264 who died of sickness while serving in the Satsuma Rebellion were enshrined in 1879 (YJ 1973, 34–38).

91. *Yōhai* is a ceremony in which the participants pay tribute to an object of worship from a distant site. In the case of Tokyo Shōkonsha, these ceremonies paid tribute to the tomb of Emperor Kōmei on January 23 (later rescheduled to January 30), Kashihara, Nara for Kigensetsu (the anniversary of Emperor Jimmu's accession) on January 28 (later rescheduled to February 11), Emperor Jimmu's tomb on April 3, and Ise Shrine for the Kanname festival on September 17 (later rescheduled to October 17).

92. Tenchōsetsu: emperor's birthday. Meiji's birthday on November 3 in this case.

93. "Rikugunshō ukagaisho" (Inquiry from the Army Ministry), dated October 24, 1879 (YJ 1983–1984, vol. 1, 79–80).

94. "Daijōkan Hōseikyoku gian" (Council of the State Legislation Department Bill) dated November 11, 1878 (ibid., 80–81).

95. "Rikugunshō daiichi ukagaisho" (First Inquiry from the Army Ministry), dated December 17, 1878 (ibid., 81). Up until this point, rites at the Tokyo Shōkonsha were conducted by army and navy ministers.

96. The three ministries agreed on the following: Rituals and ceremonies would be conducted in Shinto style and administered by the army and navy ministries; the Ministry of the Interior would oversee the promotion and demotion of priests; all three ministers had to agree on any change in the number or the salary of priests; the army would be in charge of building maintenance; and all three ministries had to agree on any changes to the main shrine or the worship hall.

97. The name Yasukuni derives from "Wu yi jingguo ye," a passage in the Chinese history book *Chunqui zuoshi zhuan,* meaning "creating a peaceful country."

98. The text of the message is included in Ikeda (1967, 67).

99. Murakami (1974).

100. Sakamoto (1984).

101. Kobayashi and Terunuma (1969), Kuwa (1935), Ikeda (1967), and Mihashi (1986).

102. Hardacre (1989, 22, 27–29).

103. Ibid., 47–51.

104. Miyaji Naokazu, *Jinja Kōyō* (1938), cited in Terunuma (1983).

105. For example, a shrine would be built in the spring, and a festival conducted to invite the gods. In the fall, a festival would be held to send off the gods, and the building would be dismantled. Based on Yanagita Kunio's work, cited in Ono (1963, 12–13).

106. Between 1872 and 1878, nine shrines dedicated to historical figures were designated as Special Government Shrines.

107. "Rikugunshō daiichi kyoku ukagai sho, December 17, 1878," cited in YJ (1983–1984, vol. 1, 81).

CHAPTER 2: INSTITUTIONALIZING JOY

Epigraph. The nameless cat is describing a conversation among the women of his household.

1. Natsume Sōseki (1972, 378). In the original Japanese text, the girl calls the shrine "Tokyo Shōkonsha" rather than "Yasukuni Shrine," the name that appears in the translation. I have replaced the shrine name to match the original.

2. Sōseki also refers to the lighthouse and the statue at Kudan in his later novel *Sanshirō*. Literary works that refer to Yasukuni Shrine or Shōkonsha are compiled in YJ (1983–1984, vol. 2).

3. At the time of the restoration, career soldiers constituted 5.7 percent of the population, while 93.4 percent were commoners (Katō Y. 1996, 17).

4. Mosse's idea of the Myth of the War Experience is discussed in chapter 1.

5. Saitō G. ([1882] 2004, vol. 3, 212–213).

6. Ibid., 215.

7. Ibid., 240.

8. *Yomiuri shinbun,* September 4, 1875, morning edition.

9. Although Yūshūkan Museum dates the print as 1868, it must have been completed after 1871, when the lighthouse was built (YJY 1986).

10. The prints I examined are from the catalog "Woodblock Prints of Tokyo's Famous Sites: The Dawn of Yasukuni Shrine as Seen through Woodblock Prints" (YJY 1986) for the 1986 exhibition at Yūshūkan.

11. Aoki K. (2004, 21).

12. Descriptions of these memorials, including names and dates of the rituals, are available in YJ (1983–1984, vol. 1), chapters 3 and 4. Details of the battles and the

names of casualties dating from the restoration to the early 1930s in China are compiled in YJ (1933–1935).

13. Fujitani (1998b).

14. YJ (1983–1984, vol. 2, 49–51).

15. An inquiry by army minister Yamagata Aritomo dated February 2, 1878, requests permission to build a votive gallery on the shrine grounds. YJ (1983–1984, vol. 2, 49).

16. *Nichi-nichi shinbun* (Tokyo), November 22, 1877.

17. YJY (1883).

18. Author interview with Yūshūkan staff member Iki Hiroshi, January 28, 2005.

19. YJY (1883).

20. According to an inquiry by the Army Ministry to the Department of the Imperial Household, dated April 26, 1883, the military requested a loan of weapons for a period of thirty days each. The Department of the Imperial Household, in its reply of May 2, granted a loan of one weapon at a time for a period of one month each (YJ 1983–1984, vol. 2, 60–61).

21. For an overview of foreigner specialists hired in Meiji Japan, see Muramatsu et al. (1995). For a detailed account of foreigner architects hired in Meiji Japan, see Muramatsu (1976).

22. Murai (2006, 4).

23. After the memorial event, a group of sympathizers established a Bronze Statue Erection Committee (Dōzō Zōryū Iin) and sought donations for the construction. Upon consultation with a member of the Iwakura Mission, who studied bronze monuments on his European tour from 1871 to 1873, in April 1885 the committee commissioned sculptor Ōkuma Ujihiro, a graduate of the Imperial School of Art, to create the statue. For the process of the construction, see Murata (1919). Information on the sculptor is available in Tanaka S. (1994).

24. *Nichi-nichi shinbun* (Tokyo), February 7, 1893.

25. It seems that Ōmura is no longer widely known in Japan. One veteran who requested anonymity told me that when he had recently gotten together with his former fellow soldiers (*sen'yūkai*) at Yasukuni, nobody knew whom the statue commemorated. The veteran himself expressed distaste for the imposing presence of the Ōmura statue. E-mail correspondence, July 22, 2003.

26. Hattori (1992, 99–103).

27. Ishii (1908, 482).

28. YJ (1983–1984, vol. 1, 663; vol. 2, 87). The track was five hundred ken, or approximately 990 meters long.

29. Prince Yoshihito visited Yasukuni five times in 1887, including a visit to the Yūshūkan museum on January 29, Sumo tournament on May 8, and another visit on June 18 (YJ 1973, 46).

30. In his entry under "Horse and Bicycle Racing" in the encyclopedia of Edo-Tokyo studies, folklorist Ōtsuki Takahiro credits these events with creating urban spaces that enabled Tokyoites to fully experience modernity (Ogi et al. 1987, 783–784).

31. Yamamoto S. (1971, 32–33).

32. It did not take long for horse races to become gambling opportunities in Japan. In the early twentieth century, the government tolerated the sales of betting tickets in the name of "improvement of military horses" (Ogi et al. 1987, 783).

33. Saitō G. ([1882] 2004, vol. 3, 240).

34. Ibid.

35. Kawabata Y. (1959); Yasuoka (1986).

36. Yasuoka (1984).

37. Ashihara (1984).

38. Masaoka Shiki's comparison of his initial encounter with Yasukuni in the late 1860s with his visit twenty years later is included in Masaoka (1927, 77–79).

39. Katai recalls that when he was a child, the shrine ground was still quite empty, with only young cherry trees and Ōmura's statue to occupy the space. He also notes that the *torii* seemed unnaturally large for the space (Tayama 1981, 68–72).

40. Kubota (1880, 2).

41. Six of the eight cannons were removed in February 1943 and donated to the military. The remaining two have been relocated to the space in front of Yūshūkan, the military museum (YJ 1973, 152).

42. Futabatei ([1907] 1919).

43. Although domestic expositions (*naikoku hakurankai*) held at Ueno starting in 1878 are often regarded as the earliest examples in Japan, the *bussankai* (product exhibition) by Daigaku Nankō (predecessor to Tokyo University) was held on the Yasukuni grounds in May 1871. For details on the Daigaku Nankō bussankai, see Kinoshita (1997).

44. Yoshimi S. (1987, 156).

45. For a history and description of such freak shows (*misemono*), see Markus (1985).

46. The Ryōgoku amusement district was extremely popular by the late eighteenth century. It centered around the Ryōgoku Bridge and had large open spaces on each end as places of refuge during Edo's frequent fires. These open spaces were created after the big fire of 1703. For a description of *misemono* at Ryōgoku Bridge, see Figal (1999, 25–26).

47. A typical panorama building was a cylindrical structure, about twenty feet in diameter and twenty-five feet tall. A dark tunnel-like passageway connected the entrance to a platform situated at the center of the building, onto which visitors ascended via an internal, spiral staircase. On the platform, the view opened up to a nearly 360-degree view of battlefield scenery brought to life by clever uses of perspective and diffused light. The images on the cylindrical wall continued onto the floor, with foreground objects built as three-dimensional models and placed on the floor. Landscapers often installed live trees and bushes. The ceiling, which often incorporated a skylight to enhance the effect, was hidden from view by a canopy placed above the platform.

48. Initially, the icons were the main attraction. But after the 1770s, most of the visitors were attracted by the vendors and entertainers that opened shop in front of the temples (Zaino 1988, 80–81; Yoshimi S. 1987, 154–155).

49. For the relationship between religious spaces and amusement, see Yoshimi S. (1987, 153–157). The use of temple grounds for commercial purposes that profited the temple is noted in Kawazoe (1993, 121–124). For an analysis of Buddhist temples' strategies to increase popular support through entertainment, see Hur (2000).

50. Other sites were Shiba (Zōjōji), Fukagawa (Tomioka Hachimangū), and Asukayama (THHI 1972–1980, vol. 2, 1175–1176).

51. The districts were as follows: (1) Sensōji Temple and Asakusa Shrine; (2) shopping arcade (*nakamise*); (3) training hall (*denpōin*) for the monks of Sensōji Temple; (4) ponds and woods of the park (Ōike, Hyōtan-ike); (5) Oku-yama, where Hanayashiki is located; (6) amusement district; and (7) southeastern part of the park (Haga 1992, 261).

52. When the lack of popular entertainment led to declining numbers of visitors to Asakusa, restrictions on performance were lifted, and performers were given total freedom as long as they stayed within the Sixth District (Takeuchi 1991).

53. The exhibitions in Ueno Park took place in 1878, 1882, and 1891. The fourth national industrial exhibition was held in Kyoto (1895), and the fifth in Tennōji, Osaka (1903). The first private exposition took place on top of Kudan Hill in 1871. The following year, another exposition was held in Yushima Seidō. The Exposition Office (*hakurankai jimukyoku*) was established immediately after this second exposition (THHI 1972–1980, vol. 2, 1139).

54. Yoshimi Shun'ya describes Ueno as the "exhibition grounds for the image of a modern nation-state" (Yoshimi S. 1987, 131–133).

55. Emperor Meiji attended the annual festival of 1874 and the special festivals of 1875, 1877, 1895, 1898, 1906, and 1907. Meiji and his empress also visited the Noh stage several times toward the end of his reign. Hirohito attended special festivals every year between 1937 and 1945 and returned for annual or special festivals six times after the war. His last visit was in 1969 (YJ 1983–1984, vol. 2, 3–8).

56. Yoshimi S. (1987, 157–162).

57. The Ishiki Kaii ordinance regulated two types of minor crimes: *ishiki* (violation with intent) and *kaii* (violation without intent). The Meiji government strictly enforced this ordinance: In 1876, a total of 2,499 people were charged with the *ishiki* crime, and 8,461 people with the *kaii* rule in Tokyo alone (Yoshimi S. 1987, 159).

58. YJ (1983–1984, vol. 1, 25–36).

59. Other places included Asakusa Okuyama (behind Sensōji temple), central Ginza, and Kanda Sakuma-chō (current Akihabara). The series of government regulations focused particularly on chasing performers and vendors away from the riverbanks and bridges, where the majority of amusements and commerce took place during the Tokugawa era (Yoshimi S. 1987, 163).

60. THHI (1972–1980, vol. 2, 1187). A description of a Yasukuni freak show during a postwar festival is included in Yoshiyuki (1971).

61. THHI (1972–1980, vol. 2, 1446–1449).

62. *Yomiuri shinbun* (Tokyo), February 11, 1905.

63. The panorama building was invented by British painter Robert Parker, who obtained a patent for it in 1787. Parker constructed his first panorama building in 1794. These structures became popular attractions throughout Europe from the late eighteenth century to the first half of the nineteenth century. Unlike Japan, the subject matter of European panorama buildings was not necessarily war (Kinoshita 1999, 164–165).

64. An exception was the panorama building at the Asakusa Hanayashiki amusement park, which showed popular tourist sites from around the world.

65. Hashizume (1990, 135).

66. YJ (1983–1984, vol. 2, 270–271). Murakami Tsuruzō was a resident of Kanda Misaki-chō, not far from Yasukuni. He also sent a proposal to Yasukuni in 1903 to host a "sumo offering" (*sumo hōnō*) at the shrine. He proposed operating the Kokkōkan for eighty-seven days, after which the facility would belong to Yasukuni (YJ 1983–1984, vol. 2, 208–209).

67. For an analysis of visual information that the homefront populace was able to receive during the Sino-Japanese and Russo-Japanese wars, see Dower, "Throwing Off Asia," parts 2 and 3.

68. Edogawa (1987, 85).

69. *Jiji shinpō*, August 1–2, 1904.

70. Nihon Panorama-kan in Asakusa, the most popular panorama building, closed in 1909.

71. Hashizume (1998).

72. *Mainichi shinbun* (Tokyo), February 11, 1904.

73. *Jiji shinpō,* September 3, 1904.

74. *Shōkon* ceremonies for the Russo-Japanese War dead began in May 1905, and most were enshrined by May 1907. Altogether, 30,883 people were enshrined in May 1905; 29,960 in 1906; and 24,657 in 1907. The numbers decreased to 1,943 in 1908; 767 in 1909; and 32 in 1910 (YJ 1973, 69–78).

75. *Jiji shinpō,* December 8, 1895. According to the official chronology of the Yasukuni Shrine, the number of enshrined deceased was 1,496 (YJ 1973, 54).

76. *Jiji Shinpō,* December 17, 1895.

77. For example, Nihon Railway Company (Nihon Tetsudō Gaisha) offered a discount of 10–50 percent for *izoku* traveling to Tokyo for a *shōkon* ritual (*Yomiuri shinbun*, Tokyo, March 22, 1906).

78. Ibid., April 1, 1906, morning edition.

79. A 1906 photo album is available at http://www2.kokugakuin.ac.jp/kaihatsu/maa/taisai_thumb1_m3905_01.html.

80. The precise number is not clear from the *Jiji shinpō* articles, as the descriptions are vague. For example, an article dated December 17 notes that "some seventy people attended with invitation cards in the morning [of the 16th], with approximately four people per group," but on December 18 "approximately 130 bereaved [were] in attendance yesterday," and on December 19 "the number of bereaved (*izoku*) in attendance yesterday was 77, with an estimate of 280 to 290 including family members." It is thus unclear whether the numbers on the first and second days indicate the number of invitations or the total number of visitors related to the enshrined.

81. *Jiji shinpō,* May 4, 1905.

82. Carol Gluck places the emergence of the so-called emperor system ideology at around 1890 (Gluck 1985, 17–21). Takashi Fujitani notes that Tokyo was not considered an imperial capital in the early Meiji years, as Edo castle burned down in a 1873 fire and was not reconstructed as the Imperial Palace until 1884, and the emperor was mostly absent from the capital on his frequent tours throughout the country (Fujitani 1998b, 31–92). Helen Hardacre also argues that Shinto in the early Meiji period underwent many organizational changes and did not increase its influence until after the Russo-Japanese War. In fact, during the Meiji period Shinto had not yet fully achieved its status as a national rite, nor was its ideological content (as opposed to its popular ritual practice) yet recognized by the general public (Hardacre 1989, 21–27; see also Gluck 1985, 138–143).

83. *Miyako shinbun,* December 15, 1895. Cited in Fujitani (1998b, 198).

84. *Kokumin shinbun,* May 6, 1906. Cited in Fujitani (1998b, 198).

85. Hardacre (1989, 109).

86. Fujitani (1998b, 214).

CHAPTER 3: NETWORKS OF GRIEF AND PRIDE

1. Ubukata ([1926] 1978, 47).

2. Ibid., 167.

3. Kagotani (1994, 133–138).

4. Koizumi (1928, 249–255).

5. It is also possible that the student, on seeing his former mentor on his way to active duty, merely expressed what he had been instructed to say. I explore this kind of coerced (or institutionalized) behavior in chapter 4.

6. Initially, only those who were killed in action or those who died as a result of wounds sustained on the battlefield were eligible for enshrinement. Due to the large number of deaths resulting from illness during the Sino-Japanese War, however, the Army Ministry announced in 1898 that men who died as a consequence of illness contracted during active duty during the war would be eligible for enshrinement at Yasukuni Shrine (Hata I. 2010, 55–57).

7. For scholarly analyses of conscription in modern Japan, see Ōe (1981), Katō Y. (1996), Kitamura (1999), and Harada (2001).

8. Conscription was managed at the local level in town and village halls and based on the existing family register system (*koseki*), with additional information required of each household.

9. Requirements for conscription, including age, changed frequently in the early years but for the most part remained at twenty. It was lowered to nineteen in 1943. Katō Y. (1996, 46–50).

10. Harada (2001, 30–31).

11. George Mosse also discusses ways in which soldiering was presented in interwar Europe as an attainable and much admired profession (Mosse 1990, 19).

12. The lottery was eliminated in March 1939 (Kitamura 1999, 11).

13. Ōe (1981, 128).

14. Men between seventeen and nineteen years of age were considered auxiliary members of the military.

15. The data were recorded with such detail that one historian researching surviving records even noted that "It is probably impossible today, even at the government or corporate level, to compile personal information in such detail." Cited in Harada (2001, 37–38).

16. I continue with Ubukata's narrative as one case study worth examining. Other works that examine the use of everyday culture to promote nationalism and rationalize the Sino-Japanese War include Inui (2008), Ōtani and Harada (1994), and Keene (1971).

17. Dower, "Throwing Off Asia II."

18. Ubukata ([1926] 1978, 41).

19. Inui (2008).

20. Ubukata ([1926] 1978, 37–38).

21. Iguchi (1998, 151).

22. *San'in shinbun,* April 24, 1895; cited in Kitamura (1999, 18).

23. Some areas formed military-related associations even before the Sino-Japanese War. In Sakai City, Osaka, for example, the local military affairs association (*heiji-kai*) was formed as early as May 1888. By the time of the Russo-Japanese War, the city had thirteen such associations that could engage in a variety of war-related activities from celebrations to funerals (Iguchi 1998, 140).

24. Ibid., 148.

25. *Yomiuri shinbun,* March 1, 1904.

26. Ibid., March 2 and 3, 1904.

27. Ibid., June 23, 1904.

28. Ibid., March 3, 1904.

29. Iguchi (1998, 138–139).

30. Kagotani (1994, 135).

31. Iguchi (1998, 145–146).

32. Harada (2001, 243–250).

33. The total number of war-related deaths for conscripts in the Sino-Japanese War was 13,488, with the national population around 42.27 million.

34. Approximately eighty-four thousand troops lost their lives during the Russo-Japanese War.

35. Tanakamaru (2002, 94).

36. Kagotani (1994, 135).

37. Oral history interview conducted by ethnologist Tanakamaru Katsuhiko in Ichigi County, Nagasaki Prefecture; cited in Tanakamaru (2002, 34–36).

38. Ibid., 52–53, 95.

39. The government required each institution to submit a document requesting the portrait in order to obtain one, which all public schools and municipal institutions in fact were required to own. Initially, distribution of the portrait was limited. In the case of schools, distribution started with the normal schools for teacher training, after which it expanded to include high schools and, finally, elementary schools. Even in elementary schools, distribution began with schools of excellence. This method of distribution turned the portrait into a valued commodity and created a strong desire among schools to receive the portrait. Schoolmasters eagerly sent their request as soon as their school became eligible. Through this calculated distribution, the state fabricated the impression that the portrait was not imposed but was something that the schools sought and were grateful to receive (Taki 1988). For a historical survey and analyses of the Imperial Rescript on Education, see Soeda (1997) and Umetani (2000).

40. Most textbooks published in modern Japan, including all government-produced textbooks for every subject published between 1904 and 1941, are reprinted in their entirety in Kaigo (1961–1967). For an analysis of Yasukuni Shrine in textbooks, see Kitajima (2013).

41. *Jinjō shōgaku shūshinsho* 4 (2nd ed.), chapter 4 (Kaigo 1961–1967, vol. 3, 86).

42. Guidebooks designed for elementary school trips typically included Yasukuni Shrine on the list of possible places to visit. One example is Yamada K. (1990).

43. Yamamoto and Imano (1976, 307–313).

44. Works examined here include writings by folklorist Yanagita Kunio, along with more recent interpretations by Japanese historians and cultural anthropologists. Yanagita rarely gave a specific time frame or location for his descriptions of "local" and "folk" customs. He was trying to create an image of a timeless, unchanging view of the Japanese countryside as part of his attempt to critique the government's policies for modernization at the expense of rural areas. Although Yanagita is often criticized for constructing narratives that concerned, in the words of Harry Harootunian, "a no-place, neither here nor there, past nor present, true nor false," his works on death and the afterlife, such as *Nihon no matsuri* [Japanese Festivals] and *Senzo no hanashi* [The Story of Our Ancestors], are useful for understanding the kind of customs many people

in modern Japan nostalgically assumed to represent "the way things used to be." I believe that the ideology of the family nation and Yasukuni memorialization were successful in part because of their appropriation of such longings and nostalgia (Harootunian 1999a, 107). My work is also informed by works that critically drew on Yanagita's studies on death and the afterlife, including Kamishima (1961), Yasumaru (2001), Itō M. (1982), and Tanakamaru (2002).

45. Not coincidentally, the Japanese term for nation-state, *kokka,* uses the characters "country" and "family."

46. The mortuary tablet (*ihai*) is a wooden plaque inscribed with the dead's posthumous Buddhist name (*kaimyō*) that is typically placed on the family Buddhist altar. It was believed that as long as the tablet remained intact, the *ie* could be reestablished (Kamishima 1961, 263).

47. Kawamura (2000, 51–71). See also Itō M. (1982).

48. Itō Mikiharu believes that the concept of nation-state, which situated the emperor as the father figure, was easily and widely accepted in Meiji Japan because the traditional family structure, led by the father figure (*kafuchō-sei*), existed not only in the warrior class but also in agricultural communities (Itō M. 1982, 56–57). Fujita Shōzō argues that wars were necessary in modern Japan in order to reinforce the relationship between *ie* and the state (Fujita S. 1998, 1–12).

49. Irokawa Daikichi lists the imperial myth, the religious tradition of ancestor worship, the social structure of the family system, and the customary heritage of folk morality as the elements used to join the household (*ie*) to the nation (*kuni*) (Irokawa 1985, 282–283).

50. Even though the family register system was first introduced as early as 1872, it was not until the late 1870s and early 1880s that the register system started to take on an administrative function, thus connecting the *ie* unit to the nation-state unit (Itō M. 1982, 4–5).

51. Inoue (1891, 17–32).

52. Yasukuni Shrine also received considerable attention for the first time in the second edition of the ethics textbooks. Reprints of the ethics textbooks are included in Kaigo (1961–1967, vol. 3).

53. Karasawa (1989, 285–286). Kawamura Kunimitsu analyzed second-edition textbooks for all six grades and concluded that topics on ethical values concerning the state (the emperor and the national polity) and *ie*-related values had increased dramatically in comparison to the content of the first edition. According to Kawamura, a similar trend could be observed in the language textbooks (Kawamura 1990, 177–178).

54. Morioka (1977, 188).

55. Hozumi Yatsuka, *"Ie" no hōriteki kannen* (1898), cited in Itō M. (1982, 14–15).

56. The term *eirei* does not appear in the *Genkai* dictionary of 1889. The *Dai-Genkai* of 1929 defines *eirei* as the spirit of a great man. In 1932 *Jien* lists the definition as the spirit of a superior man. In postwar dictionaries, however, the definition of *eirei* is restricted to members of the military killed in war (Tanakamaru 2002, 13–14).

57. Tanakamaru (2002, 15–16). In Tanakamaru's examples, the word *eirei* is used to supplement, not replace, the words "war dead."

58. Kamo (1911b, n.p.).

59. Tanakamaru (2002, 18).

60. Ibid., 27.

61. Yoshino Sakzō, "Seijika no atama," in *Watashi domo no shuchō* (Tokyo: Bunka seikatsu kenkyūkai, 1826); cited in ibid., 37.

62. Orikuchi ([1943] 1968).

63. *Mainichi shinbun* (Tokyo), August 14, 1993, morning edition.

CHAPTER 4: INSTITUTIONALIZING GRIEF

1. *Shufu no tomo* (June 1939), 98–105.

2. See chapter 1 for my discussion of the Myth of the War Experience, which is based on George Mosse's (1990) analysis.

3. Aoki S. (1976, 80).

4. An inventory of these objects is available in Sakai (2006). I reconstruct Umekichi's journey using material included in this volume.

5. See L. Young (1998, 55–114) for the media's role in Japan's colonization of Manchuria.

6. The transportation log is reprinted in Sakai (2006).

7. For example, the photo series *Shasihin kiroku Shōwa no rekishi* includes a pair of striking photographs taken at the same location two years apart. In a photograph dated December 13, 1935, several troops take off from the Shizuoka barracks in a large group. In a photograph shot from the same location and dated December 18, 1937, many fewer troops are returning, and numerous men are carrying a white box (Matsumoto et al. 1984, 105–106). These portable boxes were less than a foot long on each side.

8. Sakai (2006, 221).

9. For the willing collaboration of women's groups in the national war effort, see Suzuki Y. (1986).

10. The documents are part of the *Rikugunshō dainikki,* a collection of all official documents preserved by the army. They are maintained by the National Institute for Defense Studies (Bōeishō Bōei Kenkyūjo) and available online at http://www.jacar.go.jp/.

11. Iwata (2005b).

12. In 1939 the Ministry of the Interior mandated one *gokoku jinja* per prefecture. Each prefecture was required to either designate an existing shrine as a *gokoku jinja* (whenever appropriate) or construct a new one.

13. Takenaka (2009a).

14. One death from the restoration was also enshrined during this ritual.

15. A regular festival (*rei taisai*) took place each year in April and October. A special festival (*rinji taisai*) took place only following a *shōkon* ritual.

16. The number was decreased to two soon after.

17. Ken'anfu is an imperial facility that held the spoils of the Russo-Japanese War. It comprises the Gyofu and four additional buildings that contained plunder from other Japanese wars of imperialism. After 1945 these items were returned, and the buildings are now used for storage.

18. The itinerary is in my possession. Since the groups (*han*) were organized according to the unit that the deceased belonged to, members typically were from the same or neighboring prefectures.

19. The document is undated. Since it mentions the total number of spirits enshrined by 1921, it was likely written around 1922. "Yasukuni Jinja reisaibi ni kansuru ikensho" (YJ 1983–1984, vol. 1, 404–409).

20. This proposal was still being debated in the Imperial Diet seventeen years later, in 1938. "Teikoku kaigi ni okeru Tsutsumi Yasujirō shitsumon," January 22, 1938 (YJ 1983–1984, vol. 1, 409–410).

21. A temporary structure opened in 1924 and stayed in operation until the new building was completed and opened in 1931. This museum still operates today, with a new entrance hall added and the interior renovated in 2002. The postrenovation museum is discussed in chapter 6.

22. *Asahi shinbun,* November 14, 1931.

23. My description is based on an account of a walk-through by Matsuda Jōta, the head curator of Yūshūkan at the time (Matsuda 1933, 14–18).

24. Maruyama (2007).

25. Matsuda (1933, 13).

26. *Asahi shinbun,* April 26, 1932.

27. This facility was built with money from a bereaved widow, Mitsuya Teiko, who had donated half a million yen to the Army Ministry in accordance with her late husband's last wishes. The National Defense Hall was built using fifty thousand yen from the donation (YJ 1983–1984, vol. 2, 73–74).

28. YJY (1934, 1).

29. Since a brief description and the floor plan of Kokubōkan are included in YJ (1983–1984, vol. 2), several works on Yasukuni Shrine have mentioned the presence of this amusement park–like facility. But to my knowledge, the existing scholarship on Yasukuni Shrine does not discuss this booklet and its descriptions of the exhibits.

30. My description of Kokubōkan is based on YJY (1934).

31. Ibid., 10.

32. Ibid., 26.

33. *Yomiuri shinbun,* October 7, 1939. A description of this Filmon equipment is available in Iijima et al. (2001).

34. A description of Kokubōkan was featured in an issue of *Shōnen kurabu* (Boys' Club), a popular monthly magazine for young boys. *Shōnen kurabu* 21 (6) (June 1934), cited in T. Yoshida (2007).

35. *Asahi shinbun,* April 14, 1942.

36. Damage was limited during Tokyo's first air raid, on April 18, 1942. From November 14, 1944 to August 10, 1945, Tokyo was attacked by air 106 times, including the devastating firestorm of March 10, 1945, which killed more than one hundred thousand people. For detailed information and archival documents associated with air raids on Japan, see http://www.japanairraids.org.

37. *Yomiuri shinbun,* April 27, 1935.

38. Ibid., April 24, 1940. In addition to newspaper articles, I have relied on descriptions of the ritual by people who were in attendance. See Ōishi (1941, 17–29), Katō Takeo (1941, 58–67), and Orikuchi ([1943] 1968).

39. *Yomiuri shinbun,* April 24, 1940.

40. Typically four or six legged, a *karahitsu* is used to store the *shintai* (the object in which the god is understood to reside) and other treasures at Shinto shrines.

41. Its name, *ohaguruma,* is derived from its original structure, with wheels that were likened to a bird's wings (YJY 1987, 10, 81). A model of the palanquin procession is on display in the Yūshūkan museum.

42. *Asahi shinbun,* April 24, 1940.

43. *Yomiuri shinbun,* April 24, 1940.

44. Sakai (2006, 314–315).

45. *Asahi shinbun,* evening edition, April 26, 1940.

46. Ken'anfu viewing was limited to one family member per deceased individual.

47. It is not entirely clear which special festivals the albums were produced for. Holdings of the albums in major libraries are incomplete. With fifteen volumes, the reading room at Shōwakan Museum has the most comprehensive colletion. Both the Organization for the Advancement of Research and Development at Kokugakuin University and the National Diet Library have ten volumes each. The oldest volume available is from 1906 (Kokugakuin University), and the most recent volume is from October 1942 (Kokugakuin and Shōwakan).

48. The arrival scene is missing from the April 1940 volume.

49. Tanakamaru (2002, 69).

50. The album was among the objects maintained by Umekichi's brother. On April 24, 1938, Tokyo *Asahi* newspaper printed a short article on the completion of the album that mentions they will be sent to the families. A research team at Kokugakuin University also supports this claim: http://www2.kokugakuin.ac.jp/kaihatsu/maa/taisai_index.html.

51. The numbers are based on my calculations using the information provided in YJ (1983–1984, vol. 1, 340–347).

52. Ibid., 347.

53. Harada (1998, 2001).

54. The *ryō* was a currency unit used in premodern and early modern Japan. It was replaced by yen in 1871.

55. Harada Keiichi speculates that this most likely resulted in almost all dead being buried by the military as, at the time, two days would not have given families enough time to receive the news of death and request an alternative burial (Harada 1998).

56. "Senji rikugun maisō kisoku," Army Ordinance 16 (July 17, 1894), and "Senji kaigun shibōsha toriatsukai kisoku," Navy Notice 157 (September 21, 1894), cited in ibid., 418.

57. "Senji rikugun maisō kisoku," Army Ordinance 16 (Jul 17, 1894), cited in ibid.

58. Army Ministry file 604 and Army Ordinance 22, cited in Harada (2001, 213).

59. Harada (2001, 213).

60. They were also ordered to retrieve the enemy (Russian) dead and bury them, albeit using a different procedure. While the Japanese bodies were to be cremated on site, the Russians were buried without cremation unless it was feared that they carried a disease.

61. Ōe S. (1988, 132–133).

62. In contrast, the majority of the Sino-Japanese deaths were due to illness.

63. Another often-used method was cremation of the little finger. Namihira notes many instances in which the little finger was cut off corpses and cremated, often using the soldier's mess kit. (Namihira 2004, 139–141).

64. The Battle of Guadalcanal (August 7, 1942–February 7, 1943) produced such a tremendous number of deaths that the military gave up any ostensible attempt to retrieve ashes or body parts. The military created a manual to assist those in charge at city hall, explaining to the bereaved families the reason for the absence of ashes and body parts. According to the published history of Toyota City, for example, the city hall personnel were to explain the following situations: (1) since the enemy had obtained the air rights over the island, on-site cremation was not possible; (2) their loved one's death was a great contribution to the war effort in that, by directing enemy attention to the island for many months, Japan was able to strengthen its position for the later battles; (3) other troops made sure that the spirit of the deceased resides in the sand and stones. *Toyotashi-shi* 4, cited in Ichinose (2004a, 176).

65. From "Prayer for Peace," by Ono Eiko, winner of the 2004 Chiran City speech contest. http://www.chiran-tokkou.jp/contest/index_2014.html.

66. Namihira (2004, 169).

67. Shijō Shirai, *Gatō ni shisumade: Ichi heishi no tegami yori;* cited in ibid., 172–173.

68. Sometimes additional information was provided by comrades or hospital staff (Ichinose 2005, 176–178).

69. For a bibliography of publications on activities that involve searching for remains of the dead on battlefields, see Tamagawa (2008).

70. A parallel can be observed in the Self-Defense Forces' treatment of those who died while on duty. See Field (1993) and Tanaka N. (2003a).

71. *Yokosuka bōei shinpō,* June 13, 1934.

72. *Tōkyō nichi nichi shinbun,* Kanagawa edition, June 13, 1934.

73. L. Young (1998).

74. Yano (2006, 49–57).

75. All aspects of the media, including the press, film, and radio, were subject to censorship prior to publication, release, or broadcast. The Public Order of 1931 subjected the press to extensive censorship. State control of printed matter was strictly enforced after the Marco Polo Bridge incident on July 7, 1937. The public list of topics banned from publication included issues deemed sensitive to national security (e.g., accounts of troop movements, news on army and navy mobilization) and morale (e.g., any news that might weaken the public's confidence in the military, antimilitary or pacifist comments, and articles critical of Japan's foreign policy) (Mitchell 1983, 283–284).

In the final years of the war, when Japan was struggling in its battles against the Allied forces, the Imperial Headquarters censored information on battle outcomes prior to announcement in order to create impressions favorable to Japan. For example, the number of enemy casualties, as well as battleships and aircraft lost, were inflated, while numbers on the Japanese side were decreased significantly. For a comparison of actual and announced outcomes of battles in 1942 and 1943, see Kawashima (1997, 76–85).

76. Niki (1972, 11–16).

77. Abel (2012, 15–16).

78. For an examination of the role of radio in wartime Japan, see Takeyama (1994) and Kishi Toshihiko et al. (2006).

79. *Asahi shinbun,* October 20, 1938, and April 26, 1939.

80. Especially after October 1937, when the one-hour time difference between Japan and Manchuria was eliminated, imperial subjects were instructed to participate in this collective experience on a number of occasions. Some of the events were those during which people had previously been observing the *yōhai* practice (see chapter 3), but live radio made possible the simultaneity of the activities throughout the empire (Hara 2004).

81. A partial script for the April 1940 ceremony is available in Nakamura and NHK Shuzai-han (2007).

82. *Asahi shinbun,* April 24, 1942.

83. While most of these children were not technically orphans since their mothers were still alive, such children were broadly publicized as war orphans (*sensō iji*).

84. Those eligible that year included schoolchildren up to the sixth grade whose fathers had died in Manchuria or China (YJ 1973, 134).

85. The description of the orphans' visit comes from the first photo album of the annual visits (Gunjin Engokai 1939).

86. *Asahi shinbun,* September 7, 1939.

87. Ibid., October 15, 1941. This report parallels a chapter of the third-grade ethics reader (fifth edition), which describes a conversation between a younger brother (presumably the same age as the reader) and his brother, his mother, and his eldest brother, who came home after being wounded in battle. The mother tells the younger brothers that it is their turn now to become soldiers. At this, the two younger brothers smile at each other. The textbook demonstrates the honorable mind-set of a mother who is proud and honored to send her sons to war regardless of the dangers (Kaigo 1961–1967, vol. 3, 398–399).

88. The mass media popularized *bidan* stories not only to promote patriotism but also to stimulate sales (L. Young 1998, 106–114).

89. *Shufu no tomo,* May 1938, 488–496.

90. Ibid., May 1939, 66–74.

91. Ibid., June 1939, 98–105.

92. Hashikawa (1974).

93. Takahashi T. (2005c, 21–26, 33–37).

94. *Shufu no tomo* (June 1939), 100–101.

95. See, for example, Takahashi (2005c, 2006).

96. *Yokosuka bōei shinpō,* June 13, 1934.

97. *Tōkyō nichi nichi shinbun,* Kanagawa edition, June 13, 1934. This type of reporting, which revealed the sadness and grief of the family left behind, decreased considerably as the war intensified. This perspective is seldom observed in relation to war deaths in the Pacific theater.

98. Sakai (2006, 69).

99. Aoki S. (1976, 80). Aoki, the author of the text from which this quote is taken, is a newspaper reporter and a critic. Born in 1929, he grew up in the very climate of the institutionalized grief discussed in this chapter. For him, Yasukuni Shrine was a playground that was transformed into a holy site during the Asia-Pacific War. In this essay on his peceptions of Yasukuni Shrine, Aoki quotes a veteran announcer (whom he does not name) who revealed this episode to him.

100. Orikuchi ([1943] 1968, 28).

101. *Tokkō geppō* (January 1942), 13. *Tokkō geppō* is a monthly report by the Special Higher Police (*Tokubetsu Tokkō Keisatsu,* i.e., the Japanese "thought police" during the war). For a close analysis of the report as well as other voices of dissent during the war, see Kawashima (1997).

102. *Tokkō geppō* (June 1942), 18.

103. Statement by a shoemaker, *Tokkō geppō* (March 1942).

104. *Tokkō geppō* (April 1942), 29.

105. Ibid. (June 1942), 20.

106. Kitamura (1999, 75).

107. Ibid., 78–93, 199–200.

108. *Asahi shinbun,* April 22, 1942.

109. YJ (1983–1984, vol. 1, 158–159).

110. The shrine did not extend invitations to the bereaved families (including those living in Tokyo), citing issues of safety, transportation, lodging, and finances. Tokyo's bereaved families, however, were encouraged to attend the ceremony on their own (ibid., 259, 266).

111. Ibid., 265–267.

112. Itō T. (1989).

113. YJ (1973, 165).

CHAPTER 5: WHO HAS THE RIGHT TO MOURN?

Epigraph. Editorial for *Tōyō keizai shinpō,* October 13, 1945.

Epigraph. Father Bitter was here reflecting the advice he gave to Douglas MacArthur on the postwar treatment of Yasukuni Shrine.

1. Ishibashi ([1945] 1970).

2. See chapter 4 for the limited number of war dead memorialized at Yasukuni Shrine as of August 1945.

3. Ishibashi ([1945] 1970).

4. The prime minister made the statement at a Diet meeting on September 5, 1945. For an analysis of Higashikuni's statement, see Hosaka M. (1985).

5. For the history and an analysis of State Shinto, see Murakami (1970), Hardacre (1989), and Sakamoto (2006a). For a detailed analysis of the Shinto Directive, see Ōhara (1993).

6. The blueprint for the amusement park is reproduced in Yasukuni no Inori Henshūkai (1999, 167).

7. By definition, *izoku* includes the spouse, siblings, parents, grandparents, children, and grandchildren of the military dead.

8. For an overview of postwar history of Yasukuni Shrine, see Tanaka (2002) and Akazawa (2005).

9. For a historical overview and an analysis of the Izokukai in English, see Seraphim (2006).

10. As suggested in the introduction, the so-called Yasukuni issue, or *Yasukuni mondai,* which many Japanese scholars and journalists have written and argued about, results from the conflation of various histories, practices, traditions, and beliefs associated with Yasukuni Shrine. For a chronological overview of *Yasukuni mondai,* see Takahashi F. (1990).

11. For an analysis of the controversies stemming from prime ministers' visits to Yasukuni Shrine from the viewpoint of the Izokukai, see Itagaki (2000).

12. Several years had passed since the revelation of the enshrinement on April 19, 1979, and two former premiers, Ōhira Masayoshi and Suzuki Kantarō, had visited

Yasukuni Shrine since then. Nonetheless, Nakasone's visit drew intense criticism because of its deliberately public nature. A *New York Times* article dated August 24, 1985, notes that China issued an "unusually sharp" criticism of Japan," suggesting that such critiques of prime ministers' visits had not occurred earlier (*New York Times,* August 25, 1985). For the enshrinement of Class-A war criminals at Yasukuni Shrine, see Takenaka (2007) and Mainichi Shinbun "Yasukuni" Shuzai-han (2007).

13. Films include *Annyeong, Sayonara,* which follows a Korean woman whose father was enshrined at Yasukuni Shrine (directed by Kim Tae-il and produced by the Institute for Research in Collaborationist Activities, 2005), and *Shussō no uta* (Headhunter's Song: The Cry of the Aboriginal People of Taiwan), a compilation of scenes of protest against Yasukuni Shrine by Taiwanese aboriginals (filmed and directed by Inoue Osamu and produced by Jōhō Kobo Spiriton, 2006).

14. Along with these demands for the removal of names from the register are cases in which family members have requested Yasukuni enshrinement of their loved ones. See, for example, Nishimura (2003).

15. Although the term *tsuitō* encompasses both memorial and mourning, I use "mourning" throughout when referring to *tsuitō* in order to distinguish between *tsuitō* and *irei,* which I translate as "memorial."

16. Other works that deal with these terms include Yano (2006), Nishimura (2006), and Akazawa (2005).

17. Akazawa traces the origin of the lawmakers' explanations to an influential opinion by the late literary critic Etō Jun, who, as a key member of the Committee on the Cabinet Ministers' Visits to Yasukuni (Kakuryō no Yasukuni Jinja Sanpai ni Kansuru Kondaikai), defended lawmakers' visits to the shrine. Etō has argued that, in accordance with the traditional Japanese belief that the living cohabitate with the dead, the *eirei* at Yasukuni are protecting the living. Therefore, it is a matter of rectitude for key lawmakers to pay tribute at the shrine. Etō's argument is summarized in Etō (1986).

18. For a detailed account of the discussions that took place in the SCAP, see Nakamura and NHK Shuzai-han (2007) and Haruyama (2006).

19. *Asahi shinbun,* October 19, 1951. Forty-fourth prime minister Shidehara Kijūrō visited in the fall of 1945.

20. *Yomiuri shinbun,* October 16, 1952, evening edition.

21. Ibid.

22. Before its privatization, the operating budget of Yasukuni Shrine was included in the Imperial Army's budget as "Offering money to Yasukuni Shrine [*Yasukuni Jinja gushin kin*]" (KKT, item 287, 2007, 392). Administrators at Yasukuni Shrine continue to devise ways to generate revenue in the postwar years. One notable move was the 1985 decision to convert the *shōkon saitei,* the space in which the rituals took place until 1945, into a commercial parking lot. As of March 2013, each parking space was leased for fifty thousand yen per month.

23. Tanaka (2002, 23). For an overview of the accomplishments of the Japan League, see Jōshita (2013).

24. Engohō provided much-needed financial support for the bereaved families, but many recipients disapproved of the name of the law. They argued that, as family members of those who had died in a wrongful war that the Japanese state waged, they were entitled to reparation (*hoshō*) rather than relief (*engo*). Historian Ishihara Masaie argues that, in the case of Okinawa, the name of this monetary compensation reinforces the idea that Okinawan civilians willingly participated in the war effort and obfuscates the reality of Okinawan war experience (Ishihara 2007, 2008).

25. Information about Izokukai history is available at the Izokukai website, http://www.nippon-izokukai.jp/.

26. Journalist Tanaka Nobumasa describes an interview with a man whose war-widowed mother decided to join Izokukai so that she could participate in regular bus tours to Yasukuni Shrine. The man explains that his mother regarded Izokukai as something akin to a travel office that planned bus tours to the shrine (Tanaka N., Tanaka H., and Hata 1995, 11–14).

27. Ibid., 32–33.

28. In June 1969 a group of Christians formed Kirisuto-kyō Izoku no Kai (Association for War-Bereaved Christian Families). In July 1982 approximately seventy Christians and Buddhists in the Asahikawa region withdrew their membership in Izokukai and formed Asahikawa Izokukai (Asahikawa Association for War-Bereaved Families). Similar organizations were formed in Kanagawa, Iwate, and Tokyo prefectures in 1986. Also in 1986 Shin Buddhists formed the Shinshū Izokukai (Shin Buddhist Association for War-Bereaved Families). These groups came together to form Heiwa Izokukai Zenkoku Renrakukai (National Committee on Peaceful War-Bereaved Families) in response to Nakasone's visit to Yasukuni Shrine on August 15, 1985. A strong anti-Yasukuni sentiment unites members of this group (Hōsei Daigaku Ōhara Shakai Mondai Kenkyūjo 1987).

29. At the end of the war, the wartime ministries of both army and navy were reorganized as the Demobilization Ministry, which was absorbed into the Ministry of Welfare in 1948.

30. Army Ministry, "Yasukuni Jinja gōshi tō ni kansuru ken" and "Yasukuni Jinja no gōshi tō ni kansuru iken," dated September 21, 1945 (YJ 1983–1984, vol. 1, 268–269).

31. Navy Ministry, "Dōken iken" (YJ 1983–1984, vol. 1, 269–270).

32. Yasukuni Jinja, "Dōken iken" (YJ 1983–1984, vol. 1, 270).

33. Kunaishō, "Dōken iken" (YJ 1983–1984, vol. 1, 270–271).

34. On the exchange between these ministries, see also KKT, items 104–106 (2007, 113–114).

35. YJ (1973, 167–167).

36. YJ (1983–1984, vol. 1, 278–290).

37. *Yomiuri shinbun,* November 21, 1945.

38. For example, Kishimoto advised against any kind of publicity of the Yasukuni festival. On visiting the shrine at the end of the *shōkon* ceremony, which took place on the night before the festivals, Kishimoto convinced the military officials to reduce

the military presence by wearing civilian clothing rather than uniforms for the duration of the festival (Nakamura and NHK Shuzai-han 2007, 152–153). See also KKT, item 141 (2007, 135).

39. According to the diary of Kishimoto Hideo, religious consultant to the general headquarters (GHQ), Yasukuni authorities had no idea that their institution was in danger until October 24, 1945, when Kishimoto visited the shrine to consult with the deputy chief priest. At the meeting, Kishimoto advised the priest against publicizing the memorial ceremony through media such as radio, newspapers, and posters to prevent provoking the GHQ. At the meeting, the two discussed possible changes that might encourage the GHQ to allow Yasukuni to continue operation, such as terminating its management by the military, including public figures in the deities, and changing the shrine's name (Nakamura and NHK Shuzai-han 2007, 138–139).

40. Tanaka N. (2002, 10–11).

41. Deputy head priest Ikeda Ryōhachi explained this process using the term *aiden* (enshrinement of two or more deities in one shrine) but did not give details of the form of this dual enshrinement (KKT, item 390, 2007, 397).

42. Kuramoto Keijirō, head of the administrative department, First Demobilization Ministry, "Gōshi horyū no omonaru riyū," dated June 5, 1946 (KKT, item 129, 2007, 126).

43. The number is from both YJ (1983–1984, vol. 1) and YJ (1973). KKT gives the much lower figure of 16,861. "Yasukuni Jinja gōshi gyōmu oyobi saishiryō ni tsuite (June 28, 1946)," KKT, item 131 (2007, 128).

44. YJ (1973).

45. Tanaka Nobumasa argues that the sudden growth in the number for this year is due to cooperation by the Ministry of Welfare (Tanaka N. 2002, 66–68).

46. KKT, item 147 (2007, 137).

47. "Yasukuni Jinja gōshi tetsuzuki yōkō," dated June 28, 1946 (KKT, item 133, 2007, 129).

48. "Shibotsusha kyūmei ni tsuite," dated September 15, 1946 (KKT, item 137, 2007, 133).

49. "Summary," dated late 1947 (KKT, item 150, 2007, 138).

50. "Senbotsusha chōsa gyōmu no ikan ni tsuite," dated August 2, 1948 (KKT, item 151, 2007, 140).

51. This eligibility resulted from a revision of Engohō. Initially, the beneficiaries of Engohō included veterans. In August 1953, when a new law, Onkyū-hō (Veterans' Pension Law), was established to provide a pension to veterans, revisions were made to Engohō that extended eligibility to families of war criminals who were executed or died in prison.

52. "Kōwa jōyaku hakkō go no shibotsu sha gōshi ni tsuite," dated April 11, 1985 (KKT, items 333 and 334, 2007, 335–337).

53. Tsunoda (1977, 264–265).

54. Ibid., 265–267.

55. *Asahi shinbun* (Tokyo), January 9, 1986, morning edition.

56. For an analysis of this court case, see, for example, Arai R. (1971) and Nakayama (1972).

57. See, for example, Hirano (1990) and Morone (1998).

58. The Supreme Court ruled the Iwate case unconstitutional in 1997.

59. For a detailed account of the extended lawsuit, see Tanaka N. (2003a) and Field (1993).

60. Koizumi ultimately visited the shrine on August 13, 2001.

61. The number is from 2002 (Tanaka N. 2007, 42).

62. *Asahi shinbun* (Tokyo), April 16, 1978, morning edition.

63. Other demands included the return of ashes, information about the death (date, location, cause, condition, etc.), compensation equivalent to what the Japanese *izoku* had received, including interest (Korean and Taiwanese nationals were not eligible for a pension), and a public apology in a number of Japanese and Korean newspapers (TDC 2006).

64. Tanaka (2007, 37).

65. *Asahi shinbun* (Tokyo), April 22, 2002.

66. Ibid. November 2, 2001.

67. The plaintiffs lost (ODC 2003).

68. Takahashi T. (2005b, 29–46).

69. See the Introduction for my discussion of the "emotional alchemy" of Yasukuni Shrine.

70. The case was filed against Prime Minister Koizumi Junichiro, Yasukuni Shrine, and the Japanese state for Koizumi's visits to Yasukuni Shrine on August 13, 2001; April 21, 2002; and January 14, 2003 (ODC 2004).

71. Ibid., 24.

72. Ibid., 25.

73. Ibid., 55–64.

74. OHC (2005).

75. The three visits were on January 14, 2003; January 1, 2004; and October 17, 2005.

76. Tanaka N. (2007, 40–41).

77. I am indebted to an anonymous reviewer of the manuscript for pointing out this parallel.

78. The second case, presented on February 14, 2003, was brought by 124 people from Taiwan, many of whom had family members on the Yasukuni register.

79. Taiwanese Yasukuni supporters are favorites of conservative media outlets such as the journal *Seiron*. In its special feature, "Yasukuni and the Japanese Spirit (*Yasukuni to Nihon jin no kokoro*)," in August 2003, the journal spotlighted multiple Taiwanese contributors who argued for the importance of Yasukuni Shrine the for spirits of the Taiwanese war dead (Rin 2003; Shie 2003).

80. ODC (2004, 12–13).

81. *Asahi shinbun* (Tokyo), June 14, 2005, evening edition.

82. "Saisan sanpai, Koizumi shushō ni NO. Yasukuni iken 'kakkiteki,' hyōka no koe," *Asahi shinbun* (Osaka), evening edition, September 30, 2005.

83. Engohō carried over the payment structure of the military pension system, which allotted no privileges to those without Japanese nationality, thus resulting in the exclusion of Korean and Taiwanese war-bereaved families from payment (Tanaka N. 1997, 33).

84. "Dai 44 kai kokkai shūgiin shakai rōdō iinkai giroku dai 28 gō," dated April 12, 1962 (KKT, item 416, 2007, 457).

85. Testimony by Takahashi is not included in the written judgment of the case. The transcript is available in Tanaka N. (2009).

86. Ibid., 38–39.

87. Ibid., 26–27.

88. Ibid., 32.

89. ODC (2009).

90. Ibid.

91. Ibid.

92. The shrine personnel often use the metaphor of a candle flame to explain the impossibility of removing a particular spirit. According to this explanation, the spirits merge into each other just as a candle flame can merge with another. And just as it is impossible to divide a flame, so it is impossible to remove the individual spirits.

93. Tanaka N. (2009, 48).

94. Tokoro (2007a).

95. An abbreviated transcript of the original complaint is available in *Tsubute* 59 (Summer 2008), 83–94, as an appendix to an article by Kawabata (2008).

96. NDC (2010). For analyses of this ruling, see, for example, Sawaki (2011). Okinawans filed a lawsuit against Prime Minister Koizumi for the pain and suffering caused by his visits to Yasukuni. Contempt for civilian enshrinement at Yasukuni was a large underlying factor. The case was rejected on October 12, 2006 (Tanaka N. 2007, 54–91).

97. The official category is "Rank: Civilian Employed in Army (Non-Salaried)" (NDC 2010, 4–6).

98. http://www.yasukuni.or.jp/history/detail.html.

99. "Soko ni hisomu mono: Okinawa to Yasukuni, engohō 1," *Ryūkyū shinpō*, March 1, 2009, morning edition, 31.

100. Ryūkū Izokukai, established in February 1952; predecessor of the Association of Bereaved Families of Okinawa Prefecture (Okinawa-ken Izoku Rengōkai).

101. In 1981 the relief law was further expanded to include children who were six years and younger at the time of a parent's death.

102. "Soko ni hisomu mono: Okinawa to Yasukuni, engohō 6," *Ryūkyū shinpō*, March 8, 2009, morning edition, 31.

War death opened prospects for income, and the urgent need for *izoku nenkin* for the bereaved family members was not limited to Okinawa. In 2002 ethnographer Ishida Shigenori conducted an interview with an elderly woman in a Yamanashi village. When discussing her late husband, who returned home from the war weak and sickly, she admitted that she wished he had died in battle. When asked to explain further, she commented that her response was a result of *izoku nenkin*. Although her husband had returned, he remained unhealthy and was unable to work. But since he had returned home alive, the family was not eligible for the pension (Iwata 2005a).

103. "Soko ni hisomu mono: Okinawa to Yasukuni, engohō 5," *Ryūkyū shinpō,* March 6, 2009, morning edition, 31.

104. Cited in Ishihara (2007, 46).

105. Also to be noted is the state's use of the term *engo* (relief, protection) rather than *hoshō* (compensation). Ishihara Masaie argues that the term *engo* suggests the protection and support of people in need, while *hoshō* indicates compensation for a loss ("Soko ni hisomu mono: Okinawa to Yasukuni, engohō 12," *Ryūkyū shinpō,* March 17, 2009, morning edition, 31).

106. "Soko ni hisomu mono: Okinawa to Yasukuni, engohō 7," *Ryūkyū shinpō,* March 10, 2009, morning edition, 33.

107. "Eirei ka inu jini ka: Okinawa kara tou Yasukuni saiban," documentary film broadcast through Ryūkyū Asahi Hōsō in 2010, available in three installments at YouTube. The first installment is available at http://www.youtube.com/watch?v=zolHhY8Sd5Q.

108. According to the document *Taiheiyō sensō ni okeru waga kuni no higai sōgō hōkokusho* (Overall Report of Damage Sustained by the Nation during the Pacific War), compiled by the Economic Stabilization Agency in the Office of the Secretary General in 1949, the number of civilian deaths in all prefectures excluding Okinawa was 299,485. Accessed through the Digital Archive of the National Archives of Japan, http://www.digital.archives.go.jp/.

109. These military documents are reproduced in Ishihara (1983, 1984, 1985).

110. The term *shūdan jiketsu* was not used during the Asia-Pacific War. Journalist Ōta Yoshihiro invented the term in 1950 while he was interviewing individuals for his publication *Tetsu no bōfū* (Typhoon of Iron), the first collection of Okinawans' testimonies of their wartime experience (Ōta, "Dohyō o machigaeta hito: Sono Ayako shi e no hanron," in *Okinawa Times,* May 11, 1985; cited in Ishihara 1991, 82–83).

111. Bōeichō Senshi Shitsu, *Senshi sōsho: Okinawa hōmen rikugun sakusen,* cited in Yakabi (2005).

112. Ishihara (1991, 11).

113. "Okinawa-ken Seikatsu Fukushibu Engoka sentō sankasha gaikyō hyō," cited in Kawabata (2008, 88).

114. Ishihara (2007, 47).

115. Sawaki (2011, 172).

116. Ishihara (2007, 45).

117. At the start of the occupation, the US military attempted to mandate the study of English beginning in the first grade, but the plan failed due to lack of personnel. The military rulers also used the precolonial name Ryūkyū, rather than Okinawa, to diminish the sense of connection with the rest of Japan (ibid., 37).

118. "Dai 24 kai kokkai shūgiin kaigai dōhō hikiage oyobi ikazoku engo ni kansuru chōsa tokubetsu iinkai giroku dai 14 gō," dated May 23, 1956, in KKT, item 398 (2007, 423).

119. Ishihara (2007, 38–39).

120. Regardless of the anti-Yasukuni sentiment prevalent in the prefecture, the rhetoric that the shrine presents is identical to that of other *gokoku jinja* as well as Yasukuni Shrine (http://www.okinawa-gokoku.jp/index.jsp).

121. Article 20: Freedom of religion is guaranteed to all. (1) No religious organization shall receive any privileges from the State, nor exercise any political authority. (2) No person shall be compelled to take part in any religious acts, celebration, rite or practice. (3) The State and its organs shall refrain from religious education or any other religious activity.

Article 89: No public money or other property shall be expended or appropriated for the use, benefit or maintenance of any religious institution or association, or for any charitable, educational or benevolent enterprises not under the control of public authority.

122. Kawabata (2008, 85).

123. NDC (2010, 22–23, 26).

124. Ibid., 26–27.

125. "Yasukuni soshō: Gōshi wa seishinteki kutsū; Naha chisai, genkoku gawa, han-heiwateki to shuchō," *Ryūkyū shinpō,* March 11, 2009, morning edition, 27.

126. NDC (2010, 11).

127. Ibid., 32.

128. Ibid., 59.

129. Ibid., 66.

130. " 'Sensō sanbi o inpei,' Yasukuni soshō izokuno ikari todokazu; namida tame 'hanashi ni naran,' " *Okinawa Taimusu,* October 27, 2010, morning edition.

131. NDC (2010, 62).

132. "Shasetsu: Yasukuni gōshi soshō: sensō kagaisha to dōretsushi suruna," *Ryūkȳu shinbun,* October 28, 2010, morning edition.

133. Tanaka N. (2007, 166–167).

134. Ibid., 181.

135. Sugahara (2005, 42–54).

136. Ibid., 46.

137. Ibid., 45.

138. Bitter (1973, 118).

CHAPTER 6: MOBILIZING MEMORIES

1. The film is also available as a DVD of the same title, produced and distributed by Yasukuni Shrine. The film was first screened at Yūshūkan on September 1, 2008. The DVD is undated.

2. John Breen discusses three mnemonic strategies utilized by Yasukuni Shrine: text, display, and ritual. Here I focus on display (Yūshūkan Museum) as a mnemonic apparatus that seeks to reshape the Yasukuni narrative to appeal to younger audiences (Breen 2008).

3. I introduce a representative website and mailing list in the Epilogue. For analyses of war and peace museums in Japan, see Takenaka (2007, 2014), Yamane (2009), and Rekishi Kyōikusha Kyōgikai (2000).

4. Hirsch discusses the postmemory generation as a singular entity. But I use the plural here since, in the twenty-first century, now almost seven decades after 1945, the experiences of postmemorial remembrance are more diverse. For the purposes of this chapter, I separate postmemorial Japanese into two groups: the first postmemory generation, whose parents experienced the war; and the second postmemory generation, whose parents did not experience the war (Hirsch 1996; 1997, 22; 2008).

5. I am not arguing here that inherited trauma is more difficult but rather that the process of overcoming trauma can be more problematic for the postmemory generations due to the complex nature of the trauma.

6. The trajectory of postwar Japan has often been compared with that of Germany, particularly in the area of war reparation. But for the area of civilian experience I find the literature on Holocaust memories and their representation more useful for thinking through the Japanese situation due to the prevailing victim consciousness in Japanese memories. For scholarship on the Japan-Germany comparison, see Buruma (1994), Fujiwara K. (2001), Awaya et al. (1994), and Nakamasa (2005).

7. Sūkei Hōsankai is the successor of Yasukuni Jinja Hōsankai, introduced in Chapter 5.

8. Here, I rely primarily on Herman (1997). Brison's account of overcoming her own traumatic experience is also useful (1999). The concept of postmemory has been developed in relation to Holocaust studies, and I am aware of the criticisms regarding the retroactive use of currently available trauma theory on the events of World War II. In short, the Holocaust has come to appear as an event "that can be fully understood only in the light of our knowledge of PTSD," as Ruth Leys has pointed out. My intention here is not to analyze the actual experiences of World War II, nor do I suggest that members of the postmemory generation are suffering from posttraumatic stress disorder (PTSD). Rather, I am interested in the social and political dynamics that affected them in the postwar decades, the processes through which they became familiarized with wartime narratives of the survivor generations, as well as the debates on war responsibility that have had a strong presence in the society they grew up in. The use of trauma theory, I believe, suggests one useful way of thinking about these

processes. Leys is cautioning against the simplified understanding of the Holocaust that results from using only the currently available theory to understand the events that occurred before the development of our PTSD knowledge. But she also acknowledges that current literature on PTSD "represents the culmination of an attempt to do justice to the earlier psychiatric literature on the Holocaust survivor by integrating it into a unified theory" that applies to the victim of diverse kinds of trauma, both before and after our knowledge of PTSD. I use ideas that were produced with the knowledge of PTSD, but I do so cautiously in order to offer a possible reason for the efforts of the postmemory generation to comprehend the past (Leys 2000, 15–16).

9. Treat (1995), J. Young (1988), Scarry (1985), Caruth (1996).

10. LaCapra (2001).

11. Attie (1998). Scholarly analyses of Attie's works include Muir (2010), J. Young (2000), Apel (2002).

12. Levinthal (1996, 1997).

13. Baer (2002), Apel (2002).

14. J. Young (2000, 4).

15. Spiegelman (1991).

16. Hirsch's discussion of postmemory is specific to the Holocaust experience in that the succeeding generation attempted to bridge not only the temporal gap but also the spatial, neither of which can be achieved: temporal, because of the impossibility of going back in time, and spatial, because the site from which their parents were exiled no longer exists (Hirsch 1996, 662).

17. For information on and an analysis of Tsukuru-kai, see Saaler (2005). For museum controversies, see Takenaka (2014).

18. Interview with Iki Hiroshi, January 28, 2005. The term "cornerstone" is from Breen (2008, 156).

19. See chapter 5 for the relationship between Izokukai and Yasukuni Shrine.

20. The shift from the display of objects to an exhibit with a historical narrative is part of a larger trend in history museums. Hiroshima Peace Memorial Museum, for example, took this strategy for its 1994 renovation. In a 2005 interview, the then curator of Shōwakan Museum discussed the plan to gradually shift from displays to exhibits with a historical narrative as well. Author interview with Watanabe Kazuhiro, January 26, 2005.

21. I am aware that the relationship between an increase in the number of the museum visitors and the historical narrative presented is not so straightforward; I discuss the phenomenon in further detail later in the chapter.

22. http://www.yasukuni.jp/~sukei/message.html.

23. *Yasukuni Jinja Sūkei Hōsankai setsuritu shui,* http://www.yasukuni.jp/~sukei/message.html.

24. Joining the Asanagi does not require a separate fee, as membership in either Hōsankai or the Friends of Yūshūkan (depending on the member's age) is a prerequisite. http://asanagi.com/nyuubunitsuite.html.

25. As was the case with many life insurance companies, Fukoku Seimei was a "conscription insurance (*chōhei hoken*)" company until 1945. For the early history of Fukoku Seimei, see FSHSG.

26. A special exhibit mounted at this temporary space is detailed in Skabelund (2011).

27. The opening day was scheduled to coincide with the first day of Mitama Matsuri (Itō Y. 1988, 50).

28. At the outset, fifteen display rooms contained approximately three thousand objects (Ōyama 1994, 96). For a brief description of the museum displays prior to the renovation, see Tokoro (2007a).

29. The number of monthly visitors between July 1986 and November 1987 is available in Itō Y. (1988, 51).

30. Ibid.

31. The film *Mitama o tsugu mono* also has English subtitles.

32. Interview with curator Iki Hiroshi, January 28, 2005. Iki, who was chief curator of the museum at the time of the interview, also held the title of deputy priest (*gon negi*) at the shrine. Iki and others who had the curatorial position received no training as a curator. Instead, they came to the shrine to train as a priest and were appointed for a limited period to the museum.

33. Ibid.

34. The description is based on my visits to the museum, the museum catalog, and unofficial guidebooks to the museum. Unofficial guidebooks published to date include Nishikawa (2003) and Zushi (2007). Kokugakuin University scholar Ōhasa Yasuo also published a guidebook on the renovated museum in cooperation with Yasukuni Shrine (Ōhara 2003). See also Matayoshi (2004) for a detailed review of the museum exhibits.

35. Text at the time of my visit on March 13, 2011.

36. Zushi (2007, 122).

37. This experience of ascension can be considered a contemporary version of the spatial practice that early public museums offered as part of their role of enlightening the masses. For example, in her analysis of the first public art museums, Carol Duncan describes the entrances of museum buildings that readied the visitors for an enlightening experience by having them ascend grand staircases into the building and walking through massive pillars (Duncan 1995).

38. The sculptor Hinago Jitsuzō's other works include the monumental tower situated in Heiwadai Park, Miyazaki Prefecture, on which the infamous characters "hakkō ichiu (eight corners of the world under one roof)" are engraved.

39. "Umi yuka ba" gained popularity through the same venue as the poem "Yasukuni no," with which I began this book. Although the accompanying music was composed in 1880 in response to a commission by the Imperial Navy, it did not gain popularity outside the military until the song was picked up by the NHK for the national song series (Ogawa 2006).

40. Even though historians have come to some basic agreement on what happened in the city of Nanjing in December 1937, depictions of this tragedy vary significantly not only in Japan but also internationally. See, for example, Fogel (2000).

41. See chapter 4 for a detailed discussion of the ceremony and associated activities planned for the visiting families.

42. In Room 9 the documents related to the *shōkon* ceremony are obscured by the palanquin replica as well as the dim lighting.

43. Literally translated as "stitches by one thousand," *sen-nin bari* is a piece of cloth on which one thousand women sewed one stitch each. The cloth was meant to protect men from bullet wounds.

44. For an analysis of how the deaths of these men were politicized by wartime media and popular culture, see Dorsey (2009).

45. *Yomiuri shinbun* (Tokyo), December 8, 1941, front page.

46. For an analysis of these bride dolls, see Schattschneider (2009).

47. The photographs are exhibited with the permission of the family. The number of the photographs has increased considerably since the opening of the new museum in 2002.

48. For analyses of writings by *tokkō* pilots, see Ohnuki-Tierney (2006).

49. For the use of nostalgia as a marketing strategy, see Ivy (1995).

50. Visitors with family members enshrined at Yasukuni can participate in an official worship service that takes place inside the main shrine. Typically, Izokukai organizes group tours to Tokyo that include this service. During the summer festival Mitama Matsuri, individuals can also register to participate in the official worship. A monetary offering is required for this, and worshippers later receive a token gift on the Yasukuni theme based on the amount of the donation. As part of the registration process it is also necessary to write the name of a relative enshrined, but shrine personnel do not check for accuracy (author's experience, July 2003).

51. Interview with Iki Hiroshi, January 28, 2005.

52. Photocopy of three architectural renderings in the author's possession.

53. Correspondence between *sūkei hōsankai* member Sakuta Masaaki and Yasukuni Chief of General Affairs Hanada Tadamasa, dated January 10 and 14, 2000. Correspondence photocopy in the author's possession.

54. According to Miwa Yūji, who represented the planning company Nomura Kōgei, which designed the exhibit for the Yūshūkan renovation, the glass wall, against which the plane is situated, can open up to connect the entrance hall to the open space immediately outside. The initial plan to open up the wall and pull the fighter plane to the outdoor space, however, was never realized (Miwa Yūji, interview with the author, January 28, 2005).

55. The father's role is that of the typical *kigyō senshi,* or "corporate warrior," whose function was to sacrifice his private life for the rebuilding of postwar Japan. We see here a parallel between the grandparents' generation, who fought in the Asia-Pacific War, and the father's generation.

56. Japanese Culture Channel Sakura, http://www.ch-sakura.jp/about.html.

57. When Yasukuni initially approached Matsuda, the rough idea for the film was to have an elderly woman walking through Yūshūkan with her granddaughter, recounting memories of her experiences, which were triggered by the objects on display (interview with Matsuda Takeyuki, October 8, 2009, http://www.ch-sakura.jp/hodo/election.html?id=628).

58. According to the museum, "the Association for Friends of Yūshūkan was established in order to further strengthen the connection between Yūshūkan and people twenty-five years [of age] or younger, so that they might inherit the noble spirits of the *eirei,* who sacrificed their precious lives for the sake of their nation, and learn the accurate history of modern Japan" (Nishikawa 2003, 45).

59. The shrine has commemorated Girls' Festival and Children's Day since 1947, but until 2004 it was not part of an organized group such as the Association for Friends of Yūshūkan.

60. One objective of this "quiz rally" is to entice children, who might otherwise be turned off by the wordy panels, into the museum and develop in them an interest in the material displayed (interview with Iki Hiroshi, January 28, 2005).

61. *Sūkei hōsankai dayori* 106, August 2010, "Heisei 22 nen tanabata matsuri oyako no tsudoi hōkoku."

62. The objective of these children's events seems to be twofold: to cultivate young children as followers and to encourage their parents, typically in their thirties and forties, to participate in events at Yasukuni (interview with Iki Hiroshi, January 28, 2005).

63. http://www.yasukuni.or.jp/precincts/dovehouse.html.

64. For an English translation of the pamphlet, see Gardener (1999).

65. "Yasukuni daihyakka: Watakushi tachi no Yasukuni Jinja," pamphlet obtained at Yasukuni Shrine on June 1, 2008.

66. The Allied forces are explained in parentheses as "America, Britain, Dutch, and China," echoing the ABCD powers, which, according to the Yūshūkan narrative, surrounded and pressured Japan to wage war against the United States.

67. These are the dates for the Bon Festival of the lunar calendar (*kyū bon*).

68. *Ichigaya keizai shinbun,* July 14, 2010. http://ichigaya.keizai.biz/headline/892/. A more updated sociological analysis of the festival's popularity is available at http://trendy.nikkeibp.co.jp/article/column/20130828/1051741/.

69. These lanterns, which demonstrate appreciation for the *eirei* and represent prayers for a peaceful world, provide a major source of revenue for the shrine. The fee to have a lantern placed on the shrine is twelve thousand yen for a large one and three thousand yen for a small one. For more substantial prices of two hundred thousand yen (large) and seventy thousand yen (small) one can arrange to have a lantern hung during the festival every year. http://www.yasukuni.or.jp/schedule/mitama.html.

70. Yanagita seems to have become sympathetic to the discourse. In a lecture he presented to Tokyo University students in fall of 1941, he said that the Japanese *matsuri* made him reconsider his objection to the Japanese government's stance that Shinto

was not a religion. In the lecture, he argued that worship of god is the essence of Japanese life and, at the same time, of Japanese politics (Yanagita 1990, 236–237).

71. Yasukuni no Inori Henshū Iinkai (1999, 174).

72. Foucault (1995).

73. In March 2009 Okinawan newspaper *Ryūkyū shinpō* published a series on Yasukuni enshrinement in thirteen installments. The beginning of the first installment, which portrayed a typical scene at Yasukuni Shrine, included a description of the site as "even evoking a sense of tranquility (*heiwa sae kanji saseru*)." "Soko ni hisomu mono: Okinawa to Yasukuni, engohō 1," *Ryūkyū shinpō,* March 1, 2009, morning edition, 31.

74. There is only one other shrine in Tokyo where a *misemono goya* is showcased on a regular basis: the Hanazono Shrine in Shinjuku (Iwata 2006, 180).

75. *Nihon keizai shinbun,* March 17, 1995.

76. *Asahi shinbun* (Tokyo), March 18, 1995.

77. Editorial, *Kikan sensō sekinin kenkyū* 11 (spring 1996), cited in Taguchi, 1996, 24–25.

78. The phrase "postwar responsibility" has existed since the 1970s, but it was mobilized in the last two decades of the twentieth century and resulted in a flurry of publications that use the phrase to formulate innovative ideas for breaking through the stagnant postwar period. For recent discussions on postwar responsibility, see Ōnuma (2007), Takahashi T. (2005b), and Kōketsu (2009).

79. Ienaga (2002).

80. See, for example, Kōketsu (2009) and Takahashi T. (2005b).

81. Examples of transnational scholarship include Shin, Park, and Yang (2006), Hasegawa and Tōgō (2008), and Kawakami (2006).

82. For a detailed analysis of the Shōwakan exhibit, see K. Smith (2002). An overview of the exhibit hall's difficult path to completion is provided in Hammond (1997) and Tanaka N. (1997).

EPILOGUE

1. This categorization also has its limits, as with my division of the postmemory generations into two. The structure of the survivor generation is more complex inasmuch as it is based not only on their age but also on demographic factors such as gender, class, economic status, educational background, birthplace, and place of residence. But I introduce this division here to make some important points.

2. It is an open mailing list, with the age of participants ranging from middle-school age to a small (and dwindling) number of veterans in their nineties. Topics range from narratives of the wartime experiences of the survivor generation and debates on political issues surrounding Yasukuni Shrine, to, more recently, critiques of the Tokyo Electric Company on its handling of the nuclear crisis following the Great East Japan

earthquake of 2011, the island disputes with China, and the reinterpretation of several articles of the constitution.

3. The group's research on Yasukuni Shrine, on which Hasegawa bases his tours, was published as a booklet titled *Fieldwork on Yasukuni Shrine and Yūshūkan Museum: For Studying, Researching, and Thinking* (Tōkyō no Sensō Iseki o Arukukai 2006).

4. He maintained and constantly updated a website of survivors' experiences and often responded to requests from US veterans wanting to return Japanese items that they had had since the Asia-Pacific War. His website and mailing list are still maintained by volunteers. See http://www.rose.sannet.ne.jp/nishiha/senso/.

5. See, for example, Yamanaka (1974–1981, 1982, 1989, 2003).

6. Shrine personnel, however, close their eyes to the tour, although guides are instructed not to use a microphone during the visit. Hasegawa speculates that the shrine management decided not to interfere as long as the tours bring in "customers," that is, paying visitors to the museum, café, and gift shop.

7. Tōkyō no Sensō Iseki o Arukukai (2006, 3).

8. J. Young (1992).

9. J. Young (1993, 5).

10. http://www.yasukuni.or.jp/english/precinct/index.html.

11. Hata I. (2001).

12. The relationship between the two is not clear. The Liberal Democratic Party established the Committee for the State Support of Yasukuni Shrine in March 1964, but the shrine bill was not officially presented to the Diet until 1969.

BIBLIOGRAPHY

NEWSPAPERS AND PERIODICALS

Asahi shinbun
Ichigaya keizai shinbun
Jiji shinpō
Mainichi shinbun
Nichi-nichi shinbun
Okinawa taimusu
Ryūkyū shinpō
Sankei shinbun
Shufu no tomo
Tokkō geppō
Yomiuri shinbun
Yūbin hōchi shinbun

BOOKS, ARTICLES, AND OTHER WORKS

Abe Yasunari, Miichi Masatoshi, Morimura Toshimi, and Koseki Takashi, eds. 1999. *Kioku no katachi: Komemoreishon no bunkashi.* Tokyo: Kashiwa shobō.

Abel, Jonathan. 2012. *Redacted: The Archives of Censorship in Transwar Japan.* Berkeley: University of California Press.

Adachi Yoshio. 1981. *Aizu Tsurugajō no onna tachi.* Tokyo: Rekishi shunjūsha.

Bibliography

Adorno, Theodor W. 1986 (originally published 1959). "What Does Coming to Terms with the Past Mean?" In *Bitburg in Moral and Political Perspective,* edited by Geoffrey Hartmen, 114–129. Bloomington: Indiana University Press.

Agamben, Giorgio. 1999. *Remnants of Auschwitz: The Witness and the Archive.* New York: Zone Books.

Akazawa Shirō. 1989. "Review of Takahashi Hikohiro's *Minshū no gawa no sensō sekinin.*" *Rekishi hyoron* 474: 64–69.

———. 2002. "Sensō giseisha no tsuitō to Yasukuni Jinja." *Rekishi hyōron* 628: 2–14.

———. 2003. "Sengo Nihon ni okeru senbotsusha 'irei' to tsuitō." *Ritsumeikan Daigaku Jinbunkagaku Kenkyūjo kiyō* 82: 117–133.

———. 2004. "Senbotsusha tsuitō to Yasukuni Jinja mondai o dou kangaeruka." *Sekai* 730: 86–103.

———. 2005. *Yasukuni Jinja: Semegi au "senbotsusha tsuitō" no yukue.* Tokyo: Iwanami shoten.

Akune Iwao. 1977. *Sāākasu no rekishi: Misemono goya kara kindai saakasu e.* Tokyo: Nishida shoten.

Anderson, Benedict. 1983. *Imagined Communities: Reflections on the Origin and Spread of Nationalism.* London: Verso.

Anno Tadashi. 2006. "Kokumin kokka no riron to Yasukuni mondai." In *Yasukuni to mukiau,* edited by Nakano Kōichi and Jochi Daigaku 20 seiki COE Program, 141–196. Tokyo: Mekon.

Antoni, Klaus. 1988. "Yasukuni-Jinja and Folk Religion: The Problem of Vengeful Spirits." *Asian Folklore Studies* 47: 123–136.

Aoki Kōichirō. 2004. *Meiji Tōkyō shomin no tanoshimi.* Tokyo: Chūō kōronsha.

Aoki Masami. 1987. *Senjika no shomin nikki.* Tokyo: Nihon tosho sentā.

Aoki Sadanobu. 1976. "Watashi no Yasukuni Jinja." In his *Buraun kan no shisō: Taishū sōsa no kōzu,* 73–88. Tokyo: Sekai shisōsha.

Apel, Dora. 2002. *Memory Effects: The Holocaust and the Art of Secondary Witnessing.* New Brunswick, NJ: Rutgers University Press.

Arai Ryūichi. 1971. "Tsu-shi jichinsai iken soshō kōsoshin kantei iken." *Waseda hōgaku* 47 (1): 173–193.

Arai Shin'ichi, ed. 1994. *Sensō hakubutsukan.* Iwanami booklet, no. 328. Tokyo: Iwanami shoten.

———. 2005. *Sensō sekinin ron: Gendaishi kara no toi.* Tokyo: Iwanami shoten.

Arakawa Shōji. 2008. "Heishi ga shinda toki: Senshisha kōsō no keisei." *Kokuritsu Rekishi Minzoku Hakubutsukan kenkyū hōkoku* 147: 35–63.

Arendt, Hannah. 1970. *On Violence.* Orlando, FL: Harcourt, Brace & World.

Asahi Shinbunsha. 1971. *Tōkyō hibaku ki.* Tokyo: Asahi shinbunsha.

Asahi Shinbun Shuzai-han. 2006. *Sensō sekinin to tsuitō 1: Rekishi to mukiau.* Tokyo: Asahi shinbunsha.

Asahi Shinbun Teema Sōdan-shitsu. 1987. *Sensō.* Tokyo: Asahi sonorama.

Ashihara Eiryō. 1984. *Sākasu kenkyū.* Tokyo: Shinjuku shobō.

Attie, Shimon. 1998. *Sites Unseen: Shimon Attie's European Projects: Installations and Photographs*. Burlington, VT: Verve.

Awaya Kentarō, Hirowakari Seigo, Mishima Ken'ichi, Mochida Yukio, Tanaka Hiroshi, and Yamaguchi Yasushi. 1994. *Sensō sekinin, sengo sekinin: Nihon to Doitsu wa dou chigauka*. Tokyo: Asahi shinbunsha.

Baer, Ulrich. 2002. *Spectral Evidence: The Photography of Trauma*. Cambridge, MA: MIT Press.

Ballinger, Pamela. 2003. *History in Exile: Memory and Identity at the Border of the Balkans*. Princeton, NJ: Princeton University Press.

Bessatsu Takarajima Henshūbu, ed. 2005. *Nipponjin nara yonde okitai Yasukuni Jinja no hon*. Tokyo: Takarajimasha.

Bevan, Robert. 2006. *The Destruction of Memory: Architecture at War*. Chicago: University of Chicago Press.

Bird, Kai, and Lawrence Lifschultz, eds. 1998. *Hiroshima's Shadow (Writings on the Denial of History and the Smithsonian Controversy)*. Branford, CT: Pamphleteer's Press.

Bitter, Bruno, with Asahi Sonorama Henshūbu. 1973. *Makkāsā no namida: Brūno Bitteru shinpu ni kiku*. Tokyo: Asahi sonorama.

Bix, Herbert P. 1992. "The Showa Emperor's 'Monologue' and the Problem of War Responsibility." *Journal of Japanese Studies* 18 (2): 295–363.

———. 2000. *Hirohito and the Making of Modern Japan*. New York: HarperCollins.

Bōeichō Bōei Kenshūjo Senshi Shitsu. 1968. *Okinawa hōmen rikugun sakusen*. Tokyo: Asagumo shinbunsha.

Breen, John. 2004. "The Dead and the Living in the Land of Peace: A Sociology of the Yasukuni Shrine." *Mortality* 9 (1): 76–93.

———. 2008. "Yasukui and the Loss of Historical Memory." In *Yasukuni, the War Dead, and the Struggle for Japan's Past*, edited by John Breen, 143–162. New York: Columbia University Press.

———, ed. 2008. *Yasukuni, the War Dead, and the Struggle for Japan's Past*. New York: Columbia University Press.

Brison, Susan J. 1999. "Trauma Narratives and the Remaking of the Self." In *Acts of Memory: Cultural Recall in the Present*, edited by Mieke Bal, Jonathan Crew, and Leo Spitzer, 39–54. Hanover, NH: Dartmouth College.

Buruma, Ian. 1994. *The Wages of Guilt: Memories of War in Germany and Japan*. New York: Farrar, Straus and Giroux.

Butler, Judith. 2004. *Precarious Life: The Powers of Mourning and Violence*. London: Verso.

Caruth, Cathy. 1995. *Trauma: Explorations in Memory*. Baltimore: Johns Hopkins University Press.

———. 1996. *Unclaimed Experience: Trauma, Narrative, and History*. Baltimore: Johns Hopkins University Press.

Christy, Alan S. 1993. "The Making of Imperial Subjects in Okinawa." *Positions* 1: 607–639.

Colfino, Alon. 1997. "Collective Memory and Cultural History: Problems of Method." *American Historical Review* 102 (5): 1386–1403.

Connerton, Paul. 1989. *How Societies Remember.* Cambridge: Cambridge University Press.

Cook, Haruko Taya, and Theodore F. Cook. 1992. *Japan at War: An Oral History.* New York: New Press.

de Certeau, Michel. 1988. *The Practice of Everyday Life.* Berkeley: University of California Press.

Dorsey, James. 2009. "Literary Tropes, Rhetorical Looping, and the Nine Gods of War: 'Fascist Proclivities' Made Real." In *The Culture of Japanese Fascism,* edited by Alan Tansman, 409–431. Durham, NC: Duke University Press.

Dower, John W. 1986. *War without Mercy: Race and Power in the Pacific War.* New York: Pantheon Books.

———. 1993. *Japan in War and Peace: Selected Essays.* New York: New Press.

———. 1996. "The Bombed: Hiroshimas and Nagasakis in Japanese Memory." In *Hiroshima in History and Memory,* edited by Michael J. Hogan, 116–142. Cambridge: Cambridge University Press.

———. 1999. *Embracing Defeat: Japan in the Wake of World War II.* New York: W. W. Norton.

———. "Throwing Off Asia II: Woodblock Prints of the Sino-Japanese War." http://ocw.mit.edu/ans7870/21f/21f.027/home/index.html.

———. "Throwing Off Asia III: Woodblock Prints of the Russo-Japanese War." http://ocw.mit.edu/ans7870/21f/21f.027/home/index.html.

Duncan, Carol. 1995. *Civilizing Rituals: Inside Public Art Museums.* London: Routledge.

Earhart, David C. 2008. *Certain Victory: Images of World War II in the Japanese Media.* Armonk, NY: M. E. Sharpe.

Edogawa Ranpo. 1987. *Panorama tō kidan.* Tokyo: Shin'yōdō.

Etō Jun. 1986. "Seisha no shisen to shisha no shisen." *Shokun* 18 (4): 58–78.

———, and Kobori Keiichirō, eds. 1987. *Yasukuni ronshū: Nihon no chinkon no dentō no tame ni.* Tokyo: Nihon kyōbunsha.

Field, Norma. 1993. *In the Realm of a Dying Emperor: Japan at Century's End.* New York: Vintage Books.

———. 1997. "War and Apology: Japan, Asia, the Fiftieth, and After." *Positions* 5 (1): 1–50.

Figal, Gerald. 1996. "How to *Jibunshi:* Making and Marketing Self-Histories of Showa among the Masses in Postwar Japan." *Journal of Asian Studies* 55 (4): 902–933.

———. 1999. *Civilizations and Monsters: Spirits of Modernity in Meiji Japan.* Durham, NC: Duke University Press.

Fogel, Joshua, ed. 2000. *The Nanjing Massacre in History and Historiography.* Berkeley: University of California Press.

Forty, Adrian, and Susanne Küchler, eds. 1999. *The Art of Forgetting.* Oxford: Berg.

Foucault, Michel. 1977. "Nietzsche, Genealogy, History." In *Language, Counter-Memory, Practice: Selected Essays and Interviews by Michel Foucault,* edited by Donald F. Bouchard, 139–164. Ithaca, NY: Cornell University Press.

———. 1980. *Power/Knowledge: Selected Interviews and Other Writings 1972–1977.* Edited by Colin Gordon. New York: Pantheon Books.

———. 1993. "Space, Power and Knowledge." In *The Cultural Studies Reader,* edited by Simon During, 161–169. London: Routledge.

———. 1995. *Discipline and Punish: The Birth of a Prison.* New York: Vintage Books.

Frühstück, Sabine. 2007. *Uneasy Warriors: Gender, Memory and Popular Culture in the Japanese Army.* Berkeley: University of California Press.

Fujimori Terunobu. 1982. *Meiji no Tōkyō keikaku.* Tokyo: Iwanami shoten.

Fujioka Nobukatsu. 1999. *Jubaku no kingendaishi: Rekishi to kyōiku o meguru tatakai.* Tokyo: Tokuma shoten.

Fujita Hiromasa. 2007. "Nihon ni okeru irei, tsuitō, kenshō kenkyū no genjō to kadai." *Jinja Honchō Kyōgaku Kenkyūjo kiyō* 12: 111–142.

———. 2011. "Irei no 'kōkyō kūkan' to shite no Yasukuni Jinja." *Gunjishigaku* 47 (3): 56–74.

Fujita Shōzō. 1998. *Tennōsei kokka no shihai genri.* Tokyo: Misuzu shobō.

Fujitani, Takashi. 1992. "Electronic Pageantry and Japan's 'Symbolic Emperor.'" *Journal of Asian Studies* 51 (4): 824–850.

———. 1998a. "Minshūshi as a Critique of Orientalist Knowledges." *Positions* 6 (2): 303–322.

———. 1998b. *Splendid Monarchy: Power and Pageantry in Modern Japan.* Berkeley: University of California Press.

———, Geoffrey M. White, and Lisa Yoneyama, eds. 2001. *Perilous Memories: The Asia-Pacific War(s).* Durham, NC: Duke University Press.

Fujiwara Akira. 2001. *Uejini shita eirei tachi.* Tokyo: Aoki shoten.

Fujiwara Kiichi. 2001. *Sensō o kioku suru: Hiroshima Horokōsuto to genzai.* Tokyo: Kōdansha.

Fukoku Seimei Hoken Sōgō Gaisha, and Shakai Hensan Iinkai. 1981. *Fukoku Seimei 55 nen shi.* Tokyo: Fukoku seimei hoken sōgō gaisha.

Furukawa Miki. 1970. *Misemono no rekishi.* Tokyo: Yūzankaku.

Fussel, Paul. 1975. *The Great War and Modern Memory.* Oxford: Oxford University Press.

Futabatei Shimei. 1919. *An Adopted Husband.* Translated by Bun'ichirō Mitsui and Gregg M. Sinclair. New York: Knopf. Originally published as *Sono omokage* (Tokyo: Shun'yōdō, 1907).

Gallicchio, Marc, ed. 2007. *The Unpredictability of the Past: Memories of the Asia-Pacific War in U.S.-East Asian Relations.* Durham, NC: Duke University Press.

Gardener, Richard. 1999. "Nationalistic Shintō: A Child's Guide to Yasukuni Shrine." *Religions of Japan in Practice,* edited by George J. Tanabe Jr., 334–339. Princeton, NJ: Princeton University Press.

Garon, Sheldon. 1997. *Molding Japanese Minds: The State in Everyday Life.* Princeton, NJ: Princeton University Press.

———. 2000. "Luxury Is the Enemy: Mobilizing Savings and Popularizing Thrift in Wartime Japan." *Journal of Japanese Studies* 26 (1): 41–78.

Gibney, Frank, ed. 1995. *Sensō: The Japanese Remember the Pacific War—Letters to the Editor of Asahi Shimbun.* New York: M. E. Sharpe.

Gillis, John R., ed. 1994. *Commemorations: The Politics of National Identity.* Princeton, NJ: Princeton University Press.

Gluck, Carol. 1978. "The People in History: Recent Trends in Japanese Historiography." *Journal of Asian Studies* 38 (1): 25–50.

———. 1985. *Japan's Modern Myths: Ideology in the Late Meiji Period.* Princeton, NJ: Princeton University Press.

———. 1992. "The Idea of Showa." In *Showa: The Japan of Hirohito,* edited by Carol Gluck and Stephen R. Graubard, 1–26. New York: W. W. Norton.

———. 1993. "The Past in the Present." In *Postwar Japan as History,* edited by Andrew Gordon, 64–98. Berkeley: University of California Press.

———. 1997. "The 'End' of the Postwar: Japan at the Turn of the Millennium." *Public Culture* 10 (1): 1–23.

———. 2009. "*Sekinin*/Responsibility in Modern Japan." In *Words in Motion: Toward a Global Lexicon,* edited by Carol Gluck and Anna Lowenhaupt Tsing, 83–106. Durham, NC: Duke University Press.

Gōda Ichidō. 1995. *Nihonjin no shinigiwa: Bakumatsu ishin hen.* Tokyo: Shōgakkan.

Gorai Shigeru. 1975. "Onryō to chinkon." In *Inochi to chinkon,* edited by Maruyama Teruo, 7–62. Asahi Karuchā Sentā kōza: Gendaijin no shūkyō 6. Tokyo: Kawade shobō.

———. 1994. *Nihonjin no shiseikan: Minzoku no kokoro no arikata o saguru.* Tokyo: Kadokawa shoten.

Gordon, Andrew. 1991. *Labor and Imperial Democracy in Prewar Japan.* Berkeley: University of California Press.

———. 2009. *A Modern History of Japan from Tokugawa Times to the Present.* 2nd ed. New York: Oxford University Press.

Gunjin Engokai. 1939. *Yasukuni Jinja sanpai kinen shashinchō.* Tokyo: Gunjin engokai.

Haga Noboru. 1992. *Dai-Tōkyō no shisō.* Tokyo: Yūzankaku.

Halbwachs, Maurice. 1980. *The Collective Memory.* New York: Harper & Row.

Hammond, Ellen. 1997. "Commemoration Controversies: The War, the Peace, and Democracy in Japan." In *Living with the Bomb: American and Japanese Cultural Conflicts in the Nuclear Age,* edited by Laura Hein and Mark Selden, 100–121. New York: M. E. Sharpe.

Hane, Mikiso. 1982. *Peasants, Rebels, and Outcasts: The Underside of Modern Japan.* New York: Pantheon Books.

Harada Keiichi. 1996. "Sensō to heiwa no shiryō ni tsuite: Jieitai gokoku jinja no shiryōkan tanbō-ki." *Kikan sensō sekinin* 14: 15–21.

———. 1998. "Rikukaigun maisōchi seido kō." In *Kinsei kindai no chiiki to kenryoku,* edited by Osaka Daigaku Bungaku-bu Nihonshi Kenkyūshitsu, 417–437. Tokyo: Seibundō shuppan.

———. 2001. *Kokumin gun no shinwa: Heishi ni naru to iukoto.* Tokyo: Yoshikawa kōbunkan.

———. 2002. "Dare ga tsuitō dekirunoka: Yasukuni Jinja to senbotsusha tsuitō." *Sensō sekinin kenkyū* 36: 2–9.

Hara Takeshi. 2001. *Kashi-ka sareta teikoku: Kindai Nihon no gyōkōkei.* Tokyo: Misuzu Shobō.

———. 2004. "Senchūki no 'jikan shihai.'" *Misuzu* 521: 28–44.

Hardacre, Helen. 1989. *Shintō and the State, 1868–1988.* Princeton, NJ: Princeton University Press.

Harootunian, Harry D. 1970. *Toward Restoration: The Growth of Political Consciousness in Tokugawa Japan.* Berkeley: University of California Press.

———. 1999a. "Disciplinizing Native Knowledge and Producing Place: Yanagita Kunio, Origuchi Shinobu, and Takata Yasuma." In *Culture and Identity: Japanese Intellectuals during the Interwar Years,* edited by J. Thomas Rimer, 99–127. Princeton, NJ: Princeton University Press.

———. 1999b. "Memory, Mourning, and Natinoal Morality: Yasukuni Shrine and the Reunion of State and Religion in Postwar Japan." In *Nation and Religion: Perspectives on Europe and Asia,* edited by Peter van der Veer and Hartmut Lehmann, 144–160. Princeton, NJ: Princeton University Press.

Harrison, Robert Pogue. 2003. *The Dominion of the Dead.* Chicago: University of Chicago Press.

Haruyama Meitetsu. 2006. "Yasukuni Jinja towa nani ka: Shiryō kenkyū no shiza kara no joron." *Refarensu* 56 (7): 49–75.

———. 2007. "Tanbōki: Yasukuni Kaikō Bunko." *Sankō shoshi kenkyū* 66: 92–95.

Harvey, David. 1989. *The Condition of Postmodernity: An Enquiry into the Origins of Cultural Change.* Oxford: Blackwell.

Hasegawa Jun'ichi, Ishibashi Seiji, and Zushi Minoru. 2009. "Yasukuni Jinja no 'heiwa riyō': Yasukuni heiwa gaido zadankai." *Kikan chūkiren* 45: 66–81.

Hasegawa, Tsuyoshi, and Kazuhiko Tōgō, eds. 2008. *East Asia's Haunted Present: Historical Memories and the Resurgence of Nationalism.* Westport, CT: Praeger Security International.

Hashikawa Bunzō. 1974. "Yasukuni shisō no seiritsu to hen'yō." *Chūō kōron* 89 (10): 227–244.

Hashizume Shin'ya. 1990. *Meiji no meikyū toshi: Tōkyō Ōsaka no yūraku kūkan.* Tokyo: Heibonsha.

———. 1998. *Shukusai no teikoku: Hana densha, gaisen mon, suginoha āchi*. Tokyo: Kōdansha.

———. 2001. *Jinsei wa hakurankai: Nihon rankaiya retsuden*. Tokyo: Shōbunsha.

Hata Ikuhiko. 2001. "Yasukuni Jinja 'chinreisha' no misuterī." *Bungei shunjū* 79 (13): 344–358.

———. 2008. "Dainiji Taisen-ki no Yasukuni Jinja." *Nihon hōgaku* 74 (2): 785–815.

———. 2010. *Yasukuni Jinja no saishin tachi*. Tokyo: Shinchōsha.

Hata Nagami. 1996. "'Sensō sekinin hitei ha' no kōdo to ronri." *Sensō sekinin kenkyū* 11: 2–9.

———. 2002a. "Koizumi shushō Yasukuni sanpai no seiji katei: 'Kokka to irei' ni kansuru joron." *Sensō sekinin kenkyū* (36): 10–18.

———. 2002b. "Kokka to irei: Nihon Izoku-kai to Yasukuni Jinja o meguru sengo no shomondai." *Rekishi hyōron* 628: 15–27.

———. 2006. "Irei to kenshō no aida: Yasukuni o meguru ikutsuka no danshō." *Rekishi hyōron* 678: 85–94.

Hatsuda Tōru. 1994. *Tōkyō, toshi no Meiji*. Tokyo: Chikuma shobō.

———. 1995. *Modan toshi no kūkan hakubutsu gaku*. Tokyo: Shōkokusha.

Hattori Seiichi. 1992. *Tokyo shin hanjōki*. Tokyo: Ryūkei Shosha. Originally published from Shūhōkaku, 1925.

Havens, Thomas R. H. 1978. *Valley of Darkness: The Japanese People and World War Two*. New York: Norton.

Hein, Laura, and Mark Selden, eds. 1997. *Living with the Bomb: American and Japanese Cultural Conflicts in the Nuclear Age*. Armonk, NY: M. E. Sharpe.

———. 2000. *Censoring History: Citizenship and Memory in Japan, Germany, and the United States*. Armonk, NY: M. E. Sharpe.

———. 2003. *Islands of Discontent: Okinawan Responses to Japanese and American Power*. Lanham, MD: Rowman & Littlefield.

Heiwa o Negai Sensō ni Hantai Suru Senbotsusha Izoku no Kai, ed. 2001. *Ima "Yasukuni" o tou*. Kamogawa Booklet 137. Tokyo: Kamogawa shuppan.

Herman, Judith. 1997. *Trauma and Recovery: The Aftermath of Violence—from Domestic Abuse to Political Terror*. New York: Basic Books.

Hirano Takeshi. 1990. "Ehime tamagushi-ryō jiken chisai hanketsu no igi to shatei (shiryō)." *Ryūkoku hōgaku* 22 (4): 416–439.

Hirayama Tsutomu. 1996. "Yasukuni Jinja jiken to senjika no Jōchi Daigaku." In *Daigaku to Ajia Taiheiyō Sensō: Sensō-shi kenkyū to taiken no rekishika*, edited by Shirai Atsuhi, 124–144. Tokyo: Nihon keizai hyōronsha.

Hirsch, Marianne. 1996. "Past Lives: Postmemories in Exile." *Poetics Today* 17 (4): 659–686.

———. 1997. *Family Frames: Photography, Narrative and Postmemory*. Cambridge, MA: Harvard University Press.

———. 2008. "The Generation of Postmemory." *Poetics Today* 29 (1): 103–128.

Hishiki Masaharu. 2006. "Koizumi shushō Yasukuni sanpai iken Taiwan kankei niji soshō: Kōsai hanketsu ga motarashita mono." *Sensō sekinin kenkyū* 51: 74–77.

Hiyama Yukio, ed. 2001. *Kindai Nihon no keisei to Nisshin sensō: Sensō no shakaishi*. Tokyo: Yūzankaku.

———. 2011. "Teikoku Nihon no senbotsusha irei to Yasukuni Jinja (1): Nihon tōchika Taiwan ni okeru Taiwan-jin no Yasukuni gōshi o jirei to shite." *Chūkyō Daigaku Shakai Kagaku Kenkyūjo shakai kagaku kenkyū* 31 (1): 37–171.

Hobsbawm, Eric, and Terence Ranger, eds. 1983. *The Invention of Tradition*. Cambridge: Cambridge University Press.

Holtom, Daniel C. (1943) 1963. *Modern Japan and Shinto Nationalism: A Study of Present-Day Trends in Japanese Religions*. Chicago: University of Chicago Press. Reprint, New York: Paragon Book Reprint Corp.

Homans, Peter, ed. 2000. *Symbolic Loss: The Ambiguity of Mourning and Memory at Century's End*. Charlottesville: University Press of Virginia.

Honda Katsuichi. 1999. *The Nanjing Massacre: A Japanese Journalist Confronts Japan's National Shame*, edited by Frank Gibney; translated by Karen Sandness. New York: M. E. Sharpe.

Honda Sadao. 2008. *Shōwa no sensō, Nihonjin no senō ishiki ni tsuite: "Sensō sekinin" "Tōkyō saiban" "Yasukuni Jinja" "shin kenpō seitei" o megutte*. Tokyo: Bungeisha.

Hornstein, Shelley, and Florence Jacobowitz, eds. 2003. *Image and Remembrance: Representation and the Holocaust*. Bloomington: Indiana University Press.

Hosaka Hiroshi. 2003. "Okinawa-sen no kioku: Sensō torauma to sono katachi." *Ryūkoku Daigaku Hōgakubu kiyō-ningen kagaku* 12: 57–131.

Hosaka Masayasu. 1983. "Nihonjin ga ichiban nekkyō shita hi: Dokyumento Shōwa 16 nen 12 gatsu 8 nichi." *Ushio* 285: 226–249.

———. 1985. *Haisen zengo no Nihonjin*. Tokyo: Asahi shinbunsha.

———. 2007. *"Yasukuni" to iu nayami: Shōwashi no taiga o yuku*. Tokyo: Mainichi shinbunsha.

Hōsei Daigaku Ōhara Shakai Mondai Kenkyūjo. 1987. *Nihon rōdō nenkan* 57. Tokyo: Rōdō junpōsha.

Hoshi Ryōichi. 1990. *Haisha no ishinshi: Aizu hanshi Arakawa Katsushige no nikki*. Tokyo: Chūō kōronsha.

———. 2005. *Aizu sensō zenshi*. Tokyo: Kōdansha.

Hur, Nam-lin. 2000. *Prayer and Play in Tokugawa Japan: Asakusa Sensōji and Edo Society*. Cambridge, MA: Harvard University Press.

Huyssen, Andreas. 1995. *Twilight Memories: Marking Time in a Culture of Amnesia*. New York: Routledge.

Hyōdō Akiko. 2007. "Kagaisha de ari, higaisha de aru to iukoto: 'Eirei' tachi no sei to shi." *Kikan Nihon shisōshi* 71: 87–103.

Ichinose Toshiya. 2004a. *Meiji, Taishō, Shōwa guntai manyuaru: Hito wa naze senjō e ittanoka*. Tokyo: Kōbunsha.

———. 2004b. "Nichiro sensō~Taiheiyō sensōki ni okeru senshisha kenshō to chiiki." *Nihonshi kenkyū* 501: 149–175.

———. 2005. *Jūgo no shakaishi: Senshisha to izoku.* Tokyo: Yoshikawa kōbunkan.

Ichisaka Tarō. 2008. *Bakumatsu eiketsu tachi no hīrō: Yasukuni zenshi.* Tokyo: Asahi shinbunsha.

Ienaga Sabrō. 1987. *The Pacific War, 1931–1945.* Translated by Frank Baldwin. New York: Pantheon Books.

———. 2002. *Sensō sekinin.* Tokyo: Iwanami shoten.

Igarashi, Yoshikuni. 2000. *Bodies of Memory: Narratives of War in Postwar Japanese Culture, 1945–1970.* Princeton, NJ: Princeton University Press.

Iguchi Kazuki. 1986. "Nan no tame no sensō rekishikan ka: 'Heiwa Kinen Sōgō Sentaa' no kiken na kuwadate." *Nihonshi kenkyū* 281: 162–166.

———. 1994. "Gendaishi kenkyū to tenji: Sensō tenji o chūshin ni." *Rekishi hyōron* 256: 38–47.

———. 1998. *Nichiro sensō no jidai.* Tokyo: Yoshikawa kōbunkan.

Iijima Mitsuru, Nagai Miwako, and Nakayama Shunsuke. 2001. "Filmon ontai ni kansuru chōsa hōkoku." *Research and Reports on Intangible Cultural Heritage* 5: 53–76

Ikeda Ryōhachi. 1967. "Yasukuni Jinja no sōsetsu." *Shintō shi kenkyū* 15 (5–6): 50–70.

Ikegami Yoshimasa. 2003. *Shisha no kyūsaishi: Kuyō to hyōi no shūkyōgaku.* Tokyo: Kadokawa shoten.

Ikeo Yasushi, ed. 2006. *Sensō no kioku to wakai.* Tokyo: Shōyō shobō.

Imai Akihiko. 2002. "Bakumatsu ni okeru Aizu hanshi no junan to sono maisō." In *Jinrui ni totte tatakai towa 5: Ideorogii no bunka sōchi,* edited by Fukui Katsuyoshi and Shintani Takanori, 244–267. Tokyo: Tōyō shorin.

———. 2005. *Kindai Nihon to senshisha saishi.* Tokyo: Tōyō shorin.

Inoue Tetsujirō. 1891. *Chokugo engi.* Tokyo: Bunkaidō.

Inui Yoshiko, ed. 2008. *Sensō no aru kurashi.* Tokyo: Suiseisha.

Irie Yōko. 2000. *Nihon ga "kami no kuni" datta jidai: Kokumin gakkō no kyōkasho o yomu.* Tokyo: Iwanami shoten.

Irokawa Daikichi. 1985. *Culture of the Meiji Period.* Translation edited by Marius B. Jansen. Princeton, NJ: Princeton University Press.

———. 1990. *Shōwashi sesōhen.* Tokyo: Shōgakkan.

———. 1996. *Irokawa Daikichi chosakushū,* vol. 3. Tokyo: Chikuma shobō.

Ishibashi Tanzan. (1945) 1970. "Yasukuni Jinja haishi no gi: Gataki o shinonde aete teigensu." *Tōyō keizai shinpō* editorial. Reprint, *Ishibashi Tanzan zenshū* 13, 54–56. Tokyo: Tōyō keizai shinpōsha. Citations refer to the Tōyō Keizai Shinpōsha edition.

Ishihara Masaie. 1983. "Okinawa-sen no zentaizō kaimei ni kansuru kenkyū 1: Shiryōhen (1)." *Okinawa Kokusai Daigaku bungakubu kiyō* 11 (1): 23–43.

———. 1984. "Okinawa-sen no zentaizō kaimei ni kansuru kenkyū 2: Shiryōhen (2)." *Okinawa Kokusai Daigaku bungakubu kiyō* 12 (1): 23–49.

———. 1985. "Okinawa-sen no zentaizō kaimei ni kansuru kenkyū 3: Shiryōhen (3)." *Okinawa Kokusai Daigaku bungakubu kiyō* 13 (1): 73–79.

———. 1991. *Okinawa sen ni okeru Nihon gun to jūmin gisei (kyōkasho saiban (dai sanji soshō kōso shin) no shōgen "iken sho")*. Tokyo: Kyōkasho Kentei Soshō o Kōen Suru Zenkoku Renraku-kai.

———. 2007. "'Engo-hō' ni yotte netsuzō sareta 'Okinawa sen ninshiki': 'Yasukuni shisō ga gyōshuku shita 'engo-hō yōgo no shūdan jiketsu." *Okinawa Kokusai Daigaku shakai bunka kenkyū* 10 (1): 31–54.

———. 2008. "Beigunseika Okinawa ni okeru 'Yasukuni Jinja gōshi' mondai (1): 'Yasukuni-ka sareta Okinawa' kara no dakkyaku o mezashi." *Okinawa Kokusai Daigaku shakai bunka kenkyū* 11 (1): 23–41.

———. 2010. "Beigunseika Okinawa ni okeru 'Yasukuni Jinja gōshi' mondai (2): 'Engo-hō' ga motarashita 'Yasukuni Jinja gōhi.'" *Okinawa Kokusai Daigaku shakai bunka kenkyū* 12 (1): 33–83.

———, Ōshiro Masayasu, Hosaka Hiroshi, and Matsunaga Katsutoshi. 2002. *Sōten, Okinawasen no kioku*. Tokyo: Shakai hyōronsha.

Ishii Kendō. 1908. *Meiji jibutsu kigen*. Tokyo: Kyōnandō.

Ishimure Michiko. 1986. *Yō no kanashimi*. Tokyo: Asahi shinbunsha.

Ishizuka Hiromichi, and Narita Ryūichi. 1986. *Tōkyōto no hyakunen*. Tokyo: Yamakawa shuppansha.

Itagaki Tadashi. 1999. "Senryō-ka no Yasukuni Jinja." *Gekkan karento* 36 (2): 39–41.

———. 2000. *Yasukuni kōshiki sanpai no sōkatsu*. Tokyo: Tentensha.

Itō Chūta. (1909) 1982. "Kenchiku shinka no gensoku yori mitaru wagahou kenchiku no zento." *Kenchiku zasshi* 265. Reprint, Itō Chūta, *Ronsō zuisō manpitsu,* Itō Chūta chosakushū, vol. 6, 21–55. Tokyo: Hara shobō, 1982. Citations refer to the Hara shobō edition.

Itō Mikiharu. 1982. *Kazoku kokkakan no jinruigaku*. Tokyo: Mineruva shobō.

Itō Tatsumi. 1987. "Tōjō-ke no iibun." *Shokun* 19 (1): 26–47.

———. 1989. "Tennō to Yasukuni Jinja." *Shokun* 21 (3): 186–193.

Itō Tomonaga. 2009. *Ki o terawazu: Rikugunshō kōkyū fukukan Miyama Yōzō no Shōwa*. Tokyo: Kōdansha.

Itō Yoshikuni. 1988. "Yasukuni Jinja Yūshūkan kaikan ichinen-han no genjō to kadai." *Hakubutsukan kenkyū* 23 (1): 49–53.

Ivy, Marilyn. 1995. *Discourses of the Vanishing: Modernity, Phantasm, Japan*. Chicago: University of Chicago Press.

Iwai Tadakuma. 2008. *"Yasukuni" to Nihon no sensō*. Tokyo: Shin Nihon shuppansha.

Iwata Shigenori. 1996. *Mura no wakamono, kuni no wakamono: Minzoku to kokumin tōgō*. Tokyo: Miraisha.

———. 2003. *Senshisha reikon no yukue: Sensō to minzoku*. Tokyo: Yoshikawa kōbunkan.

———. 2005a. "Seikatsu no naka no senshisha saishi." *Kikan Tōhokugaku* 4: 162–166.

———. 2005b. "Senshisha tajū saishiron." *Gendai shisō* 33 (9): 138–147.

———. 2006. *"Ohaka" no tanjō: Shisha saishi no minzokushi*. Tokyo: Iwanami shoten.

———. 2007. "Tajū saishi no naka no Yasukuni Jinja." *Quadrante* 9: 269–280.

Jay, Martin. 1993. *Force Fields: Between Intellectual History and Cultural Critique*. New York: Routledge.

Jinja Shinpōsha, ed. 1971. *Shintō shirei to sengo no Yasukuni*. Tokyo: Jinja shinpōsha.

Jinnai Hidenobu. 1985. *Tōkyō no kūkan jinruigaku*. Tokyo: Chikuma shobō. Translated into English by Kimiko Nishimura as *Tokyo: A Spatial Anthropology*. Berkeley: University of California Press, 1995.

———, and Hōsei Daigaku Tōkyō no Machi Kenkyūkai. 1989. *Edo Tōkyō no mikata shirabekata*. Tokyo: Kajima shuppankai.

Jōshita Ken'ichi. 2013. "Senryōki no Nihon Izoku Kōsei Renmei no katsudō to sono seijiteki eikyōryōku." *Ritsumeikan Daigaku Jinbun Kagaku Kenkyūjo kiyō* 97: 91–114.

Kagotani Jirō. 1994. "Shisha tachi no Nisshin sensō." In *Nisshin sensō no shakaishi: "Bunmei sensō" to minshū*, edited by Ōtani Tadashi and Harada Keiichi, 107–154. Osaka: Forum A.

———. 2002. "Senshisha no sōgi to chōson: Chōsonsō no suii ni tsuite no kōsatsu." *Rekishi hyōron* 628: 41–54.

Kaigo Tokiomi. 1961–1967. *Nihon kyōkasho taikei kindaihen*. 27 vols. Tokyo: Kōdansha.

Kamata Sadao. 1996. "Nagasaki genbaku shiryōkan no kagai tenji mondai." *Sensō sekinin kenkyū* 14: 22–31.

Kamisaka Fuyuko. 2006. *Sensō o shiranai hito no tame no Yasukuni mondai*. Tokyo: Bungei shunjū.

Kamishima Jirō. 1961. *Kindai Nihon no seishin kōzō*. Tokyo: Iwanami shoten.

Kamo Momoki. 1911a. *Yasukuni Jinja jireki taiyō*. Tokyo: Kokkōkan.

———. 1911b. *Yasukuni Jinja shi*. Tokyo: Yasukuni jinja.

Kaneko Atsuhi. 2006. "Sensō shiryō no riaritii: Mono o baikai to shita sensō taiken no keishō o megutte." In *Ajia Taiheiyō Sensō*, vol. 6, *Nichijō seikatsu no naka no sōryokusen*, edited by Kurasawa Aiko, Sugihara Tōru, and Narita Ryūichi, 327–352. Tokyo: Iwanami shoten.

Kanō Mikiyo. 1987. *Onnatachi no jūgo*. Tokyo: Chikuma shobō.

Karasawa Tomitarō. 1989. *Kyōkasho no rekishi 1.2, Karasawa Tomitarō chosakushū*, vols. 6–7. Tokyo: Gyōsei.

Kasza, Gregory J. 1988. *The State and Mass Media in Japan, 1918–1945*. Berkeley: University of California Press.

Katayama Tadashi. 1984. "'Eirei' fukkatsu no kiken na kōzu: Gakkō kyōiku ni mochikomareru 'Yasukuni Jinja.'" *Bunka hyōron* 282: 67–78.

Katō Takahisa. 1967. "Shōkonsha no genryū." *Shintō-shi kenkyū* 15 (5–6): 9–27.

Katō Takeo. 1941. *Aokusa*. Tokyo: Dōzokusha.

Katō Toshihiko, and Maeda Ai. 1980. *Meiji media kō*. Tokyo: Chūō kōronsha.

Katō Yōko. 1996. *Chōheisei to kindai Nihon, 1868–1945*. Tokyo: Yoshikawa kōbunkan.

Kawabata Kōzen. 2008. "Okinawa-sen kara Yasukuni soshō made." *Tsubute* 59: 74–94.

Kawabata Yasunari. 1959. "Shōkonsai ikkei." In *Kawabata Yasunari zenshū*, vol. 1, 41–56. Tokyo: Shinchōsha. Originally published in *Shin-shichō* (April 1921).

Kawade Shobō. 2006. *Yasukuni mondai nyūmon ketteiban: Yasukuni no datsu shinwaka e*. Tokyo: Kawade shobō shinsha.

Kawakami Tamio, Pak Ch'ang-hŭi, and Nishimura Tōru, eds. 2006. *Kaikyō no ryōgawa kara Yasukuni o kangaeru: Hisen, chinkon, Ajia*. Tokyo: Oruta shppanshitsu.

Kawamura Kunimitsu. 1990. *Genshi suru kindai kūkan: Meishin, byōki, zashikirō, aruiwa rekishi no kioku*. Tokyo: Seikyūsha.

———. 1996. *Minzoku kūkan no kindai: Wakamono, sensō, saiyaku, takai no fōkuroa*. Tokyo: Jōhō shuppan kabushiki gaisha.

———. 2000. *"Minzoku no chi" no keifu: Kindai Nihon no minzoku bunka*. Kyoto: Shōwadō.

———. 2001. "Senshisha-ron josetsu: Senshisha to wa dareka." *Nihon shisōshi kenkyūkai kaihō* 19: 1–14.

———. 2005. "Tomurai-ron e mukete: Shisha, bōrei, senshisha kara." *Gendai shisō* 33 (9): 148–156.

———. 2006. "Senshisha no bōrei to Yasukuni." *Asoshie* 17: 148–157.

———. 2007. *Seisen no ikonogurafii: Tennō to heishi, senshisha no zushō, hyōshō*. Tokyo: Seikyūsha.

———, ed. 2003. *Senshisha no yukue: Katari to hyōshō kara*. Tokyo: Seikyūsha.

Kawashima Takane. 1997. *Jūgo: Ryūgen, tōsho no "Taiheiyō sensō."* Tokyo: Yomiuri shinbunsha.

Kawazoe Noboru. 1993. *Tōkyō no genfūkei*. Tokyo: Chikuma shobō.

Keene, Donald. 1971. "The Sino-Japanese War of 1894–95 and Its Cultural Effects in Japan." In *Tradition and Modernization in Japanese Culture*, edited by Donald H. Shively, 121–175. Princeton, NJ: Princeton University Press.

Kido Takayoshi. 1983. *The Diary of Kido Takayoshi*, vol. 1. Translated by Sidney Devere Brown and Akiko Hirota. Tokyo: University of Tokyo Press.

Kikuchi Kunisaku. 1977. *Chōhei tōhi no kenkyū*. Tokyo: Rippū shobō.

Kim Han. 2007. "Yasukuni to Kita Chōsen: Kioku to sekyuritii o megutte." *Quadrante* 9: 313–324.

Kimura Norito. 2003. *Sensōchū wa "gokuraku" datta: Kioku fairu, mura no 1940 nendai*. Tokyo: Daisan shokan.

Kimura Shigeru. 2000. "Ajia Taiheiyō Sensō kaigai senbotsusha no ikotsu shūshū jigyō: Sono keii to mondaiten." *Ottemon Gakuin Daigaku bungakubu kiyō* 36: 1–18.

Kin Birei. 2003. "Kuni no ishizue to natta sofu tachi tono 'yaskusoku' o hogo ni shite wa naranai: Gōgan to seiji shugi no giron o imashimeru." *Seiron* 374: 164–171.

Kinoshita Naoyuki. 1992. "Yasukuni Jinja ni nemutte ita kyodai abura-e." *Geijutsu shinchō* 43 (5): 90–97.

———. 1995. "Gaisenmon no kō: Nisshin sensō o meguru senshō imeeji no dōin." *Bijutsushi* 44 (2): 252–254.

———. 1996. *Haribote no machi*. Tokyo: Asahi shinbunsha.

———. 1997. "Daigaku Nankō bussankai ni tsuite." *Gakumon no arukeorojii*. Tokyo: Tokyo University. http://www.um.u-tokyo.ac.jp/publish_db/1997Archaeology/01/10700.html.

———. 1999. *Bijutsu to iu misemono: Aburae chaya no jidai*. Tokyo: Chikuma shobō.

Kira Yoshie. 2003. "Shōwa-ki no chōhei heiji shiryō kara mita heishi no miokuri to kikan." *Kokuritsu Rekishi Minzoku Hakubutsukan kenkyū hōkoku* 101: 285–305.

Kisaka Jun'ichirō. 1993. "Ajia Taiheiyō sensō no koshō to seikaku." *Ryūkoku hōgaku* 25 (4): 386–434.

Kishi Toshihiko, Kawashima Shin, and Son An-sŏk, eds. 2006. *Sensō, Rajio, Kioku*. Tokyo: Bensei shuppan.

Kitajima Junko. 2013. "Kindai kyōkasho no naka no Yasukuni: Kyōkasho sōgō kenkyūjo no shiryō kara." In *Yasukuni Jinja to rekishi kyōiku: Yasukuni, Yūshūkan fiirudo nōto*, edited by Matayoshi Seikiyo, Kimizuka Yoshihiko, and Kuroo Kazuhisa, 79–101. Tokyo: Asahi shoten.

Kitamura Riko. 1996. "Chōhei nogare kigan." *Minzoku to rekishi* 27: 24–28.

———. 1999. *Chōhei, sensō to minshū*. Tokyo: Yoshikawa kōbunkan.

———. 2006. "Senjō no shi no uketomekata o megutte." *Nihon minzokugaku* 247: 195–217.

Kobayashi Kenzō, and Terunuma Yoshifumi. 1969. *Shōkonsha seiritsu no kenkyū*. Tokyo: Kinseisha.

Kobayashi Yoshinori. 1998. *Sensōron*. Tokyo: Gentōsha.

———. 2005. *Yasukuniron*. Tokyo: Gentōsha.

Kobori Keiichirō. 1998. *Yasukuni Jinja to Nihonjin*. Tokyo: PHP shuppan.

Koizumi Yakumo (Lafcadio Hearn). 1928. "Kanaeru negai." In *Koizumi Yakumo zenshū*, vol. 5, 244–264. Tokyo: Daiichi shobō.

Kojima Tsuyoshi. 2007. *Yasukuni shikan: Bakumatsu ishin toiu shin'en*. Tokyo: Chikuma shobō.

Kōketsu Atsushi. 2009. *Watashi tachi no sensō sekinin: "Showa" shoki 20 nen to "Heisei" ki 20 nen no rekishi teki kōsatsu*. Tokyo: Gaifūsha.

Kokugakuin Daigaku Kenkyū Kaihatsu Suishin Sentā, ed. 2008. *Irei to kenshō no aida: Kingendai Nihon no senshisha kan o megutte*. Tokyo: Kinseisha.

———. 2010. *Reikon, irei, kenshō: Shisha e no kioku sōchi*. Tokyo: Kinseisha.

———. 2013. *Shōkon to irei no keifu: "Yasukuni" no shisō o tou*. Tokyo: Kinseisha.

Kokuritsu Kokkai Toshokan Chōsa Oyobi Rippō Kōsakyoku (KKT). 1976. *Yasukuni Jinja mondai shiryōshū*. Research Material Series 76–2. Tokyo: Kokuritsu kokkai toshokan.

———. 2007. *Shinpen Yasukuni Jinja mondai shirōshū*. Tokyo: Kokuritsu kokkai toshokan.

Kokuritsu Rekishi Minzoku Hakubutsukan, and Yasuda Tsuneo, eds. 2010. *Sensō to heiwa: Sōgō tenji dai 6 shitsu "gendai" no sekai 1*. Tokyo: Tōkyōdō shuppan.

Kokusai Shūkyō Kenkyūjo, ed. 2004. *Atarashii tsuitō shisetsu wa hitsuyō ka*. Tokyo: Perikansha.

Komatsu Kazuhiko. 2002. *Kami naki jidai no minzokugaku*. Tokyo: Seika shobō.

Komori Yōichi, Chie Uonshiku, and Pak Yuha, eds. 2008. *Higashi Ajia rekishi ninshiki ronsō no meta historii: "Kan-Nichi rentai 21" no kokoromi*. Tokyo: Seikyūsha.

Kosher, Rudy. 2000. *From Monuments to Traces: Artifacts of German Memory, 1870–1990*. Berkeley: University of California Press.

Koshizawa Akira. 2001. *Tōkyō toshi keikaku monogatari*. Tokyo: Chikuma shobō.

Koyanagi Kiyotaka, ed. 1983. *Yasukuni: Kokumin jinja to sensō no nai kuni*. Tokyo: Shōbunkan.

Koyasu Nobukuni. 2004. *Kokka to saishi: Kokka shintō no genzai*. Tokyo: Seidodsha.

Krystof, Nicholas D. 1998. "The Problem of Memory." *Foreign Affairs* 77 (6): 37–49.

Kubota Ryōzan, ed. 1880. *Kiji ronsetsu shūsei*. Tokyo: Suedō.

Kuroda Toshio. 1981. "Shinto in the History of Japanese Religion." Translated by James C. Dobbins and Suzanne Gay. *Journal of Japanese Studies* 7 (1): 1–21.

Kurushima Hiroshi. 1986. "Kinsei ni okeru matsuri no 'shūhen.'" *Rekishi hyōron* 439: 12–24.

Kuwa Sadahiko. 1935. "Tokyo Shōkonsha ni tsuite." *Jinja kyōkai zasshi* 34 (4/6).

LaCapra, Dominick. 1998. *History and Memory after Auschwitz*. Ithaca, NY: Cornell University Press.

———. 2001. *Writing History, Writing Trauma*. Baltimore: Johns Hopkins University Press.

Lefebvre, Henri. 1991. *The Production of Space*. Translated by Donald Nicholson-Smith. Oxford: Blackwell.

Levinthal, David. 1996. *Mein Kampf*. Santa Fe, NM: Twin Palms.

———. 1997. *David Levinthal, Work from 1975–1996: Essays and Interview*. New York: International Center of Photography in association with Distributed Art Publishers.

Leys, Ruth. 2000. *Trauma: A Genealogy*. Chicago: University of Chicago Press.

Li Ying. 2009. *Yasukuni*. Tokyo: Asahi shinbun.

Linenthal, Edward, and Tom Engelhardt, eds. 1996. *History Wars: The Enola Gay and Other Battles for the American Past*. New York: Metropolitan Books.

Maeda Ai. 1989. *Gen'ei no Meiji*. Maeda Ai chosaku-shū, vol. 4. Tokyo: Chikuma shobō.

Mainichi Shinbun "Yasukuni" Shuzaihan. 2007. *Yasukuni sengo hishi: A-kyū senpan o gōshi shita otoko*. Tokyo: Mainichi shinbunsha.

Makihara Norio. 1994. "Banzai no tanjō." *Shisō* 845: 118–136.

———. 1998. *Kyakubun to kokumin no aida: Kindai minshū no seiji ishiki*. Tokyo: Yoshikawa kōbunkan.

Markus, Andrew L. 1985. "The Carnival of Edo: Misemono Spectacles from Contemporary Accounts." *Harvard Journal of Asiatic Studies* 45 (2): 499–541.

Maruyama Masao. 1969. *Thought and Behavior in Modern Japanese Politics*. Expanded and edited by Ivan Morris. London: Oxford University Press.

Maruyama Yasuaki. 2007. "Heishi no shi o meguru tenji: Yūshūkan ni okeru shisha no tenji no tanjō to tenkai." *Nihongakuhō* 26: 37–49.

———. 2010a. *Kogoeru teikoku: Hakkōdasan sekichū kōgun sōnan jiken no minzokushi*. Tokyo: Seikyūsha.

———. 2010b. "Pafōmansu to shiteno sensō tenji: Yūshūkan kara kangaeru." *Kōshō bungei kenkyū* 33: 109–113.

Masaoka Shiki. 1927. *Byōshō rokushaku*. Tokyo: Iwanami shoten.

Matayoshi Seikiyo. 2004. "Tōkyō no naka no Okinawa to Ajia." *Kyōiku jissen ākaibuzu* 1: 27–45.

———, Kimizuka Yoshihiko, and Kuroo Kazuhisa, eds. 2013. *Yasukuni Jinja to rekishi kyōiku: Yasukuni, Yūshūkan fiirudo nōto*. Tokyo: Asahi shoten.

Matsuda Jōta. 1933. "Yasukuni Jinja to Yūshūkan." In *Minshū bunko*, vol. 74. Tokyo: Shakai kyōiku kyōkai.

Matsumoto Seichō, Miki Jun, and Fujiwara Akira, eds. 1984. *Shashin kiroku Shōwa no rekishi*. 6 vols. Tokyo: Shōgakkan.

Matsuzaki Kenzō. 1998. "Eirei oyobi gunba gunken gunkyū saishi: Yasukuni Jinja o jirei to shite." *Minzoku kenkyū kiyō* 22: 39–59.

McCullough, Helen Craig, ed. 2003. *The Taiheiki: A Chronicle of Medieval Japan*. Boston: Tuttle.

Mihashi Ken. 1986. "Tōkyō Shōkonsha kara bekkaku kanpeisha Yasukuni Jinja e." *Shintō shūkyō* 122: 78–106.

Minamoto Junko. 2009. "Yasukuni Jinja mondai o kangaeru: Gakusei no ankeeto chōsa kara mieru tōsaku shita jidai jōkyō." *Sekai Jinken Mondai Kenkyū Sentaa kenkyū kiyō* 14: 1777–1798.

Minear, Richard H. 1972. *Victors' Justice: The Tokyo War Crimes Trial*. Tokyo: Tuttle.

Mitchell, Richard H. 1983. *Censorship in Imperial Japan*. Princeton, NJ: Princeton University Press.

Mitsuchi Shūhei. 2002. "Yasukuni Jinja no 'kōkyōsei' to 'shūkyōsei' o meguru tairitsu no kōzu." *Tokyo Rika Daigaku kiyō kyōyōhen* 35: 131–151.

———. 2005. *Yasukuni mondai no genten*. Tokyo: Nihon hyōronsha.

———. 2007. *Atama o hiyasu tame no Yasukuni-ron*. Tokyo: Chikuma shobō.

Miyata Noboru. 1970. *Ikigami shinkō: Hito o kami ni matsuru shūzoku*. Tokyo: Hanawa shobō.

Miyazaki Tetsuya, ed. 1995. *Bokura no "shinryaku sensō": Mukashi atta ano sensō o dō kangaetara yoi no ka*. Tokyo: Yōsensha.

Mori Tatsuya, Suzuki Kunio, and Miyadai Shinji. 2008. *Eiga Yasukuni: Jōei chūshi o meguru dai giron*. Tokyo: Tsukuru shuppan.

Morioka Kiyomi. 1977. "The Appearance of 'Ancestor Religion' in Modern Japan: The Years of Transition from the Meiji to the Taisho Periods." *Japanese Journal of Religious Studies* 4 (2–3): 183–212.

———. 1993. *Kesshi no sedai to isho: Taiheiyō sensō makki no wakamono no sei to shi*. Tokyo: Yoshikawa kōbunkan.

———, and Imai Akihiko. 1982. "Kokuji junan senbotsusha, tokuni hanseifugun senshisha no irei jittai (chōsa hōkoku)." *Seijō bungei* 102: 1–37.

Morone Sadao. 1998. "Ehime tamagushi-ryō iken soshō no kiseki." *Shakaikagaku kenkyū* 35: 1–11.

Morris-Suzuki, Tessa. 1984. *Showa: An Inside History of Hirohito's Japan*. London: Athlone Press.

———. 1998. *Re-Inventing Japan: Time, Space, Nation*. Armonk, NY: M. E. Sharpe.

———. 2005. *The Past within Us: Media, Memory, History*. London: Verso.

Mosse, George L. 1990. *Fallen Soldiers: Reshaping the Memory of the World Wars*. New York: Oxford University Press.

Motoyasu Hiroshi. 2002. *Gunto no irei kūkan: Kokumin tōgō to senshisha tachi*. Tokyo: Yoshikawa kōbunkan.

Muir, Peter. 2010. *Shimon Attie's Writing on the Wall: History, Memory, Aesthetics*. Farnham, England: Ashgate.

Murai Osamu. 2006. "Koizumi shushō no sanpai o kyohi shinai Yasukuni Jinja ga wakaranai." In *Yasukuni Jinja nyūmon: Yasukuni no datsu shinwa-ka e*, 2–11. Tokyo: Kawade shuppan.

Murakami Shigeyoshi. 1970. *Kokka Shintō*. Tokyo: Iwanami shoten.

———. 1974. *Irei to shōkon: Yasukuni no shisō*. Tokyo: Iwanami shoten.

———. 1984. "Nisshin Nichiro sensō to Yasukuni Jinja." *Hōgaku seminā* 354: 120–123.

———. 1986. *Yasukuni Jinja, 1869–1945–1985*. Tokyo: Iwanami shoten.

Muramatsu Teijirō. 1976. *Oyatoi gaikokujin. Vol. 15, Kenchiku doboku*. Tokyo: Kajima shuppankai.

———, Lynn E. Riggs, and Takechi Manabu. 1995. *Westerners in the Modernization of Japan*. Tokyo: Hitachi.

Murata Minejirō. 1919. *Ōmura Masujirō sensei jiseki*. Tokyo.

Nagae Tarō, and Takahashi Hisashi. 2006. "Beichū no Yasukuni 'Yūshūkan' hihan ni kotaeru." *Shokun* 38 (11): 94–103.

Naha District Court (NDC). 2010. "Gōshi torikeshi oyobi songai baishō seikyū jiken, October 26, 2010." http://www.courts.go.jp/hanrei/pdf/20101202213911.pdf.

Naikakushō Jinja-kyoku. 1939. "Gokoku jinja seido no kakuritsu." *Shūhō* 131: 2–8.

Nakagawa Dōji. 1969. *Rankaiya ichidai: Waga hakurankai 100 nen shi*. Tokyo: Kōdansha.

Nakamasa Masaki. 2005. *Nihon to Doitsu: Futatsu no sengo shisō*. Tokyo: Kōbunsha shinsho.

Nakamura Naofumi, and NHK Shuzai-han. 2007. *Yasukuni: Shirazareru senryōka no kōbō*. Tokyo: NHK Shuppan.

Nakano Kōichi, and Jōchi Daigaku 21 Seiki COE Puroguramu, eds. 2006. *Yasukuni to mukiau*. Tokyo: Mekon.

Nakayama Takeo. 1972. "Nihon kenpō ni okeru seikyō bunri no gensoku: Tsu-shi jichinsai jiken o chūshin to shite." *Meijō hōgaku* 21 (4): 1–23.

Namihira Emiko. 2003. "Heishi no 'itai' to heishi no 'irei.'" *Kokuritsu Minzoku Rekishi Hakubutsukan kenkyū hōkoku* 102: 493–513.

———. 2004. *Nihonjin no shi no katachi: Dentō girei kara Yasukuni made*. Tokyo: Asahi shinbunsha.

Natsume Sōseki. 1972. *I Am a Cat*. Translated by Aiko Ito and Graeme Wilson. Tokyo: Tuttle.

Nelson, John. 2003. "Social Memory as Ritual Practice: Commemorating Spirits of the Military Dead at Yasukuni Shinto Shrine." *Journal of Asian Studies* 62 (2): 443–467.

Nelson, Robert S., and Margaret Olin. 2003. *Monuments and Memory, Made and Unmade*. Chicago: University of Chicago Press.

Nihon Senbotsu Gakusei Kinenkai. 1988. *Kike wadatsumi no koe*. Tokyo: Iwanami shoten.

Nihon Shiseki Kyōkai, ed. (1916) 1981. *Kōhon mori no shigeri*. 2 vols. Reprint, Tokyo: Tōkyō daigaku shuppankai.

Niki Etsuko. 1972. *Imōto tachi no kagaribi: Senshi shita niisan o itamu*. Tokyo: Kōdansha.

Nishijima Hiroshi. 2002. "Gakkō ongaku wa ikanishite 'kokumin' o tsukutta ka." In *Hensei sareru nashonarizumu 1920–1930s*, edited by Komori Yōichi, Chino Kaori, Sakai Naoki, and Narita Ryūichi, Vol. 5, *Iwanami kōza kindai Nihon no bunkashi*, 235–270. Tokyo: Iwanami shoten.

Nishikawa Shigenori. 1988. *Tennō no jinja "Yasukuni."* Kyōkasho ni kakarenakatta sensō, part 5. Tokyo: Nashinokisha.

———. 2003. *"Shin Yūshūkan" monogatari*. Tokyo: Inochi no kotobasha.

Nishimura Akira. 2002. "Irei to bōryoku: Sensō shisha e no taido rikai no tameni." *Gendai shūkyō* (2002): 120–137.

———. 2003. "Shi shite nao dōinchū no gakuto tachi: Hibaku Nagasaki Ikadai-sei no irei to Yasukuni gōshi." *Nishi Nihon shūkyōgaku zasshi* 25: 1–12.

———. 2006. *Sengo Nihon to sensō shisha irei: Shizume to furui no dainamizumu*. Tokyo: Yūshisha.

———. 2008. "Ikotsu shūshū, senchi hōmon to senshisha izoku: Shisha to seisha no jikūkanteki hedatari ni chūmoku shite." *Shōwa no kurashi kenkyū* 6: 39–52.

Nishisato Fuyuko. 2007. "'Yasukuni gōshi' no shikumi towa? Shōkon sareta 'eirei' wa shikaku shinsa o hete 'saishin' e!?" *Sensō sekinin kenkyū* 57: 54–65.

Nora, Pierre. 1989. "Between Memory and History: *Les Lieux de Mémoire*." *Representations* 26: 7–24.

Numata Takuji. 1984. "Sakka tachi no '8.15.'" *Bunka Hyōron* 282: 104–115.

O'Connor, Brian. 2010. "Adorno on the Destruction of Memory." In *Memory: Histories, Theories, Debates,* edited by Susannah Radstone and Bill Schwarz, 136–149. New York: Fordham University Press.

Ōe Kenzaburō. 1971. *Itami Mansaku Esseishū*. Tokyo: Chikuma shobō.

Ōe Shinobu. 1981. *Chōheisei*. Tokyo: Iwanami shoten.

———. 1984. *Yasukuni Jinja*. Tokyo: Iwanami shoten.

———. 1988. *Heishi tachi no Nichiro sensō: 500 tsū no gunji tsūshin kara*. Tokyo: Asahi shinbunsha.

Ogawa Kandai. 2006. *"Umi yukaba" o utatta koto ga arimasuka: Gunka ni komerareta kindai Nihonjin no kokoro*. Tokyo: H&I.

Ogi Shinzō. 1980. *Tōkei jidai: Edo to Tōkyō no hazama de*. Tokyo: Nihon hōsō kyōkai.

———. 1991. *Edo Tōkyō-gaku kotohajime*. Tokyo: Chikuma shobō.

———, ed. 1986. *Tōkyō kūkan: 1868–1930*. 3 vols. Tokyo: Chikuma shobō.

———, ed. 1991. *Edo Tōkyō o yomu*. Tokyo: Chikuma shobō.

———, Takeuchi Makoto, and Maeda Ai, eds. 1987. *Edo Tōkyō gaku jiten*. Tokyo: Sanseidō.

Oguma Eiji, and Ueno Yōko. 2003. *"Iyashi" no nashonarizumu: Kusanone hoshu undō no jisshō kenkyū*. Tokyo: Keiō gijuku daigaku shuppankai.

Ōhama Tetsuya. 2003. *Shomin no mita Nisshin Nichiro sensō: Teikoku e no ayumi*. Tokyo: Tōsui shobō.

Ōhara Yasuo. 1986. "A-kyū senpan wa naze gōshi saretaka." *Shokun* 18 (4): 80–92.

———. 1991. "Shintō shirei to Yasukuni Jinja, gokoku jinja." *Kokugakuin Daigaku Nihon Bunka Kenkyūjo kiyō* 68: 1–50.

———. 1993. *Shintō shirei no kenkyū*. Tokyo: Hara shobō.

———. 2003. *Yasukuni Jinja Yūshūkan no sekai: Kindai Nihon no rekishi tanbō gaido*. Tokyo: Sankei shinbunsha.

Ohnuki-Tierney, Emiko. 2002. *Kamikaze, Cherry Blossoms, and Nationalisms: The Militarization of Aesthetics in Japanese History*. Chicago: University of Chicago Press.

———. 2006. *Kamikaze Diaries: Reflections of Japanese Student Soldiers*. Chicago: University of Chicago Press.

Ōishi Moritarō. 1941. *Kamon no homare: Izoku yori izoku e*. Shizuoka: Shizuoka-ken senshisha izokukai.

Ōkado Masakatsu. 2006. "Kodomo tachi no sensō, kodomo tachi no sengo." In *Ajia Taiheiyō Sensō*, vol. 6, *Nichijō seikatsu no naka no sōryokusen,* edited by Kurasawa Aiko, Sugihara Tōru, and Narita Ryūichi, 93–122. Tokyo: Iwanami shoten.

Ōkawa Ichirō. 1980. "Yasukuni mondai no shin dōkō." *Rekishi hyōron* 358: 77–84.

Okuno Shūji. 1980. "Hachigatsu jūgonichi no Yasukuni Jinja." *Ushio* 257: 134–141.

Olick, Jeffrey. 1998a. "Memory and the Nation: Continuities, Conflicts, and Transformations." *Social Science History* 22 (4): 377–387.

———. 1998b. "What Does It Mean to Normalize the Past?" *Social Science History* 22 (4): 547–571.

———, and Joyce Robbins. 1998. "Social Memory Studies: From 'Collective Memory' to the Historical Sociology of Mnemonic Practices." *Annual Review of Sociology* 24: 105–140.

Onoda Hiroo, and Nakajō Takanori. 2007. *"Yasukuni" no koto o katarou*. Tokyo: WAC.

Ono Sokyō. 1963. *Shintō no kiso chishiki to kiso mondai*. Tokyo: Jinja shinpōsha.

Ōnuma Yasuaki. 2007. *Tōkyō saiban, sensō sekinin, sengo sekinin*. Tokyo: Tōshindō.

Orikuchi Shinobu. (1943) 1968. "Shōkon no ongi o haishite." *Geinō* 9 (7). Reprinted in *Orikuchi Shinobu zenshū*, vol. 28. Tokyo: Chūō kōronsha. Citations refer to the Chūō kōronsha edition.

———. 1956. "Minzoku shikan ni okeru takai kan'nen." In *Origuchi Shinobu zenshū*, vol. 16, edited by Orikuchi Hakase Kinenkai, 309–366. Tokyo: Chūō kōronsha.

Orr, James J. 2001. *The Victim as Hero: Ideologies of Peace and National Identity in Postwar Japan*. Honolulu: University of Hawai'i Press.

Osaka District Court (ODC). 2003. "Songai baishō seikyū, September 26, 2003." http://www.courts.go.jp/hanrei/pdf/6D9D1974B2F36AAD49256DB2000444C7.pdf.

———. 2004. "Songai bakshō seikyū jiken, May 13, 2004." http://www.courts.go.jp/hanrei/pdf/20070521164927.pdf.

———. 2009. "Reijibo kara no shimei masshō-tō seikyū jiken, February 26, 2009." http://www.courts.go.jp/hanrei/pdf/20090410182748.pdf.

Osaka High Court (OHC). 2005. "Songai baishō seikyū soshō jiken, September 30, 2005." http://www.courts.go.jp/hanrei/pdf/261F2926F7BBCF26492570BC0019B4D2.pdf.

O Sonfa. 2003. "Kankokujin wa itsuno hika 'Yasukuni' o rikai dekirunoka." *Seiron* 374: 184–194.

Ōta Michiko. 1997a. "Nihon no matsuri: Sono kigen to kyōikuteki yakuwari," part 1. *Hikaku bunka kenkyū* 35: 117–132.

———. 1997b. "Nihon no matsuri: Sono kigen to kyōikuteki yakuwari," part 2. *Hikaku bunka kenkyū* 36: 13–39.

Ōtani Tadashi. 2006. *Heishi to gunpu no Nisshin sensō: Senjō kara no tegami o yomu*. Tokyo: Yūshisha.

———, and Harada Keiichi, eds. 1994. *Nisshin sensō no shakaishi*. Osaka: Forum A.

Ōyama Shingo. 1994. "Yasukuni Jinja Yūshūkan." *Gunjishigaku* 30 (1): 92–97.

PHP Kenkyūjo, ed. 2002. *Kenshō: Yasukuni mondai towa nani ka*. Tokyo: PHP kenkyūjo.

Powless, Cyril. 1976. "Yasukuni Jinja Hōan: Religion and Politics in Contemporary Japan." *Pacific Affairs* 49 (3): 491–505.

Pye, Michael. 2003. "Religion and Conflict in Japan with Special Reference to Shinto and Yasukuni Shrine." *Diogenes* 50 (3): 45–59.

Quigley, Christine. 2005. *The Corpse: A History.* Jefferson, NC: McFarland.

Rekishi Kyōikusha Kyōgikai, ed. 2000. *Heiwa hakubutsukan sensō shiryōkan gaido bukku.* Rev. ed. Tokyo: Aoki shoten.

Rekishi Ninshiki to Higashi Ajia no Heiwa Fōramu, ed. 2010. *Higashi Ajia no rekishi ninshiki to heiwa o tsukuru chikara: Higashi Ajia heiwa kyōdōtai o mezashite.* Tokyo: Nihon hyōronsha.

Rév, István. 2005. *Retroactive Justice: Prehistory of Post-Communism.* Stanford, CA: Stanford University Press.

Rikugunshō Chōsa-han. 1932. *Yasukuni Jinja Rinji Taisai ni arite.* Tokyo: Rikugunshō chōsa-han.

Rikugunshō Shinbun-han. 1938. "Yasukuni Jinja Rinji Taisai o mukaete." *Shūhō* 79: 1–16.

Rin Kenryō. 2003. "Sengo sedai no Taiwanjin kara mita Yasukuni mondai." *Seiron* 374: 176–182.

Rynn, Midori Yamanouchi, and Joseph L. Quinn. 2000. *Listen to the Voices of the Sea: Writings of the Fallen Japanese Students.* Scranton, PA: University of Scranton Press.

Saaler, Sven. 2005. *Politics, Memory and Public Opinion: The Textbook Controversy and Japanese Society.* Munich: IUDICIUM Verlag.

Safier, Joseph. 1996. "The Yasukuni Shrine and the Constraints on the Discourse of Nationalism in Twentieth-Century Japan." Master's thesis, University of Kansas.

Saitō Gesshin. (1882) 2004. *Bukō nenpyō.* 3 vols. Annotated by Imai Kingo. Tokyo: Chikuma shobō.

Saitō Hideo. 2003. "Kūshū o kiroku suru undō." In *Nihon no kūshū* 10, edited by Nihon no Kūshū Henshū Iinkai, 207–241. Tokyo: Sanseidō.

Sakai Hisayoshi, ed. 2006. *Meiyo no senshi: Rikugun jōtōhei Kurokawa Umekichi no senshi shiryō.* Tokyo: Iwata shoin.

Sakai Tokiwa. 1938. *Yasukuni Jinja dokuhon.* Osaka: Kōtensha.

Sakamoto Koremaru. 1984. "Meiji kokka to shōkonsha taisei: Yasukuni Jinja no seiritsu to chihō shōkonsha gyōsei." *Shintōgaku* 122: 1–29.

———, ed. 2006a. *Kokka shintō saikō: Saisei itchi kokka no keisei to tenkai.* Tokyo: Kyūbundō.

———. 2006b. "Yasukuni Jinja zen gūji Yuzawa Tadashi-shi ni kiku: Yasukuni no shizukani aogu sakura kana." *Gendai shūkyō:* 99–122.

———. 2007. "'Kokka Shinto taisei' to Yasukuni Jinja: Irei to shōkon no shisōteki keifu, josetsu." *Jinja Honchō Kyōgaku Kenkyūjo kiyō* 12: 1–21.

Saki Akio. 1971. "Yasukuni Jinja no 'kokueika' hōan ni tsuite." *Kyōiku* 260: 103–109.

Sakurai Tokutarō. 1984. "Onryō kara goryō e: Chūseiteki shireikan no tenkai." In *Goryō shinkō,* edited by Shibata Minoru, 3–12. Tokyo: Yūzankaku.

Sand, Jordan. 2001. "Monumentalizing the Everyday: The Edo-Tokyo Museum." *Critical Asian Studies* 33 (3): 251–278.

Santino, Jack, ed. 2006. *Spontaneous Shrines and the Public Memorialization of Death*. New York: Palgrave Macmillan.

Satō Kazunori. 2011. "Meiji Taishō no Shōkonsha an'naiki: Yasukuni Jinja, gokoku jinja no yuisho to bungei." *Kokugakuin Daigaku Kenkyū Kaihatsu Suishin Sentā kenkyū kiyō* 5: 39–57.

Satō Nobuo. 1980. "Kokumin ni totte 'Yasukuni' towa: Shinryaku sensō no kōtei ika ni tsuzuku mono." *Bunka hyōron* 235: 184–190.

Satō Toshiyuki. 2001. "Kokka kinen no ba ni kansuru Kishida Hideto no kōsō to kenkai: 'Yasukuni Jinja shin'iki kakuchō keikaku' ni tsuite (1) Ritsuan no rekishiteki keii." *Kenchikushigaku* 37: 41–53.

Sawaki Keizō. 2011. "Okinawa Yasukuni soshō o ou dokyumento." *Zen'ei* 866: 171–173.

Scarry, Elaine. 1985. *The Body in Pain: The Making and Unmaking of the World*. New York: Oxford University Press.

Schattschneider, Ellen. 2009. "The Work of Sacrifice in the Age of Mechanical Reproduction: Bride Dolls and Ritual Appropriation at Yasukuni Shrine." In *The Culture of Japanese Fascism*, edited by Alan Tansman, 296–317. Durham, NC: Duke University Press.

Seaton, Philip. 2005. "Reporting the 2001 Textbook and Yasukuni Shrine Controversies: Japanese War Memory and Commemoration in the British Media." *Japan Forum* 17 (3): 287–309.

Sebald, W. G. 2003. *On the Natural History of Destruction*. New York: Random House.

Seki Yoshihiro. 2004. "Hakubutsukan to iu kūkan: kioku no denshō ni kansuru ichi kōsatsu." *Osaka Daigaku Daigakuin Ningen Kagaku Kenkūka kiyō* 30: 177–192.

Seraphim, Franziska. 2006. *War Memory and Social Politics in Japan, 1945–2005*. Cambridge, MA: Harvard University Press.

Sherman, Daniel J. 1999. *The Construction of Memory in Interwar France*. Chicago: University of Chicago Press.

Shibuichi, Daiki. 2005."The Yasukuni Shrine Dispute and the Politics of Identity in Japan: Why All the Fuss?" *Asian Survey* 45 (2): 197–215.

Shibukawa Ken'ichi. 1967. "Senryōka no Yasukuni Jinja." *Shintōshi kenkyū* 15 (5–6): 185–206.

Shie Yamei. 2003. "Nihon ni koi shita shinsedai no hitori to shite keii o arawashitai: Ano jidai o ikita Taiwanjin to Nihonjin ni omoi o komete." *Seiron* 374: 172–175.

Shin Gi-Wook, Soon-Won Park, and Daqing Yang, eds. 2006. *Rethinking Historical Injustice and Reconciliation in Northeast Asia: The Korean Experience*. London: Routledge.

Shintani Takanori. 2006. "Irei to gunshin: Saikō." *Kokuritsu Rekishi Minzoku Hakubutsukan kenkyū hōkoku* 133: 155–171.

———. 2009. *Osōshiki: Shi to irei no Nihonshi*. Tokyo: Yoshikawa kōbunkan.

Shin'ya Masaaki. 2007. "Yasukuni mondai no yukue." *Butsudai shakaigaku* 32: 19–29.

Shu Chin-Chiang. 2005. "Chūgoku no Yasukuni sanpai hihyō wa futō da." *Nippon* 9 (5): 61–63.

Skabelund, Aaron. 2011. "'By Running . . . /By Fighting . . . /By Dying . . .': Remembering, Glorifying, and Forgetting Japanese Olympian War Dead." *Sport in Society: Cultures, Commerce, Media, Politics* 14 (4): 504–517.

Smith, Henry. 1978. "Tokyo as an Idea: An Exploration of Japanese Urban Thought until 1945." *Journal of Japanese Studies* 4 (1): 34–80.

Smith, Kerry. 2002. "The Shōwa Hall: Memorializing Japan's War at Home." *Public Historian* 24 (4): 35–64.

Soeda Yoshiya. 1997. *Kyōiku chokugo no shakaishi: Nashonarizumu no sōshutsu to kussetsu*. Tokyo: Yūshindō kōbunsha.

Soja, Edward W. 1989. *Postmodern Geographies: The Reassertion of Space in Critical Social Theory*. London: Verso.

Sontag, Susan. 2003. *Regarding the Pain of Others*. New York: Picador.

Spiegelman, Art. 1991. *Maus: A Survivor's Tale*. 2 vols. New York: Pantheon.

Sturgeon, William Daniel. 2006. "Japan's Yasukuni Shrine: Place of Peace or Place of Conflict? Regional Politics of History and Memory in East Asia." Master's thesis, International Christian University.

Sturken, Marita. 1991. "The Wall, the Screen, and the Image: The Vietnam Veteran's Memorial." *Representations* 35: 118–142.

———. 2007. *Tourists of History: Memory, Kitsch, and Consumerism from Oklahoma City to Ground Zero*. Durham, NC: Duke University Press.

Sugahara Ryūken. 2005. *"Yasukuni" to iu ori kara no kaihō*. Kyoto: Nagata Bunshōdō.

———. 2011. "'Osaka Yasukuni gōshi torikeshi soshō' kōsoshin hanketsu o tou." *Ajenda: Mirai e no kadai* 32: 80–85.

Sugawara Nobuo. 2003. *Sensō to tsuitō: Yasukuni mondai e no teigen*. Tokyo: Hassakusha.

Sugimori Hisahide. 1954. "Yasukuni Jinja." In *Tōkyō tsūshin*, edited by Inoue Tomojirō, 302–309. Tokyo: Ōdosha.

Suzuki Hiroyuki. 1996. *Mieru toshi, mienai toshi: Machizukuri, kenchiku, monyumento*. Tokyo: Iwanami shoten.

Suzuki Kenji. 1995. *Sensō to shinbun*. Tokyo: Mainichi shinbunsha.

Suzuki Risei. 1988. *Edo no toshi keikaku*. Tokyo: Sanseidō.

Suzuki Yūko. 1986. *Feminizumu to sensō: Fujin undōka no sensō kyōryoku*. Tokyo: Marujusha.

Taguchi Hiroshi. 1996. *Sengo sedai no sensō sekinin*. Tokyo: Kinohanasha.

Takahashi Fumito, ed. 1990. *"Yasukuni" mondai kanren nenpyō*. Tokyo: Nagata bunshōdō.

Takahashi Hikohiro. 1989. *Minshū no gawa no sensō sekinin*. Tokyo: Aoki shoten.

Takahashi Ryūji. 1981. "12 gatsu 8 nichi to senchū sedai." *Asahi jānaru* 23 (51): 26–27.

Takahashi Shirō. 1996. "Heiwa hakubutsukan būmu no shōtai." *Voice* 228: 202–213.

Takahashi Tetsuya. 2005a. *Kokka to gisei.* Tokyo: NHK hōsō shuppankai.

———. 2005b. *Sengo sekinin ron.* Tokyo: Kōdansha.

———. 2005c. *Yasukuni mondai.* Tokyo: Chikuma shobō.

———. 2006. "The National Politics of the Yasukuni Shrine." Translated by Philip Seaton. In *Nationalisms in Japan,* edited by Naoko Shimazu, 155–180. Abingdon, England: Routledge.

———, and Tanaka Nobumasa. 2007. *"Yasukuni" to iu mondai.* Tokyo: Kabushiki gaisha kin'yōbi.

Takaishi Fumito, ed. 1990. *"Yasukuni" mondai kanren nenpyō.* Tokyo: Nagata bunshōdō.

Takeda Hideaki. 1996. "Yasukuni Jinja, gokoku jinja to tamagushi ryō." *Jinja Honchō Kyōgaku Kenkyūjo kiyō* 1: 213–256.

Takenaka, Akiko. 1998. "Pan-Asianism vs. Changeless, Timeless Japan: The Construction of a Wartime National Identity." *Thresholds* 17: 63–68.

———. 2004. "The Aesthetics of Mass-Persuasion: War and Architectural Sites in Tokyo, 1868–1945." PhD diss., Yale University.

———. 2007. "Enshrinement Politics: War Dead and War Criminals at Yasukuni Shrine." *Japan Focus.* http://japanfocus.org/-Akiko-TAKENAKA/2443.

———. 2009a. "Architecture for Mass Mobilization: The *Chūreitō* Memorial Construction Movement, 1939–1945." In *The Culture of Japanese Fascism,* edited by Alan Tansman, 235–253. Durham, NC: Duke University Press.

———. 2009b. "Politics of Representation or Representation of Politics? Yasukuni the Movie." *Review of Japanese Culture and Society* 21: 117–136.

———. 2014. "Reactionary Nationalism and Museum Controversies: The Case of Peace Osaka." *Public Historian* 36 (2): 75–98.

———, and Laura Hein. 2007. "Exhibiting World War II in Japan and the United States since 1995." *Pacific Historical Review* 76 (1): 61–94.

Takamori Akinori. 2007. *Nihonjin nara shitte okitai Yasukuni mondai.* Tokyo: Seirindō.

Takeuchi Makoto. 1991. "Sensōji no keidai, monzen sekai." In *Edo Tōkyō o yomu,* edited by Ogi Shinzō, 167–184. Tokyo: Chikuma shobō.

Takeyama Akiko. 1994. *Sensō to hōsō: Shiryō ga kataru senjika jōhō seisaku to puropaganda.* Tokyo: Shakai shisōsha.

———. 2002. *Rajio no jidai: Rajio wa chanoma no shuyaku datta.* Tokyo: Sekai shisōsha.

Taki Kōji. 1988. *Tennō no shōzō.* Tokyo: Iwanami shoten.

Tamagawa Hiroko. 2008. "Shōwakan shozō ikotsu junpai, ikotsu shūshū kanren shiryō." *Shōwa no kurashi* 6: 100–110.

Tamamuro Taijō. 1963. *Sōshiki bukkyō.* Tokyo: Daihōrinkaku.

Tanaka Nobumasa. 1997. *"Sensō no kioku" sono inpei no kōzō: Kokuritsu sensō memoriaru o tōshite.* Tokyo: Ryokufū shuppan.

———. 2002. *Yasukuni no sengoshi.* Tokyo: Iwanami shoten.

———. 2003a. *Gōshi wa iya desu: Kokoro no jiyū o motomete.* Tokyo: Kinohanasha.

———, ed. 2003b. *Kokuritsu tsuito shisetsu o kangaeru: "Kuni no tame no shi" o kurikaesanai tame ni.* Tokyo: Kinohanasha.

———. 2007. *Dokyumento Yasukuni soshō: Senshisha no kioku wa dare no mono ka.* Tokyo: Iwanami shoten.

———, ed. 2009. *Koreni masu kanashiki kotono nani ka aran: Yasukuni gōshi kyohi, Osaka saiketsu no shatei.* Tokyo: Nanatsumori shokan.

———, Tanaka Hiroshi, and Hata Nagami. 1995. *Izoku to sengo.* Tokyo: Iwanami shoten.

Tanaka Shūji. 1994. *Kindai Nihon saisho no chōkokuka.* Tokyo: Yoshikawa kōbunkan.

Tanaka, Yuki. 1998. *Hidden Horrors: Japanese War Crimes in World War II.* Boulder, CO: Westview Press.

Tanakamaru Katsuhiko. 2002. *Samayoeru eirei tachi: Kuni no mitama, ie no hotoke.* Tokyo: Kashiwa shobō.

Tanamoto, Masaru. 2001. "A Land without Patriots: The Yasukuni Controversy and Japanese Nationalism." *World Policy Journal* 18 (3): 33–40.

Tawara Yoshifumi. 2008. "'Tsukuru kai' no rekisi wankyoku kyōkasho to '2005 nen mondai.'" In *Higashi Ajia rekishi ninshiki ronsō no meta hisutorī,* edited by Komori Yōichi, Chie Uonshiku, and Pak Yuha, 73–81 Tokyo: Seikyūsha.

Tayama Katai. 1981. *Tōkyō no sanjūnen.* Tokyo: Iwanami shoten.

Terunuma Yoshifumi. 1983. "Hihyō, keishō, tō ni kansuru kenkyū: Tokuni shōkonhi, chūkonhi, tō o chūshin ni." *Shintō Shūkyō* 110: 18–52.

Tōgō Kazuhiko. 2007. "'Yasukuni Jinja mondai' no shikō teishi o ureu." *Gendai* 41 (7): 58–67.

Tōkairin Tsuguo. 2008. "Shōi gunjin to 'Shōkeikan.'" *Rekishi chiri kyōiku* 748: 26–27.

Tokoro Isao. 2007a. *Ofisharu gaido bukku: Yōkoso Yasukuni Jinja e.* Tokyo: Kindai shuppansha.

———. 2007b. "Yasukuni Jinja Mitama Matsuri no seiritsu to hatten." *Meiji Seitoku Kinen Gakkai kiyō* 44: 204–225.

Tokyo District Court (TDC). 2006. "Yasukuni gōshi zesshi jiken, May 26, 2006." http://www.courts.go.jp/hanrei/pdf/20070518154155.pdf.

Tōkyō Hyakunenshi Henshū Iinkai (THHI), ed. 1972–1980. *Tōkyō hyakunenshi.* 6 vols. Tokyo: Tōkyō-to.

Tōkyō no Sensō Iseki o Aruku Kai, ed. 2006. *Fiirudo wāku Yasukuni Jinja, Yūshūkan: Manabi, shirabe, kangaeyou.* Tokyo: Heiwa bunka.

Tōkyō-shi. 1895. *Tōkyō-shi shukushō taikai.* Tokyo: Tōkyō-shi.

Tōkyō-to. 1995. *Engo to irei no ayumi: Sengo 50 shūnen kinen.* Tokyo: Tōkyō-to.

Tominaga Takeshi. 2012. "Yasukuni Jinja reijibotō masshō soshō ni tsuite." *Kōgakukan Daigaku Shintō Kenkyūjo kiyō* 28: 199–213.

Totani, Yuma. 2008. *The Tokyo War Crimes Trial: The Pursuit of Justice in the Wake of World War II*. Cambridge, MA: Harvard University Asia Center.

Treat, John Whittier. 1995. *Writing Ground Zero: Japanese Literature and the Atomic Bomb*. Chicago: University of Chicago Press.

Tsubouchi Yūzō. 1999. *Yasukuni*. Tokyo: Shinchōsha.

Tsuda Michio. 2000. *Kimi wa kyōiku chokugo o shitte iruka: "Kami no kuni" no kioku*. Tokyo: Shakai hyōronsha.

Tsuda Tsutomu. 2002. "Bakumatsu Chōshū han ni okeru shōkonsha no hassei." *Jinja Honchō Kyōgaku Kenkyūjo kiyō* 7: 127–169.

———. 2011. "Yasukuni Jinja ni matsurareru shinrei." *Yamaguchiken shintōshi kenkyū* 23: 1–10.

Tsunasawa Mitsuaki. 1998. *Yanagita Kunio sanka e no ginen: Nihon no kindaichi o tou*. Nagoya: Fūbōsha.

Tsunoda Saburō. 1977. *Yasukuni to chinkon*. Tokyo: San'ichi shobō.

Tsurumi Shunsuke. 1986. *An Intellectual History of Wartime Japan, 1931–1945*. New York: Routledge.

Ubukata Toshirō. (1926) 1978. *Meiji Taishō kenbunshi*. Tokyo: Shunjūsha. Reprint, Tokyo: Chūō Kōron. Citations refer to the Chūō Kōron edition.

Uchida Hyakken. 1971. "Yūshūkan." In *Uchida Hyakken zenshū*, vol. 1. Tokyo: Kōdansha.

Ueda Hiroaki. 2003. *Sokai enikki: Gakudō sokai dosa mawari*. Tokyo: Bungeisha.

Ueno Masumi. 2008. "Shōkei kan (Senshō byōsha shiryō kan)." *Gunji shi gaku* 43 (3–4): 510–514.

Umetani Noboru. 2000. *Kyōiku chokugo seiritsushi*. Tokyo: Seishi shuppan.

Verdery, Kathrine. 1999. *The Political Lives of Dead Bodies: Reburial and Postsocialist Change*. New York: Columbia University Press.

Wakabayashi, Bob Tadashi. 1986. *Anti-Foreignism and Western Learning in Early Modern Japan: The New Theses of 1825*. Cambridge, MA: Harvard University Press.

Wakakuwa Midori. 1995. *Sensō ga tsukuru joseizō: Dainiji Sekaitaisen-ka no Nihon joseidōin no shikakuteki puropaganda*. Tokyo: Chikuma shobō.

Walkowitz, Daniel J., and Lisa Maya Knauer, eds. 2009. *Contested Histories in Public Space: Memory, Race, and Nation*. Durham, NC: Duke University Press.

Watakushitachi no Rekishi o Tsuzurukai, ed. 1987. *Fujin zasshi kara mita 1930 nendai*. Tokyo: Dōjidaisha.

Watanabe Katsuyoshi. 1993. "Nihon no 'matsuri' ni kansuru ichi kōsatsu: Matsuri no honshitsu kōzō o megutte." *Shintōgaku* 156: 27–57.

Wert, Michael. 2013. *Meiji Restoration Losers: Memory and Tokugawa Supporters in Modern Japan*. Cambridge, MA: Harvard University Asia Center.

Winter, Jay. 1995. *Sites of Memory, Sites of Mourning: The Great War in European Cultural History*. Cambridge: Cambridge University Press.

———. 2006. *Remembering War: The Great War between Memory and History in the Twentieth Century.* New Haven, CT: Yale University Press.

———, and Emmanuel Sivan, eds. 1999. *War and Remembrance in the Twentieth Century.* Cambridge: Cambridge University Press.

Woodard, William R. 1972. *The Allied Occupation of Japan 1945–1952 and Japanese Religions.* Leiden: E. J. Brill.

Wray, Harold J. 1971. "Changes and Continuity in Japanese Images of the Kokutai and Attitudes and Roles toward the Outside World: A Content Analysis of Japanese Textbooks, 1903–1945." PhD diss., University of Hawai'i.

———. 1973. "A Study in Contrasts: Japanese Textbooks of 1903 and 1941–5." *Monumenta Nipponica* 28 (1): 69–86.

Yakabi Osamu. 2005. "Tsuitō suru chiiki no ishi." *Gendai shisō* 33 (9): 216–224.

Yamabe Masahiko. 1996. "Chiiki ni nezasu heiwa no tame no sensō tenji: Sensōten undō o chūshin ni." *Rekishi hyōron* 556: 12–22.

———. 2000. "Sensō taiken o keishō suru undō no igi to tenbō." *Kikan Chūgoku* 61: 2–12.

———. 2007. "Yasukuni Jinja Yūshūkan no jōsetsu tenji to tokubetsu ten 'kokyō no gokoku jinja' ni tsuite." *Nihonshi kenkyū* 533: 60–63.

Yamada Akira. 2007. "Yasukuni Jinja Yūshūkan no tenji to sono rekishi ninshiki." *Nihonshi kenkyū* 533: 64–67.

Yamada Kai. 1900. *Shōgakkō yō shūgaku ryokō ensoku no tomo.* Tokyo: Matsuzaki Hanzō et al.

Yamamoto Hichihei. 1986. "Kūki to shite no 'Yasukuni.'" *Shokun* 18 (4): 42–56.

Yamamoto Jōhō, ed. 2010. *Kokka to tsuitō: "Yasukuni Jinja ka, kokuritsu tsuitō shisetsu ka" o koete.* Tokyo: Shakai hyōronsha.

Yamamoto Nobuyuki, and Imano Toshihiko. 1976. *Gakkō gyōji no shūkyōteki seikaku.* Taishō Shōwa kyōiku no tennōsei ideorogii, vol. 1. Tokyo: Shinseisha.

Yamamoto Shōgetsu. 1971. *Meiji sesō hyakuwa.* Tokyo: Arimine shoten.

Yamanaka Hisashi. 1974–1981. *Bokura shōkokumin.* 5 vols. and supplement. Tokyo: Henkyōsha.

———. 1982. *Kodomo ga "shōkokumin" to iwareta koro.* Tokyo: Asahi shinbunsha.

———. 1989. *Kurashi no naka no Taiheiyō sensō: Hoshigarimasen katsumade wa.* Tokyo: Iwanami shoten.

———. 2003. *Sukkiri wakaru "Yasukuni Jinja" mondai.* Tokyo: Shōgakkan.

Yamane Kazuyo. 2009. *Grassroots Museums for Peace in Japan: Unknown Efforts for Peace and Reconciliation.* Saabrücken: VDM Verlag Dr. Müller.

Yanagita Kunio. 1910. *Jidai to nōsei.* Tokyo: Shuseidō.

———. 1976. *Meiji Taishō shi, sesō hen.* 2 vols. Tokyo: Kōdansha.

———. 1990. "Nihon no matsuri." *Yanagita Kunio Zenshū,* vol. 13. Tokyo: Chikuma shobō.

Yano Keiichi. 2006. *Irei, tsuitō, kenshō no kindai.* Tokyo: Yoshikawa kōbunkan.

Yasukuni Jinja (YJ). 1906–1943. *Yasukuni Jinja rinji taisai shashin chō*. Tokyo: Yasukuni jinja.

———. 1933. *Yasukuni Jinja saishin saijitsu rekiryaku*. Tokyo: Yasukuni jinja.

———. 1933–1935. *Yasukuni Jinja chūkonshi*. 5 vols. Tokyo: Yasukuni jinja.

———. 1973. *Yasukuni Jinja ryakunenpyō*. Tokyo: Yasukuni jinja.

———. 1983–1984. *Yasukuni Jinja hyakunenshi*. 3 vols. Tokyo: Yasukuni jinja.

———. 1986. *Yasukuni Jinja: Saiten to gyōji no subete*. Tokyo: Yasukuni jinja.

———. 1987. *Yasukuni Jinja hyakunenshi, jireki-nenpyō*. Tokyo: Yasukuni jinja.

Yasukuni Jinja Yūshūkan (YJY). 1883. *Yūshūkan reppin mokuroku* 1, microfiche.

———. 1933. *Yūshūkan yōran*. Tokyo: Yūshūkan.

———. 1934. *Yūshūkan fuzoku kokubōkan yōran*. Tokyo: Yūshūkan.

———. 1986. *Yasukuni Jinja Yūshūkan shozō Tōkyō meisho nishikie ten: Nishikie ni miru Yasukuni Jinja no akebono*. Tokyo: Yasukuni jinja yūshūkan.

———. 1987. *Yasukuni Jinja Yūshūkan: Shahō to senbotsusha no ihō*. Tokyo: Yasukuni jinja, Yūshūkan.

Yasukuni no Inori Henshūkai, ed. 1999. *Yasukuni no inori: Me de miru Meiji Taishō Shōwa Heisei*. Tokyo: Sankei shinbun nyūsu sābisu.

Yasumaru Yoshio. 2001. *Kindai ten'nōzō no keisei*. Tokyo: Iwanami shoten.

Yasuoka Shōtarō. 1984. *Dai seikimatsu sākasu*. Tokyo: Asahi shinbunsha.

———. 1986. "Sākasu no uma." In *Yasuoka Shōtarō shū*, 163–171. Tokyo: Iwanami shoten. Originally published in *Shinchō* (October 1955).

Yokoyama Atsuo. 2008. "Senbotsusha no ikotsu to rikugun bochi." In *Kokuritsu Rekishi Minzoku Hakubutsukan kenkyū hōkoku* 147: 93–131.

Yomiuri Shinbun Sensō Sekinin Kenshō Iinkai (YSSSKI). 2006. *Kenshō sensō sekinin*. 2 vols. Tokyo: Chūō kōronsha.

Yoneyama, Lisa. 1999. *Hiroshima Traces: Time, Space, and the Dialectics of Memory*. Berkeley: University of California Press.

Yoshida Mitsukuni. 1982. "Sensō to shikaku media: Panorama kara eiga e." *Jinbun gakuhō* 53: 143–155.

Yoshida, Takashi. 2007. "Revising the Past, Complicating the Future: The Yūshūkan War Museum in Modern Japanese History." *Asia-Pacific Journal: Japan Focus*. http://www.japanfocus.org/-Takashi-YOSHIDA/2594.

Yoshida Yutaka. 1995. *Nihonjiin no sensōkan: Sengoshi no naka no hen'yō*. Tokyo: Iwanami shoten.

———. 1997. *Gendai rekishigaku to sensō sekinin*. Tokyo: Aoki shoten.

Yoshimi Shun'ya. 1987. *Toshi no doramatsurugii: Tōkyō sakariba no shakaishi*. Tokyo: Kōbundō.

———. 1991. "Tennō jnukō to 'teito' to shite no Tōkyō." In *Edo Tōkyō o yomu*, edited by Ogi Shinzō, 241–256. Tokyo: Chikuma shobō.

———. 1996. "Media ibento gainen no shosō." In *Kindai Nihon no media ibento*, edited by Tsuganesawa Toshihiro, 3–30. Tokyo: Dōbunkan.

Yoshimi Yoshiaki. 1987. *Kusa no ne no fashizumu: Nihon minshū no sensō taiken*. Tokyo: Tōkyō daigaku shuppankai.

Yoshino Kōsaku. 1997. *Bunka nashonarizumu no shakaigaku: Gendai Nihon no aidentitii no yukue*. Nagoya: Nagoya daigaku shuppankai.

Yoshino Sakuzō. 1976. *Yoshino Sakuzō shū*. Kindai Nihon shisō taikei, vol. 17. Tokyo: Chikuma shobō.

Yoshiyuki Jun'nosuke. 1971. "Sairei no hi." In *Yoshiyuki Jun'nosuke zenshū*, vol. 1, 93–109. Tokyo: Kōdansha.

Young, James E. 1988. *Writing and Rewriting the Holocaust: Narratives and the Consequences of Interpretation*. Bloomington: Indiana University Press.

———. 1992. "The Counter-Monument: Memory against Itself in Germany Today." *Critical Inquiry* 18 (2): 267–296.

———. 1993. *The Texture of Memory: Holocaust Memorials and Meaning*. New Haven, CT: Yale University Press.

———. 2000. *At Memory's Edge: After-Images of the Holocaust in Contemporary Art and Architecture*. New Haven, CT: Yale University Press.

Young, Louise. 1998. *Japan's Total Empire: Manchuria and the Culture of Wartime Imperialism*. Berkeley: University of California Press.

Zaino Hiroshi. 1988. *Kaiwai: Nihon no toshin kūkan*. Tokyo: Kajima shuppankai.

Zelizer, Barbie. 2000. *Visual Culture and the Holocaust*. New Brunswick, NJ: Rutgers University Press.

Zushi Minoru. 2003. *Shinryaku jinja: Yasukuni shisō o kangaeru tame ni*. Tokyo: Shinkansha.

———. 2007. *Yasukuni no yami ni youkoso: Yasukuni Jinja, Yūshūkan, hikōshiki gaido bukku*. Tokyo: Shakai hyōronsha.

INDEX

ABOUT THE AUTHOR

AKIKO TAKENAKA is associate professor of Japanese history at the University of Kentucky. She specializes in the social and cultural history of modern Japan and conducts research on the historiography of and memories associated with the Asia-Pacific War. Her work has appeared in a number of peer-reviewed journals and edited volumes on wide-ranging topics such as Japanese aesthetics, fascism, totalitarianism, history museums, and world's fairs.

STUDIES OF THE WEATHERHEAD EAST ASIAN INSTITUTE COLUMBIA UNIVERSITY

SELECTED TITLES

(Complete list at http://www.columbia.edu/cu/weai/weatherhead-studies.html)

Neither Donkey nor Horse: Medicine in the Struggle over China's Modernity, by Sean Hsiang-lin Lei. University of Chicago Press, 2014.

When the Future Disappears: The Modernist Imagination in Late Colonial Korea, by Janet Poole. Columbia University Press, 2014.

Bad Water: Nature, Pollution, & Politics in Japan, 1870–1950, by Robert Stolz. Duke University Press, 2014.

Rise of a Japanese Chinatown: Yokohama, 1894–1972, by Eric C. Han. Harvard University Asia Center, 2014.

Beyond the Metropolis: Second Cities and Modern Life in Interwar Japan, by Louise Young. University of California Press, 2013.

From Cultures of War to Cultures of Peace: War and Peace Museums in Japan, China, and South Korea, by Takashi Yoshida. MerwinAsia, 2013.

Imperial Eclipse: Japan's Strategic Thinking about Continental Asia before August 1945, by Yukiko Koshiro. Cornell University Press, 2013.

The Nature of the Beasts: Empire and Exhibition at the Tokyo Imperial Zoo, by Ian J. Miller. University of California Press, 2013.

Public Properties: Museums in Imperial Japan, by Noriko Aso. Duke University Press, 2013.

Reconstructing Bodies: Biomedicine, Health, and Nation-Building in South Korea since 1945, by John P. DiMoia. Stanford University Press, 2013.

Taming Tibet: Landscape Transformation and the Gift of Chinese Development, by Emily T. Yeh. Cornell University Press, 2013.

Tyranny of the Weak: North Korea and the World, 1950–1992, by Charles K. Armstrong. Cornell University Press, 2013.

The Art of Censorship in Postwar Japan, by Kirsten Cather. University of Hawai'i Press, 2012.

Asia for the Asians: China in the Lives of Five Meiji Japanese, by Paula Harrell. Merwin-Asia, 2012.

Lin Shu, Inc.: Translation and the Making of Modern Chinese Culture, by Michael Gibbs Hill. Oxford University Press, 2012.

Occupying Power: Sex Workers and Servicemen in Postwar Japan, by Sarah Kovner. Stanford University Press, 2012.

Redacted: The Archives of Censorship in Postwar Japan, by Jonathan E. Abel. University of California Press, 2012.

Empire of Dogs: Canines, Japan, and the Making of the Modern Imperial World, by Aaron Herald Skabelund. Cornell University Press, 2011.

Planning for Empire: Reform Bureaucrats and the Japanese Wartime State, by Janis Mimura. Cornell University Press, 2011.

Realms of Literacy: Early Japan and the History of Writing, by David Lurie. Harvard University Asia Center, 2011.

Russo-Japanese Relations, 1905–1917: From Enemies to Allies, by Peter Berton. Routledge, 2011.

Behind the Gate: Inventing Students in Beijing, by Fabio Lanza. Columbia University Press, 2010.

Imperial Japan at Its Zenith: The Wartime Celebration of the Empire's 2,600th Anniversary, by Kenneth J. Ruoff. Cornell University Press, 2010.

Passage to Manhood: Youth Migration, Heroin, and AIDS in Southwest China, by Shao-hua Liu. Stanford University Press, 2010.

Postwar History Education in Japan and the Germanys: Guilty Lessons, by Julian Dierkes. Routledge, 2010.

The Aesthetics of Japanese Fascism, by Alan Tansman. University of California Press, 2009.

The Growth Idea: Purpose and Prosperity in Postwar Japan, by Scott O'Bryan. University of Hawai'i Press, 2009.

Leprosy in China: A History, by Angela Ki Che Leung. Columbia University Press, 2008.

National History and the World of Nations: Capital, State, and the Rhetoric of History in Japan, France, and the United States, by Christopher Hill. Duke University Press, 2008.